Mastering QuickBooks Desktop 2024

Your Comprehensive Guide to Efficient Financial Management | Unlock the Power of QuickBooks for Smoother Finances, Seamless Bookkeeping, and Business Success

Trotter Burt

Disclaimer and Terms of Use
The author and publisher of this book and the accompanying materials have used their best efforts in preparing this book. The author and publisher make no representation or warranties with respect to the accuracy, applicability, fitness, or completeness of the contents of this book. The information contained in this book is strictly for informational purposes. Therefore, if you wish to apply the ideas contained in this book, you are taking full responsibility for your actions.

Printed in the United States of America

TABLE OF CONTENTS

INTRODUCTION

The accounting software program QuickBooks is created and sold by Intuit. QuickBooks products, which were first released in 1992, are primarily designed for small and medium-sized enterprises. They include cloud-based accounting software, on-premises accounting programs, and tools for managing and paying bills. In Mountain View, California, USA, Scott Cook and Tom Proulx founded Intuit in 1983. Following the popularity of its personal finance management software, Quicken, the company created services akin to these for small business owners. Quickens original software was not a "double-entry" accounting program. Based on the Quicken codebase, QuickBooks was first released as a DOS version. The codebase used by the Mac and Windows versions was distinct and was derived from In-House Accountant, a product that Intuit had purchased. Small business owners with no formal accounting expertise were big fans of the program. Because of this, the program quickly gained up to 85% of the market for accounting software for small businesses in the US.

As of 2013, it still held a commanding majority of this market. However, early iterations of the system did not meet the expectations of professional accountants, who pointed out issues with inadequate security measures (such as the absence of an audit trail) and non-compliance with established accounting standards. Intuit eventually included complete audit trail capabilities, double-entry accounting processes, and more to close the gap with these accounting pros. Having created Basic and Pro versions of the program by 2000, Intuit began providing industry-specific versions in 2003. These versions have reports and workflow processes tailored to certain business kinds, as well as language specific to the respective trades. Versions for manufacturers, distributors, contractors, non-profit organizations, professional service firms, and retailers are now available options, along with one created especially for professional accounting firms that work with numerous small company clients. For medium-sized organizations, Intuit introduced QuickBooks Enterprise Solutions in May 2002.

After this, Intuit went on to release more editions, bringing in diverse innovations to help meet the various needs of the consumers. Exciting new features are introduced in QuickBooks Desktop 2024 to assist small businesses in streamlining their bookkeeping. Improved bank feed matching, more comprehensive mobile receipt management, smarter transaction tagging and classification, and enhanced visual reporting with interactive dashboards are some of the standout features. With its enhanced visuals, automation, and mobile features, QuickBooks Desktop 2024 offers a significant improvement in usability and insights. This increases the efficiency of handling a company's finances.

What's New in QuickBooks 2024

Enhanced Security

To guarantee the highest level of data protection, Intuit eventually added 256-bit encrypted security measures to its software. It implies that even if it is intercepted by unauthorized parties, your data is safe. It is the safest encryption method in which the encrypted data has a 256-bit key, making it nearly difficult for a hacker to decrypt the data without trying 2256 key combinations.

Customer Prepayments (Enterprise Only)

The most beneficial addition included in the latest version is Customer Prepayments. Customers' deposits and prepayments on sales orders can be tracked by users, and when the orders are filled, the deposits and prepayments are automatically applied to bills. Prepayments can be recorded as current liabilities rather than accounts receivable, which foster consumer trust.

Efficient Item List Search

An improved search function in QuickBooks Desktop 2024 makes it simple to locate goods in your inventory quickly. It can increase user efficiency and save time. There were previously several QuickBooks regions where the list search was accessible. Intuit has updated the fixed asset list and memorized the transaction list, adding a list search function. The item list must still be finished, that is, without a dropdown, for the Payroll version.

Improved Integration Options

Several new automation tools, including automatic invoicing and account reconciliation, are included in QuickBooks Desktop 2024. It can lower your chance of making mistakes and save you time. For instance, you can now plan for the automatic processing of recurrent transactions.

Increased Automation

Among the many new automation tools in QuickBooks Desktop 2024 is the capacity to send invoices and reconcile accounts automatically. It can lower your chance of making mistakes and save you time. For instance, you can now plan for the automatic processing of recurrent transactions. Several other new features and improvements are included in QuickBooks Desktop 2024 in addition to the major new features mentioned above. For instance, QuickBooks Desktop has built-in budget creation and management capabilities. You can also monitor your business's environmental effects by using the new carbon footprint tracking option.

Overview of This Book

QuickBooks 2024 is a book that has been carefully written to help not just accountants but business owners monitor their accounts and all that has to do with the financial aspect of their business. This book has 7 mini-books embedded in it, each of which has chapters and a pop quiz at the end of each chapter to ensure that you completely remember the key aspects of each chapter.

Below is a sneak peek into all you will get to learn when you buy this amazing guide;

Book 1: Foundational Accounting Insights

Before you learn all about the use of QuickBooks, this book helps to ensure that you have some basic knowledge about accounting if you are not an accountant already, and even if you are, there is no harm in having a refresher. The first chapter takes a brief look at the purpose of accounting, refreshes your mind about the basic useful terms in accounting such as the financial statement, balance sheet, etc. and you will also learn about the philosophy of accounting. In the second chapter, you will learn about the fiddle-faddle method of accounting and you will also learn to make use of bookkeeping more efficiently. In this chapter, you will also learn about how QuickBooks works concerning bookkeeping. The third and last chapter of the book focuses on some major accounting problems which include working with accounts receivable, recording accounts payable transactions, a brief look at inventory accounting, accounting for fixed assets, and closing entry accounts.

Book 2: Preparing for QuickBooks Mastery

After you have had a refresher, it's now time to delve into QuickBooks. The first chapter in this book starts with the very basics which is setting up and installing QuickBooks and also running the QuickBooks setup wizard. In the second chapter of this book, you will get into the use of QuickBooks fully. You will learn how to set up a chart of account lists, item lists, price level lists, payroll item lists, classes, customer lists, vendor lists, fixed assets lists, billing rate level lists, your employees, profile lists, and lots more! In the third chapter, you will learn to tweak QuickBooks some more. You will learn how to set accounting preferences, bill preferences, calendar preferences, checking preferences, and general preferences. You will also learn how to control integrated applications, inventory, and how payroll works. Book 2 is quite loaded as it deals with so much that you need to know about QuickBooks hence you should have your system beside you with QuickBooks installed so that you will be able to practice what you are reading immediately.

Book 3: Simplifying Bookkeeping Tasks for Success

This chapter is another packed chapter that you will need lots of practicals with. The first chapter here teaches you about invoicing customers. You will learn how to choose an invoice form, tweak the invoice to your taste, invoice a customer, bill for time, print and email invoices, and record sales and credit memos. In the second chapter of this book, you will learn about paying vendors which includes creating a purchase order, recording the receipt of items, entering a bill, paying bills, and also reviewing the other vendor menu commands. In the third chapter of this book, you will learn to track inventory and items which includes adding items to the item list, and editing items and you will also learn about how the management of inventory should work in a manufacturing firm. Managing cash and bank accounts will be better explained in the fourth chapter. Here you will learn how to write checks, make bank deposits, transfer money between bank accounts, make better use of your register, reconcile bank accounts, and review other banking commands. The last chapter is a key part, happens almost every month and it has to do with the payment of employees. In this chapter, you will learn how to set up payroll, schedule payroll, pay your employees, and edit and void paychecks.

Book 4; Financial Choreography: Streamlining Your Accounting Tasks for Success

This chapter is a very important one for accountants. In this first chapter, you will learn about QuickBooks journal entries, how to update the company information, how to deal with memorized transactions, having to work with an accountant and tax report, and also how to create an accountant's copy of the QuickBooks data file. In the second chapter, you will learn how to make financial statements and reports which includes learning about what a financial statement is and how important it is to a business. You will also learn about how to produce a report, work with the report window, modify a report, and process multiple reports. The third chapter helps you understand how to prepare a budget which includes having to learn about the budget window and managing a budget and you will also learn a few tactics for budgeting. In the fourth chapter of this book, you will learn about activity-based costing. You will get to know how it works, how you can implement it, and how Quickbooks supports it. In the fifth chapter, you will learn about setting up a QuickBooks job, tracking job or project costs, job cost reporting, and using job estimates and you will also learn about progress billing.

Book 5: Financial Symphony: Artfully Mastering the Elegance of Wealth Management

This book has three chapters that are very important to help you learn how to effectively manage the finances of a company. The first chapter will teach you about ratio analysis, the second chapter will enlighten you about economic value-added analysis (EVA), and the last chapter will help you understand more about capital budgeting which also includes risk management.

Book 6: Strategic Canvas: Crafting the Blueprint for Business Brilliance

Every business needs a business plan. It is a very important document that any investor would need if they would like to invest in the business at all. In this book, you will learn about profit-volume-cost analysis, how to create a business plan forecast, and also you will learn how to write a business plan which also includes how to make strategic plans.

Book 7: Data Protection & Troubleshooting Skills on QuickBooks

In this book, you will learn about the care and maintenance of QuickBooks. You will learn about how to protect your data and also how to troubleshoot.

BOOK 1
FOUNDATIONAL ACCOUNTING INSIGHTS

CHAPTER 1
PRINCIPLES OF ACCOUNTING

The foundations of accounting are always discussed before moving on to how QuickBooks may help you run your business more efficiently hence the reason why you will learn just the basics of accounting in the first two chapters of this book so you can have a solid knowledge of how to make the best use of QuickBooks. Naturally, the focus is usually on the entire conversation on QuickBooks and the small-business landscape. The content covered in this chapter and the following two of the book essentially explains how QuickBooks accounting functions in a small business environment. There is no need for you to study this chapter or the ones that follow if you have any accounting expertise, can read an income statement and balance sheet, or can create a journal entry although a revision won't be a bad idea. But please take the time to properly study this chapter if you are new to accounting and business bookkeeping.

Looking at the Purpose of Accounting

The fact that accounting gives stakeholders access to financial information is the most crucial concept that must be understood. People who contact or do business with a company are known as stakeholders; these people can include management, staff members, investors, banks, vendors, taxing authorities, and government agencies. A little more discussion is necessary on stakeholders and their information needs. This is simply because the things that an accounting system must perform are determined by the information demands of these stakeholders. The management, investors, and entrepreneurs of the company make up the first group of stakeholders. To find out if a business is profitable, this group requires financial data. This group also seeks any information that sheds light on a company's state of health and wellness as well as its rate of growth or contraction. To carry out its responsibilities, this group frequently needs comprehensive data. It could be useful for a manager or business owner to know which clients are especially profitable or unprofitable. A savvy investor would be interested in learning whether product lines are expanding or decreasing.

The maintenance of asset and liability records is subject to a linked set of information standards. Anything that belongs to the company, whether money, supplies, or machinery, is an asset. Any debt or obligation that the company has, including bank loans and accounts payable, is referred to as a liability. External companies that provide loans to businesses and credit-reporting organizations that provide data to these lenders comprise a second group of stakeholders. Before making a loan, for instance, banks want to be informed about a company's financial situation. The accounting system must generate the financial data necessary for a bank to evaluate a loan application. Lenders are interested in learning if a company is successful and have a healthy cash flow. A company that is profitable and has positive cash flows may pay off debt with ease. In addition, a bank or other lender wants to see any assets that might be liquidated to pay off debts that could potentially be secured by the company's assets in the worst-case situation. Additionally, vendors usually demand financial data from a company. The information is required since a vendor frequently extends trade credit to a business to lend money. The federal and state government entities that oversee a corporation are among the predictable stakeholders who demand financial information from it. For any business operating in the United States to accurately calculate and pay the income tax owed to the federal government (as well as frequently the state government), it must report on its revenue, expenses, and profits. Businesses that employ people are also required to pay payroll taxes based on parameters including the number of workers, wages paid to workers, and unemployment benefits previously claimed by former employees, as well as to report to the federal and state governments on the wages paid to those workers.

Furthermore, the significance of financial accounting for businesses includes the following:

- **It is required by law to provide financial accounting:** Companies that are registered are legally required to provide financial statements, such as the income statement, cash flow statement, and balance sheet. Typically, the company's annual report contains these claims.
- **Representation of financial stand:** Financial statements are distributed to investors, auditors, banks, attorneys, and suppliers both internally and externally, to portray the stability of the financial position. The information provided by financial statements can be used to determine the company's level of financial stability.
- **Transparency**: Financial performance disclosures are made more transparent by releasing account and transaction data.
- **Compliance**: Companies must abide by all applicable laws, tax rules, and financial reporting requirements.
- **Data-driven decision making**: The financial accounting function's reports and statements give management the ability to make data-driven business decisions. Understanding one's financial intake and outflow is made possible for professionals by financial accounting, a crucial business function.

Reviewing the Common Financial Statements

Gaining an understanding of a company's financial situation is one of the most important talents that prospective managers, investors, and business owners ought to have. Equipped with this understanding, professionals at all levels may make more smart business decisions, and investors can more effectively spot intriguing prospects while avoiding unnecessary risk. A company's financial statements provide a window into its health, which might be challenging to assess through other channels. Many business personnel are not qualified to read and comprehend these documents, but accountants and financial specialists are. Critical information is obscured as a result. You must examine and evaluate several financial documents, including balance sheets, income statements, cash flow statements, and annual reports, to comprehend a company's financial situation both independently and with its industry. When examined collectively, these materials provide a valuable account.

Reading a Balance Sheet

A balance sheet represents a company's "book value." It lets you view the resources it has on hand as well as how they were funded as of a particular date. It displays its owners' equity, liabilities, and assets—that is, what it owns what it owes, and how much money its shareholders have invested.

Additionally, the balance sheet offers data that can be used to assess capital structure and calculate rates of return using the accounting equation:

Assets = Liabilities + Owner's Equity.

Let's break down these terms so you can understand better;

- **Assets:** these are simply whatever the company owns with a value that can be quantified.
- **Liabilities**: relate to sums of money that a business owes a debtor, including unpaid taxes, bonds payable, rent and utility, outstanding payroll costs, and debt payments.
- **Owners' equity**: refers to a company's net value. It is the sum of money that would remain after all debts are settled and all assets are liquidated. The shareholders, who could be either private or public investors, own this money.

To completely understand a company's financial situation, you must review additional financial documents, such as the income and cash flow statements, as the balance sheet by itself cannot reveal trends. A balance sheet for any given period can be created. You must comprehend that a balance sheet is created at a certain moment in time. Businesses typically create balance sheets to display their financial situation after the period for which an income statement is created. An income statement is usually prepared by a business once a year. In this conventional scenario, a company also creates a balance sheet right at the end of the year.

Reading an Income Statement

A profit and loss (P&L) statement, sometimes referred to as an income statement, provides an overview of the total effect of transactions related to revenue, gain, expense, and loss for a specific period. The report, which displays financial trends, business operations (revenue and expenses), and comparisons over certain periods, is frequently distributed as part of quarterly and yearly reports.

Generally, income statements contain the following details:

- **Revenue**: this is simply the amount of money that a business takes in.
- **Expenses:** this simply shows the amount that a business spends.
- **Cost of goods sold**: this is the cost of components and parts of whatever it takes to ensure that a business makes sales from whatever it sells.
- **Gross Profit**: this is the total revenue less of the cost of goods sold.
- **Operating income**: this is the gross profit less operating expenses.
- **Income before taxes:** this is the operating income less of the non-operating expenses.
- **Net income**: this is the income before taxes less taxes.
- **Earnings per share**: this is the division of net income by the total number of outstanding shares.
- **Depreciation**: this is the extent to which assets have lost value over a given time.
- **EBITDA:** Earnings before interest, taxes, depreciation, and amortization.

An income statement is meant to display the financial performance of a business over a certain time frame. It provides a financial account of the day-to-day operations of a business. All of the revenue and expense accounts for a given period are contained in an income statement. Trial balances from any two points in time are used by accountants to construct income statements. You can ascertain a company's profitability, whether it is spending more than it is making, when costs are highest and lowest, how much it is paying to produce its goods, and whether it has the money to reinvest in the company by looking at its income statement and other financial documents like the cash flow statement, balance sheet, and annual report. Income statements are frequently examined by accountants, investors, and company owners to gauge how well a company is performing in comparison to its anticipated future performance and to make any adjustments to its approach. When a company fails to meet goals, a business owner may decide to change course to make improvements the following quarter. In a similar vein, an investor may choose to liquidate one investment and invest in a business that is exceeding expectations.

Reading a Cash Flow Statement

A cash flow statement's main goal is to give a thorough picture of what occurred to a company's cash throughout the accounting period, which is a set amount of time. Based on how much money comes in and goes out of an organization, shows how well-run it is both short- and long-term. The three portions of cash flow statements are the cash flow from financing activities, the cash flow from investing activities, and the cash flow from operating activities. Operating operations, which comprise both revenue and expenses, describe the cash flow that is created after the business delivers its usual goods or services. The cash flow from buying or selling assets using free cash instead of debt is known as investing activity. These assets are typically non-physical, like patents, and physical, like real estate or cars. Cash flow from both debt and equity financing is broken out in the financing activities. It's critical to understand that profit and cash flow are two different things. While profit is defined as the amount of money left over after all costs have been paid, cash flow refers to the money coming into and going out of a business. Knowing both of these statistics is crucial. You can see what kinds of activities generate cash with a cash flow statement, and you can use that information to help you make financial decisions. A company's capacity to expand its operations and maintain financial stability is shown by a positive cash flow, which is why cash from operating income should ideally regularly surpass net income. But, a company may still be successful even with positive cash flow, which is why you should also review the income and balance statements.

Reading Balance Sheet

A balance sheet is the second-most significant financial statement generated by an accounting system. A balance sheet lists the assets, liabilities, and capital contributions made by owners of a company at a specific point in time.

- The things that a business owns, have worth and have been paid for are represented as assets on a balance sheet.
- A balance sheet's liabilities are the sums that a company owes to other individuals, companies, and governmental organizations.
- The sums that owners, partners, or shareholders have invested in the business or have reinvested by keeping earnings within the company are known as owner contributions of capital.

Assets can also be reported on balance sheets under the following categories: investments, long-term investments, fixtures, equipment, and accounts receivable (amounts owed by customers). Not every one of these asset types is present in the case of a small owner-operated company. However, these additional categories can be found on the balance sheet of a very large company, such as one of the top 100 in the US. The amounts that the company owes to other individuals and companies are displayed in the liabilities area of the balance sheet. The amount that the owner, partners, or shareholders have provided to the company in the form of initial investments or profits reinvested is displayed in the owner's equity section. The owner's equity part of the balance sheet only shows one line for a single proprietor. This line sums up all of the owner's contributions, including the initial investment and any subsequent investments. A balance sheet for any given period can be created. You must comprehend that a balance sheet is created at a certain moment in time. Businesses typically create balance sheets to display their financial situation after the time for which an income statement is created. An income statement is usually prepared by a business once a year. In this conventional scenario, a company also creates a balance sheet right at the end of the year. Retained earnings and contributed capital are the two main categories into which a corporation's equity amounts fall when examining its owner's equity or shareholders' equity section. Retained earnings are the profits that remain with the company after being distributed to shareholders. The first funds given to the corporation by the shareholders are known as contributed capital.

Examining the Philosophy of Accounting

The term "philosophy of accounting" may be overly stern, yet there are a few basic presumptions and ideas that underpin accounting. These foundational ideas are frequently referred to as generally recognized accounting concepts. Business accounting is based on these fundamental accounting concepts. All of the talks in this book are predicated on these ideas and presumptions. Saying that they are ingrained in practically every aspect of commercial accounting is not hyperbole.

Revenue principle

The realization principle, sometimes referred to as the revenue concept, asserts that money is received at the time of sale. When products or services are rendered, a sale is usually completed. Regarding the sale of goods, a fundamental aspect of the revenue principle is that money is received when the buyer becomes the legal owner of the products. Keep in mind that receiving payment in cash does not constitute earning revenue. It turns out that calculating revenue at the time of cash collection doesn't provide the business owner with a reliable estimate of actual sales, which may seem paradoxical. A portion of the consumer base might make early deposits before the products or services are delivered. Customers frequently like to use trade credit, which allows them to pay a business for goods or services at a later date. You shouldn't consider cash collection from consumers as a gauge of sales because cash flows can vary greatly. For example, a mail delay can have an impact on cash flow. Additionally, tracking customer cash collections is simple. So why not include the additional details regarding the actual times of sales?

Expense principle

According to the expense principle, a business incurs costs when it utilizes products or gets services. Stated differently, the revenue concept is complemented by the expense principle. Similar to the revenue concept, the mere act of obtaining items implies that you have already experienced their cost. In a similar vein, you have already paid for any services you have gotten (such as legal counsel). The fact that it takes your lawyer a few days or a few weeks to send you the bill is irrelevant. When you obtain products or services, you have to pay for them.

Matching principle

The revenue and expense principles are connected to the matching principle. According to the matching principle, relevant expenses and revenue should be matched at the time of revenue recognition. When it comes to companies that resale inventory, the matching principle is best shown. When it comes to the hot dog stand example, you need to account for the cost of both the hot dog and the bun on the day that you sell them. Count the costs when you sell the dogs and bunnies, not when you purchase them. Stated differently, ensure that the item's revenue and expenses are equal. You've probably heard of the term "accrual-based accounting," which is the result of applying the revenue, expense, and matching principles. In short, accrual-based accounting involves recording income at the time a sale is made and expenses at the time products are utilized or services are obtained.

Cost principle

According to the cost principle, amounts in your accounting system ought to be measured or quantified using previous costs. According to the cost principle, a structure that is owned by your business will appear on your balance sheet at its historical cost. A shift in a fair market value does not require you to modify the values in an accounting system. The initial historical costs are what you use.

Objectivity principle

According to the objectivity principle, objective, factual, and verifiable data should be used in accounting measurements and reports. Stated differently, there should be minimal subjectivity in accounting reports, accounting systems, and accountants. Whenever possible, an accountant prefers to employ objective data over subjective data, even in cases where the latter may be superior. The theory behind objectivity is that it shields a company's accounting records from the potentially damaging effects of subjectivity.

Continuity assumption

Accounting systems claim that a firm will continue to run. For reasons that are beyond my understanding, accountants refer to this as an assumption rather than a principle. When you think about the consequences of presuming that a firm won't survive, the significance of the continuity assumption becomes evident. It gets extremely difficult to determine how to value assets if there is no market value for them if a corporation fails. Because hot dogs and hot dog buns can be sold, it is implicit in that balance sheet that they have some worth. There's no guarantee that any inventory can be sold if a business decides not to go on. What does it mean for the owner's equity value as reported on the balance sheet if the inventory cannot be sold?

Unit-of-measure assumption

The unit-of-measure assumption assumes that the unit of measurement that a company should employ in its accounting is its home currency. Stated otherwise, the unit-of-measure assumption says that US businesses can use US dollars in their accounting, and UK businesses can use pounds sterling in their accounting system. Additionally, it is implicitly stated in the unit-of-measure assumption that it is OK for the unit-of-measure employed in the accounting system to lose purchasing power due to periodic deflation and inflation. Yes, some of the figures in a company's financial statements are distorted by inflation and deflation. However, the unit-of-measure assumption indicates that this is typically acceptable, particularly when there are no superior options available.

Separate-entity assumption

According to the separate entity assumption, a business entity—such as a sole proprietorship—is something distinct from its owner. Furthermore, according to the separate-entity assumption, a partnership is distinct from the partners who each hold a portion of the company. As a result, this assumption makes it possible to create financial statements specifically for a partnership or single proprietorship. Therefore, in addition to requiring a business to be distinct, separate, and identifiable from its owners, the separate entity premise also depends on this.

Adding a Few Words about Tax Accounting

A framework of accounting techniques known as "tax accounting" is centered on taxes as opposed to the release of publicly traded financial statements. To put it briefly, tax accounting is the process of accounting for taxes. The Internal Revenue Code regulates tax accounting and specifies the procedures that businesses and individuals need to follow to prepare their tax returns. Everyone is subject to tax accounting, including individuals, corporations, and businesses. Everyone has to take part in tax accounting, even those who are not required to pay taxes. The ability to trace money—flowing into and leaving—connected to people and organizations is the main goal of tax accounting.

- The area of accounting dedicated to preparing tax returns and filing payments is known as tax accounting.
- Individuals, companies, corporations, and other entities use tax accounting.
- An individual's income, allowable deductions, charitable contributions, and any gains or losses on investments are the main topics of tax accounting.
- Accounting for taxes is more complicated for businesses, requiring closer examination of how money is spent and what is and isn't taxable.

Tax Accounting for Individuals

Tax accounting for an individual taxpayer only considers things like income, allowable deductions, gains or losses on investments, and other activities that have an impact on the taxpayer's tax liability. This restricts the quantity of data required for a person to handle an annual tax return, and although using a tax accountant is permitted, it is not required by law. General accounting, on the other hand, would entail keeping track of every dollar that enters and leaves a person's hands, regardless of its intended use, including non-tax personal expenses.

Tax Accounting for Businesses

The tax accounting procedure needs to incorporate additional analysis of data from a business standpoint. Earnings, or incoming funds, for the firm, need to be tracked in the same way as they do for the individual, but any outgoing monies that go toward specific corporate commitments add another layer of complication. This can include money set aside for shareholders as well as money allocated to particular business expenses. Although hiring a tax accountant to handle these tasks is not necessary, it is very typical in larger businesses because of the intricacy of the records involved.

Tax Accounting for Tax-Exempt Organizations

Tax accounting is required even in situations where an organization is exempt from paying taxes. This is because the majority of companies are required to submit yearly returns.3. They have to disclose all incoming funding, including grants and donations, as well as how the money is spent while the organization is running. This makes it easier to make sure the company complies with all rules and laws about how a tax-exempt corporation should be run.

Activity

1. What is the purpose of accounting?
2. What does accounting philosophy say?
3. What is a financial statement?

CHAPTER 2
DOUBLE-ENTRY BOOKKEEPING

Using the Fiddle-Faddle Method of Accounting

The majority of small enterprises have employed the fiddle-faddle method, or at least those whose owners lack prior accounting training. Every figure displayed in the financial statement is individually calculated when using the fiddle-faddle technique of accounting. The fiddle-faddle method of accounting necessitates that you manually calculate a sales revenue figure. If you think back on every sale you made that day, you might be able to calculate this figure. Alternatively, by adding up each sale, you might be able to determine this figure if you create invoices or sales receipts. You might be able to determine this number if you have a cash register by examining the cash register tape.

Below are the downsides to the fiddle-faddle method;

- **It's not systematic enough to be automated**. Indeed, you might not give a damn if the fiddle-faddle method isn't automated. However, the following is a crucial point: Automating a methodical methodology, such as double-entry bookkeeping, is possible with QuickBooks. The process of creating financial statements now only needs, say, maybe five mouse clicks thanks to automation. Every time you need to generate financial statements, you or a helpless colleague must put in a great deal of work to gather the figures and all the raw data required to generate information because the fiddle-faddle method cannot be automated. Naturally, more complex financial statements require a great deal more work to be done by someone.
- **You can get details lost with ease**. It is rather simple to go through the check register and locate the check or checks that, for example, pay the rent if you are aware of the operating expense categories that the business incurs. You can apply a comparable strategy to the costs of wages and materials. What happens, though, if you also have a category for expenses related to advertising, a company license, or another easily forgotten category? Expenses are missed if a category is overlooked. Your income statement will be missing the entire operational expense category if you overlook accounting for your advertising expenses and, consequently, that you spent money on advertising.
- **It doesn't allow for rigorous error checking.** Error checking is crucial for bookkeeping and accounting systems, even though it may sound picky. With so many transactions and numbers in the system, mistakes are prone to occur.

Finding Out How Double-Entry Bookkeeping Works

According to the bookkeeping and accounting principle of double entry, each financial transaction affects at least two distinct accounts in an equal and opposite way. It's employed to fulfill the accounting formula:

Assets = Liabilities + Equity

- The accounting principle known as "double entry" states that assets are equal to liabilities plus owners' equity.
- Transactions are documented in terms of debits and credits under the double-entry system.
- During Europe's mercantile era, double-entry accounting was created to help streamline business dealings and increase trade efficiency.
- The origins of capitalism have been connected to the rise of double entry.

Understanding Double Entry

An entry that raises or lowers an asset or liability account is called a credit in accounting. A debt is the reverse. It is an input that makes a liability account smaller or an asset account larger. Transactions are documented in the double-entry accounting system using debits and credits. The total of all debits and credits must equal one another because credit in one account cancels out a debit in another.

Types of Business Accounts

A company's financial information can be measured, recorded, and shared via bookkeeping and accounting. An economic event that is documented for accounting/bookkeeping purposes is called a business transaction. It is, broadly speaking, an exchange of business dealings between elements of the economy, including vendors and businesses or customers and businesses. These interactions are typically categorized into accounts under the methodical accounting procedure.

All business transactions can be categorized into one of seven types of accounts:

- Assets
- Liabilities
- Equities
- Revenue
- Expenses
- Gains
- Losses

Debits and Credits

Credits and debits are necessary for the double-entry system to function. An entry on the left side of an account ledger is referred to as a debit in accounting, and an entry on the right side is referred to as a credit. For a transaction to be considered in balance, the sum of its debits and credits must match. It's not always the case that credits equal declines and debits equal rises. One account may be debited while another is debited. The standard accounting equation, **Assets = Liabilities + Equity**, is supported, for instance, when a debit boosts asset accounts while decreasing liability and equity accounts. Debits raise the amounts in the expense and loss accounts on the income statement, whereas credits lower those levels. The balances of income accounts are increased by credits and decreased by debits.

Double-Entry Accounting System

During Europe's mercantile era, double-entry accounting was created to help streamline business dealings and increase trade efficiency. Additionally, it made lenders' and retailers' costs and earnings easier to grasp. Some scholars contend that the development of capitalism was largely due to the calculative technology of double-entry accounting. The accounting equation is a succinct illustration of a concept that develops into the intricate, enlarged, multi-item display of the balance sheet. It serves as the basis for double-entry accounting. Based on the double-entry accounting system, the balance sheet shows that a company's total assets equal its total liabilities plus shareholder ownership. As debt capital translates into liabilities and equity capital leads to shareholders' equity, the representation essentially equates all uses of capital (assets) to all sources of capital. Every business transaction must be represented in two or more of the company's accounts for the accounting to be correct.

For example, when a firm borrows money from a bank or other financial institution, the borrowed funds increase the company's assets and increase the loan debt by the same amount. When a company purchases raw materials with cash, it reduces cash capital (another asset) and increases inventory (an asset). The accounting system is known as double-entry accounting because every transaction a corporation does affects two or more accounts. By using this procedure, the accounting equation is guaranteed to maintain its equilibrium, meaning that the values on the left and right sides of the equation will always add up to one. Compared to the single-entry accounting system, the double-entry accounting approach offers numerous advantages. Above all, by indicating how a transaction impacts both credit and debit accounts, it gives a company a comprehensive picture of its financial profile. Additionally, it facilitates error detection because discrepancies between debits and credits indicate a problem. Finally, it simplifies the process of creating financial statements.

Adding a Few Words about How QuickBooks Works

Here are some remarks regarding the benefits that QuickBooks offers. The majority of these journal entries are created for you by QuickBooks, which is the first and possibly most crucial aspect. That being said, working with diary entries is not something you should always avoid. A journal entry must be used to record any transaction that cannot be handled by a regular QuickBooks form, such as the Write Checks or Invoice form. If you buy a fixed asset with a check, for instance, QuickBooks records the acquisition automatically. However, you will need to create your journal entries and enter them differently to record the depreciation that will be utilized to expense the item. The trial balance data gives you the raw data you need to create your financial statement, which is another crucial point. This kind of raw data is not required to be used in the preparation of your financial statements. Predictably, QuickBooks uses this trial balance information to create your financial statements in an easy, fast, and uncomplicated manner.

The majority of journal entries are created by QuickBooks automatically. It also uses the data from journal entries to develop a trial balance and, upon request, generates financial statements. Therefore, the majority of double-entry bookkeeping labor is done in the background. Daily, you are not concerned with many journal entries. You are also free to refuse to ever see a trial balance if you so choose. Practically, all of the data required to create your financial statements is automatically gathered if you use QuickBooks solely to create invoices and write checks to pay your bills.

Activity

1. What is the fiddle-faddle method of accounting?
2. How does double-entry bookkeeping work?
3. Describe how QuickBooks works.

CHAPTER 3
SPECIAL ACCOUNTING PROBLEMS

Working with Accounts Receivable

The remaining amount owed to a business for goods or services provided or utilized but not yet paid for by clients is known as accounts receivable (AR). On the balance sheet, accounts receivable are shown as a current asset.

AR is any sum of money that customers owe for credit-based purchases.

- The asset account on the balance sheet that indicates money owed to a business shortly is called accounts receivable (AR).
- When a business permits a customer to pay for its products or services on credit, accounts receivable are formed.
- Similar to accounts receivable, accounts payable are amounts owed rather than money that is to be received.
- Days Sales Outstanding or the accounts receivable turnover ratio can be used to assess the health of a business's AR.
- To determine when the AR will be received, a turnover ratio study might be performed.

The term "accounts receivable" describes a business's unpaid bills or the money that customers owe it. The expression alludes to accounts that a company is entitled to get as a result of providing a good or service. Receivables, also known as accounts receivable, are a type of credit that a business extends and typically include terms that call for payments to be made within a limited amount of time. It usually lasts anywhere from a few days to a year, whether fiscal or otherwise. Due to the customer's legal duty to pay the debt, businesses list accounts receivable as assets on their balance sheets. Because they can be used as collateral to obtain a loan to aid with short-term needs, they are regarded as liquid assets. A company's working capital consists of its receivables. Additionally, since the account balance is due from the debtor in less than a year, accounts receivable are considered current assets. If a business has receivables, it indicates that it has completed a transaction on credit but has not yet received payment from the buyer. In essence, the client has given the business a brief memorandum of understanding. A crucial component of the fundamental examination of a corporation is accounts receivable. Being a current asset, accounts receivable gauges a business's liquidity—it's capacity to meet short-term obligations without requiring extra financial flows. The accounts receivable turnover ratio, which quantifies how frequently a business has collected its accounts receivable amount throughout an accounting period, is a common metric used by fundamental analysts to assess accounts receivable. Day's sales outstanding (DSO), which measures the typical time it takes to collect money after a sale has been made, would be another area of further investigation.

Examples of Accounts Receivable

An electric firm that invoices its customers after they receive electricity is an example of accounts receivable. The electricity provider waits for its consumers to pay their bills by recording an account receivable for overdue invoices. Most businesses function by permitting a percentage of their sales to be made on credit. Businesses occasionally give this credit to loyal or valued clients who receive invoices regularly. Customers can avoid the inconvenience of physically paying for each transaction thanks to this approach. In other instances, companies usually provide their customers the option to pay after they receive the service.

Examples of receivables

Anytime a company is owed money for goods or services given but not yet paid for, it becomes a receivable. This may result from an installment payment plan or subscription that is due after products or services are acquired, or it may come from a sale to a consumer on store credit. A company's balance sheet shows its amount of accounts receivable. They are recorded as an asset since they stand in for money that is owed to the business. To ascertain whether the business employs ethical business methods, investors can examine the figures shown under accounts receivable.

Recording Accounts Payable Transactions

A company's short-term debts that are still unpaid to suppliers or creditors are referred to as "payables," or accounts payable (AP). Payables are shown as a current liability on a company's balance sheet.

Another, less frequent use of "AP" is to designate the business division or department in charge of settling the company's debts to suppliers and other creditors.

- Amounts owed to suppliers or vendors for products or services received but not yet paid for are known as accounts payable (AP).
- On the balance sheet of the business, the accounts payable balance is the total of all outstanding monies owed to vendors.
- The cash flow statement shows the change in total AP from the previous period.
- To increase cash flow, management may decide to settle its existing debts as soon as the due dates are feasible.

A company's balance sheet's current liabilities column will show the entire amount of accounts payable at a given moment in time. Accounts payable are debts that, to prevent default, must be settled within a specified time frame. AP, or accounts payable, is the corporate term for short-term payments owed to suppliers. In essence, the payable is a brief IOU between a firm and another business or entity. The transaction would be documented by the opposite party as an equal increase to its accounts receivable. An essential number in a company's balance sheet is AP. If AP rises relative to a previous period, it indicates that the business is using credit more frequently than cash to make purchases of goods and services. If an organization's accounts payable (AP) declines, it indicates that it is making payments on its previous period's debts more quickly than it is taking out new credit purchases. Managing accounts payable is essential to controlling a company's financial flow. The cash flow from operating activities, which is the top component, displays the net increase or decrease in AP from the previous period when the cash flow statement is prepared using the indirect technique. To a certain extent, management can control the company's cash flow through the use of AP. For instance, management can prolong the amount of time the company takes to settle all outstanding accounts in AP if they wish to boost cash reserves for a specific amount of time.

Recording Accounts Payable

Every entry entered into the general ledger must always have an offsetting debit and credit for double-entry accounting to be done correctly. When the bill or invoice is received, the accountant credits accounts payable to record accounts payable. Typically, an expenditure account for the good or service that was purchased on credit receives the debit offset for this transaction. If the item that was purchased was a capitalizable asset, the debit might potentially go to an asset account. The accountant debits accounts payable after the bill is paid to lower the liability balance.

The cash account receives the counterbalanced credit, resulting in a reduction of the cash balance. Consider the scenario where a company receives a $500 invoice for office supplies. Upon receipt of the invoice, the accounts payable department records a $500 credit and the office supplies expense registers a $500 debit. The corporation has recorded the purchase transaction even if cash has not yet been paid out since the $500 debit for office supplies expense flows through to the income statement at this time. This is consistent with accrual accounting, which recognizes costs as soon as they are incurred rather than when money is transferred. After the bill is paid by the company, the accountant debits $500 from accounts payable and credits $500 to the cash account.

At any given time, a business may have numerous outstanding payments to vendors. Accounts Payable keeps track of all unpaid invoices to vendors. This means that the whole amount the company owes all of its suppliers and short-term lenders is visible to anyone viewing the accounts payable balance. The balance sheet displays this entire sum. For instance, before the company paid off those debts, the total of both entries in accounts payable would equal $550 if the business mentioned above also got an invoice for $50 worth of lawn care services.

Accounts Payable vs. Accounts Receivable

In essence, accounts payable and accounts receivable (AR) are the opposites. The money that a business owes its vendors is known as accounts payable, and the money that customers owe the business is known as accounts receivable. When two businesses deal on credit, one will record an item in its books for accounts payable and the other for accounts receivable. Anytime a company owes money for goods or services delivered but hasn't received payment from the company, it creates a payable. This may result from a credit purchase made with a vendor, or it may come from a payment plan or subscription that is due when products or services are delivered. Accounts payable are recorded as a current obligation on a company's balance sheet since they reflect money that is owed to third parties.

Looking at Inventory Accounting

The branch of accounting known as inventory accounting is responsible for valuing and recording changes in inventoried assets. Generally, a company's inventory consists of three types of commodities: finished goods that are ready for sale, in-progress goods, and raw goods. The items in each of these three procedures will be given values by inventory accounting, which will register them as assets of the business. For the business to have an exact valuation, assets—items that are expected to be valuable in the future—must be valued precisely.

- The particular value of assets at various phases of their development and production is ascertained through inventory accounting.
- The accuracy of the value of all assets within the organization is guaranteed by this accounting technique.
- A corporation that carefully examines these values may see higher profit margins across the whole product lifecycle.

The value of inventory goods can fluctuate during any of the three production stages. Depreciation, degradation, obsolescence, shifts in consumer preferences, increasing demand, reduced market supply, and other factors can all cause value changes. These changes in inventory products at each of the three production steps will be tracked by an accurate inventory accounting system, which will then modify the costs of the inventory and the asset values of the company.

How Inventory Accounting Works

To reduce the possibility of overstating profit by understating inventory value, generally accepted accounting principles, or GAAP, mandate that inventory be appropriately accounted for by a highly specific set of criteria. Revenue less expenses equals profit. Selling merchandise brings in money. The profit from the sale of the inventory may be inflated if the inventory value (or cost) is underestimated. That can raise the company's estimated value.

The possibility that a business might inflate its worth by inflating the value of its inventory is another thing that the GAAP regulations prevent. Inventory has an impact on the company's overall worth because it is an asset. An organization whose products are out of date may notice a decline in the value of their inventory. The worth of the company's assets and, consequently, the company itself, may be exaggerated if this is not appropriately reflected in the financial statements of the business.

Advantages of Inventory Accounting

The primary benefit of inventory accounting is having a precise picture of the financial standing of the business. But there are some more benefits to tracking an item's value as it goes through each stage of manufacture. Specifically, inventory accounting enables companies to evaluate potential areas of profit margin expansion for a given product at a given stage of its life cycle. The items that demand a significant amount of time or money during later phases of production are the ones where this is most noticeable. Products like technology, machinery, and medications all need significant expenditures after they are first designed. A business can modify the variables at a given stage to maintain the product value while boosting profit margins by cutting costs by assessing the product's worth at that point, such as clinical trials or product transportation.

Accounting for Fixed Assets

Any long-term, tangible piece of property or equipment that a business owns and utilizes to produce revenue is referred to as a fixed asset. When it comes to fixed assets, it's commonly assumed that they will either be consumed or turned into cash after at least a year. Because of this, businesses can write down the asset's value to reflect normal wear and tear.

The most frequent way that fixed assets show up on a balance sheet is as property, plant, and equipment (PP&E).

- Items that a business intends to employ in the long run to help create money are known as fixed assets.
- Property, plant, and equipment are the most popular terms used to describe fixed assets.
- Any assets that are anticipated to be used within a year or turned into cash are considered current assets.
- Long-term investments and intangibles are examples of noncurrent assets in addition to fixed assets.
- While intangibles are amortized, fixed assets are subject to depreciation, which accounts for the value loss as the assets are used.

A company's cash flow statement records the purchase or sale of a fixed asset under the heading "cash flow from investing activities." A sale results in a cash influx for the business, whereas the purchase of fixed assets indicates a cash outflow (negative) (positive). The asset is liable to an impairment write-down if its value drops below its net book value. This indicates that the balance sheet's recorded value is reduced to reflect the fact that it is overpriced in its market worth. A fixed asset is typically sold for its salvage value when its useful life is coming to an end. This is the approximate value of the item if it were disassembled and sold separately.

The asset can eventually become outdated and be disposed of without a refund in certain circumstances. In any case, since the corporation is no longer using the fixed asset, it is written off the balance sheet. An organization's assets, liabilities, and shareholder equity are listed in its balance sheet statement. The distinction between current and noncurrent assets is based on how long they will be useful. Since current assets are usually liquid, it takes less than a year to turn them into cash. Long-term investments, deferred charges, intangible assets, and fixed assets are examples of assets and property held by a corporation that are not readily converted to cash. These are referred to as noncurrent assets. The phrase suggests that these assets won't be sold or depleted throughout the accounting period. A fixed asset is usually represented on the balance sheet as PP&E and has a physical form.

Businesses buy fixed assets for a variety of purposes, such as:

- The production or supply of goods or services
- Rental to third parties
- Use in an organization

Benefits of Fixed Assets

Asset information is useful for conducting in-depth financial analyses, firm assessments, and accurate financial reporting. These reports are used by creditors and investors to assess a firm's financial standing and make decisions about lending funds or purchasing stock in the company. Since a company may record, depreciate, and dispose of its assets using a variety of recognized techniques, analysts must carefully review the notes on the firm's financial statements to understand how the figures are calculated. Large investments in PP&E are necessary for capital-intensive businesses like manufacturing, which makes fixed assets especially crucial. If a company consistently reports negative net cash flows for the acquisition of fixed assets, this may be a good sign that the company is expanding or investing.

Examples of Fixed Assets

Buildings, machinery, software, furniture, land, and automobiles are examples of fixed assets. For instance, delivery vehicles that a business owns and operates are fixed assets if it sells produce. A parking lot established by a firm is considered a permanent asset. Personal cars used for commuting are not regarded as fixed assets, nevertheless. Furthermore, purchasing rock salt to melt ice in the parking lot would be viewed as an expense rather than a benefit. When a fixed asset is purchased, the purchase price is debited from the asset account and credited to the cash account in the same amount. For instance, a temporary employment company spent $3,000 on furniture. To pay for the furniture, the accountant credits the cash account and debits the fixed assets account when the furniture is delivered. Include the interest rate if the asset was purchased in installments. Measure the fair market value of assets that are traded for other ones. Carry over the original asset's value if you are unable to determine the worth of the swapped asset.

Recognizing Liabilities

A liability is anything that an individual or business owes, typically money. Over time, obligations are resolved by the transfer of financial gains, such as cash, products, or services. Liabilities are listed on the right side of the balance sheet and consist of accumulated expenses, bonds, mortgages, deferred revenues, and accounts payable.

One can compare and contrast liabilities and assets. Assets are items you possess or are owed, whereas liabilities are things you owe or have borrowed.

- In general, a liability is something due to another party.
- A legal or regulatory risk or obligation can also be referred to as liability.
- Businesses record liabilities as opposed to assets in accounting.
- A company's short-term financial commitments, such as accounts payable, that are due within a year or a typical operational cycle are referred to as current liabilities.
- Liabilities recorded on the balance sheet that are not due for more than a year are referred to as long-term (non-current) liabilities.

A liability is, generally speaking, an unfulfilled or unpaid obligation between two parties. Within the accounting domain, a financial liability is an obligation that is further characterized by prior business dealings, occurrences, sales, trade of goods or services, or anything that could provide financial gains in the future. Non-current obligations are typically regarded as long-term (12 months or more), whereas current liabilities are typically regarded as short-term (anticipated to be concluded in 12 months or less). A liability's temporality determines whether it is considered current or non-current.

They may consist of an obligation to provide a service in the future to third parties (such as short- or long-term loans from banks, people, or other organizations) or an unresolved debt from a prior transaction. Larger liabilities, such as bonds payable and accounts payable, are typically the most prevalent. Due to their continued current and long-term operations, these two line items will be present on the balance sheet of the majority of corporations. Since they are used to fund operations and big expansions, liabilities are an essential component of a business. They can also increase the effectiveness of business-to-business interactions. For instance, a wine supplier selling a case of wine to a restaurant often does not request payment at the time of delivery. Instead, it bills the restaurant for the purchase to expedite delivery and facilitate the business's payment.

Types of Liabilities

Liabilities are divided into two groups by businesses: current and long-term. Long-term liabilities are obligations that must be paid off over an extended period, whereas current liabilities must be paid off within a year. A long-term liability would be a mortgage that a business takes out and must pay back for fifteen years. On the other hand, the mortgage payments due in the current year are recorded in the short-term liabilities area of the balance sheet and are regarded as the current portion of long-term debt.

Current (Near-Term) Liabilities

Analysts ideally want to verify that a company has the cash on hand to cover its present liabilities, which are due in less than a year. Payroll expenses and accounts payable, which include amounts owing to suppliers, regular utility bills, and other comparable costs, are a couple of instances of short-term liabilities. Additional instances consist of wages payable, interest payable, dividends payable, unearned revenues, and liabilities of discontinued operations.

Non-Current (Long-Term) Liabilities

Given the name, it should be clear that any non-near-term responsibility that is anticipated to be paid off in more than a year falls under the category of non-current liabilities. Using AT&T as an example, there are more items than the one or two that your garden variety firm may list. Bonds payable, another name for long-term debt, typically rank highest on the list and are the biggest burden. Businesses of all sizes use bonds, which are loans from each buyer, to finance a portion of their continuous, long-term operations.

As bonds are issued, mature, or are called back by the issuer, this line item is always changing. The ability to settle long-term debt with funds from financing deals or future earnings is what analysts look for. Companies take on long-term commitments beyond bonds and loans. Long-term liabilities may also include commitments for pensions, salaries, deferred taxes, and rent. Additional instances consist of warranty liability, contingent liability, deferred credits, and post-employment benefits.

Closing Out Revenue and Expense Accounts (Closing Entry)

When a journal entry is made to move balances from a temporary account to a permanent account after an accounting period, it is called a closing entry. Businesses utilize closure entries to set temporary accounts' balances or accounts that display balances for a particular accounting period, to zero. The corporation transfers these balances into long-term accounts on the balance sheet in this way. These permanent accounts display the historical financial data of an organization.

Temporary Accounts

In the general ledger, temporary accounts are those that are used to consolidate transactions throughout a single accounting period. Eventually, at the end of the fiscal year, the balances in these accounts are utilized to create the income statement. An organization's financial performance and operations throughout a single fiscal year are shown in the income statement, which is a financial statement.

This is the reason why "Year ended" is written on the dateline of the annual revenue statement. As previously noted, income statement accounts like sales and spending accounts make up temporary accounts in the general ledger. The balances of these accounts are moved to the income summary, another temporary account when the income statement is released at the end of the year. The balances of temporary accounts are transferred to retained earnings, a permanent account on the balance sheet, using the income summary.

Income Summary

Closing entries are made temporarily into the income summary account. After the accounting period, all temporary accounts have to be reset to zero. Their balances are emptied into the income summary account to do this. The net balance of all the temporary accounts is subsequently transferred by the income summary account to retained earnings, a permanent account on the balance sheet.

Permanent Accounts

Permanent accounts are those that display a company's long-term financial situation. Accounts on a balance sheet are ongoing accounts. The balances of these accounts are carried forward over several accounting periods. The income statement's temporary accounts are zeroed off and their balances are transferred to the permanently retained profits account in the closing entries shown below. The income summary account is used for this.

- **Close Revenue Accounts**: this clears the balance of the revenue account by getting the revenue debited and the income summary credited.
- **Close Expense Accounts**: this clears the balance of the expense accounts by getting the income summary debited and also getting the corresponding expenses credited.
- **Close Income Summary**: this helps to close the income summary account by getting the income summary debited and also getting the retained earnings credited.
- **Close Dividends**: helps to close the dividends account by getting the retained earnings debited and getting the dividends credited.

Activity

1. What are accounts receivable?
2. What are accounts payable transactions?
3. Briefly describe inventory accounting.
4. What are liabilities?
5. What does it mean to close out an entry?

BOOK 2

PREPARING FOR QUICKBOOKS MASTERY

CHAPTER 1
SETTING UP QUICKBOOKS SYSTEM

To utilize QuickBooks, you must: Launch the QuickBooks Setup application after installing the program. You get a broad overview of both of these duties in this chapter. You will also learn many things you will learn as regards the planning process before you proceed to set up your QuickBooks.

Planning Your New QuickBooks System

In this section, you will learn about the very important things you need to know especially how QuickBooks can aid in ensuring that your whole accounting process is quite simplified. You will get to know what accounting does and also what accounting systems do. With a perfect understanding of all of these, you will get to see that setting up QuickBooks is quite simple and the process makes a whole lot of sense.

What accounting does

Consider the functions of accounting. While there may be disagreements over specifics, most people would agree that accounting performs the following four crucial tasks:

- **Calculates gains and losses**
- **Reports that detail an organization's assets, liabilities, and net worth**
- **Gives thorough records of the accounting for the owner's equity, obligations, and assets.**
- **Provides financial data to all parties involved, particularly management.**

What accounting systems do

Below is a quick review of the typical functions of accounting systems, or at least those used by small businesses:

- Create financial reports, such as balance sheets, income statements, and other accounting statements.
- Create company documents such as invoices, customer statements, payroll checks, and so on.
- Maintain thorough records of all important accounts, such as cash, fixed assets, inventory, accounts payable (amounts owed to vendors by a company), accounts receivable (amounts owed by customers to a firm), and so forth.
- Carry out specific information management tasks. For instance, royalties are frequently paid to authors by book publishers in the publishing sector. Thus, the accounting systems of book publishers usually have to handle royalties accounting.

The Place of QuickBooks

Once you comprehend the functions of accounting and accounting systems in general, you will be able to view QuickBooks' functions more clearly.

- Creates financial reports.
- Creates a variety of standard business forms, such as purchase orders, credit memos, customer invoices, customer statements, and checks.
- Maintains thorough records in basic settings for a select few critical accounts: cash, inventory, accounts payable, and receivable.

The key to choosing the best accounting solution is balance, just like with many other things in life. When selecting your accounting software, you could take into account several criteria, including customer support, data security, affordability, portability, and interaction with other business tools. The majority of businesses utilize QuickBooks' desktop version because it provides a good combination of features that most users require.

Installing QuickBooks

Installing QuickBooks is similar to installing most other apps or programs: either through a disc containing the program or a download. You can evaluate several product alternatives, speak with a sales representative, and (if you're ready) buy the version of your choice at https://quickbooks.intuit.com/desktop. You ought to be able to download the product after making the purchase; if not, please contact Intuit. All you have to do is put the QuickBooks disc into the appropriate disk if you buy a copy from a physical retailer. To install QuickBooks, you just need to download the application or insert the disc containing the software. That's all. Just adhere to the directions displayed on the screen. The installation key or code is usually required to be entered. If you buy the program at a local store, you can find this code and key inside the QuickBooks packaging, which is often on the back of the envelope the disc, arrives in. If not, Intuit offers these products when making an online purchase. You can be asked questions regarding how you want QuickBooks installed during the installation process. You should almost always go with the default recommendations. To put it another way, QuickBooks might ask whether it can make a new folder for the application files to be installed in. In this instance, select "yes."

QuickBooks can function as a multi-user accounting system, allowing multiple users to access it. Usually, a computer or server that is accessible from a central location houses the QuickBooks data file, which is the repository for all of the QuickBooks information. Installing the QuickBooks software on their PCs and using it to access centrally placed QuickBooks data files is all that is required for users to operate with the QuickBooks data file.

Dealing with the Presetup Jitters

You use an on-screen wizard to configure QuickBooks for your company's bookkeeping after installing the program. The QuickBooks Setup onscreen wizard is a clever name for it. You will find out what steps you need to take to function efficiently before using QuickBooks Setup in the following sections. Additionally, you will receive a summary of the steps you need to take to complete QuickBooks Setup.

Getting ready to set up

You provide QuickBooks with a lot of information when you run QuickBooks Setup. Practically speaking, you need the following for setup and post-setup cleanup (which I cover in this chapter and the one after that):

- True financial statements as of the day of the QuickBooks conversion
- Detailed records of your inventories, fixed assets, accounts receivable, and payable
- An exhaustive or almost exhaustive roster of personnel, clients, suppliers, and inventory goods (if you purchase and sell inventory).

Before you begin QuickBooks Setup, you should gather all of this information since, depending on how you set up QuickBooks, you might be questioned about it. Gather this information in advance rather than trying to frantically search for it while the Setup Wizard is going. After that, arrange all of the required documents on the desk by your computer. Let me also add that during QuickBooks Setup, you will have to make several accounting selections. For example, you might be prompted to choose whether to employ an accounts payable system. If you would like QuickBooks to deliver monthly statements to your customers, you can use the Setup Wizard to make that decision. Additionally, you can be asked if you want to utilize classes to keep closer tabs on your income and expenses or if you want to generate estimates for clients. Generally speaking, you can just accept the default response when you are asked any accounting-related questions. It is mandatory by law, therefore, that you maintain consistency in your tax accounting. To modify your accounting, which the Internal Revenue Service refers to as a change of accounting technique, you have to apply for authorization from the IRS first.

Things happening during the setup

You work with QuickBooks to set up a chart of accounts and your bank accounts as you proceed through the setup process. Preferences control how QuickBooks functions and which capabilities are initially available. Just so you know, the accounts for income, expenses, assets, liabilities, and owner's equity that show up in your financial statements are identified in the chart of accounts. Once QuickBooks Setup is finished, you're practically set to use the program.

A crucial clarification: After installing QuickBooks and completing the setup procedure, you might believe that you're good to go. However, there are two more things you need to do:

loading your key master files and figuring out your beginning trial balance. The trial balance shows your asset, liability, and owner's equity values as of the conversion date in addition to your year-to-date income and spending figures. Repeatedly used inventory items, vendors, employees, and customer information are all stored in the master files. For instance, a customer's name, address, phone number, and contact person's name (if different) are all kept in the customer master file.

Running the QuickBooks Setup Wizard

Now that you have installed the QuickBooks program, the installation program can commence QuickBooks instantly and then commence the setting up of QuickBooks. You can also choose to commence QuickBooks setup by precisely starting the QuickBooks program you would start any other program.

All you need to do is choose **File > New Company.**

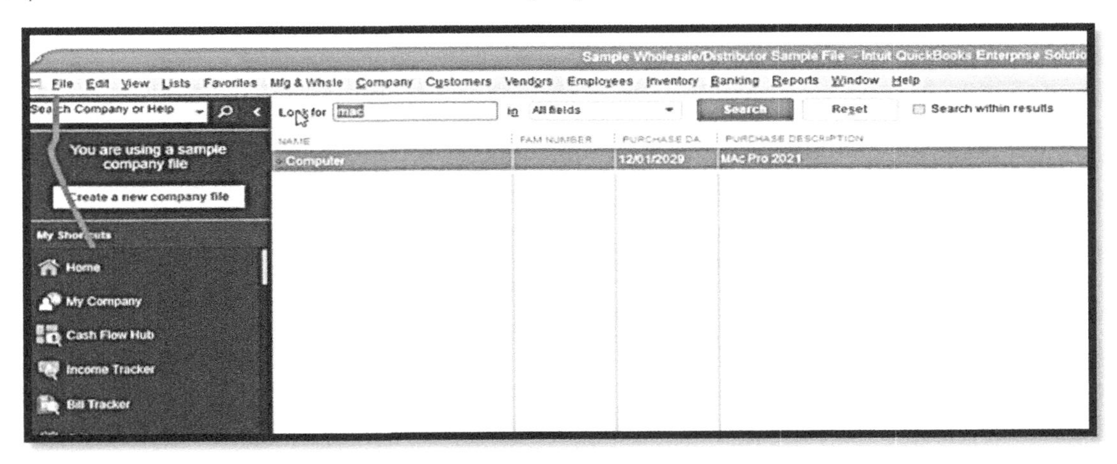

Ushering In

When you select **File > New Company in QuickBooks Setup**, the QuickBooks Desktop Setup screen appears. This screen allows you to open a new QuickBooks company file. There are two radio buttons on the screen. You can create a new file using your email address if you want to set it up as the admin by selecting the **For Myself** (I'm the Admin) button. If you like to set up the file on behalf of the admin, you can do so by using their email address by selecting the **For Someone Else button**. You can select the complex setup option from the Other Options drop-down box. This option takes you through a series of information-filled pages where you can very precisely configure the appearance of the company file that QuickBooks creates.

Providing company information

The initial screens of the EasyStep Interview gather several crucial general business data, such as your company name and legal name of the company, your company address, the industry you operate in, your federal tax ID number, the month of January as the start of the fiscal year, the type of income tax form your company files with the IRS, and the industry or type of business you operate in (retail, service, etc.). The tax accounting regulations for limited liability corporations (LLCs) are not well understood by QuickBooks. If an LLC has only one owner, it is handled as a sole proprietorship; if it has several owners, it is treated as a partnership. However, LLCs have the option to choose to be regarded as C or S corporations. Make sure to specify whether your LLC is a C or S corporation if you've made this election for it.

- Click the **Next button in the EasyStep Interview** to proceed to the next screen. Click **Back** to return to the previous screen. Click the **Leave option** if you are discouraged and want to give up. But make an effort not to give up.

QuickBooks generates the company data file containing your company's financial data after gathering this general company information. Based on the company name, QuickBooks recommends a QuickBooks data file or a default name. Accepting the proposed folder location and name is all that is required (unless you want to save the data file in the Documents folder, which is a good idea).

Personalizing QuickBooks

To set the QuickBooks settings, the EasyStep Interview asks you a series of detailed questions regarding your business operations after QuickBooks has gathered the general company data given in the previous paragraphs. Preferences essentially govern how QuickBooks functions and appears by turning on and off certain accounting features.

To configure the QuickBooks preferences, the EasyStep Interview will ask the following kinds of questions:

- Does your firm maintain inventory?
- Do you want to track the inventory that you buy and sell?
- Do you collect sales tax from your customers?
- Do you want to use sales orders to track customer orders and back orders?
- Do you want to use QuickBooks to help with your employee payroll?
- Do you need to track multiple currencies within QuickBooks because you deal with customers and vendors in other countries, and do these people regularly have the audacity to pay or invoice you in a currency different from the one your country uses?
- Would you like to track the time that you or your employees spend on jobs or projects for customers?
- How do you want to handle bills and payments (enter the checks directly, or enter the bills first and the payments later)?

Configuring your start date

The day you start using your new accounting system may be the most important choice you make throughout the system setup. It is referred to as the conversion date. Ideally, you should start using an accounting system on the first day of the month or the year. As a result, the conversion date is the subject of another often-asked topic. You are prompted to use the dialog box to determine the start date. The beginning of the year is the most convenient time to begin implementing a new accounting system. The cause? You can input a more straightforward trial balance. For instance, you only input the balances of the asset, liability, and owner's equity accounts at the beginning of the year. You can also enter the balances of your year-to-date expense accounts and revenue at any other time. Usually, this year-to-date income and expense data is only accessible at the beginning of each month. Because of this, the beginning of a month is the only other realistic start date that you may use. In this instance, your prior accounting system provides you with income amounts for the entire year as of the preceding month's end. For example, if you've been using Sage 50 Accounting, you can obtain the income and spending amounts for the current year from Sage. You're virtually done if you've specified the start date, provided the essential company details, indicated the majority of your accounting settings, and chosen the day you wish to use QuickBooks.

When you select the **"Leave" option,**

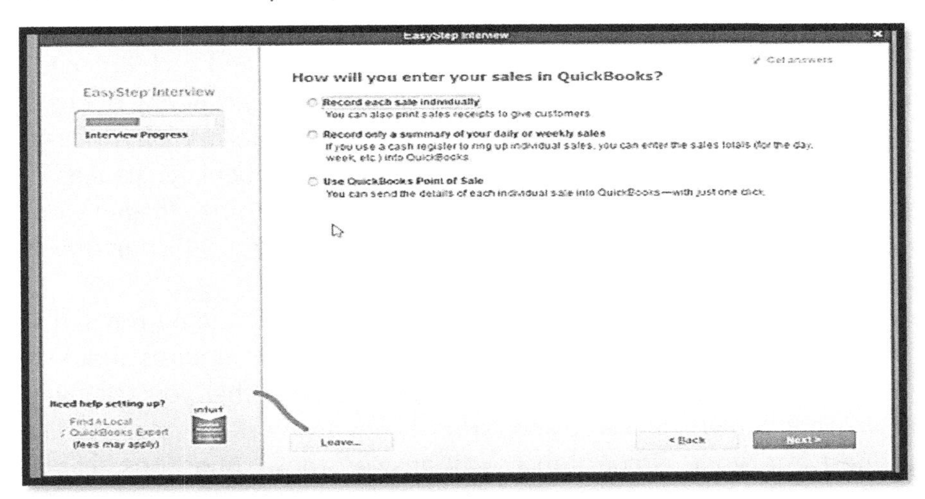

QuickBooks puts you inside the software, prepared for work. However, the EasyStep Interview procedure is not permanently lost. To resume the interview, simply open the file that you were in the middle of configuring. The EasyStep Interview then begins again when you do.

Taking a look at the suggested chart of accounts

At the very conclusion of the **EasyStep Interview,** QuickBooks recommends a starting set of accounts, known as a chart of accounts, depending on the details you provide about your industry and the tax return form you file with the IRS. You may monitor your income, expenses, assets, obligations, and owner's equity using these accounts. The suggested accounts are the ones that QuickBooks indicates with a check, as the screen indicates. These checked accounts are the ones you'll utilize in QuickBooks (at least initially) if nothing else. The check mark indicates that an account has been proposed for removal. The account will not appear in the final chart of accounts since QuickBooks removes the checkmark. Additionally, you can click on an account to include it in the initial chart of accounts by adding a checkmark. If you make modifications that you later decide you don't want, you can go back to the original recommended chart of accounts by clicking the **Restore Recommendations icon** at the bottom of the list. Once you're satisfied with the suggested chart of accounts, click **Next.** Accepting QuickBooks' recommendations is OK because you can alter the chart of accounts at a later time.

Adding your information to the company file

Following the setup of the company file by you and QuickBooks, QuickBooks will prompt you to add personal data.

- **Customers, vendors, and employees:** Select the **first Add button** to add descriptions for clients, suppliers, and staff. QuickBooks inquires as to whether you would prefer to manually enter the data into a worksheet or if it can be obtained from another source, such as an email client or service (Outlook, Gmail, etc.). Since you'll most likely be entering the data by hand, select the relevant option and click Proceed. Enter each client, supplier, or worker in a separate row when QuickBooks opens a worksheet window, being sure to include the address and name information. Once you are done, click **Continue**. Next, QuickBooks prompts you to enter opening balances for customers and vendors, which are the sums you owe or are due; using a page I won't show you. Enter the opening balances in the QuickBooks screen after selecting the **Enter Opening Balances link** to indicate that you have done so.
- **Services and inventory items you sell:** Choose **the second Add button** in the second box to add a description of the products you sell. QuickBooks inquires about your products and services, including whether you offer services, whether you sell inventory goods, and whether you would like to keep track of any such sales. After selecting the option that best fits your circumstances to answer these questions, click **Proceed**. If QuickBooks opens a worksheet window (not shown), each item you sell should have its worksheet row with a description. Don't forget to include a description of any inventory items you have when you convert to QuickBooks. Once you are done, click **Continue.** This procedure must be repeated for every kind of item you sell if you sell multiple types of items.
- **Business bank accounts**: Choose the **Add button in the third box t**o add a description of your company's bank account (or bank accounts). The name, account number, and balance of each bank account should be entered when QuickBooks shows the Add Your

Bank Accounts worksheet window (not displayed). Click **Continue** once you have finished entering all of the required data.

Identifying the Starting Trial Balance

You do not obtain a full trial balance in the QuickBooks company file by default when you set up the QuickBooks Setup procedure, whether you select the Detailed Start/EasyStep Interview version or the default Start version. In QuickBooks, you can see the balances of your bank account, accounts receivable, inventory, and accounts payable, provided that you adhere to the guidelines and advice given in the previous sections. However, to start receiving useful reports from QuickBooks and to utilize the program to provide financial data for your tax returns, you also need to enter all of the trial balance data that is missing.

Activity

1. Install QuickBooks on your device.
2. Run the QuickBooks setup wizard.
3. Identify the starting trial balance.

CHAPTER 2

LOADING THE MASTER FILE LISTS

Practically speaking, when you set up QuickBooks 2024, you establish master file lists in addition to a company file that you'll use to hold financial data about your firm. You can utilize and reuse the information that is stored in this master files lists. Every one of your clients is listed in one of the master file lists; the customer information master file contains the customer's name, address, phone number, account number, and other details. This chapter guides you through the process of populating each master file (or lists, as QuickBooks refers to them) that you must fill out (or at least fill in the majority of) before you start using QuickBooks regularly. One thing to keep in mind is that you don't have to fill up your master files before you start working. That may be all the information you need to get started if you add your current vendors into the vendor master file, your current customers into the customer master file, and so on. You might be able to add everything else on the fly with the data you submitted during the QuickBooks Setup procedure and the inclusion of a few additional lines in important master files. As you deal with windows and dialog boxes that reference master-file information, QuickBooks allows you to add entries to the various master files.

Setting Up the Chart of Accounts List

Every account in your organization, together with its balance, is listed in the chart of accounts. This list is used by QuickBooks to keep track of cash, debts, and money coming in and going out. You can see the transaction history for each account in the register. For more information, you may also run a fast report.

Account types on the chart of accounts

Your chart of accounts offers you various types of accounts for you to able to get your transactions categorized;

- **Assets:** these are various purchases for items like vehicles, equipment, and buildings that are used for your business.
- **Liabilities**: these are the funds you owe and you have not been paid yet.
- **Income**: sales transactions for various products or services that have been sold.
- **Expenses**: these are the various costs for business operations such as advertising and promotion, office supplies, and rent if applicable.

Open your chart of accounts

Choose **Company, Lists, or Accountant, and then click on Chart of Accounts**.

Accounts QuickBooks setup for you

Everybody receives identical standard accounts. QuickBooks incorporates accounts according to your sector. You can manually add the account if you don't see it. Moreover, you can modify, remove, or conceal an account.

Account	What it is	Instantly added by QuickBooks when you.....
Accounts Payable (A/P)	Keeps track of invoices and payments for your company. QuickBooks allows you to select an A/P account when entering and paying bills if your company has numerous A/P accounts.	Get a bill created for the first time.
Accounts Receivable (A/R)	Keeps track of client payments and invoices. QuickBooks allows you to select an A/R account when you invoice or get paid if you use several A/R accounts.	Gets an invoice created for the first time.
Opening Balance Equity	Balances opening balance transactions to maintain the balance of the balance sheet.	Insert the opening balance for a balance sheet account.
Payroll Expense	Keeps track of the company's payroll items, or expenses, such as commissions, bonuses, and salaries. This covers employer-paid health plan premiums as well as employer-paid tax contributions for programs like Social Security and Medicare.	Switch on the payroll for the first time.
Payroll Liabilities	Keeps track of all federal, state, and employee-paid taxes, such as	Switch on payroll for the first

	Medicare and Social Security, as well as all taxes and deductions from your employees' paychecks until you give them over to the government.	time.
Retained Earnings	QuickBooks moves net income into your retained profits account at the start of each fiscal year.	Configure a new company file.
Sales Tax Payable	Keeps track of all the sales tax you get and pay. Any outstanding payments owe money to the sales tax jurisdictions.	Switch on sales tax.
Uncategorized Expense	Expenses that aren't assigned to a particular expenditure account, such as an initial vendor balance.	Insert an opening balance for a vendor.
Uncategorized Income	Income is not assigned to a particular income account, such as a customer's initial balance.	Insert an opening balance for a customer.
Undeposited Funds	Keeps track of the money you get from customers until you deposit it.	
Inventory Asset	Monitor the value of your inventory.	Include an inventory aspect or assembly for the first time.
Reconciliation Discrepancy	Records transactions that have been previously reconciled and altered since the prior account reconciliation.	Insert an adjustment to reconcile discrepancies.

Follow the steps below to include more accounts if there is a need for you to keep track of any other type of transactions.

Windows

- Navigate to the **Lists menu,** and then choose the Chart **of Accounts.**
- Choose **New** from the **Account dropdown menu.**

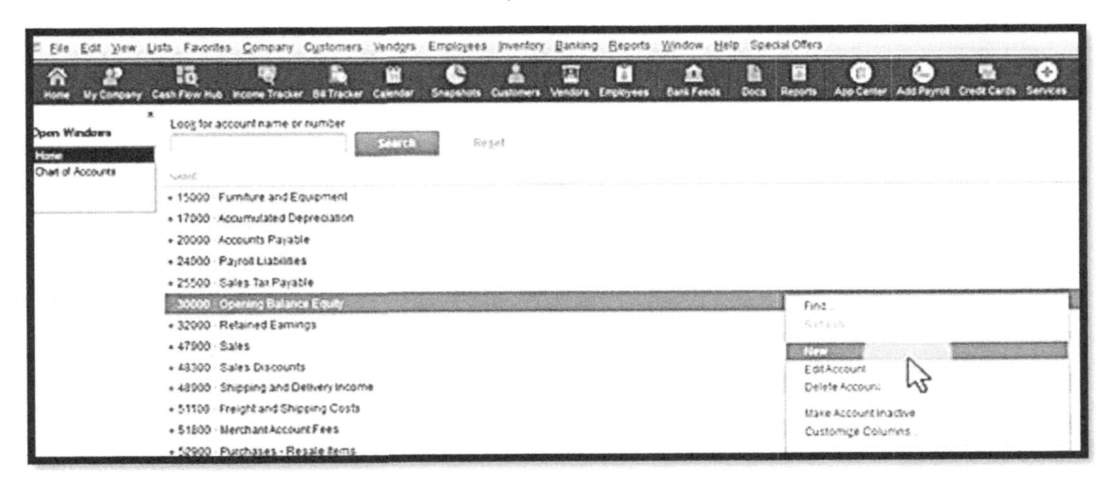

- Choose an account type, and then choose **Continue.**

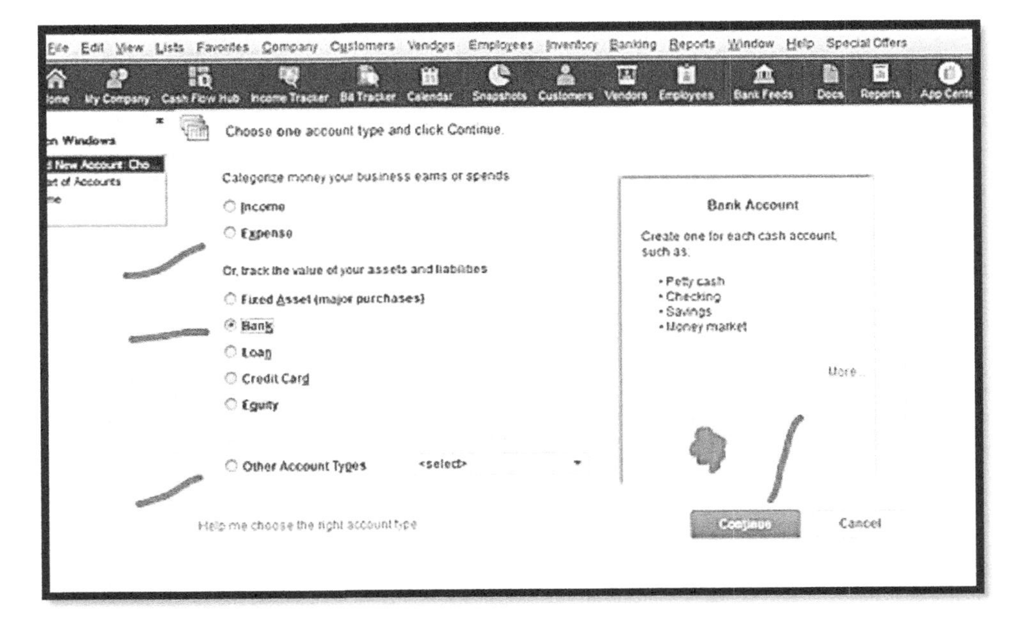

- Fill in the account details.
- Choose **Save & Close.**

To monitor particular accounts under a parent or primary account, you can further create sub-accounts. For instance, your parent's utility account contains separate subaccounts for gas, phone, and water bills.

Note: The account type of the parent and sub-account must match.

- First, navigate to the Lists menu and choose the Chart **of Accounts.**
- Choose **New from the Account dropdown menu.**
- After choosing an account type, click **Continue.**
- Input the account information.
- Check the box next to **Sub Account.**

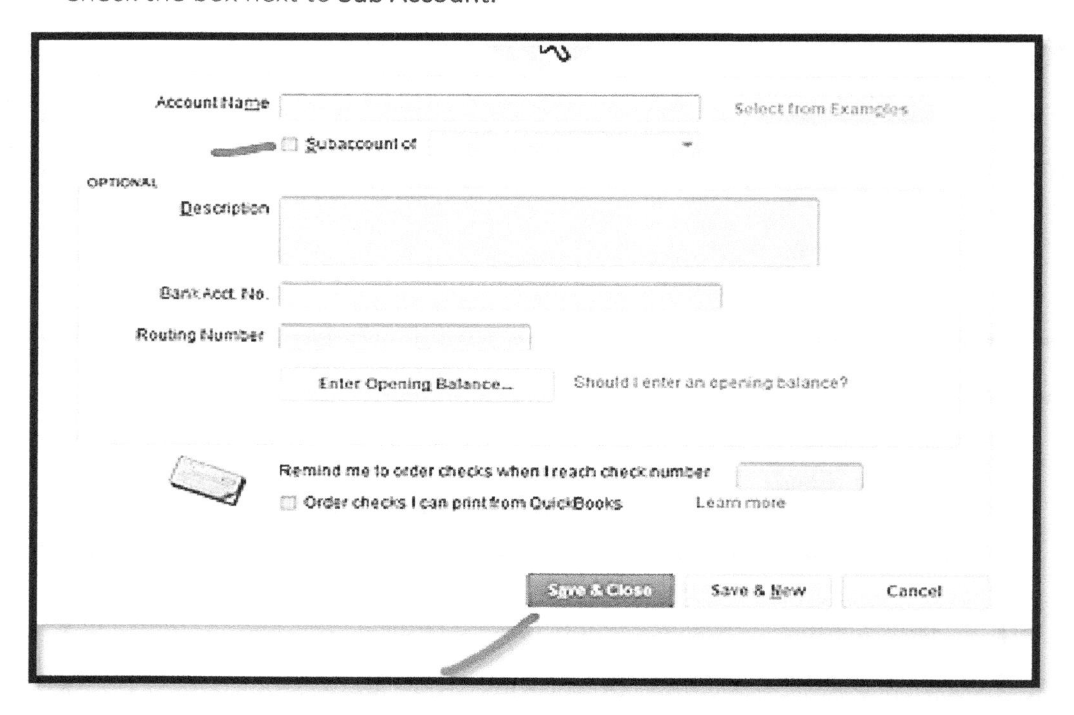

- Choose the parent account from the Subaccount of dropdown.
- Choose "Save & Close."

The Chart of Accounts window's Activities button offers a menu of commands that you can use to write checks, deposit money, record credit card charges, transfer money, create journal entries, reconcile bank accounts, use registers, and generate working trial balance reports.

- You can print reports with account information by using the menu of commands that appears when you click the **Reports button**. You can transfer files from your computer to QuickBooks by using the **Attach button.** An example of a file you can submit is a PDF receipt for an equipment purchase.

Setting Up the Item List

QuickBooks opens the Item List window when you

- Select the **Lists > Item List command.**

This window shows every item you manually entered after completing the Setup Wizard's tasks as well as everything you configured as part of executing QuickBooks Setup. Keep in mind that the item list is crucial! It enables you to maintain a record of the goods you purchase, hold, and sell to clients.

Working with the Price Level List

You can make dynamic pricing modifications using the pricing Level list when you write invoices, credit memos, and other invoices. Also, take note of the fact that the Price Level list has a direct bearing on how you handle and charge for inventory items.

Using Sales Tax Codes

You can use the codes, or acronyms, listed in the Sales Tax Code list to designate certain things as taxable or nontaxable. QuickBooks opens a window with the current sales tax codes listed in it if you select this command. (Typically, you'll see Tax and Non as the two active codes.)

Unless you instruct QuickBooks to track sales tax either during setup or subsequently, the Sales Tax Code list is not displayed. Follow these steps to add sales tax codes:

- Navigate to the **Edit menu**, and then choose **Preferences.**
- Choose **Sales Tax** then locate the **Company Preferences tab on the preferences window.**

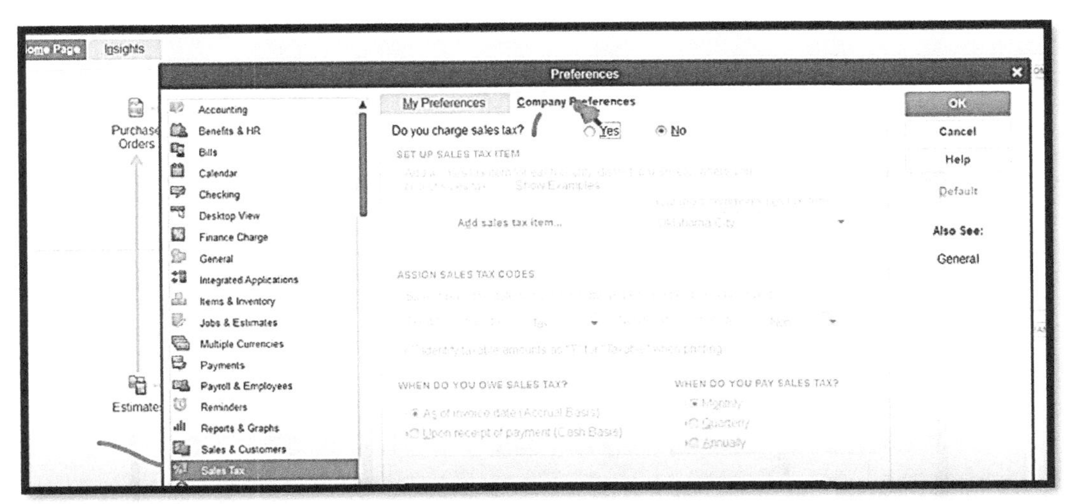

- Choose **Yes** to switch on sales tax.

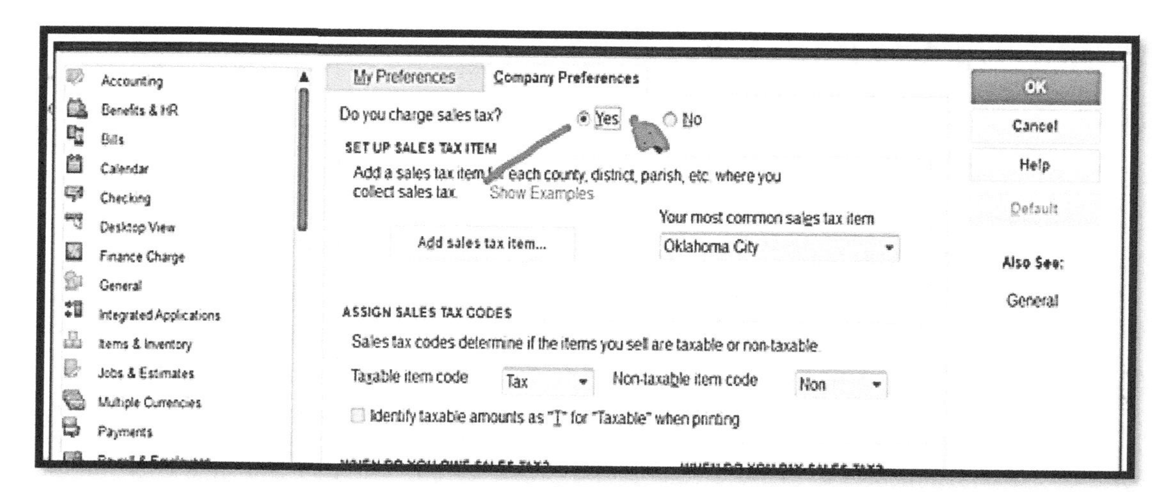

- For every county, district, city, etc. where you collect sales tax, set up the sales tax items or sales tax groups. To accomplish this, select **Add sales tax item.**

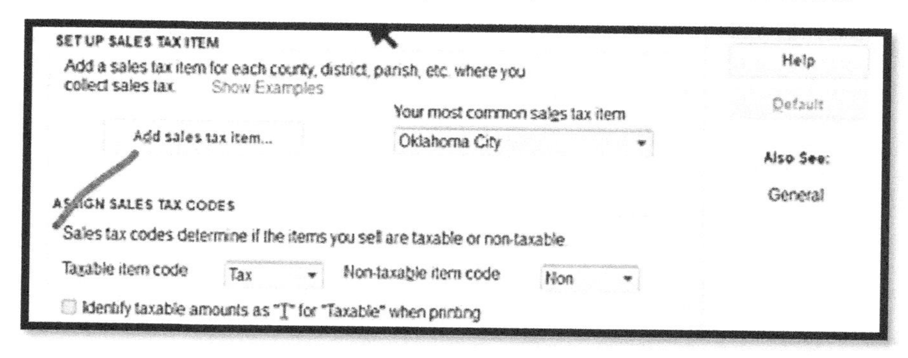

Follow the steps below to create sales tax items;

- Select **Sales Tax Item** from the drop-down menu under **Type.**

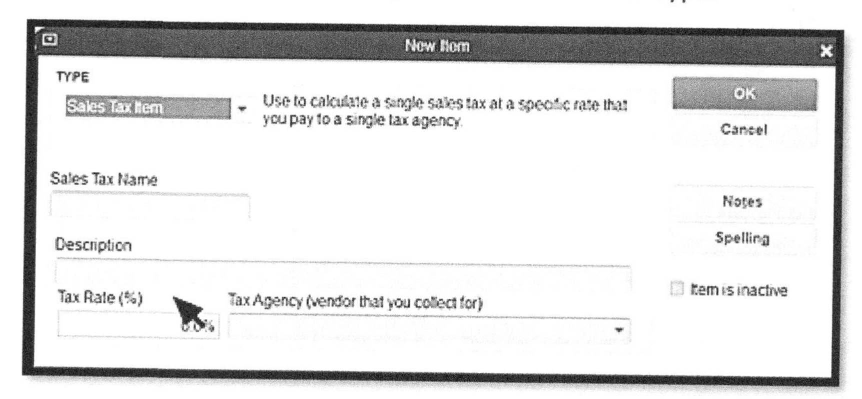

- Enter the preferred name for the tax item in the **Sales Tax Name field.** It is recommended that you choose **the tax location as the name**. The Description field is where you can add further details.
- Enter **the item's exact rate in the Tax Rate (%) area.**
- Enter **the name of the collecting agency (configured as a vendor) in the Tax Agency field**. To set up the agency if it isn't already on the list, choose **Add New.**
- Click **OK.**

To edit an already existing sales tax item, follow the steps below;

- Select **Item List from the Lists menu.**
- Locate the **sales tax item** that needs updating.
- To edit an item, right-click on it and choose **Edit Item (QB for Mac: click the pencil icon).**
- Revise details such as the tax agency, rate, and name for sales tax.
- Click **OK.**

Follow the steps below to create a sales tax group;

For several sales tax items that are included in a single sales transaction, create a sales tax group. Even while sales taxes appear as a single line item on your invoices and sales receipts, you may track and report on them separately when you set up a sales tax group.

- Give codes for sales taxes. You can track taxable and non-taxable sales and/or consumers with the use of sales tax codes. You can generate a report that separates the total amount of taxable and non-taxable sales by setting up and designating the appropriate sales tax code. Two tax codes—TAX (taxable) and NON (non-taxable)—are automatically generated in QuickBooks when you enable sales tax. When you have clients and goods for which you must collect tax, you use TAX. NON is used for consumers and goods that are not subject to taxes, such as out-of-state transactions, products that your customers will resell, and non-profit organizations.
- Decide on the sales tax basis (cash or accrual). Consider the accounting policies and preferences of your organization.
- Decide how often you would like to pay the sales tax (quarterly, annual, monthly).
- Click **OK.**

Setting up the non-taxable status of an item

- Select **Item List from the Lists menu.**
- Choose **Item then New (or Edit Item) from the Item List window.**
- Select **Non-Taxable Sales (or Non-Taxable Labor) from the tax code drop-down menu.**

Set up the non-taxable status of a customer

- Select **Customer Center from the Customers menu.**
- To put up a client as non-exempt, right-click on their name and choose **Edit client: job.**

Note: Choose **New Customer & Job > New Customer** if the customer hasn't been set up yet.

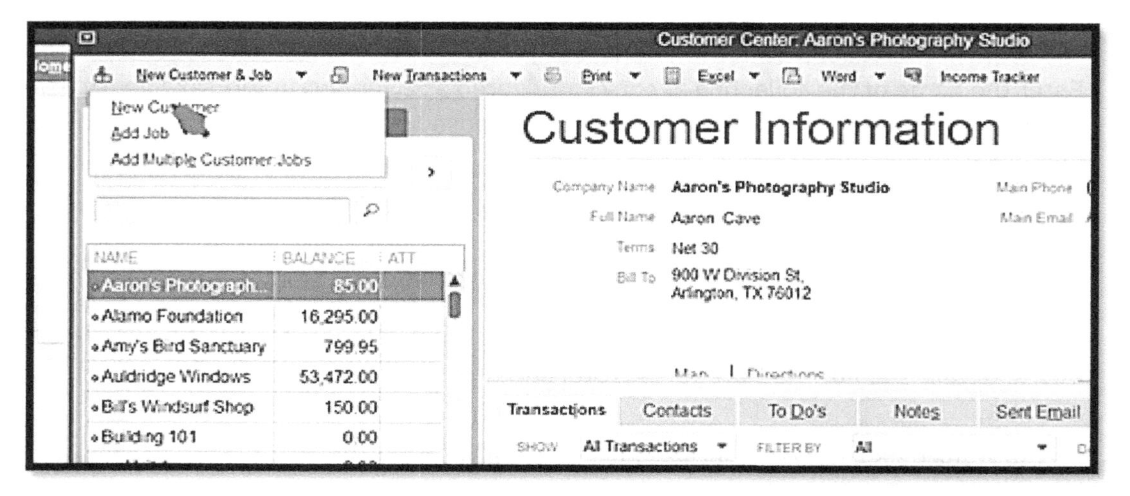

- Navigate to the **Sales Tax Settings tab on the Edit customer screen.**
- Select the **Non-Taxable Sales (or Service) option from the Tax Code drop-down menu**. Enter the customer's resale certification number in the **Resale No. column.**
- Click **OK.**

Create specific tax codes

- To generate a tax code tailored to your company's requirements, click the **Tax Code drop-down menu** and select **Add New**. The following are other non-taxable codes that you can use:

Sales tax code	When to use
OOS	**OUT-OF-SALES.** For sales made outside of the state, many states do not impose sales tax. A customer who purchased your product from your company catalog but resides in a different state may be assigned this sales tax code. This non-taxable sales tax code is already present in a lot of QuickBooks company files.
LBR	LABOR. As labor services are not taxed in many states, LBR may be assigned to a service item. This non-taxable sales tax code is already present in certain QuickBooks

	company files.
NPO	NON-PROFIT ORGANIZATIONS. Even in cases where the goods and services you offer are subject to sales tax, these organizations do not have to pay it. A customer would be allocated an NPO.
GOV	GOV. Sales to government offices that happen to not be taxed.
WHL	WHOLESALERS. Customers who happen to be reselling the goods they got from you.
RSL	RESELLERS. Clients that use your products to make their products that they then sell, or who resell the goods they purchase from you.

Setting Up a Payroll Item List

Items that show up on employee payroll check stubs are identified in the Payroll Item list. The Payroll Item list is not even a concern if you outsource your payroll processing to an external payroll service bureau, which is a wise decision. Again, don't worry about the Payroll Item list if you're utilizing the QuickBooks Enhanced Payroll Service. (In either scenario, the payroll items you use to record payroll are set up by the QuickBooks team.) Furthermore, you don't even need to track payroll inside QuickBooks when using Intuit's comprehensive "we-do-everything" Payroll Service because QuickBooks employees handle payroll on their computers at their office.

If payroll items must be added, take these actions:

- Click on **Lists > Payroll Item List command.**

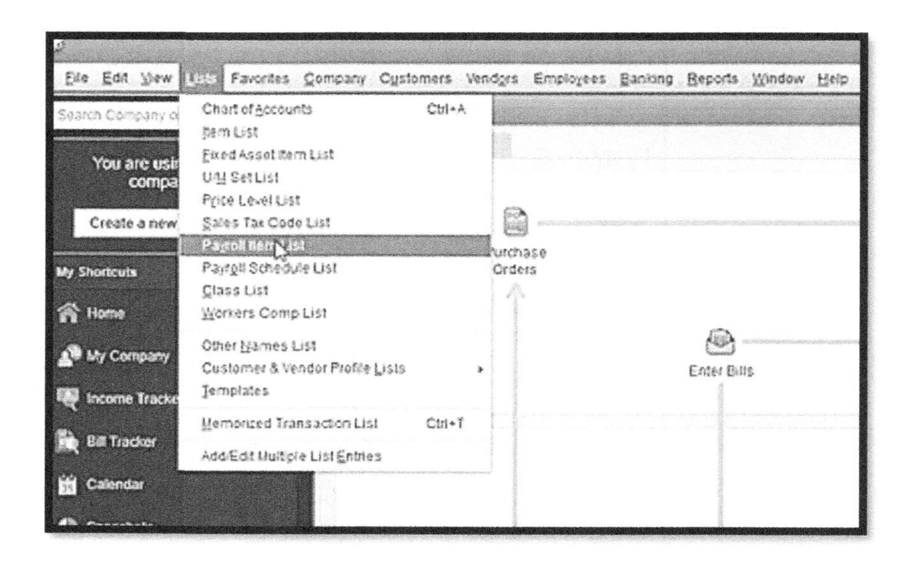

- Choose the **Payroll Item button** and then click on **Payroll Item > New for the addition of a new Payroll Item.**

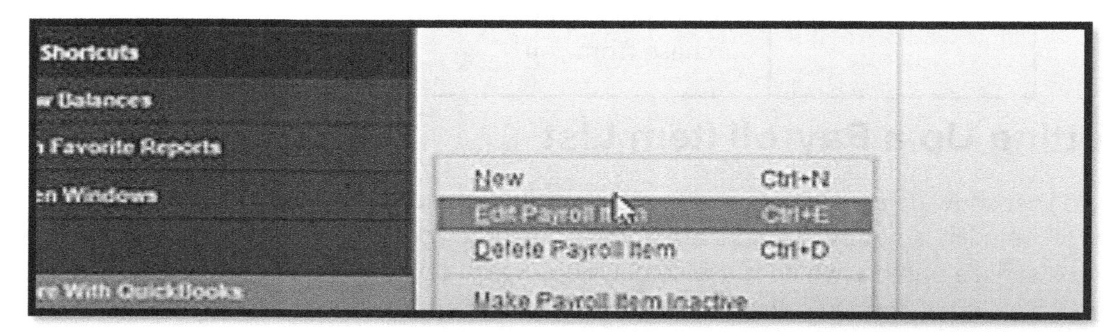

- Give the payroll item a name.
- Choose the **Next button** to go through the rest of the payroll items setup questions; this will also complete the payroll item setup.

To deal with the Payroll Item list, you can access essential commands from the Payroll Item menu. The menu contains commands to **add, delete, rename, make active, and print the list of payroll items in addition to the commands you use to add entries to the list.**

Setting up Classes

Using classes in QuickBooks allows you to track and separate financial data in ways that aren't achievable with other accounting data points like the account number, customer, sales representative, item, and so on. Classes can be used, for instance, by a company to divide up financial data according to stores, business divisions, or regions.

To arrange classes, take the following actions:

- Click on **Lists > Class List command.** Choose the **Use Class Tracking for Transaction check box after selecting Edit > Preferences, Accounting, and Company Preferences tabs if the Class List command is not visible.**
- Click on **Class > New** at the lower part of the window to have a new class created.
- Insert a name or an abbreviation in the Class Name box to give a new class a name.
- Select the **Subclass Of check box** and then select t**he parent class from the Subclass Of drop-down list** if the class you're setting up is indeed a subclass of a parent class.
- Choose **OK** to get the class saved. As an alternative, you may choose the **Next button** to save the class and bring up the **New Class dialog box again,** or you can click **Cancel** to not save the class.

You can check the **Class Is Inactive checkbox** to make the class no longer usable. When you choose the **Class button,** a menu called **Class appears.** You may use this menu to change the selected class's details, delete **the selected class,** make it inactive, print a list of classes, and perform various other helpful functions. These are all quite simple commands. Try them out to see how they function.

Setting Up a Customer List

All of your customers and their details, including shipping and billing addresses, are kept track of in a customer list.

To add a customer to the Customer list, follow these steps:

- Select **the Customers then select Customer Center Command. QuickBooks will then show the Customer Information window.**
- Choose the **New Customer Window & Job drop-down list that is located on the toolbar then proceed to the command of New Customer if you would like to add a new customer.**

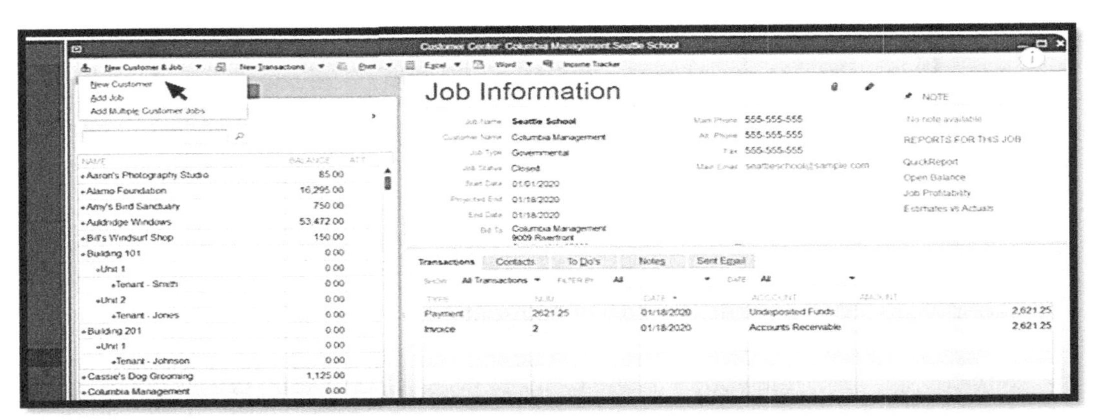

- Provide the customer with a short name with the use of the **Customer Name box.**

- Select **the very currency you use in billing your customer** if you happen to bill your customer in a different currency from your usual home currency. QuickBooks wants you to detect when you invoice a customer and collect payments from them in a currency other than your home currency. If you informed QuickBooks that you work in several currencies, you would have done this while performing the EasyStep Interview setup process.
- Ensure that you do not pay attention to the Opening Balance and As Of boxes. Using the Opening Balance and As Of boxes to establish the customer's opening balance is generally not a good idea. Setting the accounts receivable balance for your new customers in that manner is incorrect. This effectively sets up the debit portion of an entry without the associated credit portion. You'll eventually need to make bizarre journal entries to catch up on your unfinished bookkeeping. However, there is one exception to the general rule, which is covered in the tip that follows.
- To provide the company name and contact details, such as the billing and shipping addresses, phone numbers, fax numbers, email addresses, and so on, use the boxes on the **Address Info tab.**

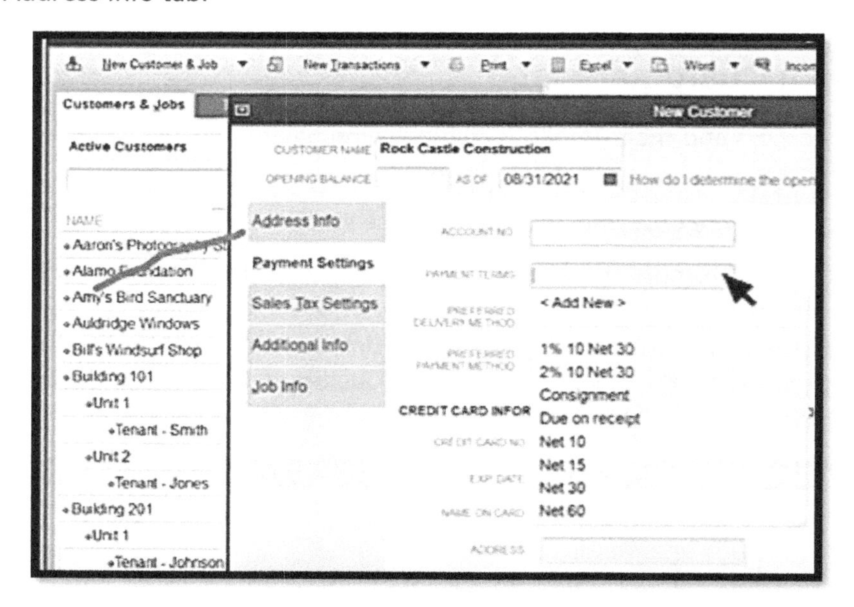

- Choose **the Payment Settings tab** to show the set of boxes available. Account numbers, credit limits, periods of payment, preferred modes of payment and delivery, and even credit card information can all be noted for a customer. It should be noted that you can indicate to customers that they can make payments to you via bank transfer or credit card by using the Online Payments check boxes, but you must first have these services set up. When you click one of these options, QuickBooks asks you to configure the services if you haven't already.

- If for any reason you happen to be tracking sales taxes, choose the **Sales Tax settings tab** to show the boxes you will make use of in identifying this customer's sales tax rate. You can select the sales tax code that applies to this specific customer using the Tax Code drop-down list on the Sales Tax Settings tab (not visible). Additionally, the actual sales tax item and, if applicable, the resale number can be found.
- Add **some more information about the customer.** QuickBooks has several additional boxes that you may use to gather and store customer information when you click the Additional Info tab.

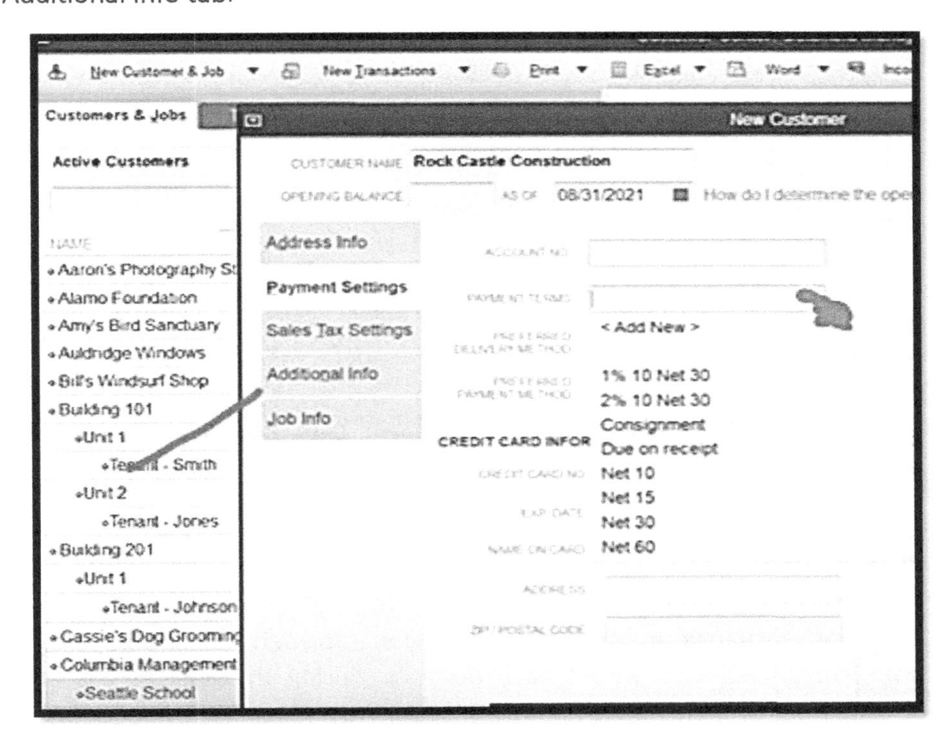

For example, you can classify a customer as belonging to a specific customer type using the Customer Type drop-down list.

- You can also get more specific by choosing the Job Info tab to make a description of the customer's job.
- Once you are through making a description of the customer, choose the Save & Close or Save & New button to ensure that your description is well saved.

Setting Up the Vendor List

A vendor list is used to maintain track of your vendors, much like a customer list is used to keep track of all of your customers. Similar to a customer list, a vendor list enables you to gather and document data, including the vendor's address and contact details.

Take these actions to add a vendor to your Vendor list:

- From the Vendor Center command, **choose the Vendors.**
- Choose the **New Vendor drop-down list** on the toolbar and then select **New Vendor to include a new vendor.**

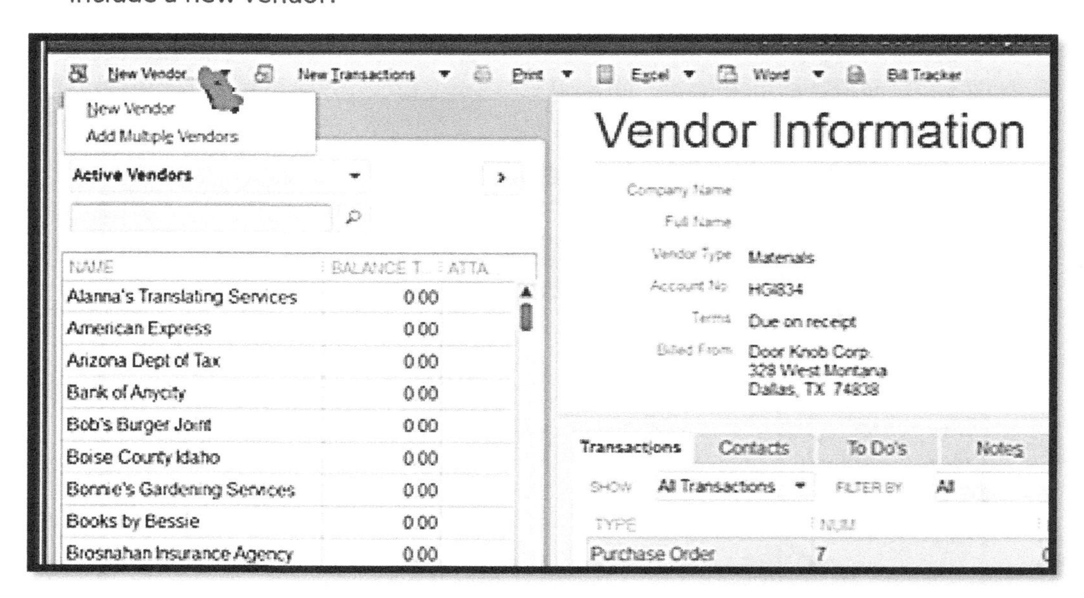

- Name the vendor in the Vendor Name box.
- If you happen to pay your vendor in another separate currency that is not the same as your usual home currency, choose the currency from the Currency drop-down list. QuickBooks wants you to recognize when you get bills from or pay vendors in a currency other than your home currency. If you informed QuickBooks that you work in various currencies, you would have done so during the EasyStep Interview setup process.
- Disregard the **As Of and Opening Balance fields.**
  The Opening Balance and As Of boxes should remain empty. The initial balance owed to a vendor and the date the amount is due are entered into those boxes by ignorant people, but these entries simply lead to issues down the road. There will be a need much later to track down and fix this mistake. There is, however, an exception to the general rule—which is covered in the tip that follows—just like when you bring on new clients.
- Provide the information and address of the vendor. You can gather vendor name and address information by using the several clear boxes provided by the Address Info tab. Naturally, you type the vendor's entire name in the Company Name field.

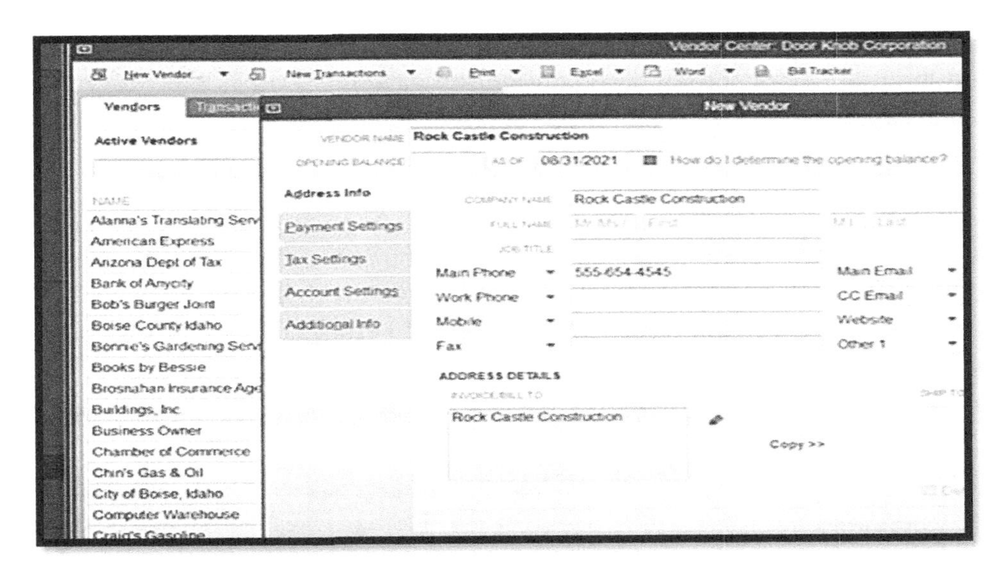

The Edit Address Information dialog box, which appears when you click the **Edit buttons on the Address Info tab**, allows you to enter the address in standard street address, city, state, and zip code format. The Address blocks for Billed From and Shipped From have the Edit buttons to the right of them.

- You can choose to include any more information as you deem necessary. The Account Settings, Tax Settings, and Additional Info tabs in QuickBooks display a few more boxes that you can use to gather and store information in addition to the most pertinent vendor data, which is collected by the Payment Settings tab (which includes account number, credit limit, and payment terms). You can obtain the vendor's tax identification number through the **Tax Settings tab,** which will enable you to provide a Form 1099 to the vendor at the end of the year, as occasionally mandated by federal tax rules.

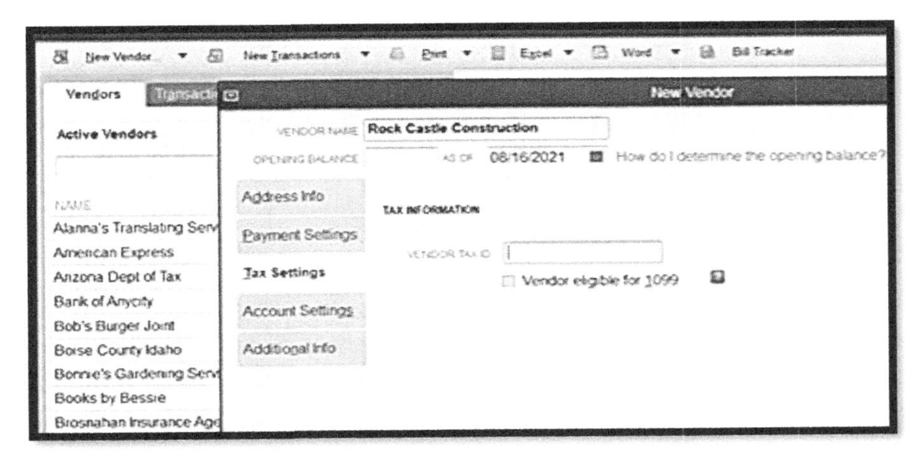

You can designate which accounts QuickBooks should use to automatically fill in account fields when you input a vendor transaction by using the Account Settings tab. You can add more custom fields and classify the vendor based on category using the **Additional Info tab.**

- Lastly, select **OK.** The vendor window will then be closed and you will be redirected to the Vendor Center.

However, take note that QuickBooks displays boxes you can use to list the accounts you want QuickBooks to fill in for you automatically when you record a check to a vendor or when you record a bill from a vendor when you click the **Account Settings tab** (the fourth tab available in the **New Vendor window**).

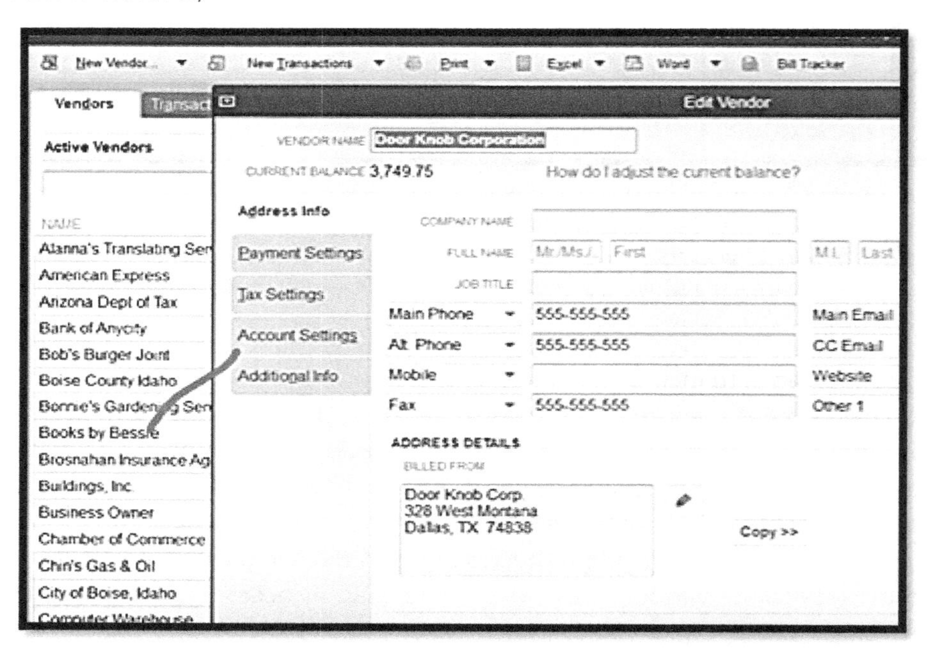

You might instruct QuickBooks to automatically fill in that expense category the next time you enter a bill or record a check to pay that vendor, for example, if the phone company receives the check for telephone expenses. If you pick this option, you won't have to look through all of your accounts to find phone charges because it won't enter an amount because, well, the amount can vary.

Setting Up a Price Level List

You can create customized pricing for various clients or tasks by using price tiers. QuickBooks will automatically get the proper custom pricing for a customer or job whenever you issue an invoice, estimate, sales receipt, sales order, or credit memo for those customers or jobs after you create a price level and associate it with one or more customers or jobs. To change an item's price on a sales form, build price levels and use them. A sales form can also be created with the prices manually changed. Billable time and reimbursable mileage items automatically use price levels connected with customers. They are not automatically applied to invoices made from estimates or reimbursable items and expenses from purchase transactions.

Follow the steps below to design a price level;

- Navigate to the **Price Level List from the Lists menu.**
- Choose **New after selecting Price Level at the bottom.**
- Choose the **pricing level type after entering the price level name.**

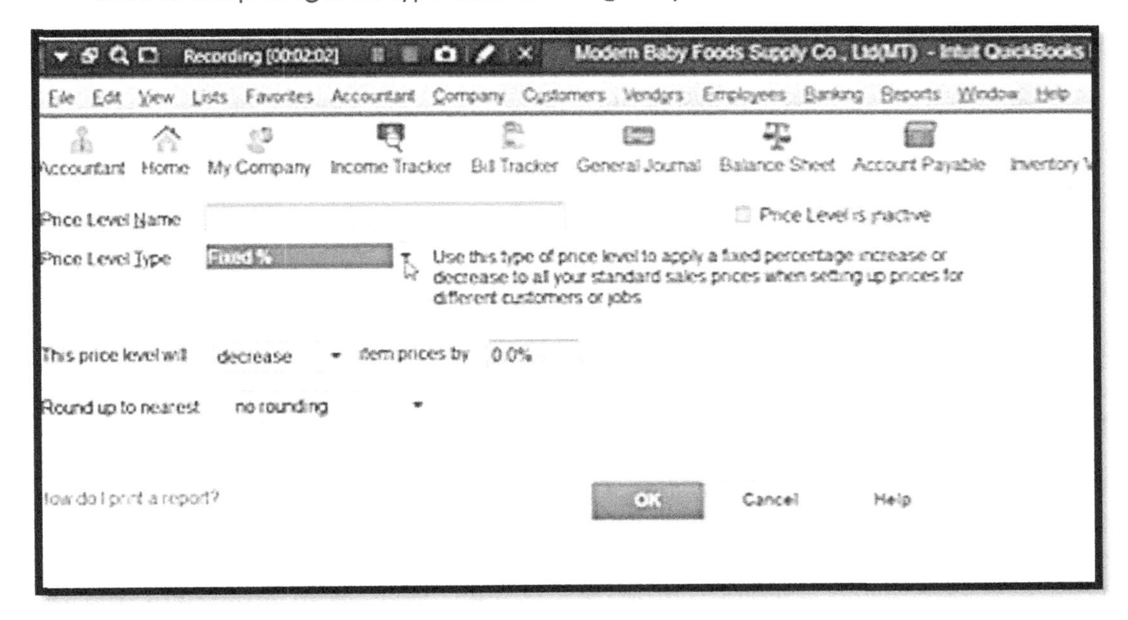

  - **Fixed Percentage Price Levels:** allows you to set a fixed % price increase or decrease for all items for a certain client or job. You could, for instance, set a fixed percentage pricing level for a consumer who receives a 10% discount on all of your goods and services. When using fixed % price levels, you have the option to set this Company preference to round sales prices up to the next whole dollar.
  - **Per Item Price Levels:** allows you to establish unique prices for products connected to various clients or tasks. For instance, you may charge $8 for product A (usually priced at $10), $5 for product B (usually priced at $5.50), and your regular pricing for product C if you want to implement a per-item price level for your preferred clients. Another example would be if you had a specific customer for whom you agreed to bill $50 per hour (normally valued at $70) for research time and $30 per hour (usually valued at $35 per hour) for administrative work. You can only access this if you have the Premier or Enterprise edition of QuickBooks Desktop.

- Select **OK.**

To make use of price levels, check the two different ways below by which you can use them;

Add a price level directly to items on a sales form

- Make **a bill of sale or other type of transaction.**
- Navigate to the Rate column, click **the drop-down menu, and select the price level that you want to apply to the item**. Take note that the adjusted amount of the item is indicated next to each pricing level.
- Ensure **you save the transaction.**

Associate a price level with one or more customers or jobs

- Click on the **Customers menu and then Customer Center.**
- Click twice **on a customer in the list.**
- Navigate to the **Payment Settings tab.**
- Choose the **Price Level drop-down** and make a choice of the price level you would like to link with the customer.
- Choose **OK.**

Note: Items will immediately display with the updated quantity anytime you create a sales form for a customer if you associate that customer with a pricing level. Invoices, estimates, sales receipts, credit notes, and sales orders are among the relevant sales documents.

Setting Up a Billing Rate Level List

The amount that you charge for services is determined by a billing rate. For instance, a law company may simply offer hours of legal consultation; yet, the item "legal advice" would be priced differently for each practitioner. A recent law school graduate's time billing could be done at one rate, while a senior partner in the firm might bill at a different, most likely considerably higher rate. You can set unique service item charges for various workers and vendors using billing rate levels. If you discover that a single standard cost for a certain service isn't always enough, you might want to employ them. For instance, depending on experience level or labor burden costs, multiple personnel doing the same service may bill at varying rates. Alternatively, you may bill an employee at various rates according to the complexity of the work. QuickBooks will automatically fill in the relevant rate for each service item based on who performed the job each time you create an invoice with billable time once you set billing rate levels and associate them with workers and vendors.

- **Assign each of the billing rate levels to people who are on the Employees, Vendors, or Other Names list.**
  - Launch the list to which you would like to include a billing rate level.
    - **For employees**: choose the **Employees menu** and then select the Employee Center.
    - **For Vendors**: choose the **Vendors menu** and then the Vendor Center.
    - **For other names**: choose the Lists menu then select **Other Names List.**

- o When in the list, click twice **on the name you would like to link a billing rate level to.**
    - o Navigate to the **Payment Settings (for vendors) or Additional Info (for employees) tab.**
    - o Choose the **Billing Rate Level drop down then click on the billing rate level you would like to link with the name.**
    - o Choose **OK.**
- Keep track of the time you wish to bill. As you monitor the clock, allocate the hours to a client or task. Keep in mind that time-tracking data can be utilized for payroll, client bills, or both. However, billing rate levels are not related to payroll; they are simply utilized when sending bills to your clients.
- Make an invoice. To enter your billable time, select **Add Time/Cost** on the Main tab at the top of the form. Then, depending on who performed the task, the proper billing rate will be applied for each service item.

Setting Up Your Employees

The Employee Center window appears in QuickBooks when you select the Employees > Employee Center command. This window allows you to view an active or inactive employee list that you have entered into QuickBooks. Employees can also be added to the list by using the New Employee button in this box.

Setting Up an Other Names List

QuickBooks shows the Other Names list box when you select the

- **Lists > Other Names List command.** The companies or individuals that you pay but who don't fit into one of these other typical categories—customers, vendors, or employees—are shown under the Other Names section. For example, you may use the Other Names list to find the government entities you pay.

Select the **Other Names button** on the Other Names window, which is located at the bottom, to add a name to the list.

- Click the **Other Names menu and select New** when QuickBooks displays. Providing a name, identifying the entity, recording an address, and other fields are available in the New Name window that QuickBooks displays when you select the New command.

Setting Up the Profile Lists

QuickBooks presents a submenu of commands that you may use to build some of the mini-lists that it utilizes to make your bookkeeping and accounting easier,

- If you choose the **Lists > Customer & Vendor Profile List command**. Sales representatives, customer and vendor categories, job types, payment terms, customer communications, payment methods, shipment methods, and vehicles are all included in the Profile lists. The majority of the Profile listings are really easy to navigate. For instance, QuickBooks shows the Sales Rep list window when you select the Sales Rep list command. Next, select **New from the drop-down list by clicking the Sales Rep. in QuickBooks, the New Sales Rep dialog box appears.**

To alleviate any remaining accounting apprehension, let me just clarify that you input the sales representative's name in the Sales Rep Name field. The sales representative's initials are then entered into the Sales Rep Initials box, heedlessly. QuickBooks adds the sales representative to your Sales Rep list when you click **OK.** The other Profile lists function in an analogous, basic manner. You select **New** after clicking the Profile List button and selecting the Profile list from the submenu. You utilize one or two boxes to describe the new Profile list when QuickBooks shows a window. You can keep a list of business cars by using the Vehicle list if you want to track vehicle mileage in QuickBooks. Keep in mind that you often need to track business vehicle mileage to claim business vehicle expenses as a tax deduction. Using this list to track your business vehicles is simple; simply select the **Company > Enter Vehicle Mileage option to get started.**

Activity

1. **Configure the following;**

- Chart of account list
- Item list
- Payroll Item list
- Classes
- Customer list
- Vendor list
- Fixed Asset list
- Price level list
- Billing rate level list
- Profile list

CHAPTER 3

FINE-TUNING QUICKBOOKS

By customizing options, you may adjust QuickBooks so that it works just for you. Just so you know, when you run QuickBooks Setup via the Detailed Start path (also called the QuickBooks EasyStep Interview), you are providing QuickBooks with a lot of information that it may use to fine-tune. For example, the EasyStep Interview uses the sales tax preferences to explain how sales tax should function for your firm if you select that you charge customers sales tax. Considering these choices affect QuickBooks's functionality and a specific user's experience with it, this chapter explains how to modify the preferences. You will learn a lot from quite a bunch of materials even though none of it is very complex because QuickBooks offers a comprehensive set of preferences options.

Accessing the Preferences Settings

You can choose to configure preferences within QuickBooks in two different ways;

During the Detailed Start/EasyStep Interview

When you perform the EasyStep Interview in QuickBooks, you set all the preferences—or at least all the initial preferences. The choices that the Detailed Start/EasyStep Interview sets are usually the right ones. QuickBooks asks highly intelligent questions and converts your responses into settings for preferences. It may still be necessary for you to check and adjust these preferences, though, if your business evolves, if you make an error during the setup interview, or if someone else in your organization conducted the Detailed Start/EasyStep Interview.

Changing the preferences manually

By selecting the Edit > Preferences command

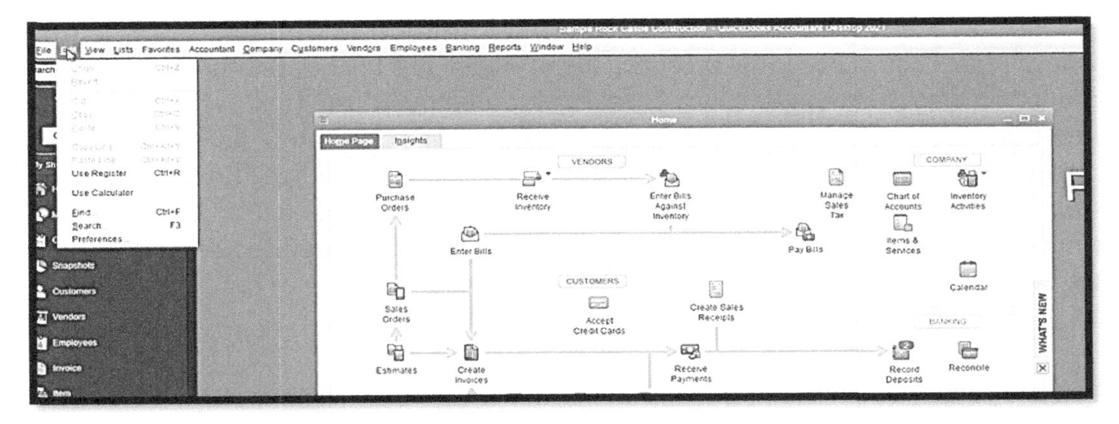

You can manually alter the preferences. QuickBooks opens the dialog box labeled Preferences. QuickBooks organizes preference categories. For example, all preferences related to accounting are organized into an accounting preference set, and all choices related to checking accounts are gathered into a checking preference set. The Preferences dialog box generally provides two tabs of preferences for each preference group, which is another thing to keep in mind. Individual user preferences can be found under the My Preferences tab. The firm Preferences tab displays preferences linked to the firm data file.

Not all My Preferences tabs offer you the ability to modify QuickBooks' operating system. A specific set of choices may or may not provide options for personalization. For example, Bill's set of choices does not offer any personalized options under the My Choices page. Put another way, you cannot inform QuickBooks that various users at your company receive different bills. Every user inside a company must be able to utilize billing in the same way. QuickBooks may provide users with several alternatives depending on other preferences and settings.

Setting the Accounting Preferences

There is only one option available in the Accounting Preferences dialog box's My Preferences tab: you can instruct QuickBooks to automatically fill in certain fields when you record a general journal entry. But don't let the lack of customization annoy you. When you consider it, this nearly complete absence of individually tailored preferences makes sense. Accounting for a business must function uniformly and without exception for all employees. However, there are many corporate options that you can specify for accounting. Once more, this makes sense when you consider it. Accounting systems are managed differently by different companies.

Making use of account numbers

QuickBooks allows you to identify accounts in the accounts list or the Chart of Accounts list by name by default. You can tell QuickBooks that you prefer to use account numbers over account names for account identification by checking the Use Account Numbers check box. For example, the account you use to track wage spending may be called "wages." Account numbers are commonly used by larger firms or those with very long lists of accounts.

You have more control over how accounts are arranged on a financial statement and how new accounts are added to the Chart of Accounts list when you use numbers. You can instruct QuickBooks to display the lowest subaccount in financial statements rather than the higher parent account by checking the Show Lowest Subaccount Only check box. Subaccounts, or accounts within accounts, can be created with QuickBooks. Additionally, sub-sub accounts—accounts inside subaccounts—can be made. Sub-accounts are used to keep a closer eye on assets, liabilities, equity levels, revenue, and expenses.

Configuring general accounting options

The Company preferences tab offers the following six general accounting check boxes date warnings and closing date configurations.

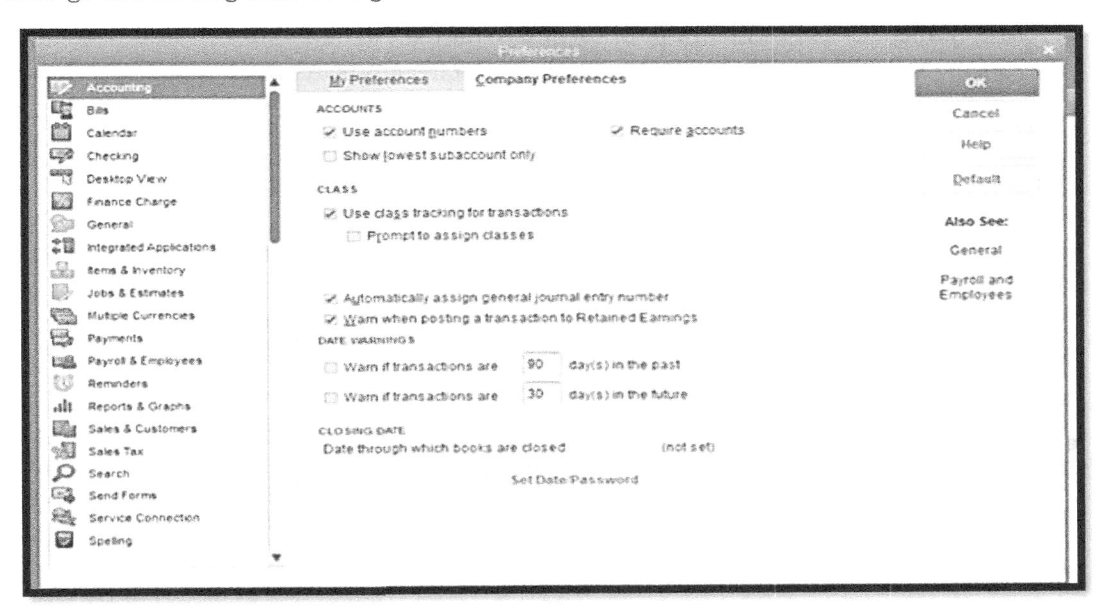

- **Use Account Numbers**: You can input an account number for a transaction if you check the Use Account Numbers check box. When you select the corresponding checkbox labeled "Show Lowest Subaccount Only," QuickBooks is instructed to show only the account number and name of any sub-accounts you may be using—not the account's whole history. This option may clean up displays and make it simpler to identify which account you are looking at if you utilize a lot of levels of subaccounts.
- **Require Accounts:** If you check the Require Accounts check box, QuickBooks is notified that a transaction needs to have an account specified. This is logical. Accounting isn't done if you aren't tracking the sums coming into and going out of the company utilizing accounts. In my humble view, there would never be a reason to deselect the Require Accounts check box.
- **Use Class Tracking for Transactions**: You can instruct QuickBooks to track your financial data using classes in addition to accounts by checking the Use Class Tracking for Transactions check box. You can divide account-level data in different ways using classes. Although it sounds difficult, this is fairly easy. You can monitor revenue and expenses by categories of revenue and expense, for instance, using the account list. Expenses can be monitored through the use of categories including supplies, rent, and wages. Thus, classes give you a mechanism to monitor this data in a different dimension. For example, you can divide your wage expense into the wages paid to your

two business sites. A restaurateur who owns two eateries might find this useful. It should be noted that QuickBooks further offers checkboxes for you to select whether or not the program should urge you to assign classes and to assign classes to names, accounts, or other objects.

- **Automatically Assign General Journal Entry Number**: When you use the Make General Journal Entries command in QuickBooks, this check box instructs the program to give numbers to the general journal entries you submit. This check box should remain selected. By the way, your professional on-staff accountant or your CPA usually enter general journal entries.
- **Warn When Posting a Transaction to Retained Earnings**: If you check this option, QuickBooks will alert you if it detects any attempt to debit or credit the retained profits account directly by you or by another party. (In general, you shouldn't debit or credit the retained earnings account directly; in any event, only qualified accountants would record transactions into retained earnings.)
- **Date Warnings:** QuickBooks is instructed to alert you through the Date Warnings boxes if you enter (or someone else enters) a transaction with a date that is either too long in the past or too far in the future. If you select one of the Date Warnings boxes, you should also provide the number of days that are too far in the past or too far in the future.
- **Closing Date Settings**: You can specify a date before which changes to your QuickBooks data file are not permitted using the Closing Date field. Put differently, you are telling QuickBooks that you do not want any modifications made to the QuickBooks data file before this date if you set the closing date to December 31, 2023. This implies that a frightening warning message will appear if someone tries to change a transaction that is dated before your closing date. Additionally, it implies that no transaction may be entered using a date that is earlier than this closure date. When someone tries to add or edit an old transaction, you can select a closing date and generate the password that will be needed. To do this, click the Set **Date/Password option.**

In earlier iterations of QuickBooks, you could use the Company Preferences tab of the Accounting Preferences dialog box to toggle the Audit Trail function on and off. However, an always-on audit trail is a feature of all modern versions of QuickBooks, so the Audit Trail check-box accounting setting is no longer present. By the way, an audit trail is only a record of the individuals who make changes to transactions. As one might expect, auditors adore audit trails. An Internal Revenue Service auditor or your CPA, for example, can use audit trails to investigate why an account balance is what it is after the fact.

Setting the Bills Preferences

You can set company-wide options for managing vendor bills by displaying the options dialog box and clicking the **Bills icon**.

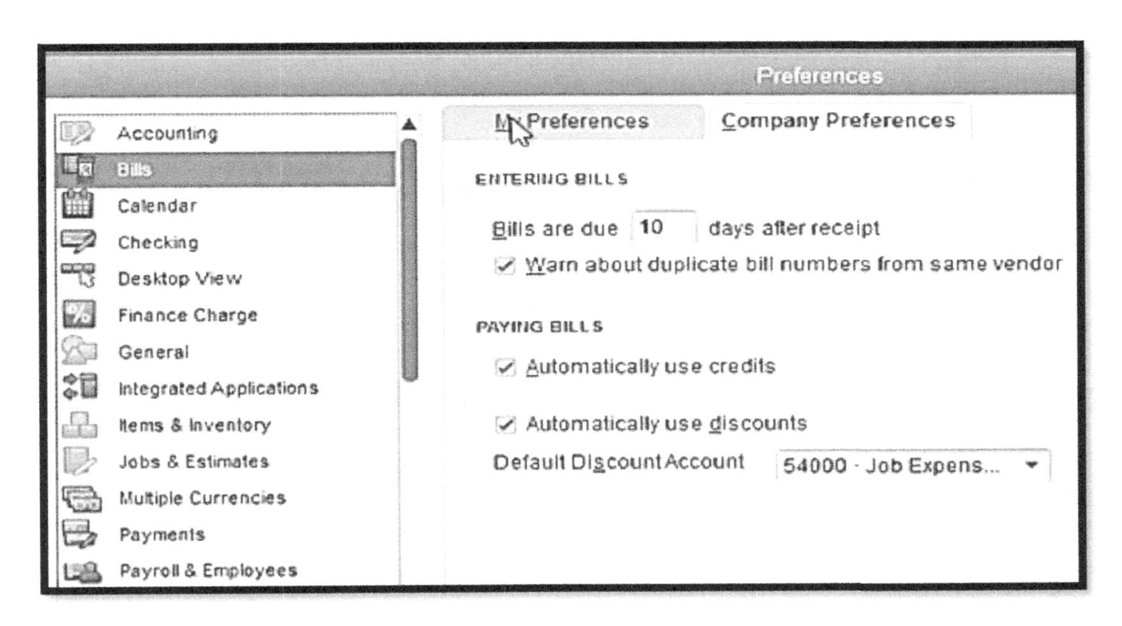

For example, by providing a value in the corresponding text box, you can designate that bills are due a specific number of days after they are received. These company-level choices can also be used to designate which account should be used to record the value of the early-payment discounts and when they should be applied.

Setting the Calendar Preferences

You can customize how QuickBooks displays calendar information by bringing up the Preferences dialog box and clicking the **Calendar icon**.

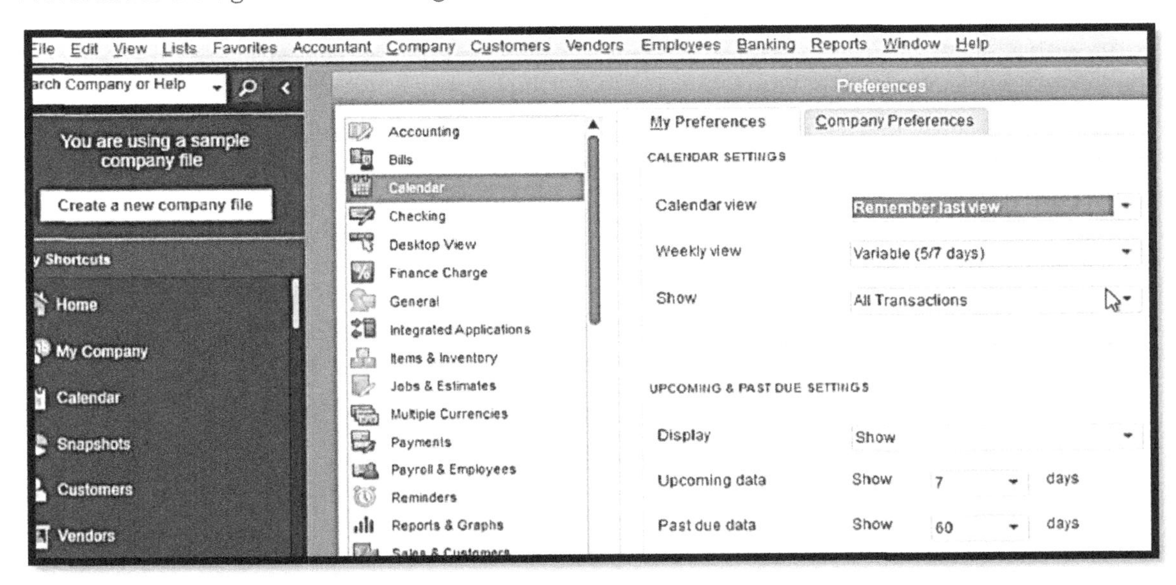

You can choose which transactions to display on the calendar, how you want calendar reminders to appear, whether you want to remember previous calendar settings, and which view to use to display weeks.

Setting the Checking Preferences

QuickBooks shows the My Preferences or the Company Preferences tab when you show the Preferences dialog box and click the **Checking button.**

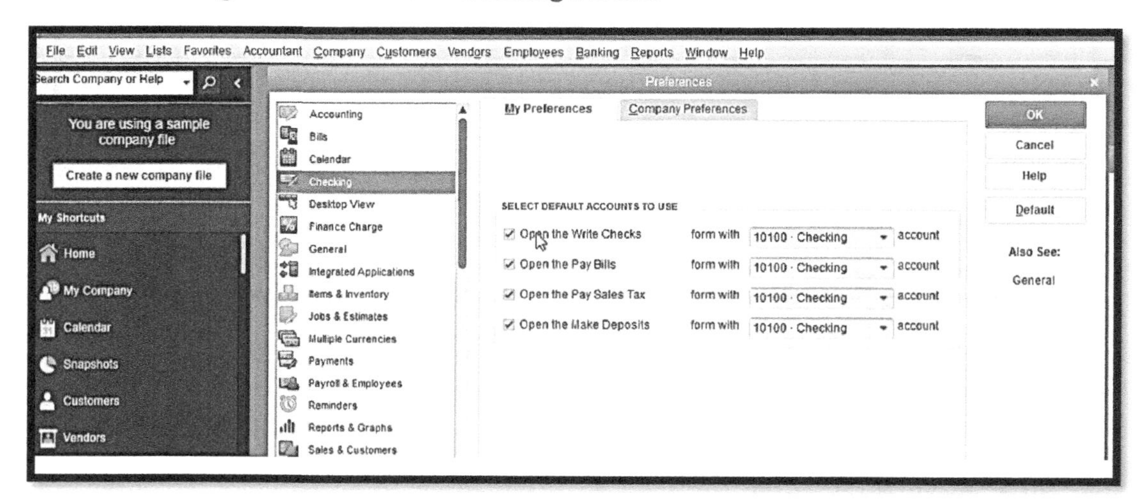

You can instruct QuickBooks as to which account it should suggest as the default account when you open specific sorts of windows inside QuickBooks by using the **My Preferences tab of the Checking Preferences dialog box**. The Form with X Account drop-down list is located to the right of the Open the Write Checks box. Selecting the **Open the Write Checks check box** opens the Form with X Account drop-down list, from which you may select an account. When you open the Write Checks window in QuickBooks, this setting instructs you to use or recommend the designated account. You can designate the default account for the Pay Bills, Pay Sales Tax, and Make Deposits windows using the checkboxes on the My Preferences tab. using the **My Preferences page** to set the default accounts is a smart idea if you have numerous checking accounts set up. It is less likely that you will accidentally write checks on or pay bills from the incorrect account if these parameters are set.

The company Preferences tab offers various choices that can be used in the description of how checks work within QuickBooks;

- **Print Account Names on Voucher**: with the use of this checkbox, you will be able to indicate to QuickBooks that it should make a print of account names on the voucher portion of the check.
- **Change Check Date When Non-Cleared Check is printed**: choose this checkbox to inform QuickBooks to employ the current system date as the printed check date.

- **Start with Payee Field on Check**: choose this checkbox to inform QuickBooks to put the insertion point, or text cursor, in the Payee field whenever you launch the Write Checks window.
- **Warn about Duplicate Check Numbers**: By checking this box, you instruct QuickBooks to notify you when there are duplicate check numbers. (Obviously, you want to leave this check box checked to avoid using duplicate or incorrect check numbers.)
- **Autofill Payee Account Number in Check Memo**: If you want QuickBooks to automatically enter the payee account number when you write a check, check this option. QuickBooks obtains the account number of a beneficiary from either the Vendor or Other Names lists.
- **Select Default Accounts to Use**: You can choose which account QuickBooks advises using when you open the Pay Payroll Liabilities or Create Paychecks windows by using these checkboxes. In essence, therefore, these boxes allow you to specify to QuickBooks which bank account you use to pay payroll-related expenses such as withholding amounts from federal income taxes and writing payroll checks.
- **Bank Feeds**: QuickBooks offers option buttons that you may use to customize the appearance of online transaction information in the online banking window if you have enabled online banking.

Changing the Desktop View

You can choose whether QuickBooks should display all of its information in one window or multiple windows by using the **View radio buttons on the My Preferences tab, labeled One Window and Multiple Windows**.

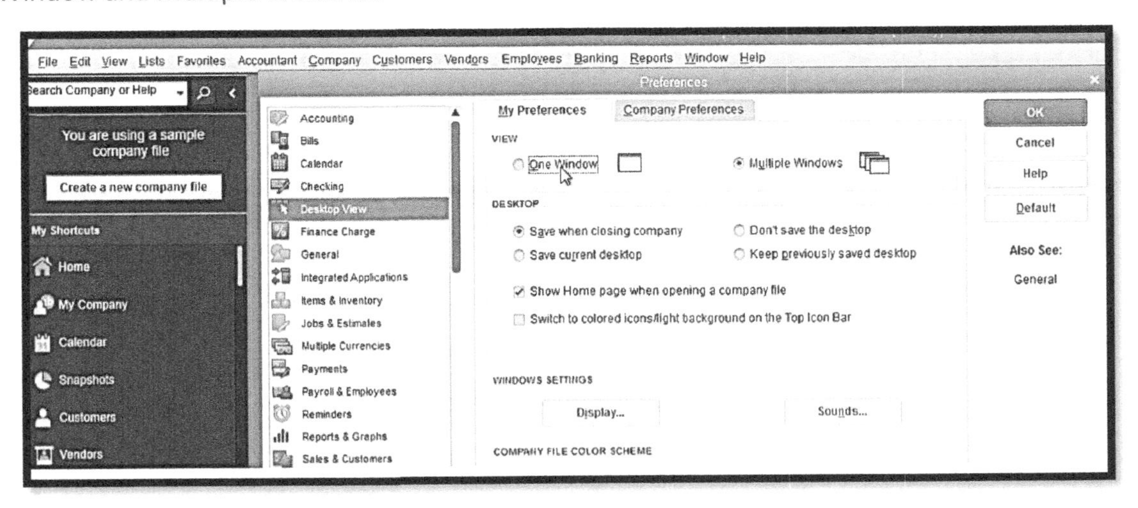

Older Microsoft Windows versions can be recognized via the Multiple Windows option. A program like QuickBooks shows several floating document windows inside the application program window when this option is used. Try both view settings first if you have any questions about how this feature operates. You can choose if and when QuickBooks should store the desktop's current view by using the Desktop radio buttons.

To instruct QuickBooks to save the desktop view when a company is closed,

- Check the **Save When Closing Company radio button**. QuickBooks keeps this desktop display when you reopen a company. To instruct QuickBooks to save the current view and then access it again later, you may also check the **Save Current Desktop option button**. Choose **the radio** choice labeled **Don't Save the Desktop** if you wish to maintain the current desktop layout.

You can configure QuickBooks to show the QuickBooks home page, utilize colored icons, and have a light background for the top icon bar by using the Desktop check boxes. QuickBooks adds the home page or modifies the icon bar color if you check a box. You can get to the Windows Display Properties and Windows Sounds Properties settings by clicking on the Windows Settings buttons. By pressing these two buttons, you can modify Windows Display Properties and Windows Sounds Properties directly from within QuickBooks instead of having to use the Control Panel tools. You may customize the icons that show up on the QuickBooks home screen using the **Company Preferences found under the Desktop View Preferences**. For example, the Customers set of checkboxes allows you to designate which accounting operations relating to customers are accessible through icons on the main page. You can indicate if you wish to use the input Bills and Pay Bills command to input and pay bills by checking the Vendors check box. You can toggle the display of other accounting task icons on and off with the hyperlinks QuickBooks provides toward the bottom of the Company Preferences tab of the Desktop View Preferences dialog box.

Setting Finance Charge Calculation Rules

To assess finance costs for any customers, whose payments are late, set up your QuickBooks preferences for finance charges.

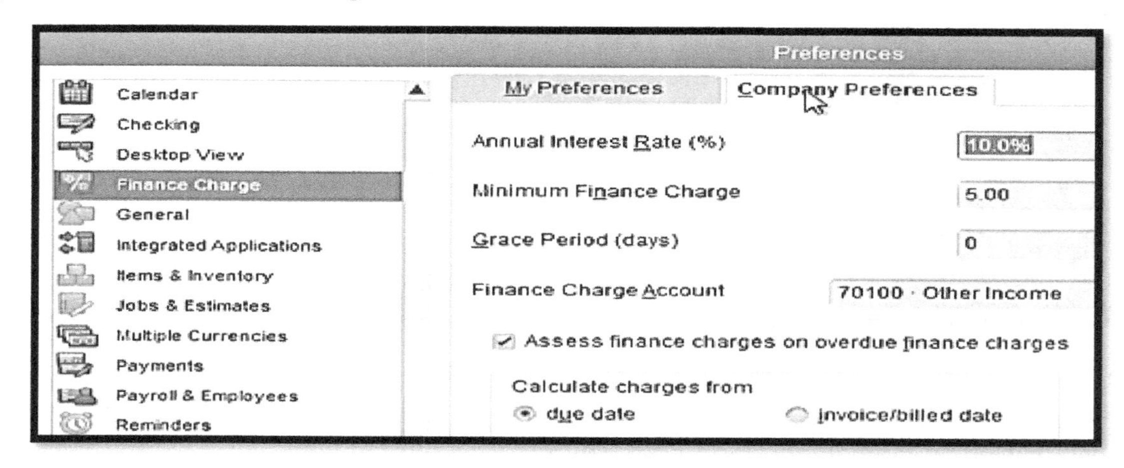

- Navigate to QuickBooks and choose **Preferences.**
- Choose **Finance Charges.** For the Annual interest rate (%), Minimum finance charge, and Grace period (days), enter the details of your finance charge.
- (Optional) A financial charge title is enterable.
- Decide when you would like to begin calculating financing charges.
    - Due date
    - Date of Invoice/Billing
- Select which account will be used to monitor finance charge income.
- (Optional) Uncheck this box if you do not want to calculate finance costs for past-due payments.
- (Optional) Choose **Mark Finance charg**e invoices if you want to print your invoices for clients. Checkbox for the print version. Leave this checkbox checked if you send statements.

Follow the set of instructions below to gain access to the finance charge;

- Navigate to Customers, and then choose **Assess Finance Charge.**

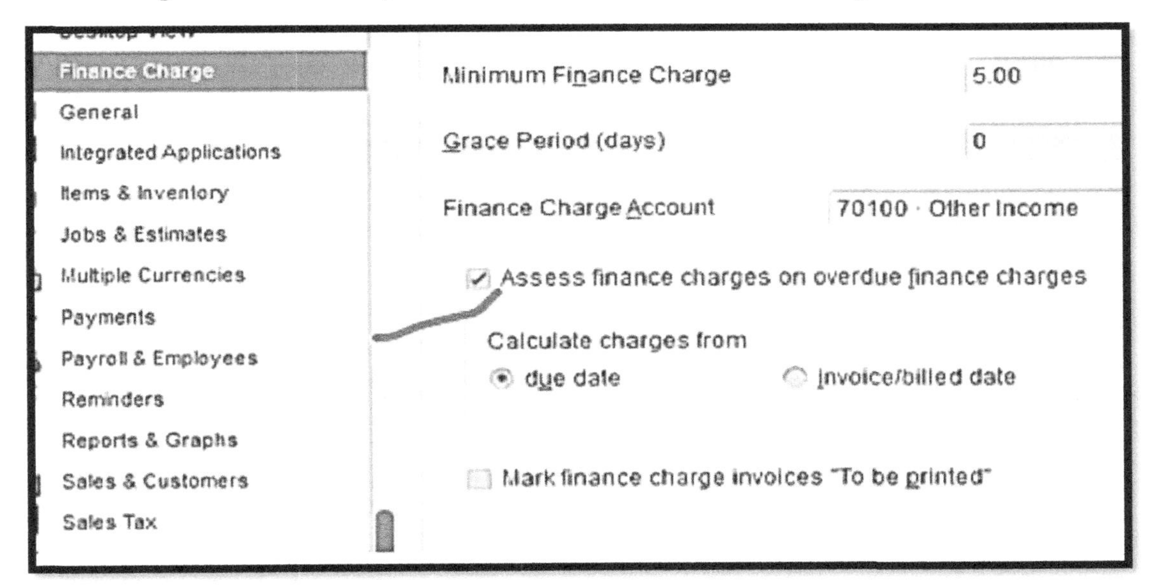

- Choose the customer and job you would like to assess finance charges from the Assess column.
- (Optional) Simply type over the values indicated in the Finance Charge column to adjust any finance charge amount. Choose **Settings and enter the new interest rate to adjust the rate.**
- (Optional) Check the box next to Mark invoices to be printed if you want to print the finance charge invoices for clients. You should leave this checkbox unchecked if you send statements.

Setting General Preferences

The general preferences tab offers check boxes that you can choose to instruct QuickBooks to get the following done;

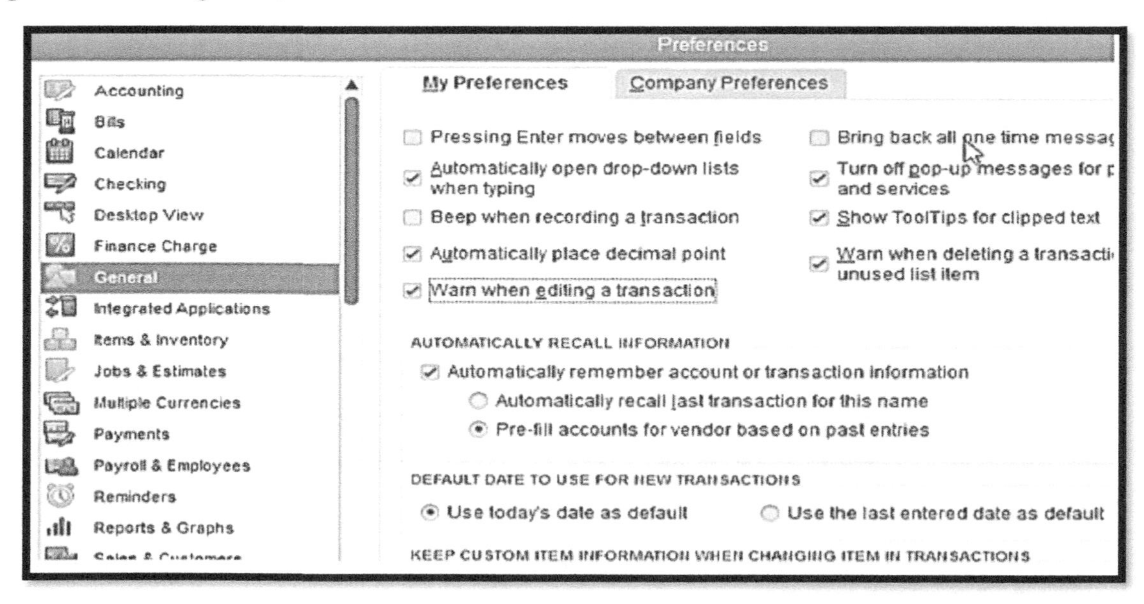

- To move the selection cursor from one field on the window to the next field when you press Enter
- To open drop-down lists automatically when you're typing
- To beep when you record a transaction
- To place a decimal point two digits from the right end of the number automatically
- To warn you when you're editing an existing transaction
- To bring back all the one-time Help messages that you may have suppressed
- To turn off pop-up messages for products and services
- To show tooltips for clipped text
- To warn you when you're deleting an existing transaction or some unused items on a list.
- To run QuickBooks in the background even when you're not using QuickBooks (to make QuickBooks start faster)
- To recall account or transaction information automatically — telling QuickBooks, for example, to automatically recall the last transaction for a particular customer, vendor, or employee
- To use either today's date or the last entered date as the default date
- To keep custom item information changed as part of entering a transaction.

Click the **Help button** that appears along the right edge of the Preferences dialog box if you have specific questions about the My Preferences checkboxes that are available for the General Preferences options. QuickBooks offers concise but helpful explanations of the functions and uses of the Preferences options.

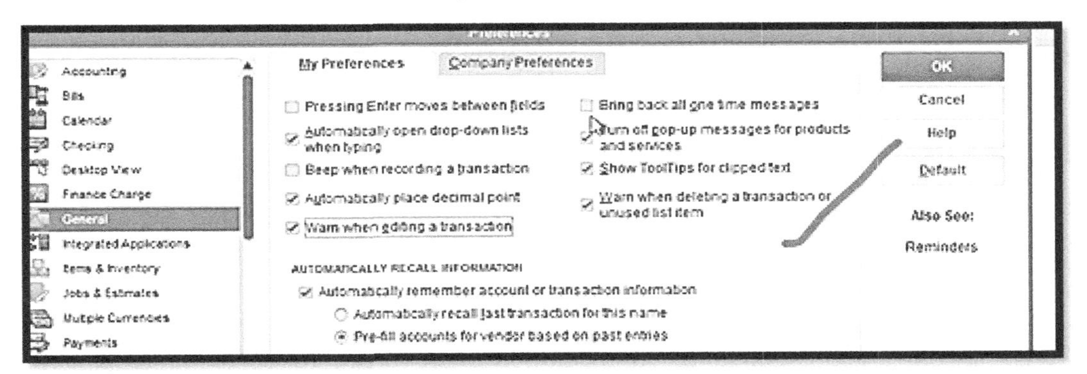

Controlling Inventory

While QuickBooks offers many Company preference capabilities about inventory and items, personal preferences are not available for inventory tracking and control. The QuickBooks buy order and inventory functionalities are toggleable. If you input a purchase order number that you have already used, you have the option to indicate that you wish to be alerted. Additionally, you can control how QuickBooks decides whether you have enough inventories to sell or not. You can also specify whether negative inventory balances are permitted in QuickBooks Enterprise Solutions. QuickBooks allows you to quantify your inventory items by utilizing multiple units of measure if you acquire or sell an item using more than one. For example, if you sell cloth both by the yard and by the bolt (the rolled-up fabric). Choose **Multiple U/M per Item from the Unit of Measure drop-down list** if you're interested in doing this.

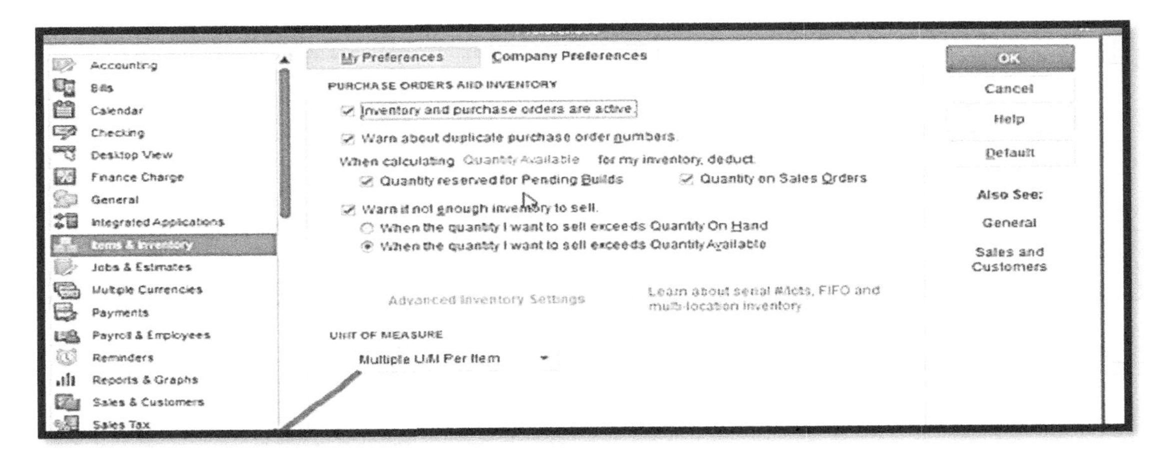

If your company handles prepayments for inventory, multiple vendor bills for a single item receipt, or multiple inventory receipts for a single vendor bill, you might want to think about turning on QuickBooks's Enhanced Inventory Receiving (EIR) feature if you use QuickBooks Enterprise Solutions. You may certainly increase your inventory item counts and prevent the kinds of item count and QuickBooks issues that frequently arise in these more complex inventory scenarios by activating this option. However, once you set on improved inventory receiving, you cannot turn it off.

Controlling How Job and Estimates Work

The My Preferences tab of this Preferences dialog box is empty since there are no options for personal preferences for Jobs & Estimates preferences. However, you can choose from several firm preferences when it comes to jobs and estimates. You can choose the word or terms to be used for tasks that have been submitted but not yet approved or denied using the Pending text box. You can include a word or description in the Awarded text box that QuickBooks will use to recognize the jobs that your clients or customers have accepted. Cleverly, "Awarded" is the default description of a job that has been awarded. For jobs that fall into these categories, you can also specify what phrase to use using the In Progress, Closed, and Not Awarded text boxes.

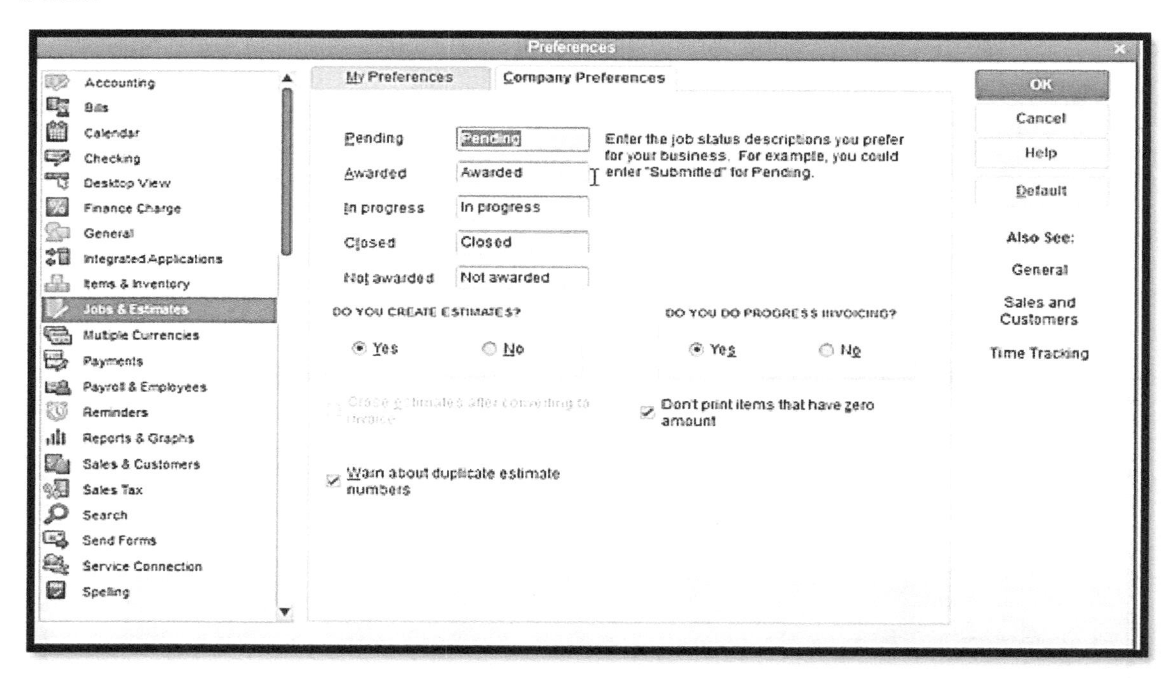

The "Do You Create Estimates"?

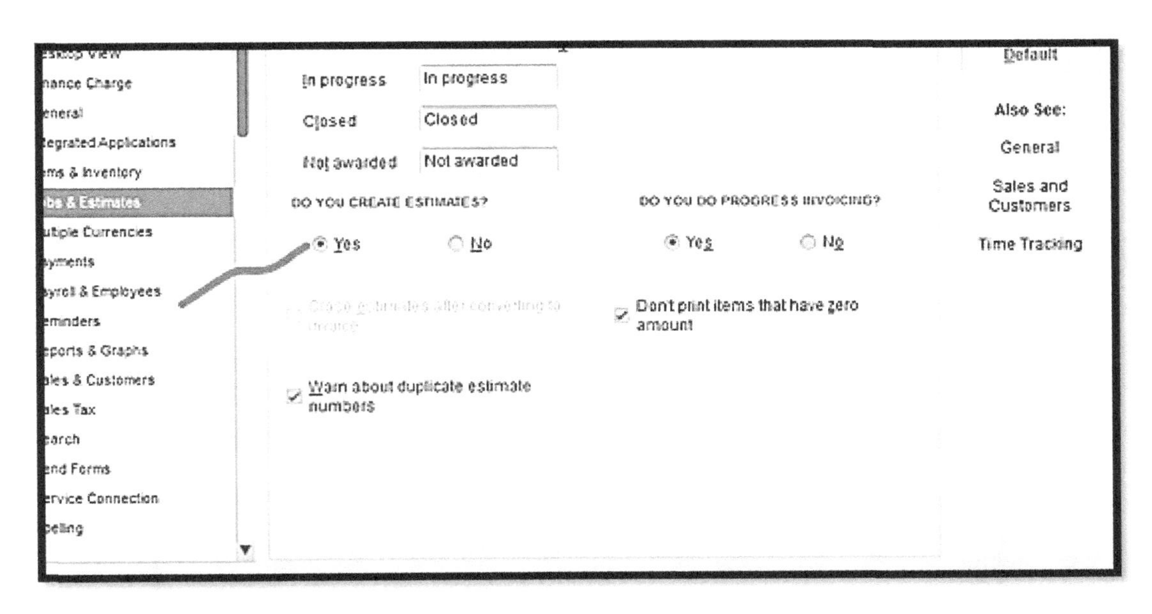

By using radio buttons, you may tell QuickBooks if you wish to generate job estimates for clients. The radio button that responds to the inquiry, either Yes or No, is selected. Is Progress Invoicing Something You Do? You can select radio buttons to indicate whether you progress to bill jobs. If checked, the alert about utilizing the Duplicate Estimate Numbers checkbox alerts QuickBooks to the possibility of utilizing duplicate estimated numbers. QuickBooks is instructed not to print estimates with zero balances if the Don't Print Items That Have Zero Amount checkbox is checked.

Dealing with Multiple Currencies

You can monitor foreign currency transactions with QuickBooks Desktop. You can designate a certain currency type to each of the following profiles and accounts using the Multicurrency feature:

- Customers
- Vendors
- Price levels
- Bank accounts
- Credit card accounts
- Accounts receivable
- Accounts payable

You must open a bank account for each additional currency you wish to work with after informing QuickBooks that you will be handling several currencies (currencies in addition to your home currency). Next, when you create a new vendor or customer, you can specify the currency that they use. For clients or vendors with whom you haven't yet done business, you can additionally choose a transaction currency. However, once you have conducted business in your native currency with a vendor or consumer, you are unable to alter the currency for them. Once this setup is complete, you can pay suppliers in foreign currency, receive money from clients in foreign currency, and move money in and out of your foreign currency bank account using foreign currency units (euros instead of dollars, or vice versa).

Switch on Multicurrency

- From the **Edit menu, choose Preferences.**
- Choose **Multiple Currencies.**
- Choose **Yes, I use more than one currency from the preferences tab of Company.**

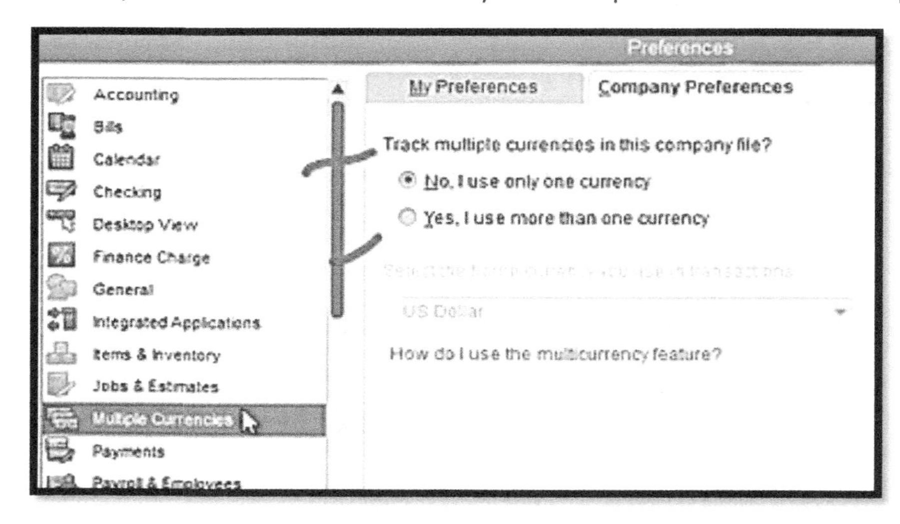

- Choose **your home currency from the drop-down menu.**

Add foreign-currency customers and vendors

Each vendor or customer profile can only have one currency assigned to it. To designate a new currency, you must establish new profiles.

- When you activate the option, your local currency will be assigned to all current clients and suppliers. Changes to the currency are not possible for names that already have transactions associated with them.
- As you close open balances, keep using these home currency customers or vendors. For any new sales or purchases you make, use your foreign-currency customers or vendors; but, you should keep using the names in your native currency until you have finished any open transactions.
- For generating foreign-currency customers or vendors, use the Customer and Vendor Centers. Give the foreign currency client or seller you generated a slightly different name if the name is already listed using your home currency.

For the addition of foreign currency Vendors or Customers, follow the steps;

- Navigate to the **Customers (or Vendors) menu, and then click on Customer Center or Vendor Center.**
- Choose the **New Customer: job or New Vendor drop-down, then click on New Customer or New Vendor in the Customer Center.**
- Add **a Customer or Vendor Name and Currency.**
- Choose **OK.**

Add foreign-currency accounts

Each account can only have one currency assigned to it. For your transactions involving foreign currencies, you must open new accounts.

- Your home currency will be applied to all current accounts. For accounts that already have transactions recorded against them, the currency cannot be altered.
- Keep using the home currency accounts to settle any outstanding balances. After closing all open balances, make transactions using the new foreign currency accounts.
- Bank, Credit Card, Accounts Receivable (A/R), and Accounts Payable (A/P) are the account types to which currencies can be allocated. Note: The customer's or vendor's currency must coincide with the currency of the A/R and A/P accounts. As you create the transactions, QuickBooks automatically creates a different account for every currency.
- As needed, create foreign-currency bank and credit card accounts using the Chart of Accounts.

Follow the steps below to include foreign-currency accounts;

- Select the **Chart of Accounts option** from the Lists menu.
- Right-click anywhere in the **Chart of Accounts and choose New.**
- After selecting the suitable account type, give **it a name.**
- Choose **"Save & Close."**

Create foreign-currency transactions

Note: For new foreign-currency transactions, only use the foreign-currency names or accounts you added. Don't use the new foreign currency version of an existing customer to accept payment against an open invoice for that customer if the invoice is in your home currency. Rather, proceed with completing the purchase using the customer's local currency version.

- Sales and purchase transactions are assigned the currency of the client or vendor you supplied on the form; you do not need to designate a currency to them.
- Every transaction involves exchange rates, which establish the transaction's value in the home currency.

- The transaction total is stated in the home currency equivalent of the amounts on sales and buys transactions, which are expressed in the currency of the vendor or the customer.
- Reports will consistently display the domestic currency, irrespective of the currency utilized during transactions.

Finally, here's a fun fact about multiple currencies: When you enable QuickBooks' many Currency functions, small currency reminders appear in various windows and dialog boxes. For example, amount boxes will display a little symbol representing the currency that should be entered into that specific box, alerting you to the fact that, for example, you should put British pounds in this text box.

Starting Integrated Payment Processing

You may manage how QuickBooks processes payments by using the various checkboxes and links found in the Payments settings. For example, the Receive Payments check boxes allow you to designate whether you wish to use the Undeposited Funds account as a temporary holding account for client payments, as well as if you want to automatically apply and compute payments.

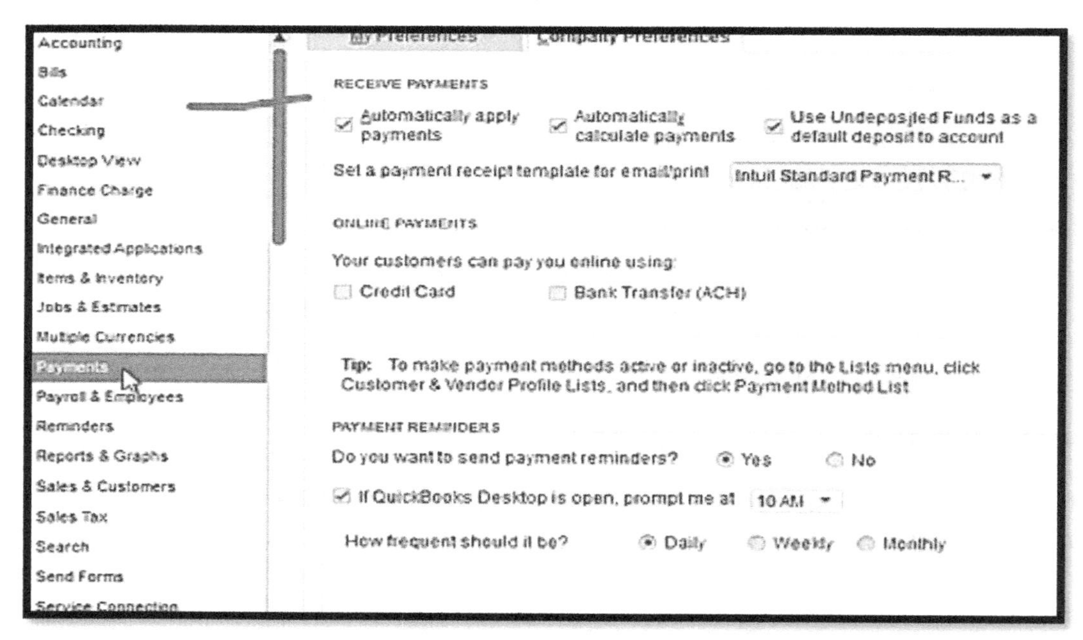

You can also specify in the Payments preferences whether you'll accept bank transfers and credit card payments from clients via the Automated Clearing House (ACH) system. QuickBooks includes a link on invoices that clients can use to pay using credit cards or bank transfers if you enable this setting. As expected, there is a small cost associated with this service from Intuit;

therefore, if this is of interest to you, carefully review the current rates that are displayed when you tick the boxes to enable this option.

Controlling How Payroll Works

The Company Preferences tab is the only one included in the Payroll & Employees Preferences package. You can instruct QuickBooks on how to handle payroll by selecting one of the three radio buttons on the Payroll Features screen: Enhanced Payroll, Payroll, or Payroll Premium. Please take note that QuickBooks only shows radio buttons that make sense for the version of the program you have chosen. You can instruct QuickBooks on what employee data to print on the payroll check, including the employee's address, the company's address, information about sick leave, vacation pay, and pay period information, by using the **Pay Stub & Voucher Printing option.** By clicking the button and examining the dialog box that QuickBooks shows, you may determine how this operates.

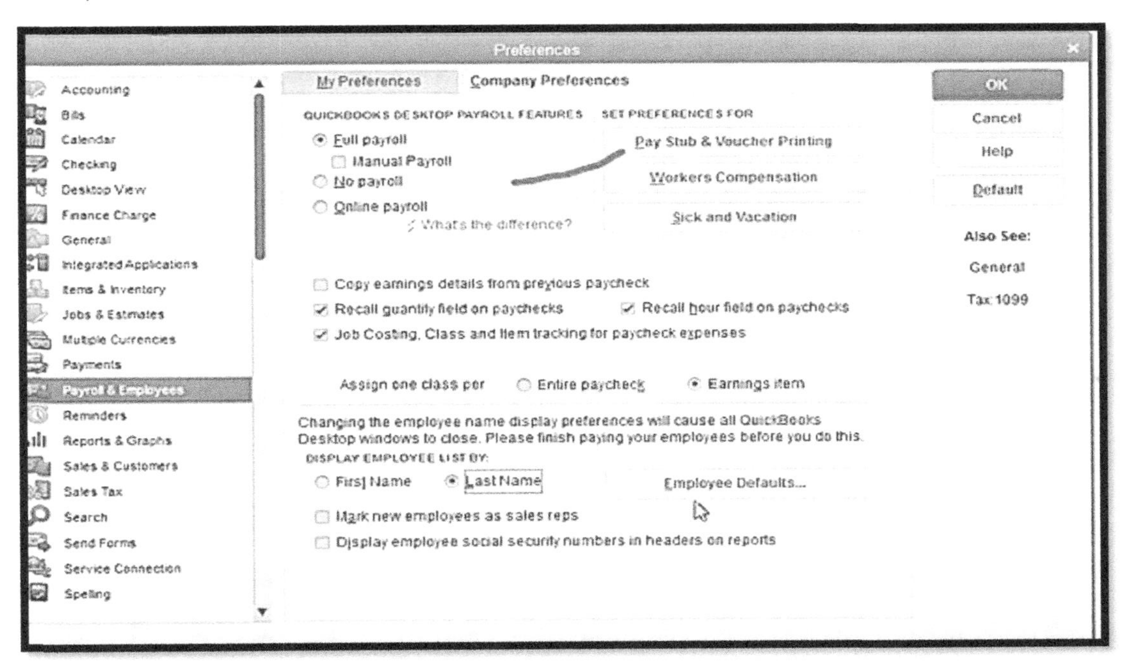

You can adjust how QuickBooks tracks the accrual and use of employee sick and vacation pay by clicking on the **Sick and Vacation button**. Once more, click any of these buttons to bring up a screen with additional details about how to use it. The Employee List Display You can select whether the personnel lists are ordered on reports by last name or by first name by using radio buttons. QuickBooks provides a dialog box that you may use to specify employee payroll defaults, including tax and health insurance deductions when you select the Employee Defaults button. Lastly, there are two additional payroll handling methods offered by QuickBooks. If the checkbox labeled **"Mark New Employees as Sales Reps"** is checked, it accomplishes the following: It designates new hires as sales representatives when you add them to the employee list. Additionally, if chosen, the check box labeled **"Show Employee Social Security Numbers in Headers on Reports"** accomplishes the following: Reports now include employee Social Security numbers.

Telling QuickBooks How Reminders Should Work

You can instruct QuickBooks to display the Reminders list whenever you open a company files by using the single check box on the **My Preferences tab of the Reminders Preferences dialog box.** The My Preferences tab is not displayed as a figure because it just has one check box.

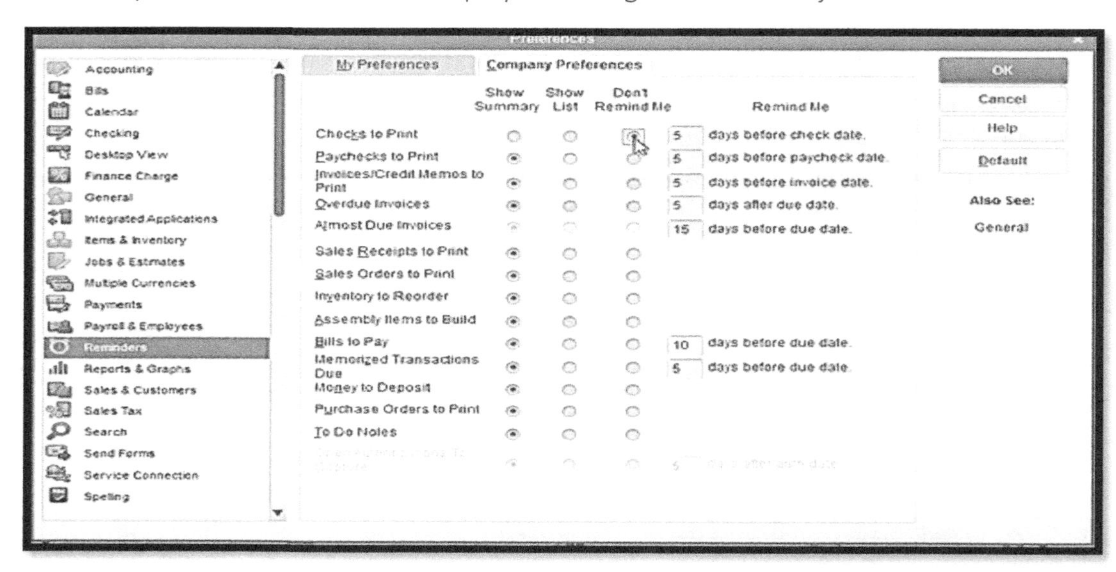

You can customize QuickBooks' reminders for accounting and bookkeeping activities by using the several radio buttons on the Company Preferences tab. These buttons include Paychecks, invoices, credit memos, sales receipts, sales orders, inventory to reorder, assembly items to build, bills to pay, paid transactions due, money to deposit, purchase orders to print, to-do notes, and open authorizations to capture. You choose whether you wish to get reminders for each of these bookkeeping or accounting chores by checking the box in the **Show Summary list that shows up in the QuickBooks Company Preferences Reminders list.** Additionally, you can select whether to view the task list in its entirety, including the list of checks that need to be printed, or you can specify that you would like not to be reminded of a specific accounting or bookkeeping category. You can specify how many work days ahead of time you wish to be notified for certain of the reminder notes. You must specify how many days in advance of the check date you want the reminder to appear, for example, if you want to be reminded to print checks. To accomplish this, type a number into one of the fields of text labeled "Remind Me."

Specifying Reports and Graphs Preferences

You can select how QuickBooks should refresh reports when the data is based on changes by using the radio buttons on the **My Preferences tab of the Reports & Graphs Preferences dialog box**. Refresh automatically is the standard refresh setting. Additionally, you can choose to have QuickBooks (gently) recommend that you refresh a report only when data changes by checking the Prompt Me to refresh radio button. If you have a lot of reports and a big data set, you might want to disable automatic refresh. Report refreshes can take a while to process.) If you don't need or want to be notified to refresh a report, you may also choose the **Don't Refresh radio button.**

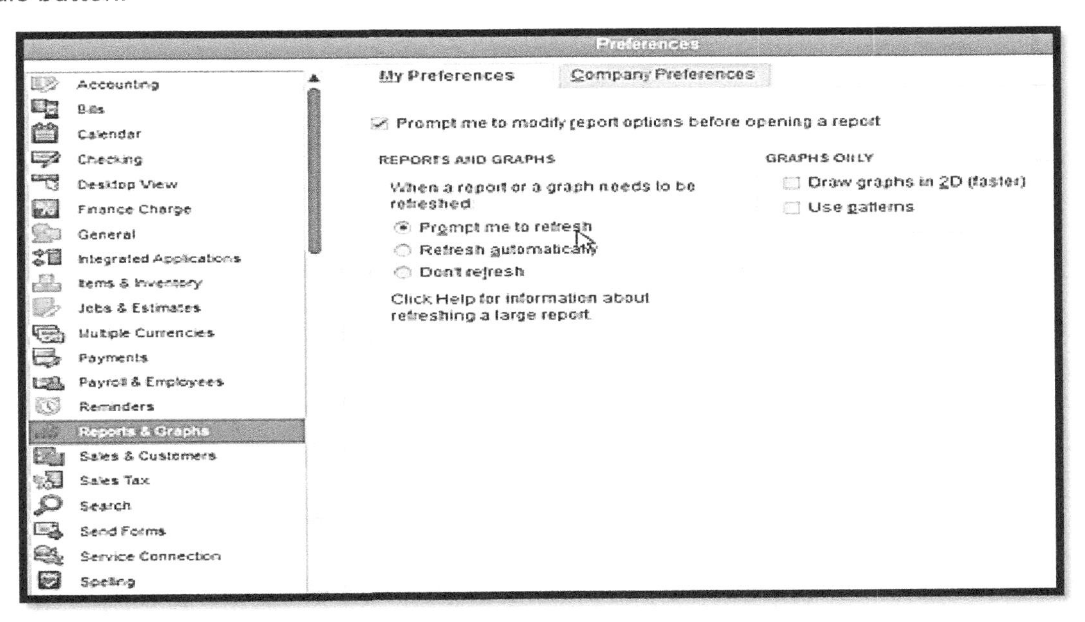

If you tick the box labeled **"Prompt Me to Modify Report Options before Opening a Report,"** QuickBooks will open the Modify Report window each time a report is created. The Modify Report box gives you control over additional reporting options as well as the information that appears in reports, including the date range on which the report is based. QuickBooks uses the standard reporting options to create reports if this check box is left unchecked. You have control over the information that QuickBooks graphs display by using the Graphs Only checkboxes. To instruct QuickBooks to draw 2D graphs instead of 3D ones, tick the Draw Graphs in the 2D check box. (QuickBooks creates 2D graphs somewhat faster; you might wish to use that kind.) Keep in mind that 2D graphs have more visual precision than 3D graphs. If you would prefer QuickBooks to create a graph with cross-hatching patterns instead of colors to represent the various parts of a chart, you can also tick the **Use Patterns checkbox.**

For example, you can select accrual-basis accounting or cash-basis accounting as the default accounting technique when creating reports using the **Summary Reports Basis radio buttons.**

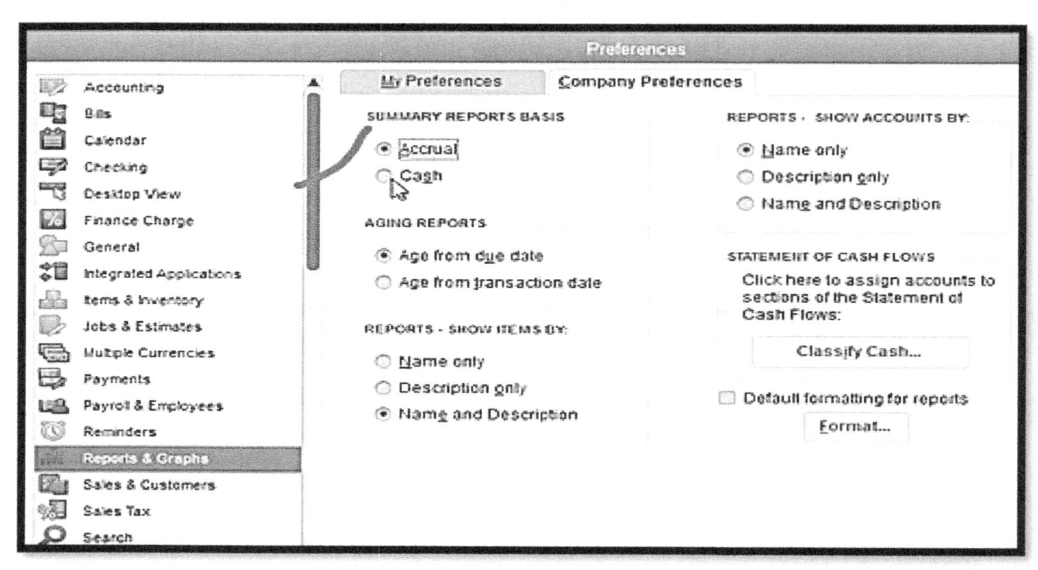

You can choose whether an invoice or bill's age should be determined from the transaction date or the due date by using the Aging Reports radio buttons. The Accounts - Display Reports You can choose how account information appears in reports by using the radio buttons to change the appearance of the account name, description, or both. Two other options are particularly important. First, when you click the **Classify Cash button,**

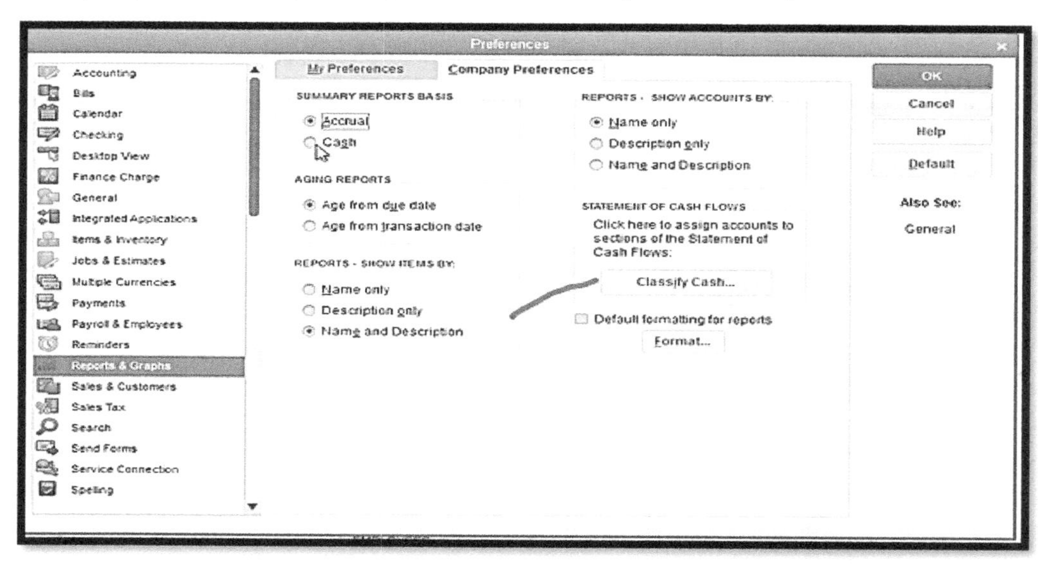

a dialog box appears and you can choose whether changes in a specific account balance should be reported in the financing, investment, or operating sections of the cash flow statement. QuickBooks shows the Reports & Graphs Preferences dialog box, where you can alter the report header and footer information if you clear the Default Formatting for Reports check box and click the Format button. You can designate the information that appears in the report header area by using the Show Header Information check boxes. You may specify the same information for the report footer by checking the **Show Footer Information check box**. You can designate the alignment of the information on the report page using the Alignment drop-down list included in the Page Layout section.

- You can choose the typeface and formatting for individual report sections using the **Fonts & Numbers tab of the Reports & Graphs Preferences dialog box.** For instance, select the **Column Labels entry in the Change Font For list box**, then click the **Change Font button** to alter the report's column labels' font. You can choose the font, font style, point size, and additional special effects in the Font Formatting dialog box that QuickBooks displays.

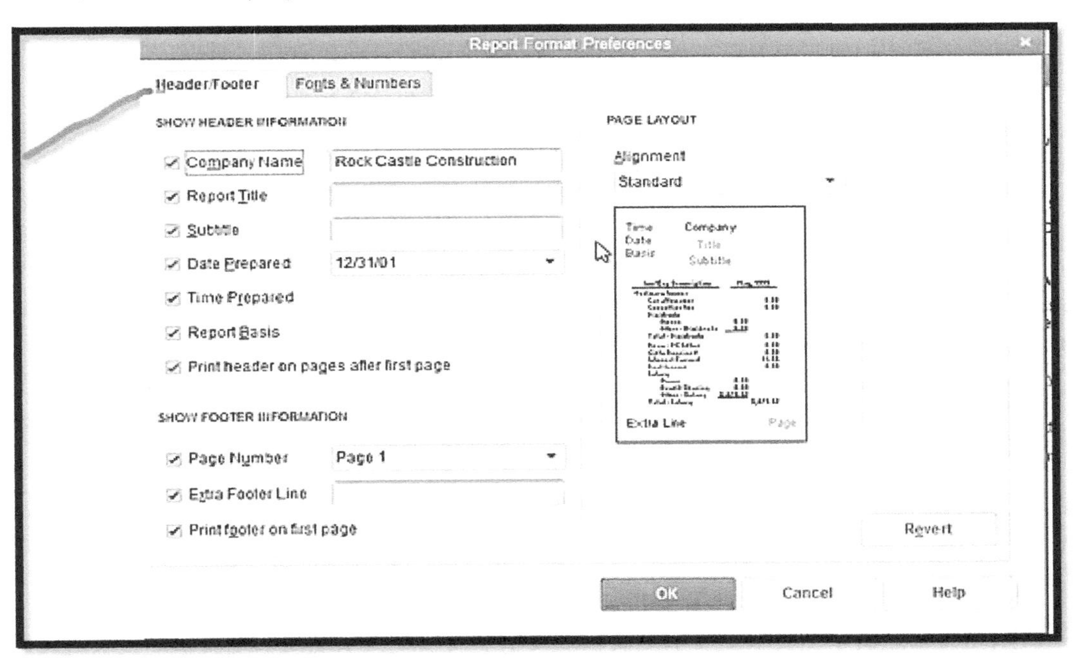

Specifying How Sales Are Taxed

There are company preferences for sales tax even when there are no personal preferences available. Do You Apply Sales Tax? Within QuickBooks, you can select whether or not to charge sales tax by using the radio buttons located at the top of the company preferences tab. To respond to the question, click **the radio button labeled "Yes" or "No."**

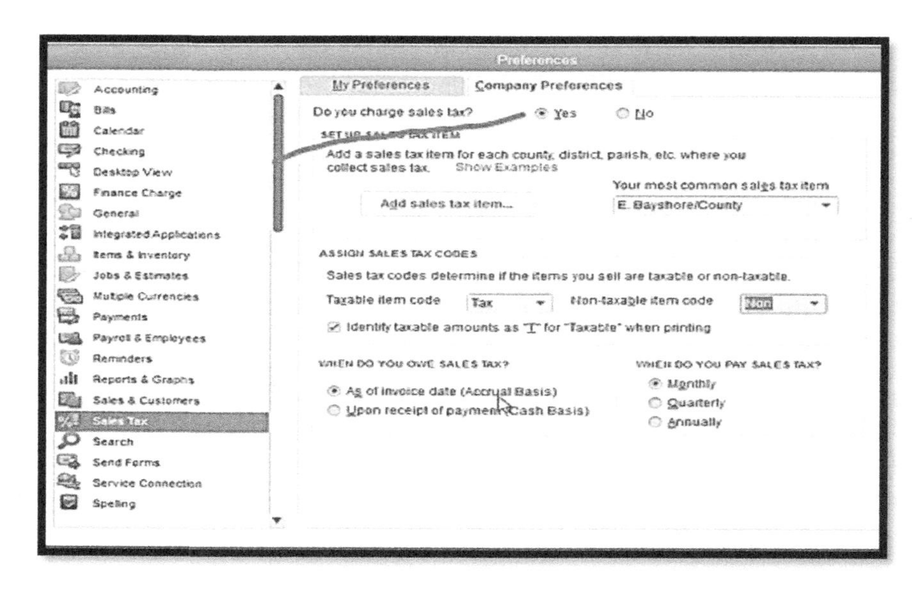

You can specify which code QuickBooks should use to distinguish between taxable and nontaxable sales using the drop-down menus for Taxable Item Code and Non-Taxable Item Code. QuickBooks uses the astute "tax" code by default for taxable sales and the similarly astute "non" code for nontaxable transactions. However, you can construct your own taxable and nontaxable codes by

- Selecting **Add New entry** from either drop-down list or using the dialog box that QuickBooks presents.

You can set up an item for the sales tax you charge on invoices by selecting the **Add Sales Tax item under the Set up Sales Tax Item section**.

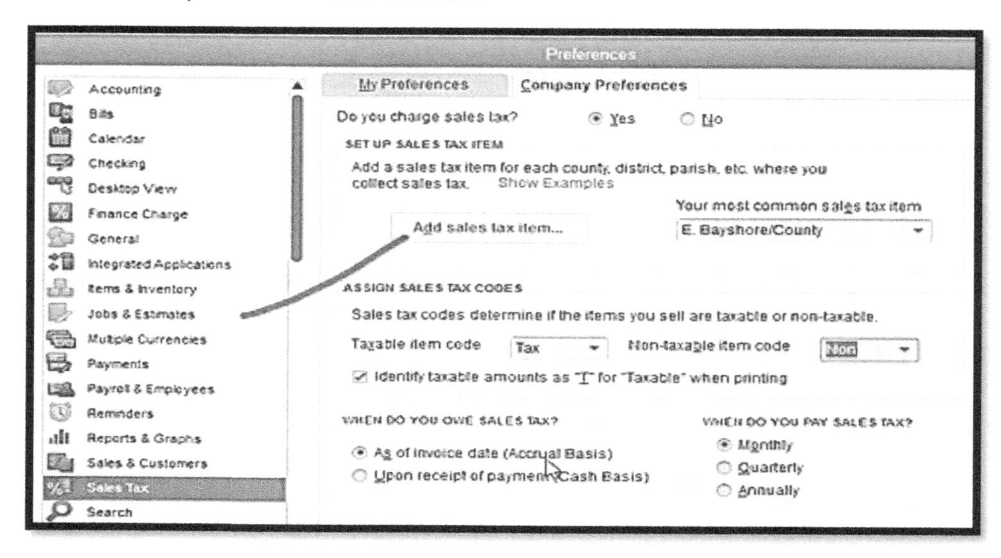

By entering the name of the sales tax item in the Your Most Common Sales Tax Item drop-down list, you can specify the default (or most common) sales tax item you wish to include.

- Select **Add New** from this list and fill out the dialog box that QuickBooks displays to add the sales tax item. You can provide the sales tax item's name and rate in the New Item dialog box.

You can choose which code words to use to mark invoice items as subject to sales tax by using the drop-down options for Taxable Item Code and Non-Taxable Item Code. The "Taxable" check box is labeled "Identify Taxable Amounts as "T." If printing is chosen, QuickBooks will be notified to mark taxable amounts on an invoice with the code T. When Does Sales Tax Become Due? You can select whether the taxing authority says you owe sales tax as of the invoice date (if accrual-basis accounting is required) or upon receipt of payment (if cash-basis accounting is permitted) by using the radio buttons. When Should Sales Tax Be Paid? The Monthly, Quarterly, and Annual radio buttons allow you to specify to QuickBooks how often you need to submit sales tax numbers. The radio button that matches the frequency of your sales tax payments is what you select.

Setting the Search Preferences

You can select whether you want the Search box to be displayed on the QuickBooks icon toolbar using the checkbox on the My Preferences tab of the Search Preferences dialog box. (This should be fairly obvious, but just in case, check the box, click **OK,** and then take a look at how QuickBooks has changed your icon toolbar.)

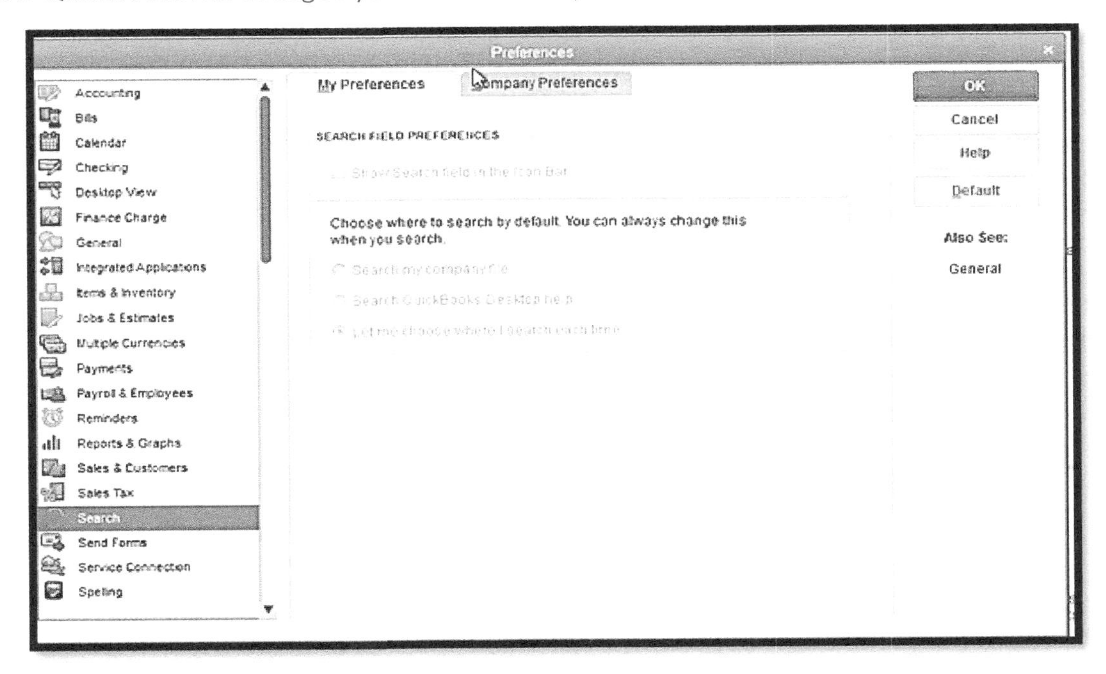

You can configure how often QuickBooks updates the index of the company data file and menu items that are utilized when you search for data within the QuickBooks application on the Company Preferences tab of the Search Preferences dialog box (not shown). QuickBooks updates automatically once per hour, but you have the option to request more or less frequent updates. It takes several minutes for the index to be updated, and QuickBooks performs more slowly during this time. You can also click a button on the Search Company Preferences tab to force an instant update of the index.

Fine-Tuning the Service Connection

There are two checkboxes on the My Preferences tab of the Service Connection Preferences dialog box that you may pick to modify QuickBooks' behavior when you establish web connections. You have the option to save downloaded files by checking one box. The other instructs QuickBooks to keep your web browser open after it has finished utilizing the internet. There are two Company Preferences settings available in the Service Connection Preferences dialog box (not displayed). For instance, you can choose whether QuickBooks should always prompt for a password or if it should connect to QuickBooks Services automatically and not prompt for one. Just choose the relevant radio button to arrive at this decision. Additionally, you can instruct QuickBooks to allow message gathering in the background by checking the Allow Background Downloading of Service Messages check box. (If you tick this box, QuickBooks will download new messages while you're not using it, preventing it from interfering with your other online activity.)

Controlling Spell Checking

Although the Spelling choices dialog box does not have any corporate choices, you can customize how QuickBooks' spell-checking functions for you with some options under the My Preferences page. If you would like to have spell-checking done automatically before sending a document to a third party, like a vendor or customer, select the box labeled **Always Select Spelling Before Printing, Saving, or Sending Supported Forms.**

To instruct QuickBooks not to spell-check words or phrases that won't appear correctly spelled because they aren't real words, use the Ignore Words With checkboxes. For example, to instruct QuickBooks not to scan Internet URL addresses, choose the Internet Addresses check box. Additionally, you can instruct QuickBooks not to try to spell-check words that are acronyms and abbreviations, such as OK and ASAP, by checking the All UPPERCASE Letters check box. You may also take custom-spelled terms out of your spell-check vocabulary in QuickBooks. (During spell checking, you can add custom-spelled terms by informing QuickBooks that a word that has been marked as potentially misspelled is spelled correctly. When the Check Spelling dialog box displays, click the **Add button** to accomplish this.)

Controlling How 1099 Tax Reporting Works

There are no inclinations regarding 1099 tax reporting. That being said, the Company Preferences tab indicates that there are company preferences. You can instruct QuickBooks on which occasions 1099-MISC forms must be filed by using this tab. (Select the Yes radio button to respond in the affirmative to the question Do You File 1099 Forms?.) Additionally, you can link QuickBooks accounts to the various fields on the 1099 form that you use to track payments to independent contractors by using this page.

- Click the **You Can Do It Here hyperlink to accomplish this**. If you have any queries concerning these boxes or the 1099 reporting threshold amounts, see www.irs.gov or speak with your tax counsel.

Setting Time and Expenses Preferences

There is a company Preferences tab in the Time Expenses Preferences dialog box. Enable Do You Track Time? by clicking the **Yes radio option** to activate time tracking in QuickBooks.

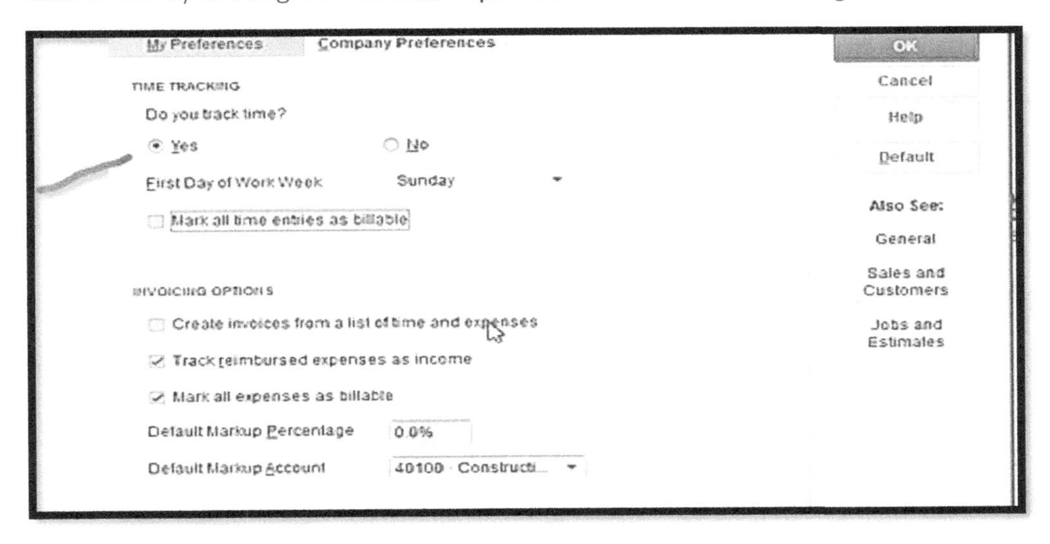

You can also specify which day should show up first on the Weekly Time Sheet window by using the First Day of Work Week drop-down list. (This parameter is where you describe the weekly billable time.) Choose the method you wish to keep track of reimbursed expenses by using the checkboxes under Invoicing Options. Check the Generate Invoices from a List of Time and Expenses check box to indicate that you occasionally want to base invoices on accrued time and expenses.

- Additionally, check the **Track Reimbursed Expenses As Income box** to indicate that you wish to keep track of reimbursed expenses that you charge and subsequently collect as income from clients or customers.

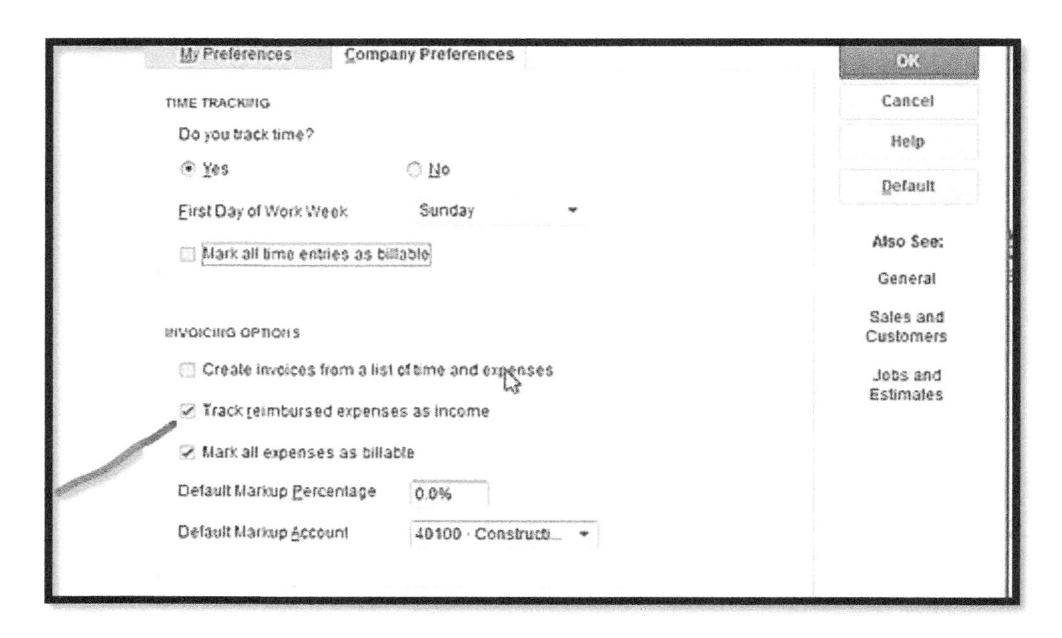

You can set a default retail markup percentage in your pricing using the Default Markup Percentage text box, but before you rely on it, make sure it's displayed correctly in estimates. The account that QuickBooks should use to track your markups can be chosen using the Default Markup Account drop-down list. You can designate expenses that need to be reimbursed when entering bills and assign them to a particular customer work by checking the Mark All Expenses as Billable box.

Activity

1. **Set the following in your QuickBooks;** accounting preferences, bills preferences, calendar preferences, finance charge calculation rules, general preferences, search preferences, sales and customer's preferences.
2. Control the following in QuickBooks, integrated applications, how payroll works, spell checking and how 1099 tax reporting works.

BOOK 3

SIMPLIFYING BOOKKEEPING TASKS FOR SUCCESS

CHAPTER 1
INVOICING CUSTOMERS

QuickBooks offers several options to help you bill your clients. These tools, along with a few other related technologies for tracking customer payments and sending credit memos, are covered in this chapter. QuickBooks will be a blessing if you have previously been sending bills to clients manually, maybe by using a word processor to prepare the invoices. In addition to simplifying procedures associated with invoicing, QuickBooks also gathers invoice data and stores it in a QuickBooks data file. Thankfully, this implies that by utilizing QuickBooks for invoicing, you may also benefit from the additional feature of documenting accounting transactions.

Choosing an Invoice Form

You can utilize an invoice form in QuickBooks that is tailored to your company's needs. Companies that sell goods, such as wholesalers and retailers, must provide an invoice with details about the goods they sell. Legal, architectural, engineering, and consulting firms are examples of businesses that sell services. These businesses require an invoice that accurately represents the services they provide. Companies that offer both goods and services require a combination of qualities.

Thankfully, QuickBooks allows you to select the invoice format that most closely suits your company's needs.

- Select the **Customers > Create Invoices command** to open the Create Invoices box and select an invoice form.

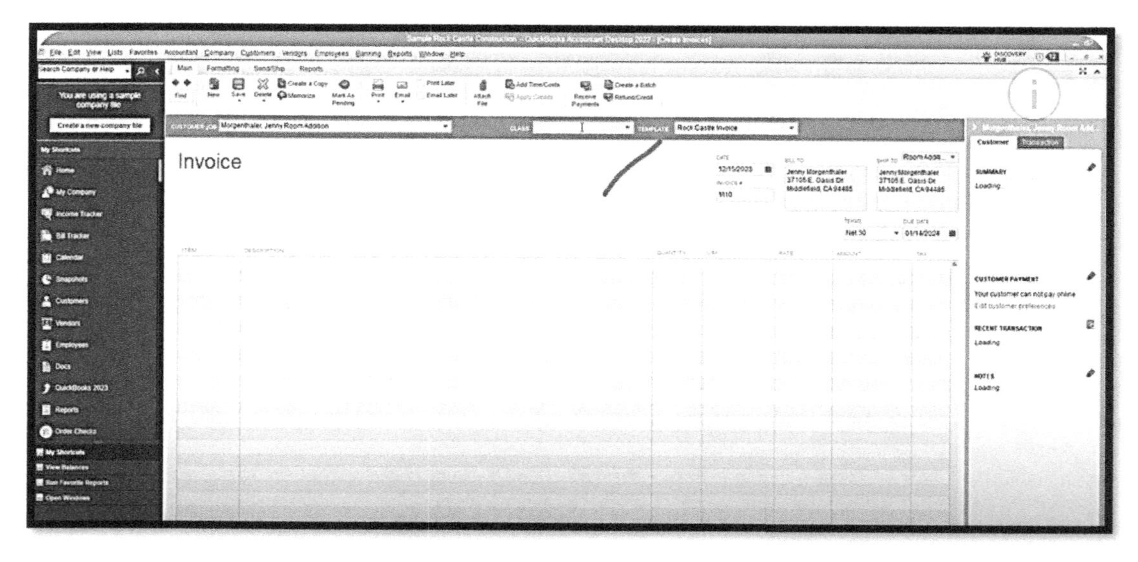

Use the Template drop-down list, which is located in the upper-right corner of the Create Invoices window when QuickBooks opens, to select the desired invoice form. Options including an attorney's invoice, a finance-charge invoice, a fixed-fee invoice, a product invoice, a service invoice, and a professional invoice are available in this drop-down list. Select the invoice template that appears to be most appropriate for your company. When you select a new invoice form template in QuickBooks, the Create Invoices window is redrawn. This implies that by selecting an option from the Template drop-down list, you can easily view the appearance of an invoice form template.

Customizing an Invoice Form

QuickBooks offers you greater flexibility even though you have the option to use a predefined invoice form design for your bills. To make an invoice that is just how you want it to look, you can also develop custom invoice form templates. You can accomplish this by starting with one of the simple invoice form templates and then modifying it to precisely meet your needs.

Choose a template

Select the **Customers > Create Invoices command** to open the Create Invoices window and select a template to modify. Next, select the template that most closely resembles the final design of your invoice from the Template drop-down list.

Customization options

The form customization features in QuickBooks can be confusing to novice users. However, tinkering with what QuickBooks refers to as its Additional change choices is usually the best place to begin any change.

- Click the **Formatting tab in the Create Invoice window**, and then select the **Customize Data Layout button** to make these adjustments. If you're using one of the premade invoice templates, you cannot use the Additional Customization dialog box; you can only use a copy. Consequently, when you select the **Additional Customization button in QuickBooks**, it can ask you to create a copy of an invoice template. Regardless, the Additional Customization dialog box appears in QuickBooks.

Header Info

You can choose what appears at the top of the Create Invoices window and on a printed invoice form by using the Header tab of the Additional Customization dialog box. The invoice number, the invoice date, and the billing and shipping details are all included in this data, which is referred to as the header. You may also select the labeling style for the information by adding or removing text boxes from the list. You can choose whether the form title should show up on the screen (within the Create Invoices window) and on the printed version of the invoice by using the Default Title check boxes, for instance. You can enter the title you want the form to have in the Default Title text box. Similarly, you may designate which label should be used to indicate the invoice date and whether the date should show in both the print and screen versions of the invoice using the Date checkboxes.

Columns Info

The items that an invoice bills for are described in detail in the columns section of the invoice. Product invoice columns list the individual products together with their price and quantity; they also list the things that are the subject of the invoice. The columns of a service invoice list the particular services that are being billed. The Additional Customization dialog box's Columns tab resembles the Header tab. To specify whether a specific column-level piece of information should show up as a column on the Create Invoices window or in the produced invoice, utilize the Screen and Print check boxes. Similarly, you may supply QuickBooks with the descriptive labels it uses in the Create Invoices window and on the printed invoice form by using the Title text boxes. The Order text boxes are the unique options available on the Columns tab. You can select the columns' order of appearance (left to right) using these boxes. Enter the value 1 in the Order box of the item row if, for example, the item number or code is to appear in the first column on the left.

Prog columns Info

When you use progress billings, information pertinent to certain circumstances can be seen in the "prog columns" section of an invoice. To add or remove details like the ordered amount, the amount that was previously invoiced, and any back-ordered amounts, selects the **Prog Cols tab in the Additional Customization dialog box.** You can make modifications to your invoice forms using the Header, Columns, and Prog Cols tabs. However, don't worry about making flawless adjustments the first time. If your eyesight is better than mine, you may use the Preview box to see exactly how your changes appear. If not, click **OK** and take your time going over the updated Create Invoices window. You can modify your invoice once more to address any errors you may have made in the past, such as using the wrong section of descriptive language or ordering the columns incorrectly.

Footer Information

You may customize the information that shows in the Create Invoices window below the columns area as well as in the printed invoice itself by selecting the Footer tab of the Additional Customization dialog box. A note to the customer, the invoice amount, payment and credit details, a balance-due area, and (optionally) a longer text box are all included in the footer information. The Footer tab can be manipulated in the same way as other tabs. You can tick both the Screen and Print check boxes to get some information to appear. Edit the text that appears in the Title text box to modify the wording that QuickBooks uses.

Print Information

You can adjust the way QuickBooks produces invoices using the customized template by using the Print tab in the Additional Customization dialog box. You can choose whether QuickBooks should print this specific invoice template using the standard old invoice printer settings or alternative, unique print settings by using the radio buttons at the top of the tab. You can also instruct QuickBooks on how to number the pages in a multi-page invoice using the Print options.

Basic Customization

There is a Basic Customization button in the Additional Customization dialog box. This button opens QuickBooks' Basic Customization dialog box, which offers some simple customization options. Click the **Manage Templates button** to select the invoice form template that you wish to alter. QuickBooks will then show the Manage Templates dialog box; select the desired invoice template. You can first personalize the custom invoice and financing charge templates that QuickBooks provides. As an alternative, you can choose one of these pre-made templates, click **Copy** to make it, and then edit it. QuickBooks returns you to the Basic Customization dialog box after it close the Manage Templates dialog box when you click **OK.**

Logo

Check the Use Logo box to include a logo on your invoices. Next, choose the graphic-image file containing your logo using QuickBooks' Select Image dialog box. The Select Image dialog box functions similarly to a typical Windows dialog box for opening files.

Color

Choose your preferred color scheme from the **Select Color Scheme drop-down list t**o add color to your invoices. For example, if you have a color printer and don't mind spending a lot of money on colored ink. Click **Apply Color Scheme** after that.

Invoice fonts

The font that QuickBooks utilizes for the text that appears on an invoice is customizable. Simply click the **Change Font button** after selecting the desired text segment in the Change Font For list box. In QuickBooks, the Example dialog box appears. To specify the appearance of the selected text, use its Font, Font Style, and Size boxes. A Sample box that displays the appearance of your font changes is included in the Example dialog box. Click OK once you've finished specifying the font. QuickBooks displays the Layout Designer when you click the **Layout Designer button**, which may be found in both the Basic Customization and Additional Customization dialog boxes. You can rearrange the information on the invoice in the printed version by using the Layout Designer. Experimenting with the Layout Designer is the greatest way to learn how to use it. It would be best if you made an example invoice form template for something completely unimportant, and then you could play around with this new template. You can try to move and resize objects, choose objects, resize multiple objects, position text within fields, change fonts, and modify margins. Also, QuickBooks has an additional form design tool called the web-based QuickBooks Forms Customization tool that you may use to create invoice forms and other QuickBooks forms that better suit your needs. Selecting the **Customize Design button** on the Formatting tab will bring up this tool from the Create Invoices window. When you execute this action, QuickBooks presents a webpage that guides you through an extensive graphic design process for the invoice form. Simply follow the directions on the website to use this method.

Invoicing a Customer

Your A/R workflow begins with preparing the invoice if your company does not need to create estimates or sales orders.

- Choose **Create Invoices from the Customers menu or the Home screen.**
- Choose **a customer or customer job from the Customer: Job drop-down menu. You can choose Add New if the client or task is not yet on the list.**

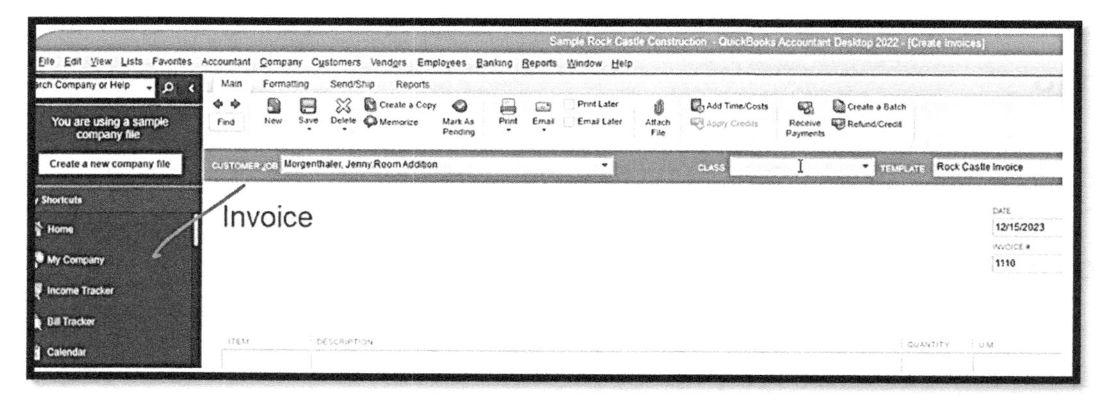

Enter a brief name for the customer in the Customer: Job list, such as an acronym for the customer's business name, if they are a new client that you haven't yet billed or described in the Customer List. When QuickBooks asks if you want to add a customer, reply that you do, even though it says the customer does not yet appear in the customer list. Provide QuickBooks with the customer information it requests when requested.

- Enter the necessary data at the top of the form, such as the Terms, Bill to/Sold to, and Date Invoice #.
- Choose **the item or items from the detail area**. Note: Based on the description and unit cost entered when it was set up, the quantity and description immediately appear when you pick or add an item. This can be changed or removed when creating invoices.

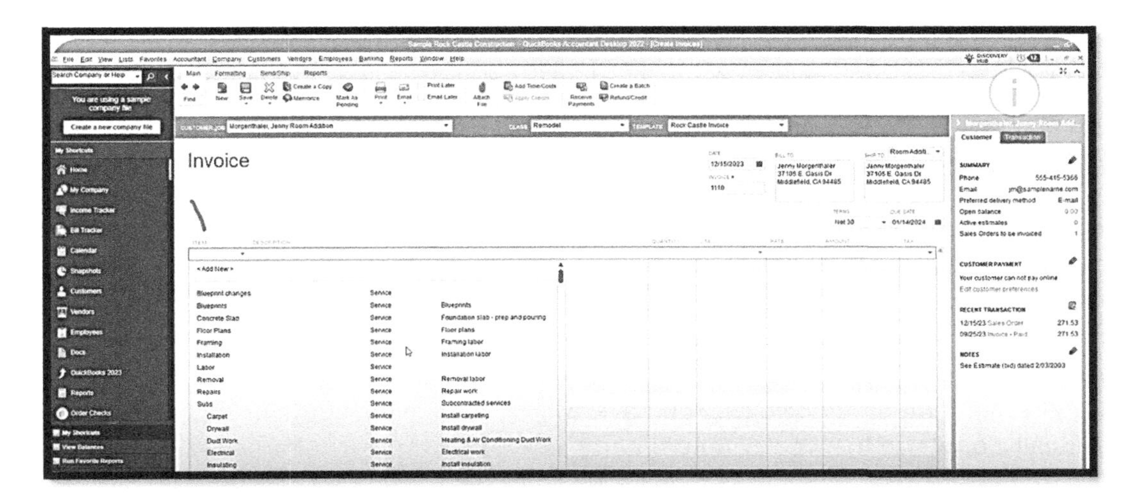

You can add more rows to the invoice by entering more items. In the columns section, each item you wish to bill for—anything that ought to show up as a distinct charge on the invoice—appears as a row. One line in the invoice's column-based area is utilized for each product you wish to bill a customer for. One line in the invoice area should be used to indicate any freight charges you wish to charge a customer. Once more, one line or row in the columns area indicates the sales tax charge if you wish to bill a consumer.

- **There is a need for you to create a discount item if there is a need for you to apply a discount to the item or items.**
  - Navigate **to the Lists menu from the Home screen.**
  - Choose **the Item List.**
  - Do a right-click anywhere, and choose **New.**
  - After choosing the **Type drop-down**, choose **Discount.**
  - Add the item's name or number and a succinct description.
  - Enter the amount or percentage of the discount in the Amount or % area. You might choose to enter the discount amount directly on your sales forms and leave the Amount or % column empty if your discount amounts vary.
  - Select **the income account** you wish to use to track the discounts you offer to clients using the Account drop-down menu.
  - Choose **the relevant tax code for the item.**
  - Click **OK.**
- Choose **Save and Close.**

QuickBooks provides the ability to add and remove historical customer information from the Create Credit Memos/Refunds window, the Create Invoices window, and most other customer information windows. Click the **Show History button**, which resembles an arrowhead and appears in the upper-right corner of the window slightly to the right of the Template drop-down lists, to add historical data about a client to a window. Within the historical information panel, you can drill down and view further details about certain transactions, for instance, by clicking on links.

Billing for Time

Line items that show up in an invoice are often ones that you describe in the item list and then immediately quantify in the invoice. However, you might genuinely sell multiple units of the same item in some service-related enterprises. An attorney may only sell a certain amount of time—hours or half hours—of legal advice. An accountant, tax preparer, or consultant may charge by the hour. There are two ways that QuickBooks allows you to track time that will be charged as an item on an invoice. You have two options: either time or record each activity individually, or utilize the weekly time sheet.

Weekly Timesheet

- Select **Customers** > **Enter Time** > **Use Weekly Timesheet** to employ the weekly time-sheet approach.

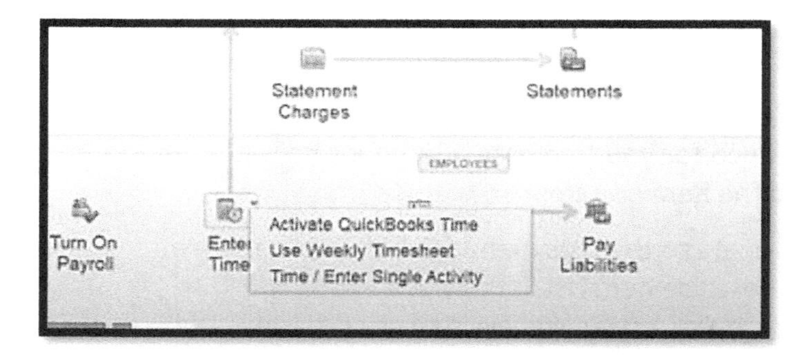

This opens the Weekly Timesheet window in QuickBooks. Use the Name field to identify the employee, vendor, or other individual completing the service before using the Weekly Timesheet window. This person's name needs to be selectable from the Name drop-down menu. If the person's name isn't available in the Name drop-down list, type it in the box and tell QuickBooks which list (vendor, employee, or other names) the name should be added to when prompted. Use the Weekly Timesheet window's columns to list the customer or job for which the work was completed, the service code, a brief description or note, the payroll item (if you use QuickBooks for payroll), the class (if you track classes), and finally the number of hours worked each day after adding the employee's name. The Weekly Timesheet window allows you to enter as many lines as you like. In an invoice, each line appears independently. The invoice's description section contains the notes information. You should therefore make use of pertinent and thorough notes.

Timing single activities

- Select **Customers > Enter Time >Time/Enter Single Activity** if you wish to capture service actions as they happen. The Time/Enter Single Activity window appears in QuickBooks.

Enter the date of the activity in the Date box to time or record it. To find out who provided the service, check the Name box. Indicate the client or the task for which the service was rendered in the Customer: Job field. Select the relevant service item from the list under Service Item and, if you are monitoring an employee, the relevant payroll item from the list under Payroll Item. Naturally, you can also categorize the action using the Class drop-down list if you're tracking classes. Write a succinct, suitable description of the service in the Notes box. It is important to write this description carefully because it will appear on the invoice.

Once you have been able to describe or offer this general information about the service, there are two ways by which you can record the time spent on the service;

- **Record time manually**: You can manually input the amount of time spent on an activity by utilizing the Duration box. For instance, if you spent ten minutes, type 0:10 in the Duration field. To enter 3:40 in the Duration box, you should type 3 hours and 40 minutes.
- **Have QuickBooks record the time**: QuickBooks has the option to track the amount of time you spend on each task. To begin an activity, simply click the Start button in the Duration box; to end an activity, click the Stop button. Click the **Pause button** to put the timer on hold (for example, while you answer a phone call).

Make that the Billable checkbox, located in the dialog box's upper-right corner, is checked. You can instruct QuickBooks to save this record of a chargeable action for use in an invoice at a later time by checking the chargeable box. The Previous and Next buttons, situated at the top of the dialog box, allow you to navigate back and forth through your activity timing records. Also, take note that there is a spelling button accessible. It's a good idea to click that option to proofread the notes description you enter, as this information will eventually appear in an invoice.

Including billable time on an invoice

Create the invoice as normal to add billable time and cost. QuickBooks asks you whether you want to bill for any of the time or costs after you identify the customer (if you've entered time for the client) and if you've been monitoring costs for the customer. QuickBooks shows the Select Billable Time and Costs dialog box if you select **"yes."** All of the times you've recorded for a customer are displayed on the Time tab of this dialog box. Click the **Use column** for the time to add these times to the invoice. (The column with a checkmark on the leftmost column is the Use column.) Alternatively, you can click the Select All button to choose every time. Next, press **OK**. These billable times are added to the invoice by QuickBooks as distinct lines. To view lists of the things, out-of-pocket costs, and business miles incurred on behalf of a customer, select the Things, Expenses, or Mileage tab. These kinds of goods are charged for on an invoice in the same manner that time is. Even your out-of-pocket expenses can be marked up.

- Selecting the **Company > Enter Vehicle Mileage command** will allow you to track and bill for the miles you drive on behalf of clients. (Use the dialog box QuickBooks displays to report the miles traveled and identify the customer when you select the **Enter Vehicle Mileage instruction.**) In case you're in the Create Invoices window and wish to go back to the Choose **Billable Time and Costs dialog box,** simply click on the **Add Time/Costs button** that shows up at the top of the window.

Printing Invoices

There are two ways that you can print invoices and mail them after that:

- Selecting the **Print button** at the top of the Create Invoices window allows you to print individual invoices.

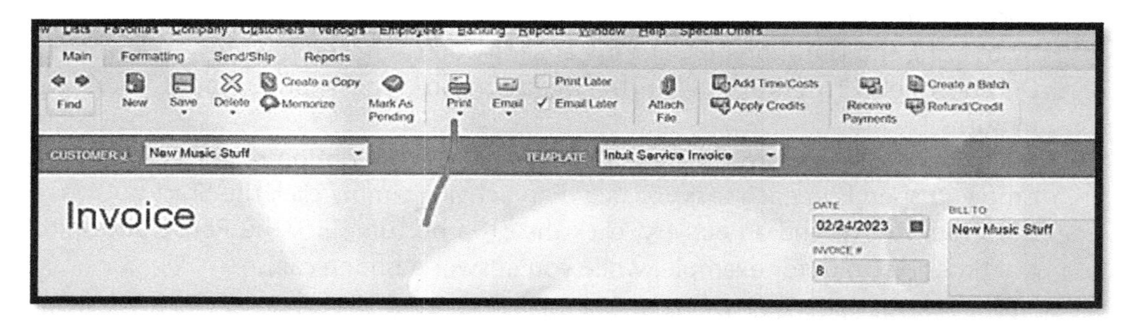

- Additionally, you can print a batch of invoices by selecting the **To Be Printed Invoices** for printing using the **Select Invoices to Print dialog box** that QuickBooks shows and selecting **Batch from the menu that QuickBooks displays**. Click **OK** after selecting the invoices you wish to print by clicking on them.

When you select the Print button in QuickBooks, a menu with the option to Preview appears. To get a preview of the printed invoice, select the **Preview command**.

Emailing Invoices

An invoice from QuickBooks can be emailed.

- Click the **Email button on the Main tab,** which is located at the top of the Create Invoice window, to accomplish this. Provide the email address and (optionally) a new email message, along with the email account you wish to use (webmail, an email program like Microsoft Outlook, or the QuickBooks emailing system) if you haven't already set up email preferences. Then, coincidentally, send the invoice by clicking the **Send Now button.**

By selecting the **Send Forms area of the Preferences dialog box** and using the **Edit > Preferences command**, you may configure email preferences. When you click the **Email button for the first time**, QuickBooks could ask you to describe your email account or accounts. Simply follow the steps on the screen to provide the information. Additionally, QuickBooks can advise you to use their mailing service, in which case the invoice is emailed to Intuit, which subsequently sends the paper invoice to your client via snail mail. Follow the on-screen instructions if you're interested in using Intuit's invoice-sending service. To the dismay of numerous users, later iterations of the QuickBooks software included a notice and a clickable link at the foot of printed and emailed invoices, encouraging the customers or clients of those users to use a free (for them) online payment system to settle your invoice. There is a monthly fee of a few dollars for this service, known as the Intuit Payment Network, and a 2 to 3 percent service charge for credit card payments.

Recording Sales Receipt

If you are paid in full at the moment of the sale, use the sales receipt. Cash, cheque, and credit card payments are included in sales receipts. You can still record your daily sales summary using Sales Receipt if you do not need to track sales by customer. Create a customer account called Daily Sales (or any other name you like), and then input each item's total sales for the day. You can set up a customer name for each cash register if you have several and wish to keep track of the sales at each one.

- Choose the **Create Sales Receipts/Enter Sales Receipts option from the Customers menu or the QuickBooks Home screen.**

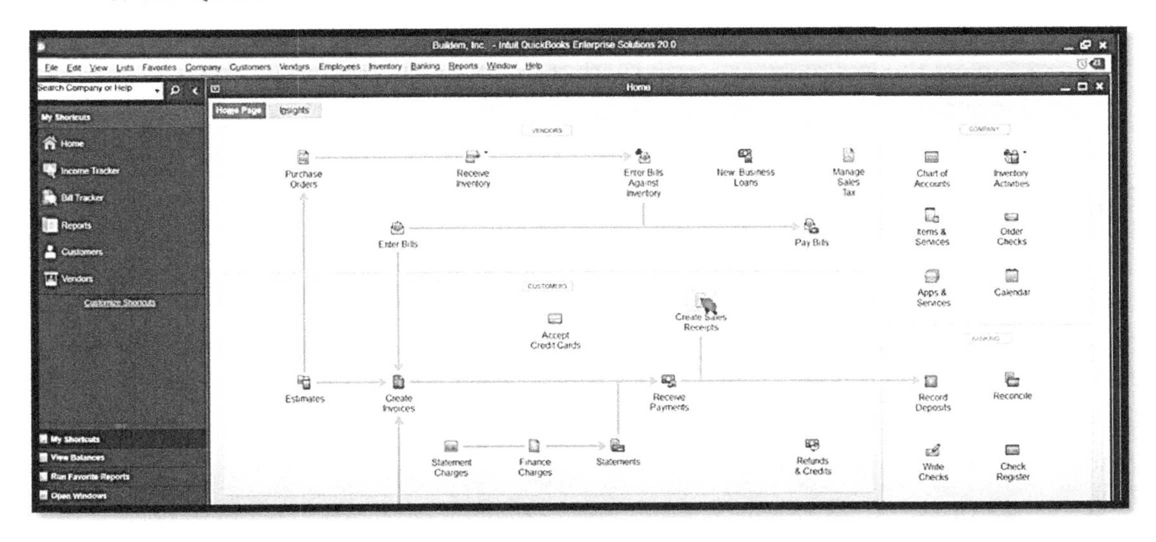

- From the Customer: Choose a customer or job from the job drop-down menu. You can click **Add New** if the customer is not already on the list.
- Enter the pertinent data, such as the sale number and date, at the top of the form.
- Select **the mode of payment.**

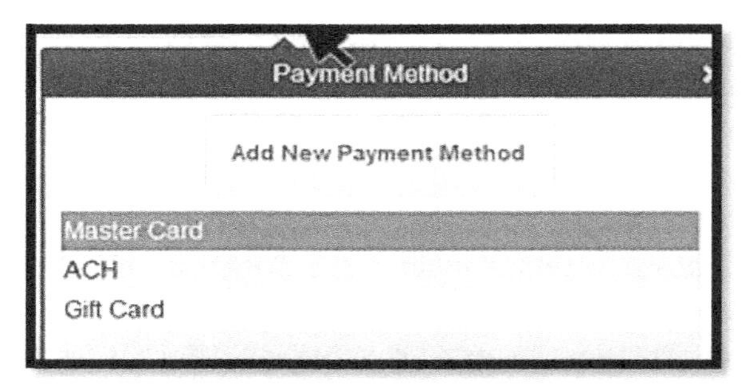

- Choose the item or items you plan to sell in the detail section.

Note: Based on the description and unit cost supplied when the item was set up, the quantity and description immediately appear when you pick or add an item. This can be changed or removed when creating invoices.

- **If there is a need for you to include a discount you then have to create a discount item.**
    - Choose **Item List from the QuickBooks Lists menu.**
    - Anywhere you do a right-click, select **New.**
    - Click the Type drop-down menu and choose **Discount in the New Item box.**
    - Add the item's name or number and a succinct description.
    - Enter the amount or percentage of the discount in the Amount or % area. You might choose to enter the discount amount directly on your sales forms and leave the Amount or % column empty if your discount amounts vary.
    - Select **the income account you wish to use to track the discounts you offer to clients using the Account drop-down menu.**
    - After choosing the proper tax code for the item, click **OK.**

Recording Credit Memos

Credit notes indicate when you owe customer money and when they owe you money. If a customer returns goods you previously sold them, credit memos could happen. Credit memos can also happen when you give a customer a refund for another legitimate reason. For example, the product might not have been as nice as you generally sell it to be, or a service might not have been rendered as it should have been.

To document a credit memo, take the following actions:

- To see the Create Credit Memos/Refunds window, select the **Customers > Create Credit Memos/Refunds command.**

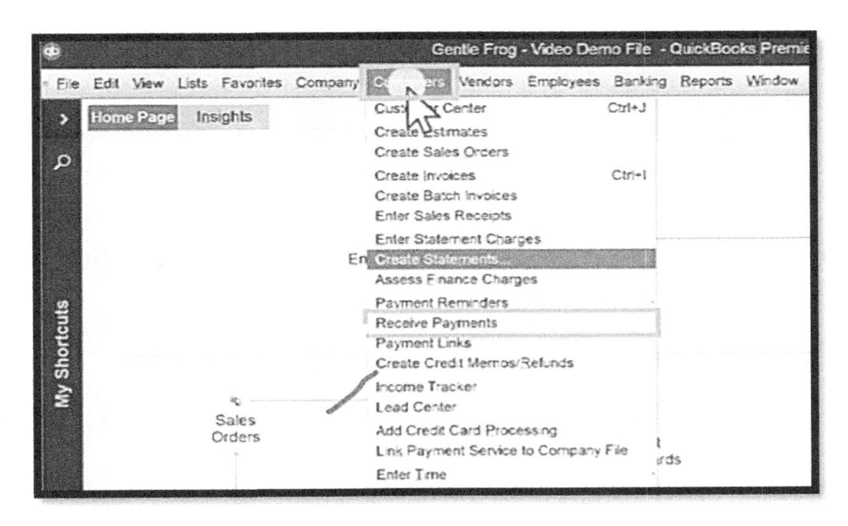

- Select the customer from the Customer: Job drop-down list, or the customer and the job.

Many of the buttons on the different tabs of the Create Credit Memos/Refunds window are functional here, just as they are in the Create Invoices window: Prior, Subsequent, and so forth. Custom credit memo forms can be created, much like invoices. You click the Customize Data Layout button on the Formatting tab to accomplish this. Personalized invoice forms and credit memos can be customized in the same manner. For information on customizing a credit memo, see the previous section on this subject.

- Give the credit memo date and number and then make a confirmation of the customer information.
- Make a description of the reason for the credit memo in the columns area.
- Choose the **Print button** to have a credit memo printed.
- Lastly, you either **Save & Close or Save & New** to have the credit memo saved.

Receiving Customer's Payments

You can handle payments directly within QuickBooks Desktop if you have QuickBooks Payments installed. You can be compensated in a few different ways. For the invoices you email to clients, you have the option to enable online payments. Clients have two options for paying invoices: ACH bank transfer or credit card. To make a payment, all they need to do is click the email's link. If a consumer comes into your store, you can also take payments over the phone or in person.

Here's how to configure QuickBooks Desktop so that your clients may pay you.

Register for QuickBooks Payments if you haven't already. Connect your current QuickBooks Payments account to QuickBooks Desktop if you already have one for another product.

Briefly carry out the following before you commence the payment exercise

- Switch on the card reader.
- With the use of the USB cable provided, connect the card reader to the computer.
- Launch QuickBooks Desktop.
- To successfully process in-person payments, make use of the card reader.

It's time for you to get paid. You can process payments in person or give your customers an invoice that they can pay online by following these steps.

Processing in-person payments

You do not have to give them an invoice if they call or visit your store to pay. Make a sales receipt instead:

- Choose **Enter Sales Receipts from the Customers menu.**
- Choose **the specific customer from the Customer: Job dropdown.**
- Include the products and the services that the customer must be paying for.
- Complete the remaining aspect of the sales receipt.
- Choose your preferred payment method; Cash, Check, or Visa (ensure you make use of Visa for credit cards).
- When you have completed the above, choose **Save & Close.**

Process payments for open invoices

You have a few choices if a consumer requests payment over the phone or in person after you send them an invoice. You might request that they click the Pay Now button in the email to complete their online payment if you issued them an online invoice.

Additionally, you can handle the payment processing and reconcile it with their current invoice:

- Click the **Customers menu, then choose Receive Payments.**

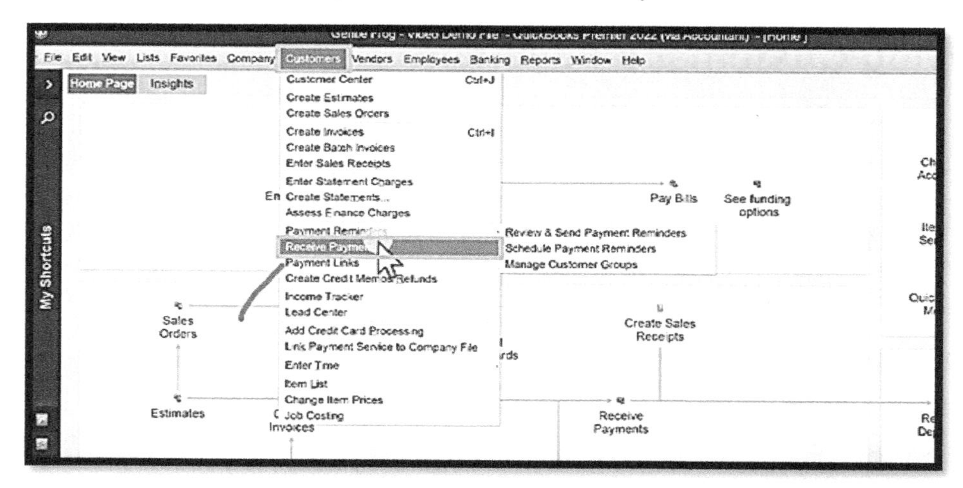

- From the Received From dropdown, choose the customer.

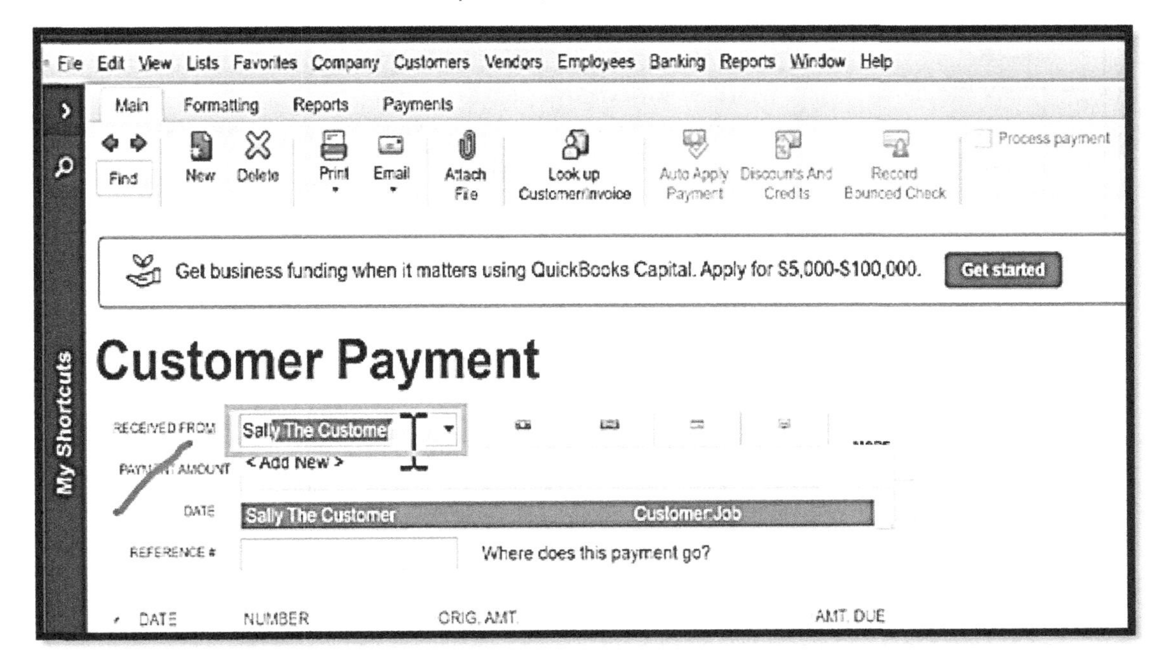

- To add the payment to an invoice, check the box next to it in the transactions area. This is the invoice that you should have sent them earlier.
- Choose the mode of payment: Payment options: Visa (used for credit cards), cash, or check.
- Once finished, choose Save & Close.

Customer Prepayments on Sales Orders

Customer deposits, often known as prepayments, are sums of money received in advance of the completion of a good or service. An invoice for the payment is not yet in your possession.

In QuickBooks Enterprise 24.0 or later, to handle prepayments:

Receive customer prepayments

Step 1: Switch on Prepayments

- Select Edit, followed by Preferences.
- After choosing Payments, select Company Preferences.
- Select Prepayment Settings after going to Prepayments.

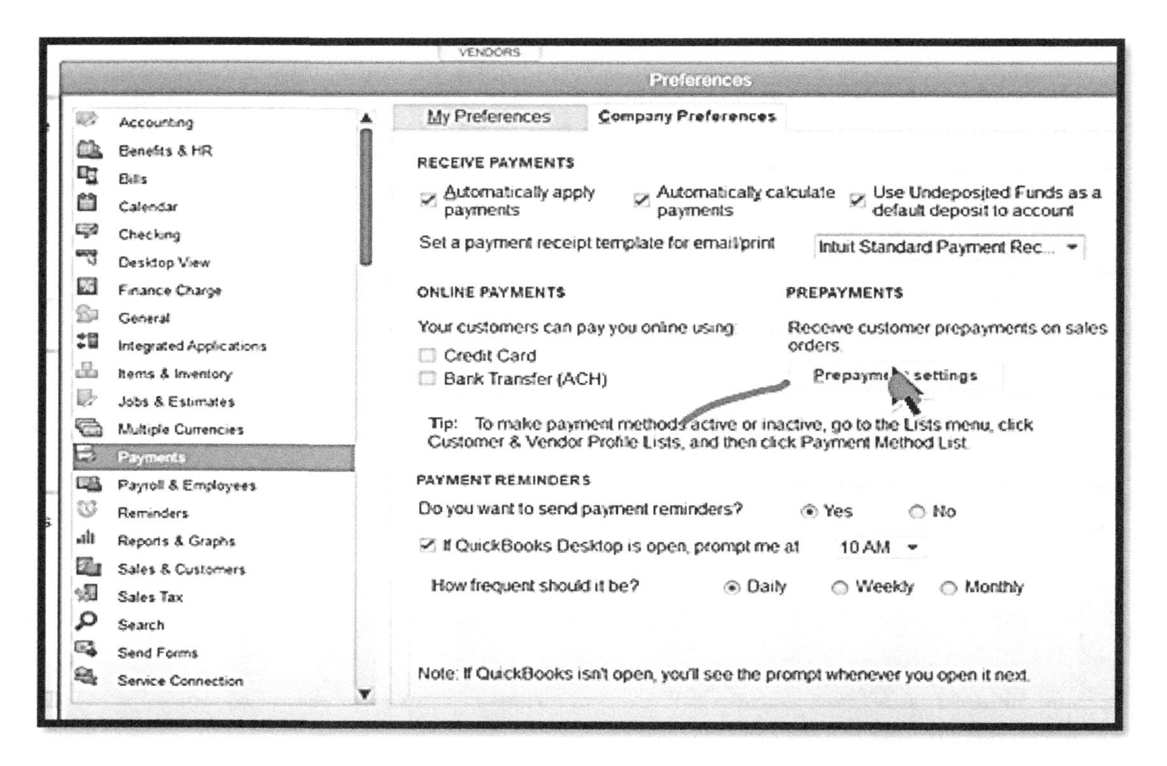

- To enable payments, select the **corresponding checkbox.**
- From the options, pick a current liabilities account. A new current liability account can be opened. Simply choose.
- When you're finished, click **OK,** and then click **OK** once again in the preferences.

Step 2: Receive prepayments on an open sales order

Create and save new sales orders or launch any sales order that exists already.

- Click Sales Order, and then choose Receive Payments.

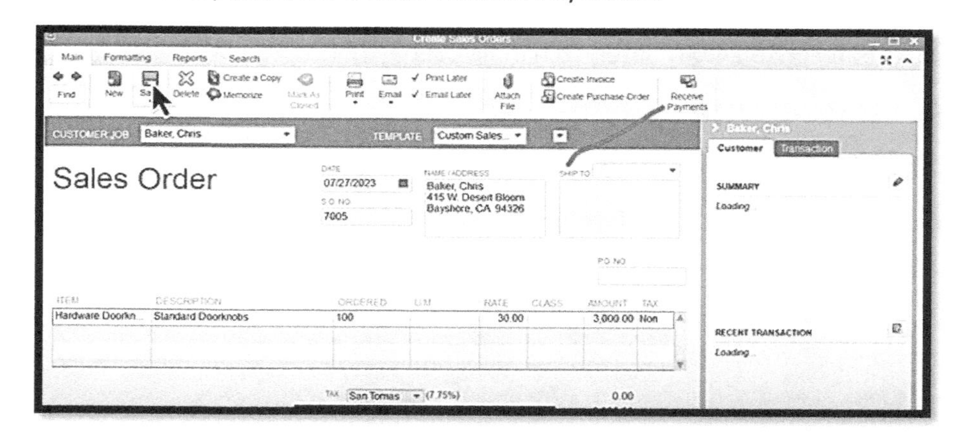

- You will reach Customer Payment by doing this. On your customer payment, there will be a checkbox labeled "**Prepayment on Sales Order.**"
  Note: You must first check the box labeled Prepayment on Sales Order to access the Customer Payment from Home or Customer Center.
- After entering the prepayment amount and any information, click **Save and Close.**
- Verify that the prepayment amount and remaining balance have been changed by checking the sales order.

Print a sales order that shows you received a prepayment

- After opening the sales order, select **Formatting.**
- After choosing **Customize Data Layout, select Footer.**
- Check the boxes under **Balance Due and Prepayments.**
  Note: In the Print template, you can change where these fields appear. Simply choose the **Layout Designer.**
- When you're finished, click **OK.**
- Select **Print** after opening the sales order. Regarding prepayments and the remaining amount owed, consult the sales order.

Apply prepayment credit to an invoice

- Select "**Create Invoice"** after opening the sales order.
- To apply prepayment credits, select **Save this invoice and then Yes.**
- For this invoice, you can view the available Prepayment Credits. It is advised that you use the prepayment credits associated with the invoice. In addition, you can view further potential credits for this customer, such as a credit memo or prepayments made for unrelated sales orders.
- To apply the prepayment credit to this invoice, select it and enter or modify the credit amount. Next, choose **Done.**
- Verify whether the balance owed and the prepayment credit has been updated. The invoice with payments/credits and the remaining amount can be printed.

Note however that if a prepayment hasn't been applied to an invoice, you can change it. Once a payment has been applied to an invoice, it cannot be changed. Once a prepayment has been applied to an invoice, it cannot be changed; therefore, it must be deleted. The generic journal entries that QuickBooks automatically generates will be removed as a result.

Using Odds and Ends on the Customer Menu

The majority of the key commands on the Customer menu are covered in this chapter. But there are a few more commands available on this menu that are interesting, even helpful, and should be included in this book.

Because of this, you will also discover more commands that could be present on your Customers menu:

- **Customer Center:** brings up the Customer Center window, which has details about your clientele, including their outstanding balances.
- **Create Estimates**: shows a window that you can use to build an estimate for a client, illustrating the price of a service or product, for instance, if you sell it to them.
- **Create Sales Orders**: shows a window where a sales order can be created. A sales order is essentially an invoice for a product or service that you haven't sold yet. To register an order from a client or customer and record the order details, you create a sales order.
- **Sales Order Fulfillment Worksheet**: Make your entire list of unfulfilled sales orders visible in the Sales Order Fulfillment worksheet window. This worksheet can also be used to print batches of sales orders. (Note: QuickBooks will prompt you to convert a sales order into an invoice anytime you begin working on one for a specific client or customer if you have created sales orders for them.)
- **Create Batch Invoice**s: brings up the Batch Invoice dialog box, where you may select which customers to charge for a certain item. Once you've organized the clients into these groups, or batches, you may instruct QuickBooks to generate a large number of invoices. For instance, if you bill clients on a monthly retainer basis, you may group the clients on a retainer and then send them individual invoices for the "monthly retainer fee" item.
- **Enter Statement Charges**: shows the Register of Accounts Receivable. This command can be used to increase the amount of accounts receivable for a certain customer, but it shouldn't be necessary. The customer's subsequent statement shows the amounts.
- **Create Statements:** this shows a window where you can make a batch of monthly statements for clients. These statements list all of the amounts owed by customers, as well as the invoices generated, credit memos issued, and payments made over the month.
- **Income Tracker**: opens the Income Tracker window, which displays the flow of sales revenue you should (hopefully) receive as well as the flow of expenses you have incurred or will incur. It does this by graphically organizing your estimates, orders, and invoices.
- **Lead Center:** brings up the Lead Center window, where you may track and save leads for customers. You can make notes, list names, and maintain a to-do list for lead-generating tasks using this window.
- **Add Credit Card Processing**: shows a particular web page that narrates and also tries to convince you to buy the credit card of Intuit's processing service.
- **Add Marketing and Customer Tools**: accessible in QuickBooks Enterprise Solutions version): shows a list of websites that you can visit to learn more about the electronic

data exchange and work-order management features that are compatible with QuickBooks.

- **Learn about Point of Sale**: gives additional details on configuring a point-of-sale system. Additionally, a 30-day free trial is available.
- **Item List**: indicates the items that might be included in the invoice or credit memo in the item list.
- **Change Item Prices**: enables you to alter many products' prices at once; for example, raising each item's price by 5%.

Activity

1. Choose and customize an invoice form.
2. Bill for time.
3. Print and email an invoice.
4. Record sales receipts and credit memos.
5. Receive customer payments.

CHAPTER 2
PAYING VENDORS

The process of tracking vendor information can be as easy or complex as you like. Nevertheless, if you don't use purchase orders or an accounts payable system, you can simplify vendor administration. When you set up QuickBooks, you choose if you would like to track accounts payable (amounts owed to vendors) and whether you use purchase orders. Ultimately, you are free to decide whether to use purchase orders or accounts payable. You use the Edit >Preferences command to accomplish this.

Creating a Purchase Order

The straightforward function of a purchase order is to inform a vendor that you wish to buy a certain item. A purchase order is an agreement to buy. Purchase orders are not used by many small enterprises. However, after they reach a certain size, a lot of companies choose to use them since purchase orders turn into permanent records of the goods they've ordered. Additionally, the use of purchase orders frequently formalizes an organization's purchasing procedure. For instance, you can determine that employees in your company are not allowed to make any purchases above $200 without a purchase order. With this process, you have successfully managed purchasing activity if only you could issue purchase orders.

Follow the steps below to create a purchase order in QuickBooks Desktop;

- To start with, if you have not switched on purchase orders, do this first
    - Choose **Preferences** after you have chosen **Edit.**
    - Choose the **Company Preferences tab** after you have chosen Items & Inventory.
    - Check the **Inventory and purchase orders are active checkboxes and then choose OK.**
- Navigate to **Vendors and then choose Create Purchase Orders.**

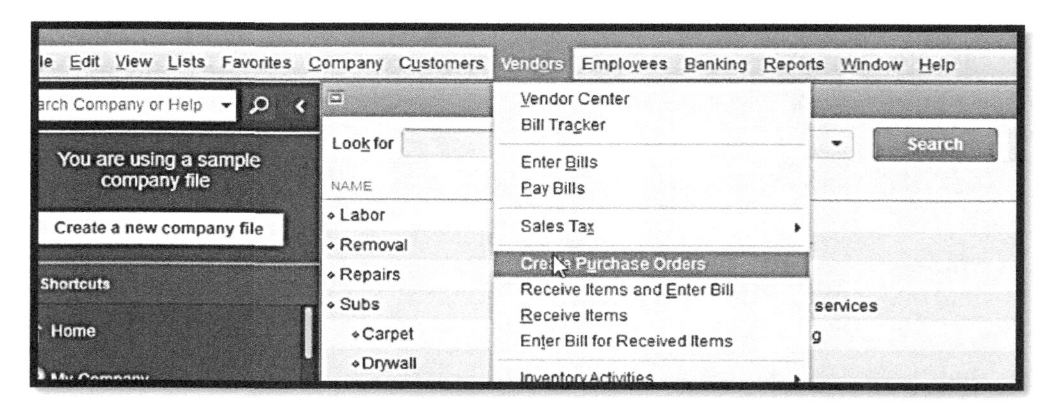

- Choose the vendor you want to make a purchase order for from the Vendor choice. To add a new vendor, choose **Add New** as well.

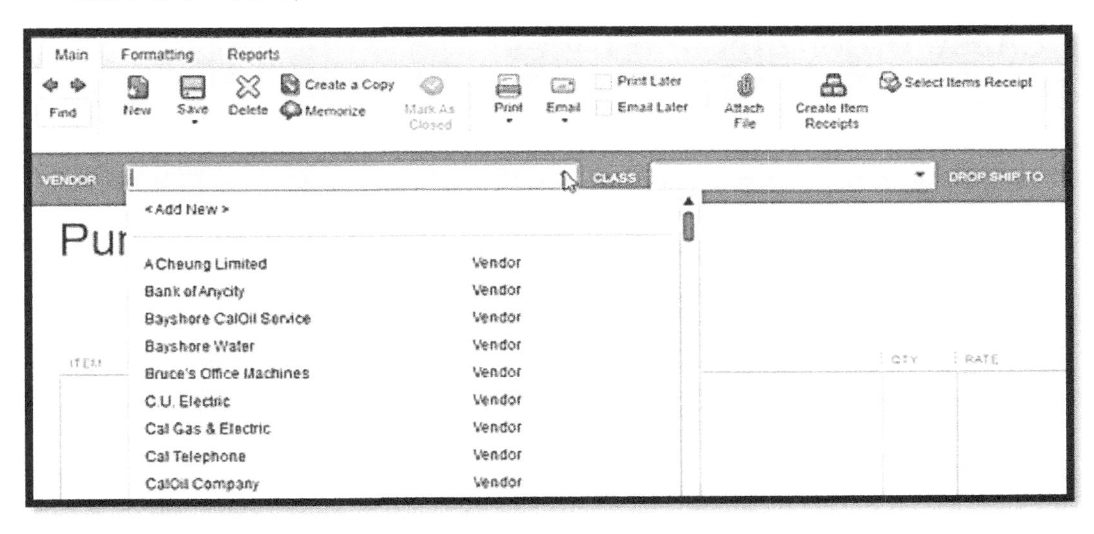

- Complete the remaining fields and include the items you want to order. Ensure you get the purchase order date confirmed and also confirm the vendor and Ship To information.
- Choose **"Save & Close."**

For users of Mac;

- Choose **Create Purchase Orders** after you have chosen Vendors.
- Choose **Create Purchase Order.**
- Choose **Save** after you has filled out the necessary fields.

To create a purchase order for an estimate, follow the steps below;

- Choose **Generate Purchase Order from the Estimates window.**
- If everything is from a single vendor, mark on the estimate For all allowed items. If there are products from several vendors, choose the ones you wish to have on your purchase order by selecting **for selected items.**
- Click **OK.**
- After completing the fields, click **Save.**

In case of a mistake, after you have created the purchase order, you can still get the purchase order altered.

Follow the steps below to edit the purchase order;

- Navigate to Vendors and choose the **Purchase Order List**.
- To make changes to a purchase order, double-click the vendor. The timeframe for buying orders opens.

- Choose the purchase order that needs editing. Choose the **Left View icon** if the purchase order list isn't visible.

Purchase order tips and tricks

- **Not all purchases need a purchase order**: When you utilize this helpful tool for the first time and are not accustomed to working with purchase orders, it's tempting to overdo it. However, remember that not every purchase requires a purchase order.
- **Utilize purchase orders in managing buying**: Purchase orders are typically used by organizations to monitor and record purchases. In actuality, a purchase order is not always necessary for transactions. Purchase orders are not necessary for amounts that you have committed to buy that are supported by regular contracts, such as your landlord's, gas companies, and phone company's bills. Furthermore, purchase orders are frequently unnecessary for small expenditures like office supplies. Purchase orders are certainly not the best approach to take, but you still need to find a means to keep these costs under control.
- **Consider other, complementary control tools:** Simple budgets or "approval from the supervisor" are two other financial restrictions that frequently function just as well.

Recording the Receipt of Items

You can keep a record of the receipts you receive from vendors. This is usually what you do when you want to document the receipt of an item even before you get the bill for it. For example, you want to know the precise amount of inventory you have in your warehouse or on your retail floor in any firm that deals with inventory. It is best to make the necessary adjustments to your inventory records for these purchases as soon as you get the vendor's invoice. In this case, you document the receipt of the goods.

To have a record of item receipts, follow the steps below;

- Click on the **Receive Items command** after you have chosen Vendors.

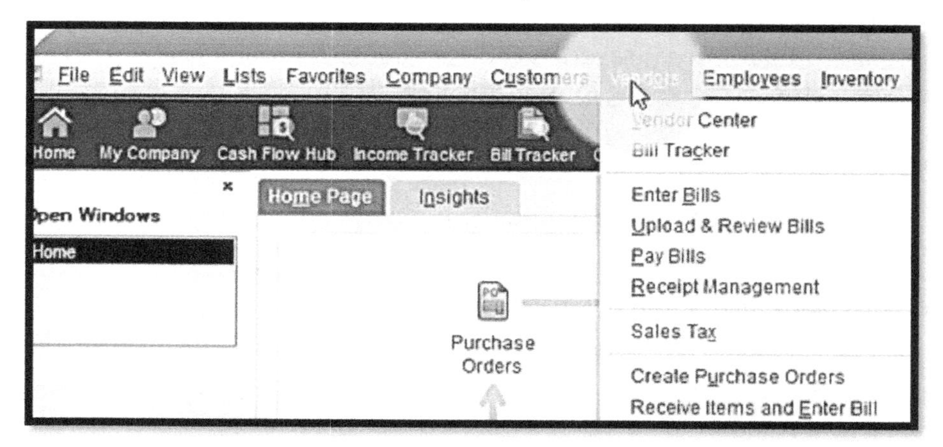

- Choose **the vendor** from which you are getting items from the drop-down list of vendors.
- Choose any purchase orders that you happen to be getting items from. QuickBooks asks you whether you wish to receive things against one of the open purchase orders or if there are any open purchase orders for the seller. Click **Yes** if the goods you receive are the ones you specified in a purchase order. Choose the purchase order that ordered the items you are now receiving when QuickBooks shows the Open Purchase Orders dialog box; click **OK to proceed.** The dialog box only contains open purchase orders.
- Make a confirmation of the receipt date.
- If need be, insert a reference number.
- Employ the use of the Total box to have a view of the total value of the order that was received if available.
- Make a description of the items you got.
- Make a description of any form of related expenses.
- Choose either the **Save & Close or Save & New button to have the receipt item saved.**

Simultaneously Recording the Receipt and the Bill

It is possible to document a bill for goods you get concurrently with the item's receipt. To accomplish this, just tick the Bill Received box, which is located toward the top of the Create Item Receipts window. You can also select **Vendors > Receive Items** and Enter Bill if you know that you will be recording a bill at the same time that you record the receipt of things. Put another way, you select the **Receive Items and Enter Bill command** rather than the **Receive Items command** from the **Vendors menu**. QuickBooks opens the Enter Bills window when you do this. Except for the Bill Received checkbox being checked, the Enter Bills window is essentially a duplicate of the **Create Item Receipts window**. You take the identical actions as you would to record the receipt of the products to concurrently record them as received and enter a bill. But one thing to keep in mind regarding recording bills and item receipts at the same time is this: When entering a bill, you must be quite accurate about the vendor's charges. Your payment will likely cover more than simply the products you ordered, like shipping and handling costs. It's not certain that these sums will appear on the Items tab. Most likely, they will be noted on the Expenses tab.

Entering a Bill

You can enter bills as you get them if you indicated in the QuickBooks setup that you wish to keep track of outstanding bills, also called accounts payable. QuickBooks tracks the bills that aren't paid as you work. Maintaining accurate and up-to-date records of accounts payable is crucial for performing accrual-basis accounting correctly.

- Navigate to the Vendors menu and then choose **Enter Bills.**
- Fill out the needed fields after you have chosen a vendor from the dropdown menu.

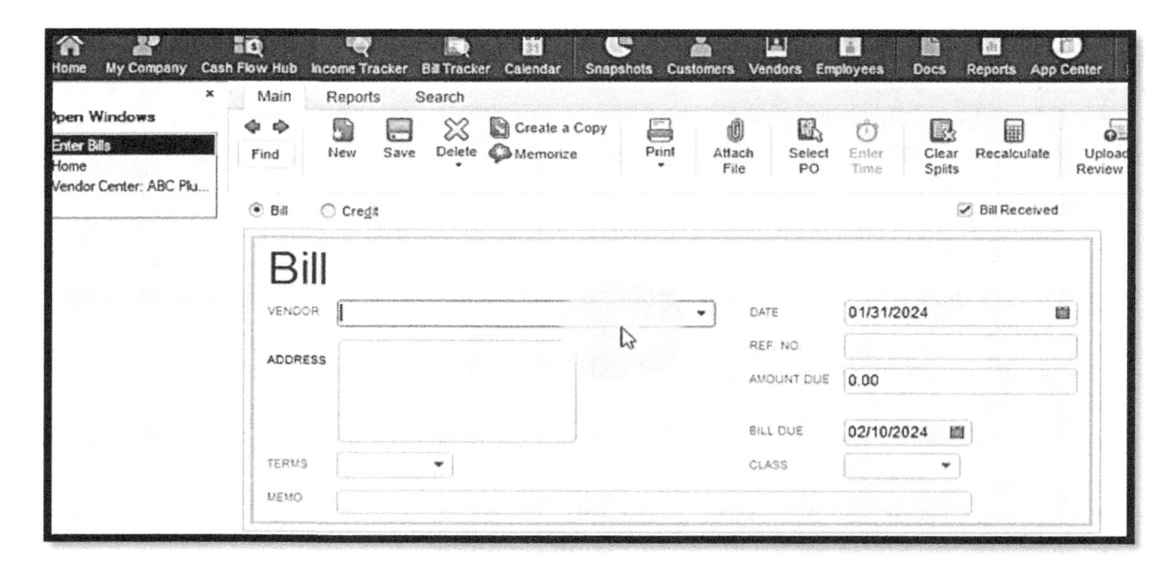

- Date: the date you got the bill.
- Amount: the total amount of the bill received.
- Due date: the due date of the bill.

- **Choose the specific type of bill you would like to record;**
  - Expenses: records a bill for expenses incurred by the business like phone service, rent, and utilities.
  - Items: this helps with the recording of a bill for just anything that your company buys, sells, or resells in the course of business like products, shipping, and getting to deal with charges and discounts.
- Choose **Save** to have the recorded bill.

Paying Bills

You don't utilize the Write Checks window to record the bills you wish to pay if you use QuickBooks to track the invoices you owe. Instead, you instruct QuickBooks to show you a list of these outstanding bills that you have already documented. From there, you may select which bills to pay and which bank account QuickBooks should debit from.

If for any reason, you are unable to see the bills you want to make payment for, follow the set of instructions;

- Verify whether the bill needs to be entered into QuickBooks still.
- In the Pay Bills window, make sure that **Show all bills is selected**. Then, scroll up or down to locate your bill.
- When you choose **Due on or before,** you may refine your search for a specific bill by entering the date in the **Show Bills area**.

- In case you have several accounts payable, see if the invoice is associated with a distinct account.
- Verify if the bill has already been paid. The Transaction List by Vendor report is available for use.
    - Navigate to the **Reports menu**.
    - Choose Vendors & Payables then click on the **Transaction List by Vendor.**
    - Choose Customize Report and then click on **Billing Status from the Column section.**
    - Choose **OK.**

To pay bills or payables this way, take these steps:

- Choose **Pay Bills from the Vendor's menu.**

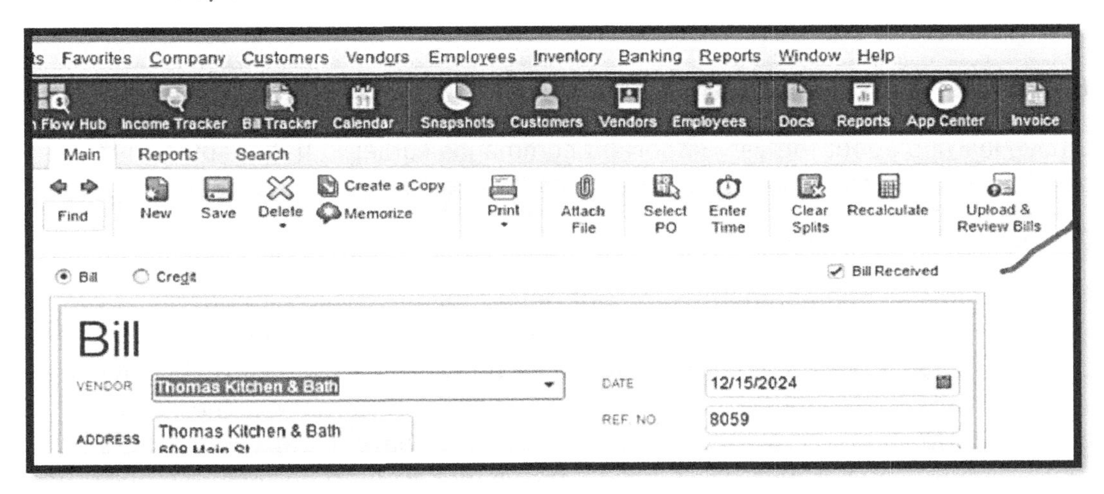

- Choose the right accounts payable from the menu that pops up.
- Choose the checkboxes of the bills you would like to pay from the table. It is worth noting that to unmark or mark all the bills in the list choose **Clear Selections or Select All Bills.**
- **Configure any discount or credit that you would like to add to the bills.**
    - **Discount**: Choose this if your vendor offered you a discount for this transaction.
    - **Credit**: choose this if you got a credit from your vendor, and you made use of it in the reduction of your total bill amount.
- Insert the date you got the bill paid.
- **Choose the preferred method;**
    - **Check**: choose Assign check number if you have a plan to write the check manually. Choose To be printed to print the check or include it in the list of checks to print.
    - **Credit Card**: you can opt to make use of credit cards to get bills paid and then also get a payment stub printed.

- **Online Bill Payment**: In QuickBooks, you can choose to directly pay your vendor bills. You are also able to record your payments instantly so that you will have reports that are quite accurate.
- **Online Bank Payment**: The payment processor will print the employee's cheque and ship it to them. If you would want your name and account number to be delivered with the bill or credit reference number, you can choose the option to include a reference number.
- Cash, Debit or ATM card, Paypal, or EFT: Even if you aren't paying with a physical check, you can still choose Check and then Assign check number. You can either leave the check number field empty or enter the type of payment.

* Choose **Pay Selected Bills.**
* Choose **Done, or choose Pay More Bills** if you feel there are other bills there is a need for you to pay.

Reviewing the Other Vendor Menu Commands

You have learned about the very important commands earlier in this chapter, in this section, you will learn about some other vendor commands and what they do also.

Vendor Center window

A list of vendors and comprehensive vendor details for the chosen vendor are shown in the Vendor Center window. To utilize it, select the vendor you wish to view detailed information about from the Active Vendors drop-down list. A vendor can view a lot of information in the Vendor Center. The Vendor list is the source of all of this information. The Vendor list is the ideal location to keep track of any information you may have about your vendors, including phone numbers. For QuickBooks to function, the vendor list must be kept up to date. Why not take the extra few minutes to store all of your vendor details there as well? If you choose this course of action, you may quickly seek information like the vendor's phone number or fax number using the Vendor Center window. For keeping track of open bills, past-due invoices, unbilled purchase orders, and debts that have been paid within 30 days, the Bill Tracker toolbar button is highly helpful. To render this information obvious at a glance, the data is displayed neatly.

Sales Tax menu commands

The Sales Tax command shows a submenu of instructions that can be used to alter the sales tax liability owed pay sales tax amounts you've collected to the relevant tax agency, and generate reports on your sales tax liability, revenue, and set up sales tax codes.

You must notify QuickBooks that you are a sales tax collector to view this menu. During the QuickBooks setup process, you can instruct QuickBooks to collect sales tax. Additionally, you can select **Edit > Preferences** to customize the company's sales tax settings.

Just select **Vendors > Sales Tax > Pay Sales Tax** to pay the sales taxes you owe.

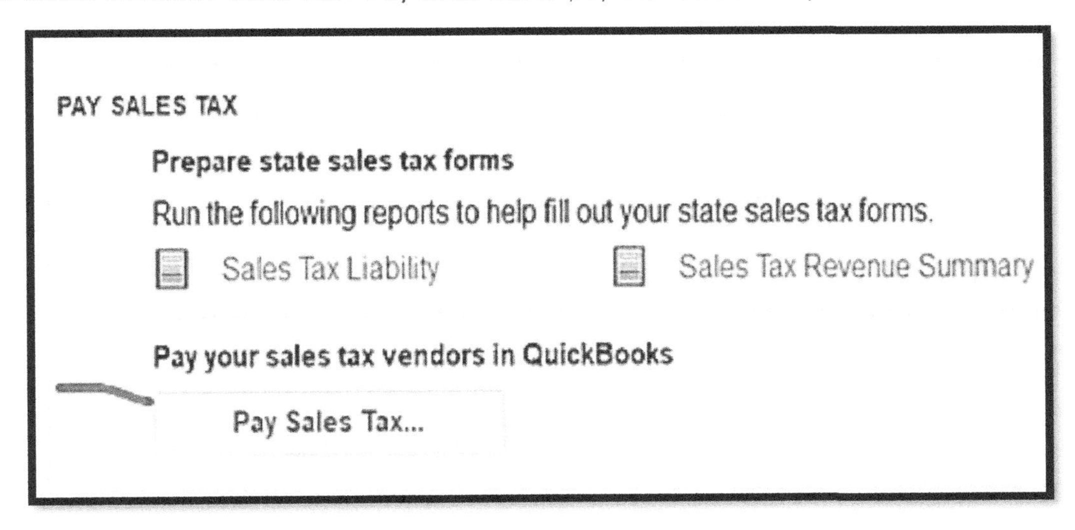

You can choose which sales tax collection agencies you want to pay or click the **Pay All Tax option** when QuickBooks shows the Pay Sales Tax dialog box, which includes the amounts you owe each agency. Checks are printed using the standard procedure, and QuickBooks registers them in the bank account register. You can select **Vendors > Sales Tax > Adjust Sales Tax Due** to change the amount QuickBooks believes you owe a sales tax collection agency.

Choose a sales tax agency in the Sales Tax Vendor box and a suitable expense or income account in the Adjustment Account box when QuickBooks displays the Sales Tax Adjustment dialog box. The adjustment amount should then be entered in the Amount box after selecting the relevant button (Increase Sales Tax By or Decrease Sales Tax By). Just choose the command that matches the report you want to print to get one of the sales tax reports. For instance, select **Vendors > Sales Tax > Sales Tax Liability to print the Sales Tax Liability report.** You can obtain sales tax information and carry out some of the operations mentioned in the previous paragraphs by using the **Manage Sales Tax command**, which opens a window with buttons and clickable hyperlinks. You can add, remove, or change codes by going to the **Sales Tax Code List**. Additionally, it offers drop-down menus with choices to carry out the previously mentioned tasks, such as paying sales tax obligations or seeing reports displaying the transactions for which sales tax was assessed.

Inventory Activities menu commands

You can interact with QuickBooks inventory features and the associated item list by using the **Inventory Activities command**, which presents a submenu of instructions.

Print/ E-File 1099s commands

You can print 1099-MISC forms for a certain calendar year by using the Print/E-file 1099s command, which presents a submenu of commands.

- By selecting the **issue/E-file 1099s > Review 1099** suppliers command, for example, you can identify the suppliers for whom you most likely need to issue 1099s. (QuickBooks displays the Vendor 1099 Review report, which includes vendors and shows which ones are eligible for 1099 based on your descriptions when you select this command.)

In general, if you own rental property or run a business, you have to send a 1099-MISC to pretty much any unincorporated vendor you pay $600 or more for services in a year. However, the reporting level may vary in the future owing to inflation. Additionally, you should be aware of two other realities before choosing to disregard this guideline. You can initiate an online wizard that assists you in determining which suppliers need 1099s and getting ready to print or electronically file those 1099s by using the **Print/E-file 1099s > 1099 Wizard command.**

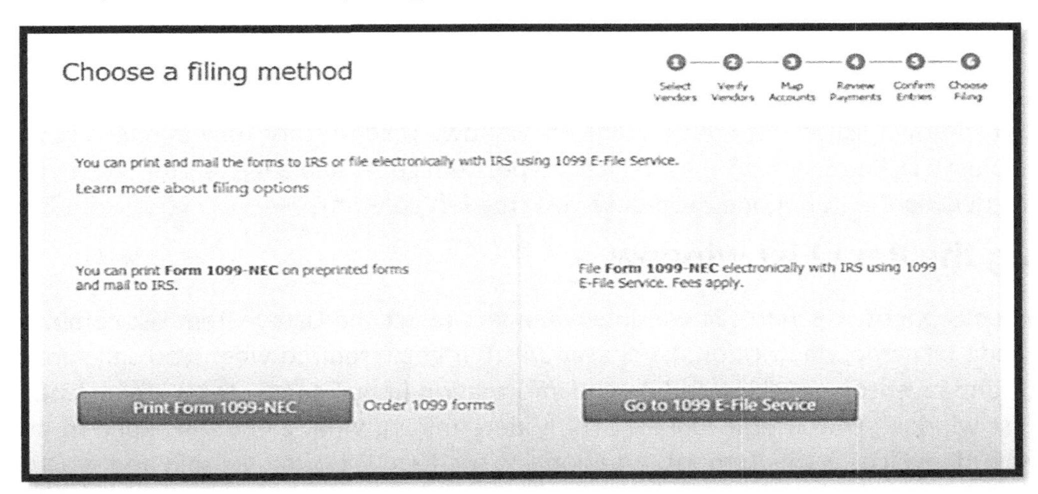

Finally, you can generate reports that you may use to determine which suppliers require 1099s and what specific information should be included in those 1099s by selecting the **1099 Summary Report and 1099 Detail Report options from the Print/E-file 1099s menu.**

Activity

1. Create a purchase order.
2. Record the receipt of items.
3. Enter a bill and pay bills

CHAPTER 3

TRACKING INVENTORY AND ITEMS

The item list is a crucial component of your QuickBooks accounting system, which shouldn't come as a surprise to anyone who has dealt with the program. All of the products you offer are listed on the item list. In addition, the item list lists additional items that show up in your purchase orders and invoices, if you use them. You will learn about how to make use of the Item list effectively in QuickBooks in this chapter. You will also learn about how you can look at and effectively utilize the various information in the Item list for the tracking and tallying of what you sell.

Looking at Your Item List

There are numerous methods to view the data you've saved in your item list in QuickBooks. If you've dealt with QuickBooks a little, you could already be familiar with some of this information; otherwise, you might not. Regardless, the following sections go over the various ways you can view the things in your item list.

Using the Item Code column

Space is a crucial factor to take into account while examining the Item Code column and Item Code drop-down list in the Create Invoices window. Take note of how condensed the Item Code column is. Keep in mind that the item type, item code, and a longer item description are all provided via the Item Code drop-down list (the left column).

Using the Item List window

QuickBooks opens the Item List window when you select the **Lists > Item List command.** The item code or name, description, kind, account that gets credited when you sell some of the things, and inventory stocking and pricing information (if you supply that) are all listed in the item list window. One useful tool for swiftly determining what can be included in purchase orders and invoices is the item list. Additionally, the item list offers a rapid and practical way to view prices and stock levels. Double-clicking an item in the Item List pane will give you more information about it. The Edit Item box appears in QuickBooks when you double-click the item. In essence, the Edit item window shows every piece of information that is accessible for a certain object. This window allows you to modify certain item details.

Using inventory reports

Numerous insightful, practical inventory reports are available through QuickBooks. For instance, QuickBooks presents an inventory report submenu when you select the

- **Report > Inventory command**. Reports on inventory valuations, stock levels, and a worksheet for physically counting the inventory on store shelves or in the warehouse, if applicable, are all available from this submenu.

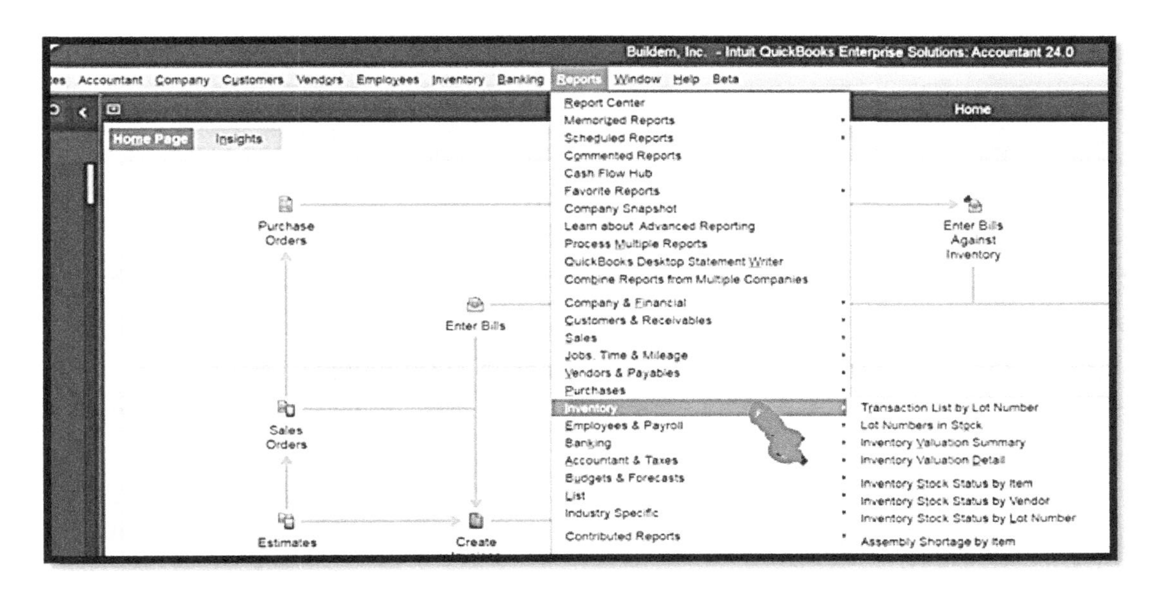

Adding Items to the Item List

A wide variety of items can be added to the item list. Recall that everything you include in an invoice or purchase order has its description stored in the Item list, as mentioned in the opening lines of this chapter. After giving this some thought, you see that you have many kinds of stuff. For example, if you're a retailer, an invoice can list the inventory you sell. If you provide different kinds of consumers different discounts, the discounts could show up as a line item on an invoice. In states where sales tax is imposed, the sales tax is shown as a line item on an invoice. You use several descriptions for different objects. There are differences between how you describe a sales tax that you have to charge and how you describe an inventory item that might show up on an invoice.

Item Types

Below is a list that can help you decide on the type of items that should be added to your list.

Service	This is any form of service provided to a customer. You can choose to create a service charged by either the job or by the hour.
Inventory Part	A thing you purchase to resell. If you haven't enabled the inventory items and inventory

	section in the preferences, you can't use this item.
Non-Inventory Part	This is simply a product you product you; purchase but do not sell, sell but do not purchase, purchase and sell but do not stock or get it tracked as an inventory.
Other Charge	This is used strictly for shipping charges, markups, or any other line items that come up on your invoices.
Subtotal	This is an item that gets the items added up before it in invoices and any other sales transactions. You can choose to subtotal Quantity, Price, Cost, and numeric custom columns.
Group	A group item can be used to combine several objects. You can make a group item with those two things, for instance, if you frequently have a shipping charge together with another charge.
Assembly	A product assembled from separate pieces that are recorded in inventory is called an assembly. There are assemblies only in the Premier and Enterprise editions.

Below are the item types that perform calculations

Discount	A discount is a percentage or flat rate applied to the price of a certain item or goods. For each discount you offer, you may have more than one discount item. For instance, a discount on volume purchases and another for wholesale clients.
Payment	You can include a deposit as a line item on an invoice with this item type if you receive payment in full or in part for it.
Sales Tax Items	For each sales tax you impose, if you charge sales tax, you can establish a sales tax item.

Sales Tax Group	This relates to various sales taxes combined into a single, bigger sales tax. For instance, you impose a sales tax equal to the sum of the sales taxes from the state, the county, and the city.

Follow the steps below to create an item

- Navigate to **Lists**, and then click on **Item List** for Windows and Items for Mac.
- Choose **Item** then click on New for Windows or Plus + for Mac and then choose **New Item.**
- Choose the type of item you would like to create.
- Complete the item fields.
- Make use of the custom fields to include your own customized fields.
- Choose **Save.**

The following are the most used fields for all item types;

Item Name/ Number	Insert your preferred name for the item. You can make use of about 31 characters.
Description	Make use of this field to include information about the item.
Sub-item of	Choose the checkbox if you would like the item to be a sub-item of an existing item.
Sales Price/ Rate/ Price/ Amount	**The field varies based on the type of item;** • Sales Price (Inventory): this is the amount charged for the product. It might be equal or much more than the cost. • Rate (Service): this is the rate you charge to your customers. You can choose to either make it a flat rate or an hourly rate. • Price (Non-Inventory part): this is the part of the price you charge to your customers. • Amount (Other charge): The charge's total amount. Both monetary amounts and

	percentages can be entered. Add a % indicator if the amount is expressed as a percentage.

Purchase Information and Sales Information

Purchase information and Sales information show during the creation of an Inventory Part or when you choose;

- The item is purchased for and sold to a certain customer: job on Non-inventory Parts.
- This service is performed by a subcontractor on various Service items.
- I purchased this assembly from a vendor on Inventory Assembly items.
- This is a reimbursable charge on Other Charge items.

Description of Purchase Transactions	This is the description that purchase orders and bills will use to describe the item.
Description of Sales Transactions	This is the description that will be printed on estimates, sales receipts, sales orders, and invoices.
Cost	Insert the cost of the item when you must have purchased it.
Expense Account	This is the account that will track the amount that is spent on buying the item.
COGS	The total amount spent on producing the items sold is known as the cost of goods sold. It is also the account that is used to monitor item payments.
Preferred Vendor	The name of the vendor where Inventory is often bought.
Sales price	This is the amount you get to charge for the item.

	It should be equal to or more than the cost.
Income Account	The account to track the amount you get from selling the item.
Tax Code (Windows) Sales Tax Code (Mac)	If the item is subject to sales tax, choose the **Sales Tax Code (Mac) or the Tax Code (Windows)**. QB will compute tax on the item when you make a taxable transaction.

Inventory Information

These fields are beneath Inventory Information and are displayed when you choose Inventory as the item type.

Asset Account	Generated by QuickBooks and instantly assigned. If you would not like to make use of the default account, below are the two types of assets; • **Current Assets:** these are often the assets that you are likely to change to cash within a year. • **Fixed Assets:** these are assets you are likely not expected to convert to cash during a year of normal operations. They are usually needed for the operation of your business.
Reorder Point	At this point, QuickBooks prompts you to place a new order for the item.
Quantity on Hand	The amount of inventory you currently possess. Note: Enter zero for items that have just been added to inventory. Enter the last count of the items you currently have in stock.
Total Value	The entire market value of the shares you now own. Note: Enter zero for items that have just been added to

	inventory. Enter the value of your most recent stock count for items that you currently have in stock.
As of	The date that your total value, amount on hand, and reorder point is applicable. **Note:** You need to enter a date that follows the item's previous transaction when converting non-inventory, service, or other charge items to inventory. For your inventory to be accurate, you must input all sales and purchases of the item up to the present date if you enter a date from the past.

Upon creating a Group Item, the subsequent fields become visible. All individual items need to be set up before you establish a group item.

Item List	A table that allows you to select the items and quantities to add to the group item
Print items in a group	If you want the individual items to appear when you utilize the group item on invoices and other transaction forms, select this option.

The following will be displayed when you design a Payment item.

Payment Method	Choose the payment method you would like to use when the payment item gets used in transactions.
Deposit option	Choose just how you would like your payment to be deposited. Group with other undeposited funds: this option includes the payment to the undeposited funds account. Deposit To: this option includes the payment to the account you must have chosen.

You don't need to exit the sales form or the invoice to create an item. To add a new item, simply type its name and hit the tab key. Next, choose Set Up (for Mac) or Yes (for Windows) when prompted to configure the item.

Create multiple items

Multiple inventory or service items can be created in two different methods.

Option 1: To open a new Item window, select **Next** as soon as you've created a new item. Once you have created all the objects you require, proceed by filling in the relevant fields and starting over.

Option 2: Bring the goods in.

- Navigate to File, choose **Import, and then choose Items.**
- Choose between the **Service, Non-Inventory, and Inventory item types.**
- Fill out all the necessary fields.
- Ensure that the items you wish to import have the **Import checkbox selected.**
- Choose **Import.**

Editing Items

Updating the information

Upon the creation of your preferred item, you can choose to modify the information you have earlier documented at any given time.

- Choose **Lists, and then choose Item Lists (for Windows) or Items (for Mac).**
- Click **twice** on the specific item you would like to alter.
- Get the info for the item chosen edited.
- Lastly, choose **OK.**

Change item type

- If an item is a charge item, non-inventory, or inventory (for Windows only), you can modify its category.
- Navigate to **Lists and choose Items (Mac) or Item List (Windows).**
- To modify an item, **double-click on it.**
- Choose the new item type after choosing the Type.
- Select **OK.**

The items you can modify the type on are limited. Not every time can the type be changed back. You can't alter an item's type, for instance, once you convert it to an inventory or service item.

Duplicate an item

You might have to make comparable products. An item can be copied or duplicated and saved under a different name. This can now be found in Mac QuickBooks 2023.

- Navigate **to Lists and choose Items (Mac) or Item List (Windows).**
- Choose **the Item you wish to duplicate.**
- Select **Duplicate Item using a right-click or, on a Mac, by selecting plus +.**
- Change the item's details and name. Recall that no two things may have the same name.
- Select **OK.**

A parent or sub-item that you duplicate will likewise become a parent or sub-item of the new item. Except for On Hand and Reorder Point, all item information is duplicated when you duplicate an inventory item. The values in these fields are 0.

Remove Items

Hide an item

In QuickBooks, an item that has ever been utilized in a transaction cannot be deleted. You can conceal it if you no longer need it. An item is deleted from the list but remains in your books when it is hidden.

To get an item hidden:

- Navigate to **Lists and choose Items (Mac) or Item List (Windows).**
- To hide an object, **double-click on it.**
- Choose the item that is either inactive (for Mac) or inactive (for Windows).
- Select **OK.**

Once an object is hidden, you may always unhide it by clearing the object's inactive checkbox. Examine whether the item is a sub-item of a concealed parent item if the checkbox isn't there and you can't unhide it. If so, either unhide the parent item or cut off the parent item's link to the sub-item. To display hidden items in your item list, check the Include inactive checkbox.

Delete an item

- Navigate to **Lists and choose Items (Mac) or Item List (Windows).**
- Choose **the item that you wish to remove.**
- Select **Delete Item under Edit.**

Multiple items cannot be deleted at once. If you accidentally remove something, you ought to pick Undo Remove from Edit right away. If you make any more changes in QuickBooks, the deletion cannot be undone.

Managing Inventory in a Manufacturing Firm

Manufacturing companies have different inventory tracking requirements than other business categories. When you strip things down to their most basic form, the issue is caused by two challenging accounting requirements:

- The manufacturer in manufacturing setting blends items made from raw resources into completed commodities. This implies that the manufacturing process lowers the inventory count and value for some items (raw materials or components) while simultaneously increasing the count and value of other finished goods items. This is the difficult aspect of the operation.
- Regulations in the manufacturing sector state that inventory values for finished goods should take into account more than only the item's value. You also add in the labor and manufacturing overhead costs incurred during the product's production.

The first manufacturing inventory problem is resolved by QuickBooks; however, the second problem is not resolved or addressed by the program. Fortunately, you generally don't have to worry too much about the second issue if you're a small company.

Taking care of manufactured inventory the easy way

You cannot account for the production of inventory in QuickBooks if you are using QuickBooks Pro or certain previous versions of QuickBooks Premier. The best you can do is arranging goods in an invoice for a customer so they can be combined into individual items. Although this strategy seems careless at first, it isn't as terrible as you might initially believe. In a customer invoice, you have the option to display just the group item. The "just use a group item" method has one drawback: it doesn't allow you to keep track of the inventory values of the final goods. You add inventory assembly items to the item list for the products you manufacture in QuickBooks Premier or QuickBooks Enterprise Solutions to account for the manufacturing of inventory. Additionally, you keep a record of the things you manufacture. Select the **Retail > Inventory Activities > Build Assemblies command** to begin building some assemblies. This opens the Build Assemblies window in QuickBooks. To construct anything, simply select the desired item from the Assembly Item drop-down menu and input the amount that you (or a foolish colleague) constructed in the Quantity to build box located at the lower-right corner. Next, you click the **Build & New or Build & Close button.** (Press the **Build & New button to record the assembly of additional parts**.)

Below are brief but useful observations about the Build Assemblies window and the Build Assemblies command;

- QuickBooks displays the number of clients that have placed orders as well as the amount of assembly you have on hand in the upper-right corner of the window. Recall that information is available as it is quite helpful.

- Within the Build Assemblies box, a table displays the components that make up your product. This table is a bill of materials, not that it matters.
- QuickBooks displays the maximum number of assemblies you can produce given your existing inventory holdings at the bottom of the bill of materials list.
- QuickBooks modifies inventory item counts when you build an item. For example, if you make boxed gift sets, each containing four red mugs, one box, and one wrapping tissue, QuickBooks will record building the assembly with higher item counts for the boxed gift sets and lower item counts for the boxes, wrapping tissues, and red mugs.

You can handle the record-keeping difficulty of having inventory spread across several sites with QuickBooks Enterprise Solutions.

- Select the **Edit > Preferences command, choose Items and Inventory, select the Company Preferences tab, and finally select the Advanced Inventory Settings button** to activate this feature, which is known as Advanced Inventory Tracking.

To track inventory items by site, the QuickBooks Enterprise Solutions edition shows dialog boxes that let you create a list of inventory sites and add fields to relevant windows and dialog boxes. QuickBooks provides instructions on how to upgrade to Enterprise Solutions if you're not currently using the Enterprise Solutions edition.

Activity

1. Add and edit items in your items list.
2. How can inventory be managed in a manufacturing firm?

CHAPTER 4

MANAGING CASH AND BANK ACCOUNTS

One of the many features that QuickBooks offers to simplify your work with bank accounts is a dedicated window for logging the checks you've written. You can also just record deposits into accounts with QuickBooks. Furthermore, QuickBooks comes with capabilities that make it simple to record transfers between accounts, reconcile bank accounts, and conduct online banking activities. A large portion of the content on this page will be recognizable to users of Quicken, QuickBooks's little brother program. For the approximately 10 million Quicken users, this is good news because the QuickBooks banking capabilities resemble the well-known Quicken checkbook program.

Writing Checks

Regular checks are used in QuickBooks Desktop to cover fixed assets, inventory and non-inventory part costs, servicing, additional fees, and any other tracked expenses. Moreover, you can pay credit card debt or deposit funds into a petty cash account using this form.

- Select **Write Checks from the Banking menu to begin writing checks.**

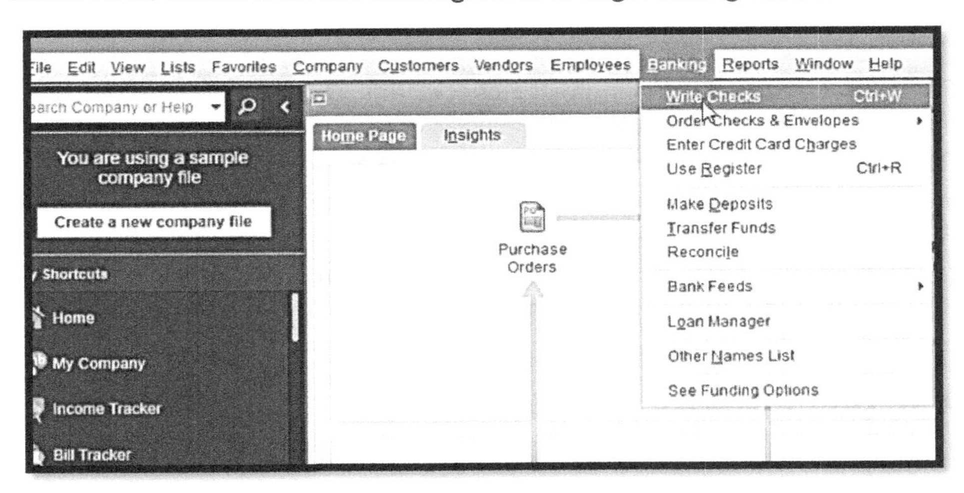

Follow the steps below to write checks accurately in QuickBooks Desktop;

- **Bank Account**: this is the account where the money written on the check will be taken from.
- **Ending Balance**: this is the balance of the amount of money in the bank account as of the day that the check is being written.
- **Pay to the Order of**: this ought to be the name of the payee or just whoever the check is issued for.

- **No:** in QuickBooks, the number is assigned depending on the check preference you configure.
- **Date**: ensure you make use of the date when you issue the check.
- **Amount:** Verify the amount in digits. The dollar amount in words will immediately appear beneath the Pay to the Order area.
- **Address**: this is the address of the payee which is instantly populated from the name setup of the payee.
- **Memo:** Although this option can be left empty, it is typically used as an informal remark for further information such as account details, payment purpose, and period.
- Print Later or Pay Online: If you require printing the check later, click the **Print Later checkbox**; if you plan to make the payment online, check the Pay Online checkbox.
- **Expense or Items tab**
    - To record shipping costs, liabilities (for payments towards loans or liabilities), and other expenses that aren't related to any item in QuickBooks, use the Expense tab.
    - To select the relevant item from the drop-down list, use **the Item tab.**
- Choose **Save & Close.**

Below are other forms of check;

- **Bill Payment Check**: this is usually generated when you choose the Pay Bills choice in QuickBooks Desktop.
- **Sales Tax Checks**: these simply are checks that are designed to get your sales tax liabilities paid with ease.
- **Paychecks**: these are checks that are given to an employee in payment of salary or wages.
- **Payroll Liability Checks:** checks made out to cover whatever your business owes as a result of your payroll, or to pay payroll taxes you withheld from employees. They include union dues, health insurance premiums, 401(k) payments, and garnishments for unpaid child support.

Delete or void a check

Make sure you know the difference between voiding and deleting a check before you begin. When a check is voided, its value is reduced to $0. The Memo field now has VOID added. A voided check is always re-enterable. If you wish to maintain a record of the check-in QuickBooks, do this. When a check is deleted, QuickBooks loses the transaction record. It will appear to have never occurred. You can re-enter a deleted check, but you cannot reverse this.

Void a written check

- Navigate to the **Banking menu and choose Use Register.**
- Select the **account that you used to write the check from the drop-down menu.**

- Pick the **check in the Bank Register.**
- To initiate a Void check; firs**t, pick the QuickBooks Edit menu.**
- Choose **Record.**

Void a blank check

- Make **a $0.00 check out to yourself.**
- In the Expenses section, **designate an account and enter the name of the payee.**
- Choose **Void Check from the Edit menu.**

Delete a check

- Navigate to the **Banking menu and choose Use Register.**
- Select **the account that you used to write the check from the drop-down menu.**
- Pick the **check in the Bank Register.**
- Choose the Edit option in QuickBooks, and then choose **Delete Check.**
- Choose **Record.**

Print checks

- **Choose the Print icon from the Write Checks window, then choose:**
    - **Check**: to produce a solitary check. Selecting this option will require you to provide a printed check number.
    - **Batch**: Print several checks that you have marked for later printing in a batch. You will be taken to the **Select Checks to print window** after selecting this option. Mark the check or checks that you wish to print, then click **OK.**
- **Do the following in the Print Checks window;**
- Choose the printer type and name in the Print Checks window.
- Select the **check type you want to print—Wallet, Standard, or Voucher—in the Check Style section.**
- Uncheck the option to **Print company name and address** if your company name and address are already printed on your pre-printed checks.
- Verify that all other settings are in order.
- When the above settings have been properly done and completed, choose **Print** to have the check printed,

Print the check register

- Choose **Use Register from the Edit menu.**
- Select the account from the drop-down menu, and then click **OK.**
- On the registration, click the **Print icon at the top.**
- Input the desired date range for printing. Note: Mark the box labeled "Print splits detail" if you wish to print the split detail.
- Click **OK,** and then click **Print.**

However, take note that QuickBooks requires users to have access to a bank account to put them in a role where they can write checks. Make a bank sub-account if you are making use of QuickBooks Desktop Enterprise and you do not want a user to view private or sensitive transactions, such as payroll, in the bank register. This allows you to restrict which of your bank accounts a specific user can access or issue checks from.

Create a sub-account of the main checking account

- Choose **Charts of Accounts** from the Lists menu.
- Right-click just anywhere and choose **New once you are in the Charts of Accounts.**
- Choose a **Bank,** and then continue to choose the **Account type.**
- In the field of Account name, insert A/P Check Register, or just about anything that separates it from other bank accounts.
- Choose the account where money will be drawn in transactions after you have put a checkmark in the Subaccount box.
- Choose **Save & Close.**

Create a user role

- As the QuickBooks Admin, log in. (ensure you log in as the Admin; this is very important)
- Choose **Users from the Company menu, and then click Set up Users and Roles.**
- Pick the **tab for the role list.**
- Make a new role or copy an existing one that has the access the user needs.
- Make alterations to the role:
    - In the front of Banking, choose **the + sign.**
    - Enable Full access to Create Checks.
- Choose the plus sign in front of the bank registers while you're still in the banking area.
- Next to the primary checking account, **select +.**
- After creating a sub-account, highlight it and provide permission to **View and Print.**
- As needed, keep changing the role to allow access to additional responsibilities.

Go to the Company menu, choose Set Up Passwords and Users, and finally choose Set Up Users. You can change an existing user's access or add a new user and provide them the necessary access in the User List box.

To grant a new user access to write checks:

- Click **Add User in the User List window.**
- Enter the new user's login credentials in the Set up user password and access window, then click **Next to go to the Banking and Credit Cards page.**
- After choosing **Full Access, choose Finish.**

To edit an existing user to have access to write checks:

- Choose **the user you wish to edit from the User List window.**
- Until you get to the Banking and Credit Cards page, keep selecting **Next.**
- After choosing **Full Access, choose Finish.**

This technique might be used in reverse to limit access to payroll or other private transactions in a sub-account to those who truly require it. For a variety of register operations, specific people may be granted access to the main account; but, they will not be able to view the private transactions from the sub-account. There is no option to include class information when you open the Write Checks window or check register. There are no source classes for checks or deposits. The Splits button located at the bottom-left of the check register window can be used to add target classes. Close the window and reopen it while holding down the Shift key if the Class field, Restore, or Record buttons are absent when you open the register. If none of these work to fix the problem, make sure your screen resolution and font DPI are set to show QuickBooks correctly.

Making Bank Deposits

You frequently deposit money from several sources at once when you deposit at the bank. Typically, the bank keeps track of everything as a single record with a single total. The way your bank records the deposit may differ from what you put in QuickBooks if you enter the same payments as separate entries. QuickBooks offers a unique method for you to merge all of these details so that your records correspond to your actual bank deposits in these situations. Transfer transactions to your Undeposited Funds account that you wish to combine. After that, register a bank deposit to merge them. This is the process for entering bank deposits into QuickBooks Desktop.

Putting payments into the Undeposited Funds account

Customer payments are stored in QuickBooks in the Undeposited Funds account until you deposit them at a physical bank. To ensure that QuickBooks matches your bank records, you can merge these payments into a single record after you obtain your deposit slip. Before combining them, follow these steps to deposit payments into your Undeposited Funds account.

Step 1: Put payments into the Undeposited Funds account

- **Payments that are being processed with QuickBooks Payments;**

QuickBooks handles all of the processing of invoice payments if you use QuickBooks Payments for Desktop. It is not necessary to transfer money to an account or combine them.

- **Invoice payments you process outside of QuickBooks;**

QuickBooks automatically transfers payments made by the workflow to the Undeposited Funds account. Proceed to **Step 2 and make the payment deposit.**

- **Sales receipts for payments you process outside of QuickBooks;**

Payments for sales receipts are automatically deposited by QuickBooks into the Undeposited Funds account. QuickBooks takes care of the rest; all you need to do is create a sales receipt.

If you would prefer to choose the specific account you would like to put payments into, follow the steps below;

- Click on the **Edit menu, and then choose Preferences.**
- Payments can be chosen from the list. Next, select **the tab for Company Preferences.**
- The **Use Undeposited Funds as a Default Deposit to Account checkbox** should be selected and unchecked.
- Click **OK.**

Every time you create a sales receipt, you may now choose to use an Undeposited Funds account or a different account.

- Choose **Create Sales Receipt from the Homepage.**
- From the **Customer drop-down menu, choose the customer.**
- Choos**e Undeposited Funds from the Deposit to drop-down menu.**
- Completion of the form is required.
- Either chooses **Save & New or Save & Close.**

To ensure you are aware of where your money is going, always check the "Deposit to" option. You don't need to combine payments with others in QuickBooks if your bank records it as a separate deposit. Alternatively, you can exclude Undeposited Funds and deposit the money straight into an account.

Step 2: Make a bank deposit

You can make a bank deposit and aggregate the payments in QuickBooks with your deposit slip in hand. The Bank Deposit pane immediately displays all payments made to the Undeposited Funds account.

- Choose **Record Deposits / Make Deposits from the Homepage.**

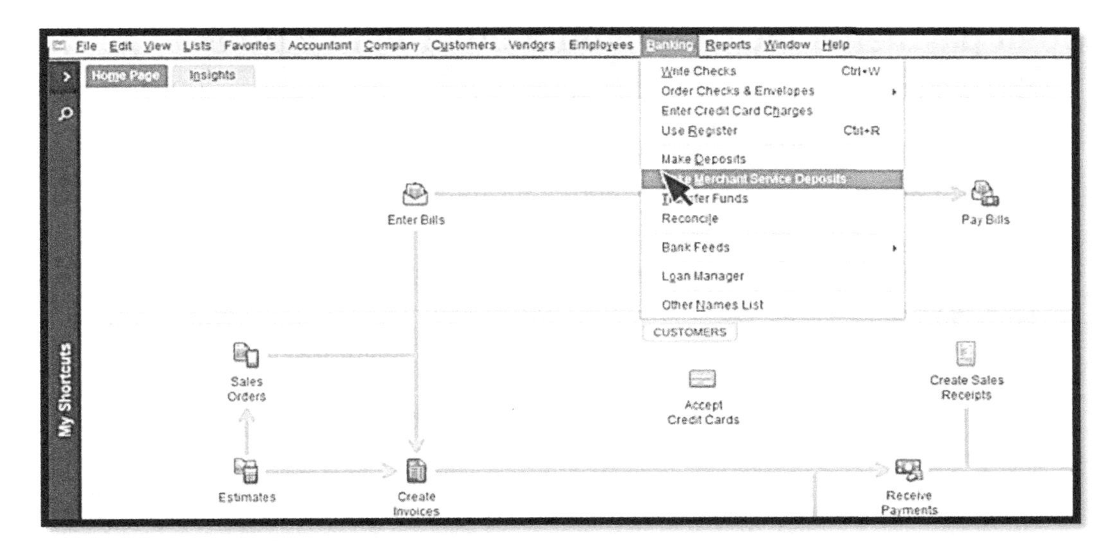

- Choose **the payments you wish to combine in the Payments to Deposit window. Next, choose OK.**
- Choose the account you wish to deposit money into from the Deposit to option in the **Make Deposits window.**
- Verify the amount of the deposit. Verify that the account and the chosen payments correspond to the bank's deposit slip. Refer to your deposit slip for guidance.
- Input the day you visited your bank to make the deposit.
- As needed, add a memo.
- Once finished, choose **Save & Close.**

Every bank deposit has its record. Put money on each of your deposit slips one at a time. The Bank Deposit pane displays only the transactions that are currently in your Undeposited Funds account. Place it in the Undeposited Funds account if you don't see one that has to be added.

Deposit payments into separate bank accounts

If you need to put money into different bank accounts, follow the steps below;

- Choose **Record Deposits / Make Deposits from the Homepage.**
- Choose t**he payments you wish to combine in the Payments to Deposit window. Next, choose OK.**
- Choose the account you wish to deposit money into from the Deposit to option in the **Make Deposits window.**
- Under the payment you wish to transfer to a different account, add a new line.
- Choose **the second account in the from account dropdown menu on the second line. Next, enter the desired amount as a negative value in the second account.** You can enter all or a portion of the amount.
- Choose **Save & Close** when you are through.

Deposit payments into an account other than a Bank Account

You often record deposits in QuickBooks for a bank or other current asset accounts, since you're simulating a real-life bank deposit.

Should you wish to transfer a deposit to a different kind of account?

- Choose **Record Deposits / Make Deposits from the Homepage.**
- Choose **the payments you wish to combine in the Payments to Deposit window. Next, choose OK.**
- Choose **the desired account to receive the deposit from the Cash Back and go to the dropdown in the Make Deposits window.**
- Enter the desired amount to be deposited into the account. To move everything at once, enter the whole amount of the deposit. The account you choose from the Deposit to section will get the remaining amount if you don't deposit the entire amount.
- Once finished, choose **Save & Close.**

Recording recurring deposits

You can set up a recurring transaction for an existing deposit if you record the same deposits regularly:

- After choosing the **Banking option, select Use Register.**
- Look for an existing deposit and open it.
- Select **Memorize Deposit with a right-click on the deposit.**
- If you would want QuickBooks to automatically record the deposit, select Automate Transaction Entry. If not, choose **Add to my Reminders List to receive a prompt to initiate the deposit.**
- Choose **how often (monthly, weekly, daily, etc.) from the How Often dropdown menu.**
- Enter the start date of the recurring deposits in the **Next Date section.** On the first day, the first recurring deposit will begin.
- Enter the number of deposits you would like QuickBooks to create in the **Number Remaining field.**
- You can specify how many days in advance QuickBooks will record the deposit in the **Days In Advance to Enter area**. If you would want to record the deposit on the day you have chosen, enter 0.
- Click **OK when you're finished.**

Once the above has been completed, QuickBooks will instantly record the deposit on the date and frequency you choose.

Delete a bank deposit

You have the option to erase a bank deposit if you ever need to start over:

- Click on the **Reports menu. Next, choose Report Center.**
- Click on the **Banking option.**
- Locate the report on **Deposit Details. Next, click the Run icon.**
- Locate and access the deposit that you wish to remove.
- All of the payments that are included in the deposit are visible in the Make Deposits window. Examine them to determine if you need to start anew.
- In the window, right-click and choose **"Delete deposit." To confirm, click OK.**

All deposit payments are returned to your Undeposited Funds account. You can make a fresh deposit and start again.

Transferring Money between Bank Accounts

To transfer money between bank accounts, use the Banking menu's helpful command. **Banking > Transfer Funds** is the option to move money across accounts. The Transfer Funds between Accounts window appears in QuickBooks when you do this.

Follow the steps below to make use of this window;

- Make use of the **Date field for the identification of the transfer date**. The date can be entered using the format mm/dd/yyyy, or it can be clicked using the little calendar button that shows up to the right of the Date field. Click the day that matches the date you wish to put in the Date field when QuickBooks shows the calendar.
- Employ the **Transfer Funds drop-down** list to choose the bank account from which you will be moving funds. The bank account name can be entered into the box, or you can select a bank account from QuickBooks' list by clicking the arrow located at the right end of the box.
- Make use of the Transfer Funds To drop-down list for the identification of the bank account that gets the funds that were transferred.
- Employ the Transfer Amount box for the identification of the amount of the transfer. The transfer amount is $10,000, for instance, if you move $10,000 from one bank account to another.
- Provide a memo description for the transfer transaction. Note that this is optional. You can enter a brief memo describing the funds transfer in the Memo box if you'd like (it's not a big deal).
- Get the transfer transaction saved. Click the **Save & Close or Save & New button to save your transfer transaction.** Alternatively, you can click the **Clear button to remove the transfer transaction from saving.**

Working with the Register

The instructions outlined in this chapter's previous paragraphs can be used to record checks, deposits, and account transfers; however, an alternative approach is also available: Using the Register window is possible. The Register window bears resemblance to the standard paper register used for recording transactions related to a bank account. You can easily enter transactions into an account register with QuickBooks.

Follow the steps below to input bank account transactions directly into an account register;

- To show an account register, click on **Banking > Use Register command.** You can also choose to click on **Banking > Use Register.** QuickBooks will then display the Use Register dialog box.
- Make use of the **Date column** of the register to record the date of the deposit, payment, or transfer. The format for entering a date is mm/dd/yyyy. Alternatively, you can select the month in which the date is shown by clicking the tiny calendar button to the right of the Date box, and then select the day button that matches the date you wish to enter.
- Assign a transaction number; although this is optional. To distinguish the transaction individually, use the **Number column**. For instance, enter the check number in the Number field when recording a check transaction. It might not be necessary to register a number for deposits and transfers.
- Make use of the **Payee field** for recording the payee for a check, the customer paying a deposit, or some other sort of information in the case of a transfer transaction. Note that by using the down-arrow button located at the right end of the Payee box, you can select an existing customer, vendor, or name from one of the QuickBooks lists. QuickBooks provides a list of names when you do this. To select one, click on it.
- Give the transaction amount. If you are reporting a check transaction or a transfer of funds out of the account, use the Payment field. If you are describing a transfer or deposit into the account, use the Deposit field. Use dollars and cents to enter the transaction amount in the relevant field (Payment or Deposit). When a transaction has been balanced in the bank reconciliation, a check mark will show up between the payment and deposit columns.
- Note the account. When a check is used to purchase an asset or pay for an expense, the Account field is used to indicate this. To determine which sales revenue account a deposit represents for a deposit transaction, use the Account field. To determine which other bank account is involved in a transfer transaction, use the Account field. You have two options: either open the Account drop-down list and choose the desired account, or type the account name into the Account box.
- You can choose to provide a memo description or split the transaction if need be. By selecting the Clear option, you can remove the Splits detail. By selecting the Recalc button, you can also instruct QuickBooks to use the split transaction data to recalculate the payment or deposit amount.
- Choose the **Record button** to have a transaction recorded in the register.

The Register window commands and buttons

The Register window has several boxes and buttons that let you customize its appearance and operate it more simply.

The Go-To button

The Go-To box appears when you click the **Go-To button**. With the help of this dialog box, you may look up a transaction in the Register window, for example, one where the Payee/Name uses a certain name. To go to the prior or subsequent transactions that also fit the search parameters, select the Back and Next buttons. Naturally, click **Cancel** to exit the QuickBooks program window and delete the Go to dialog box.

The Print button

The Print Register dialog box appears when you click the Print button. You can print a copy of the account register using this dialog box. You can choose the range of dates you'd like on the printed register by using the Date Range From and Date Range Through boxes in the Print Register dialog box. You may also choose the Print Splits Detail check box in the Print Register dialog box to instruct QuickBooks to display the split transaction detail.

The Edit Transaction button

When you click the Edit Transaction button, QuickBooks opens the window that you used to record the selected transaction in the first place. Recall that all of the bank account's transactions are displayed in the Register pane. Checking account transactions that you recorded using the Write Checks window is one example of these transactions. QuickBooks displays the transaction again in the Write Checks window if you click the **Edit Transaction button** after you have already recorded it in the Write Checks window. To preserve your changes, edit the transaction in the Write Checks window and select **Save & Close or Save & New.**

The Quick Report button

A report with a summary of the registered data for the payee or name in the chosen transaction will appear when you click the QuickReport button. By selecting QuickReport, you can quickly and easily create a report that lists all of the transactions you have made to Sagesse Energy, provided that the chosen transaction is a check issued to the company.

The Sort By list

You can select how QuickBooks arranges register information using the Sort By drop-down list. QuickBooks allows you to sort register data in several different ways, including by date, amount, order entry date, and more. Open the Sort By drop-down list and select the desired ordering sequence to modify the way QuickBooks arranges or orders the data in the register.

Using the Edit Menu Commands

You have learned how to utilize the register and record check and deposit transactions, as well as account transfers, in the paragraphs that came before this chapter. Often, all you need to know to use the windows covered and record the transactions outlined is what you already know.

However, be aware that the Edit menu offers additional helpful commands for adding new transactions, changing current transactions, and reusing transaction data while you're working with a register:

- **Edit Check/Deposit:** The Edit Transaction button (which shows up in the Register window) is the same as this command. QuickBooks opens the Write Checks window so you can use that tool to edit the transaction when you select the Edit Check/Deposit option. Depending on the transaction that is selected, the command name varies. If the transaction you have selected is a check, you get the Edit Check instruction. If the selected transaction is a deposit, you see the Edit Deposit command.
- **New Check:** To enter a new check transaction and enter it into the register, this command opens the Write Checks window.
- **Delete Check:** The selected transaction is removed from the register by using the Delete Check command. (This command's name varies based on the transaction you select in the register.)
- **Memorize Check:** This command, which shows up when it's appropriate, allows you to save the check information for later use by memorizing the selected transaction and adding it to the list of transactions you've learned. (Memorizing a transaction and then reusing it repeatedly saves you data entry time if you have a transaction that you record often, like once a month.)
- **Void Check:** You can cancel the chosen check transaction with this command, which also shows up when it's suitable.
- **Copy/Paste:** The selected check is copied by the Copy command. QuickBooks pastes the just copied check into the following blank row of the register if you select the Paste command.
- **Go To Transfer:** The other side of a transfer transaction is reached by this instruction. Naturally, the Go to Transfer command makes sense and is only functional if the specified transaction is a transfer.
- **Transaction History:** A window listing every transaction connected to the currently chosen transaction is displayed by this command. This command is usually used when the chosen transaction is a payment made by a customer. In this instance, every transaction associated with the customer payment transaction is included in the Transaction History window. To access a linked transaction fast, use the Transaction History window. Just click on the listed transaction. By selecting the transaction and

then selecting the amend Payment button, you can also amend transactions that are displayed in the Transaction History box.

- **Use Register**: The Use Register dialog box appears when you run this command, allowing you to choose which account to show in a register.
- **Use Calculator**: this command as can be predicted shows the Windows calculator.
- **Find**: Either the Simple tab or the Advanced tab of the Find window is displayed by the Find command. You may look up transactions and search your register using both tabs.

A report of every transaction the Find command has located is generated by the Report button, which may be found on both the Simple and Advanced tabs. This report can be printed using the **File > Print Report command** or by clicking the **Print button** at the top of the Report window in QuickBooks. The report is displayed in a standard report window. There is a **Reset button** on the **Find window's Simple and Advanced tabs** as well. It is important to note that you can reset your search by clicking the **Reset option and applying a different set of search or filtering parameters.**

- **Search:** You can utilize the search window that is opened by this command to look for specific information in your company file.
- **Preferences:** With this command, you can modify QuickBooks's operation to better suit the accounting needs of your company.

Reconciling the Bank Account

You should examine your accounts in QuickBooks to make sure they match your actual bank and credit card bills, just like you would with a balanced checkbook. We refer to this procedure as reconciling. Reconciling your credit card, savings, and checking accounts should be done each month. Compare the list of transactions you entered into QuickBooks with your bank statements whenever you receive them. You can be sure your accounts are accurate and balanced if everything matches.

Step 1: Reviewing your opening balance

Before the commencement of your reconciliation, ensure that you back up your company file. If this is your first time having to reconcile an account, review the opening balances. You select the day on which to begin recording transactions when you create a new account in QuickBooks. You enter the amount that is in your actual bank account on any given day. The initial balance is where it all begins. At the outset of a bank statement, this setting is advised. Your initial reconciliation will be substantially simpler as a result.

Step 2: Prepare for the reconciliation

Make sure to include every transaction for the time of the bank statement that you want to reconcile. Wait to enter any transactions that aren't on your statement or haven't cleared your bank yet.

Step 3: Start your reconciliation

Reconciling can begin as soon as you receive your bank statement. Choose your earliest bank statement to begin with if you're reconciling over several months. Take one statement at a time and reconcile each month independently. Important: QuickBooks Desktop will display a sign-in box if it detects that you are not logged in while you are reconciling a Merchant or Payments account. This guarantees that a legitimate company ID is successfully linked to your account.

- Navigate to the **Banking menu and choose Reconcile.**
- Choose **the bank or credit card account that has to be reconciled from the list in the Account box.**

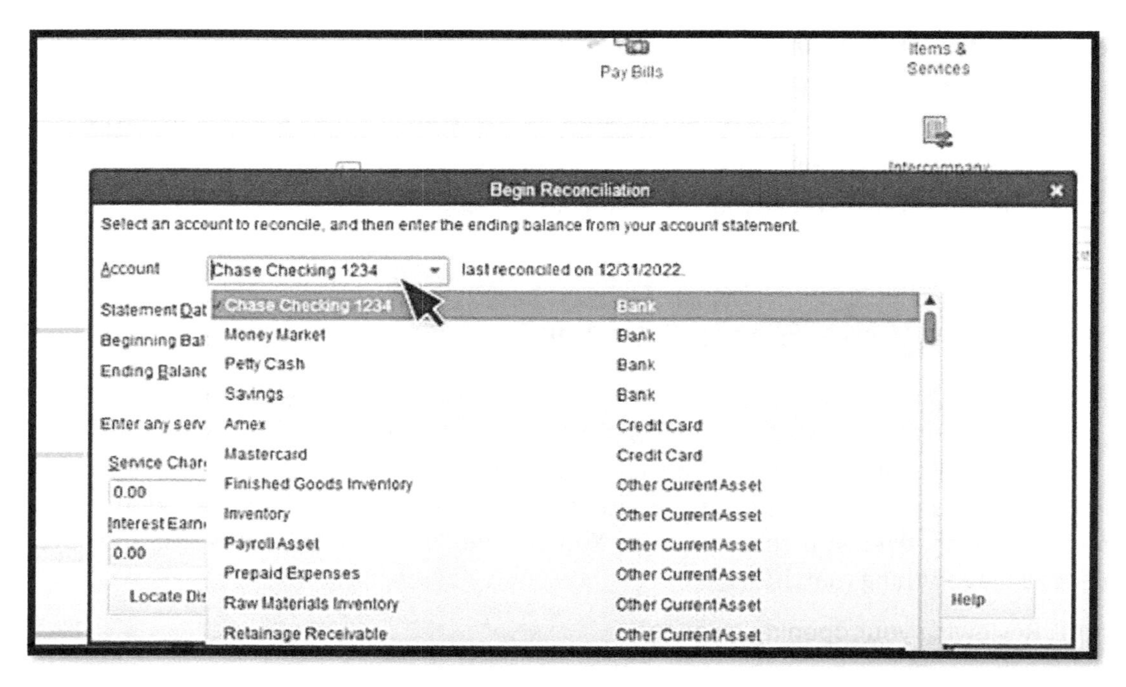

- The Statement Date is entered automatically. It usually occurs 30 or 31 days following the prior reconciliation's statement date. Adjust it to reflect your bank statement as necessary.
- Additionally, QuickBooks inputs the **Beginning Balance automatically**. This figure is obtained by using the ending balance from your most recent reconciliation.
- Using your bank statement as a guide, enter your ending balance.
- Based on your bank statement, enter the **Service Charge and Interest Earned.** Don't add charges to QuickBooks that you have previously recorded.

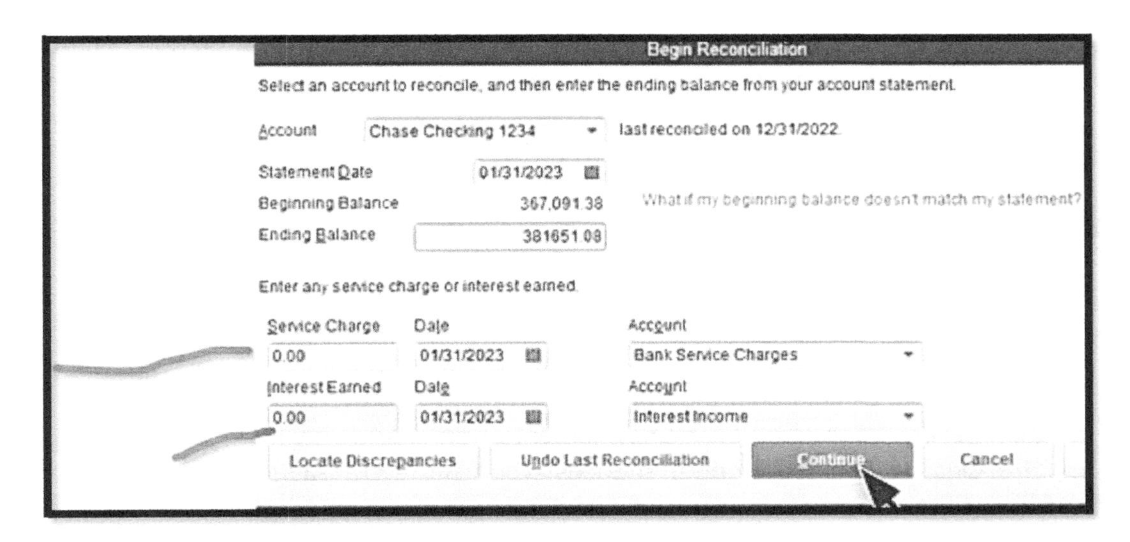

- Examine the fields. If the information is accurate, click **Continue or OK.**

Don't panic if your starting balance differs from your statement. A few tools are available to assist you.

- If the numbers don't add up, choose **Find Discrepancies**. You can utilize these reports to identify disparities and other reconciliation-related problems.
- Here's how to adjust your opening balance and beginning balance if you're still having problems.
- You can choose **Undo Last Reconciliation** if you need to restart from scratch.

Recall that your starting balance goes back to the starting balance of the prior reconciliation when you undo one. On the reconciliation, every cleared transaction becomes uncleared.

Step 4: Compare our bank statement and QuickBooks

Just compare the transactions listed on your bank statement and QuickBooks to perform reconciliation. Verify that the dates and transactions are correct. After you've finished going over your statement, you'll be aware that everything was entered into QuickBooks.

Here are a few things you may do to help your reconciliation before you commence;

- Choose **Hide transactions** after the statement's end date if you only want to see transactions for the statement period you're working on.
- Charges and Cash Advances (purchases) and Payments and Credits (payments to the credit card company) are the parts to look at while you're reconciling a credit card account. Concentrate on one area at a time.
- Choose **Matched** if you're reconciling an account for online banking. Next, input the bank statement's Statement Ending Date. Transactions that QuickBooks downloaded and matched are automatically chosen.

Note: In the register, a lightning bolt appears next to a matched transaction. When you reconcile it, the lightning bolt is replaced with a check mark.

- You can choose a column's header or title to sort the list.
- Refer to the list if QuickBooks shows more transactions than your bank statement does.

Match your transactions

- Proceed with the first transaction on your bank statement when you're ready.
- Look for the same one in QuickBooks' **Reconciliation window.**
- Examine the differences between the two transactions. Choose and place a checkmark in the checkbox column if the transactions match. The transaction is now reconciled.
- Verify every transaction on your statement by comparing it with QuickBooks' records. The Cleared Balance amount reduces when more transactions are added to the reconciliation or cleared. If you add or clear deposits or other credit amounts, the sum goes up. Don't mark a transaction as reconciled if it doesn't show up on your statement.

  Here are a few short methods to see if everything matches:
  - Look for the Items you've marked cleared section to view the total number and amount of transactions you've included in the reconciliation. The transaction summary that appears on bank statements is the same for many banks. To check whether any transactions are missing, compare the total number of transactions.
  - To modify or obtain additional details regarding a particular transaction, choose it, then **double-click or Go To it.**
  - Choose **Modify** if you need to go back and edit the data you entered when you first started your reconciliation. The portion next to it displays information about the ending balance, interest, and service costs.
- The expected difference between your bank statement and QuickBooks should be $0.00 when you get to the end. If this is what you get, choose **Reconcile now**.

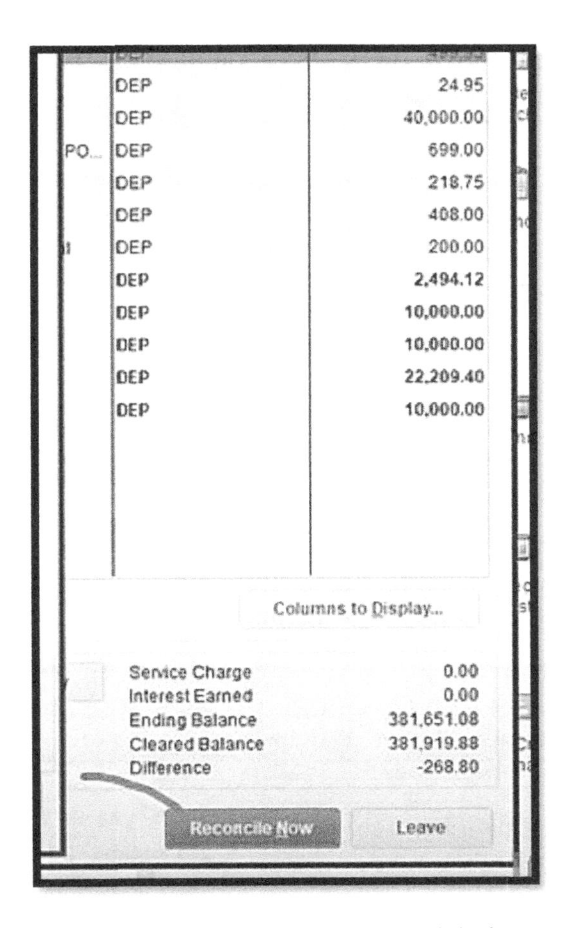

If on the other hand, the balance does not match at the end, below are the options you have;

- **Return to Reconcile**: navigate your way back to the reconciliation so you will be able to get all reviewed once more.
- **Leave Reconcile:** get the reconciliation saved so you will be able to modify or review any transaction that is giving rise to this issue. You can then return to complete the reconciliation much later.
- **Enter Adjustment**: To finish the reconciliation, you can make QuickBooks adjust to bring everything into balance. Only proceed if you are certain that all of the right transactions are in QuickBooks and that the data you entered is correct. The adjustment is automatically entered as a journal entry by QuickBooks.

You can see a Previous Reconciliation report for the reconciliation you adjusted to see all of your modifications on the list. This will display cleared transactions as well as any post-transaction modifications that might not be visible in your discrepancy.

- Select **Find from the Edit menu**.
- Choose **Memo** from the **Advanced tab in the Find window.**

- Type **Balance Adjustment** in the Memo area, then click **Find.**

Reviewing the Other Banking Commands

You have already studied the most popular and practical banking commands earlier in this chapter. Using the other commands available on the Banking menu might not be necessary. However, in case you feel that you may need to utilize them, here are a few more commands.

Order Checks & Envelopes command

You can order QuickBooks checks and envelopes or obtain information on ordering QuickBooks checks and envelopes by using the Order Checks & Envelopes command, which presents a submenu of commands.

Enter the Credit Card Charges command

You can use the **Banking > Enter Credit Card Charges command** to open an entry window for credit card charges if you set up a credit card account. This is the credit card account that you or your business will utilize to charge transactions.

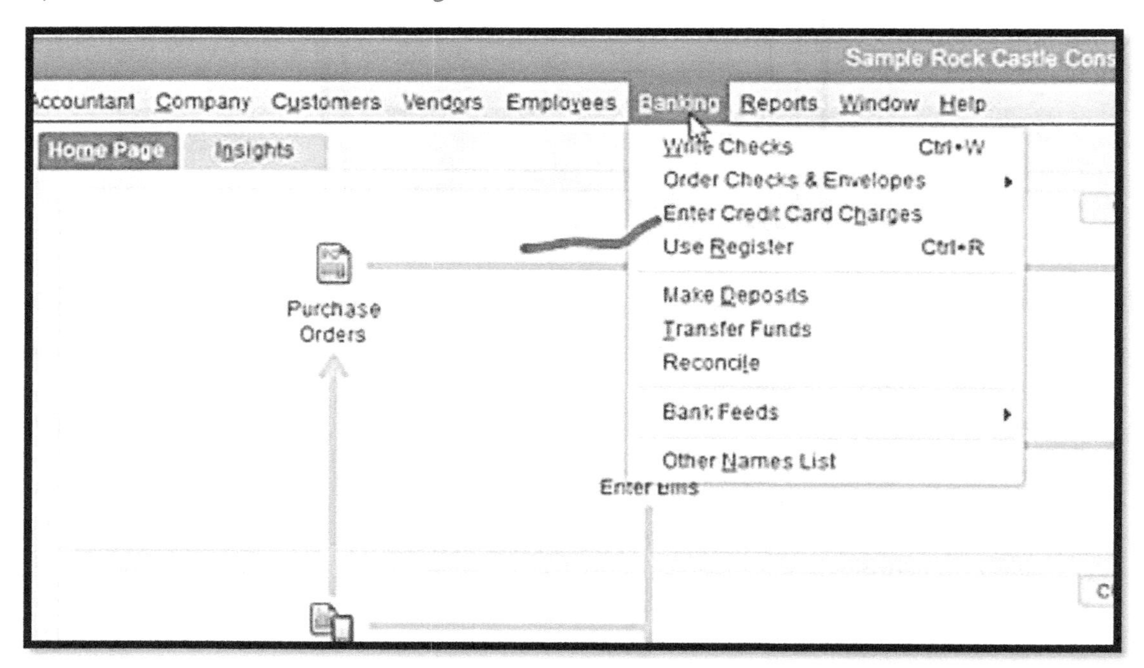

The Enter Credit Card Charges window opens when you select the Enter Credit Card Charges command. Using the area at the top of the screen, you describe the credit card purchase and select **the credit card account** for which you wish to keep track of transactions.

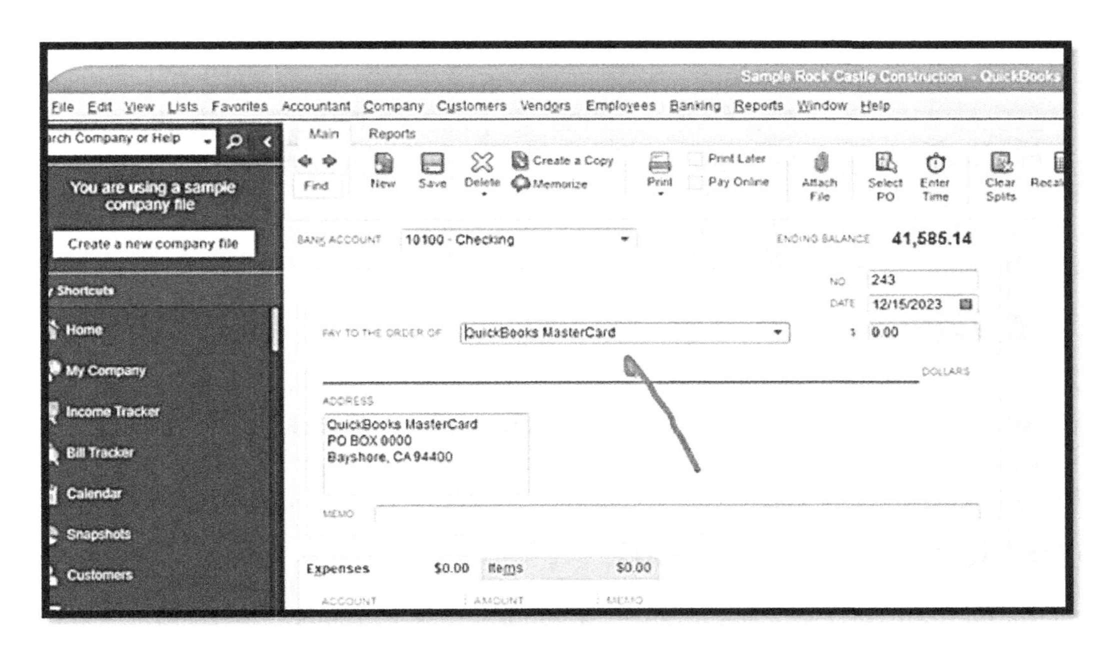

Next, you utilize the Expenses and Items tabs to describe the charges and the accounts they affect. These tabs function similarly to the tabs in the Write Checks box. Assuming you've configured credit card accounts that permit online services, clicking the **Download Card Charges button at the top of the Enter Credit Card Charges window** causes QuickBooks to download recent credit card transactions straight into the credit card register.

Quite plainly, a few requirements need to be fulfilled for this command to function:

- You need a credit card account set up.
- You need to set up a credit card account for online services.
- You need an Internet connection so that QuickBooks can grab credit card transactions from the credit card company.

Bank Feeds command

You may see which financial organizations (banks, savings and loans, and credit unions) allow you to do online banking and perform online banking by using the Bank Feeds command, which presents a submenu of commands. To take advantage of the time-saving benefits that online banking offers businesses, make sure your current bank offers online banking by giving them a call. If it does, request a sign-up package and detailed instructions on how to begin using internet banking. From the Bank Feeds submenu, select the **Set Up Bank Feed for Account command** if you would like not to call your bank directly. Using this command will take you step-by-step through the online financial services application and setup process.

Select the **Participating Financial Institutions** option to find out which banks work well with QuickBooks if you'd like to learn more about online banking. If you wish to pay your bills online but your bank doesn't work well with QuickBooks, you can select the Learn about Online Bill Payment command. You may also open a transaction file from your bank (if that's how your bank offers online banking) and modify the appearance of the online banking window using the Import Web Connect File and Change Bank Feeds Mode commands found in the Bank Feeds submenu.

Other Names list

A window listing all the other names you've used to record transactions is displayed by selecting the Other Names list. The individuals and companies included in your list of other names are not your clients, suppliers, or staff. Put differently, names that don't cleanly fall into one of the established categories are included in the Other Names list.

Load Manager Command

Your created loan accounts are listed in a window that appears when you run the Loan Manager command. While the Loan Manager window does more than just list loan accounts, it is noteworthy for the following reasons: QuickBooks gathers loan data from you when you click the **Add a Loan button** so that it can separate loan payments into principal and interest.

Activity

1. Make bank deposits.
2. Reconcile the bank account.
3. Transfer money between different bank accounts.

CHAPTER 5

PAYING EMPLOYEES

QuickBooks offers an alternative for self-paying employees called Enhanced Payroll, which entails QuickBooks assisting you with payroll tax forms. QuickBooks Assisted Payroll would be an additional payroll choice. Using this service, you pay your employees using QuickBooks, and Intuit takes care of submitting the required payroll tax forms and paying the taxes. Another choice to think about if you require payroll but are not an accountant is: Think about taking a small risk and choosing one of the full-service payroll companies, like Gusto, Paychex, or ADP. Payroll processing by one of them makes accounting much easier and, in my experience, ends up saving you money in the long run.

Create and run your Payroll

Step 1: Assign a pay schedule to your employees

Pay schedules are a useful tool to help you conduct your regular payroll more smoothly. Create and update a payroll schedule for your staff if you haven't done so already.

Creating a payroll schedule

- Navigate to **Employees and choose Payroll Center.**

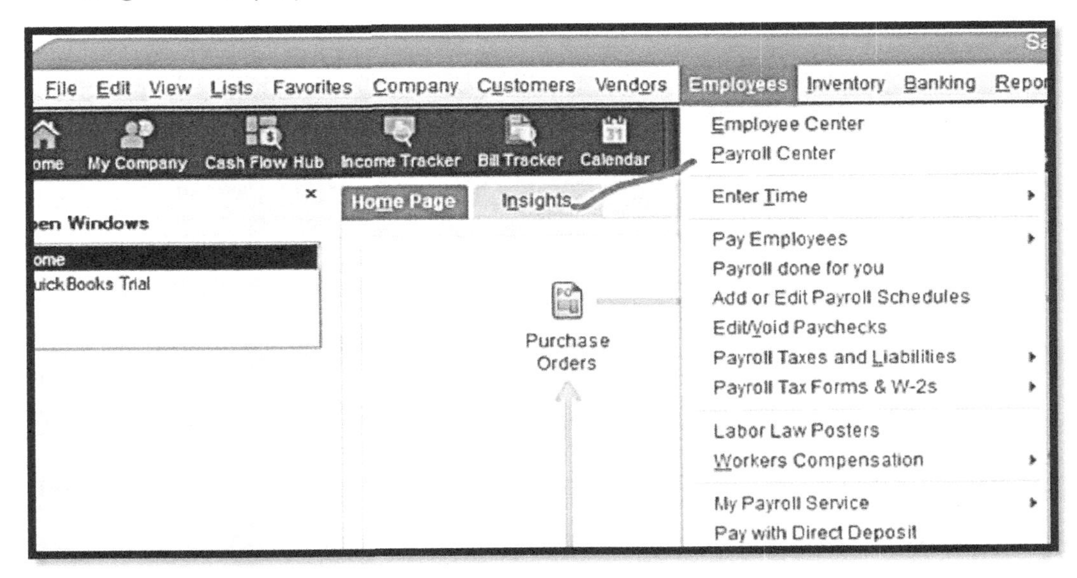

- Choose **New** from the **Payroll Schedule dropdown option.**
- Give the schedule a name and select the frequency of employee payments.
- Fill in the other fields, and then click **OK.**

- If you want to assign the revised schedule to every employee, choose Yes or No.

Assign a pay schedule to an employee

- Navigate to Employees and choose Employee Center.
- Double-click the name of the worker.

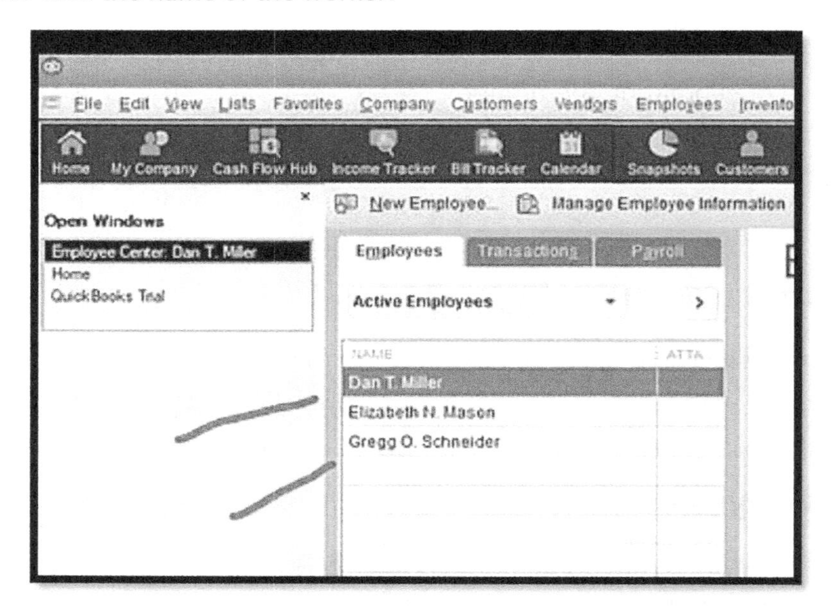

- Pick the Payroll Information tab.

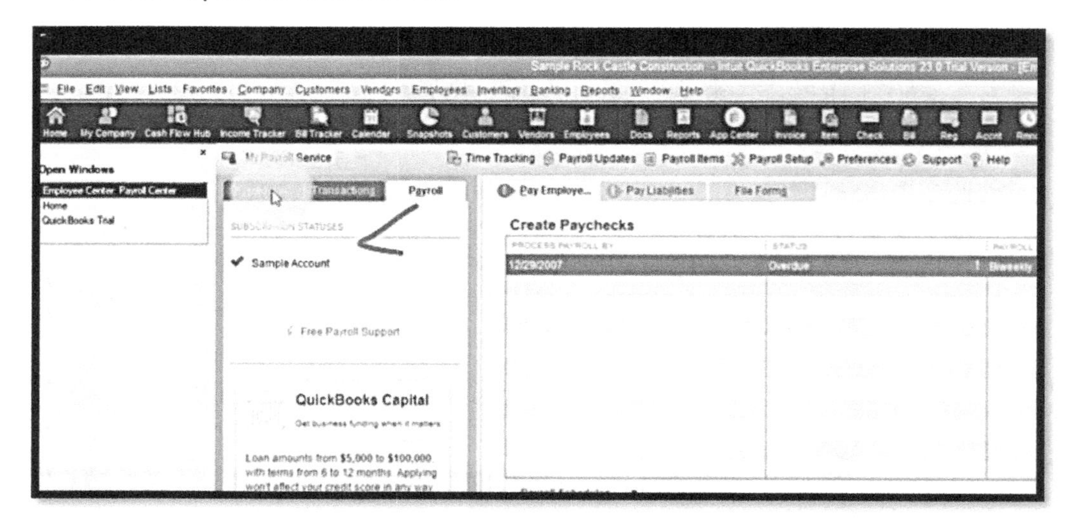

- From the menu, choose the Payroll Schedule drop-down option.
- To apply a pay schedule to this employee, select the one you want.
- To save, select OK.

Update a pay schedule

Only the current pay period is impacted if you modify the dates while creating payroll using the Enter Payroll Information window. To make any future payroll schedules up to date:

Please take note that the Process Payroll On date and Check date are modified to account for transmit lag periods and federal holidays if you use Direct Deposit or QuickBooks Desktop Payroll Assisted.

- Navigate to **Employees and choose Payroll Center.**
- Choose the payroll schedule that needs to be updated from the **Create Paychecks table.**
- Choose **Edit Schedule** from the **Payroll Schedules dropdown menu.**
- In the Edit Payroll Schedule window, make the required changes.
- Click **OK.**

Deactivate or delete a payroll schedule

You can set a payroll schedule to be inactive rather than delete it. In this manner, you may easily reactivate it if necessary without having to create a new payroll plan. To remove a pay schedule:

- Navigate to **Employees** and choose **Employee Center.**
- Choose **the payroll schedule that needs to be updated from the Create Paychecks table.**
- Choose **Edit Schedule from the Payroll Schedules dropdown menu.**
- Once you've marked **Schedule as inactive, click OK.**

There are two processes involved in totally deleting a payroll:

Remove any employees who are on the payroll schedule you would like to have deleted;

- Navigate to **Employees and choose Payroll Center.**
- Double-click **the name of the worker.**
- Select the **Payroll Info option.**
- Make sure the schedule you need to delete isn't the one that is entered in the Payroll Schedule box. If so, either clear the field or give the employee a different payroll schedule.
- To view each employee's paycheck schedule, follow these instructions.

Delete the payroll schedule

- Navigate to **Employees and choose Payroll Center.**
- Navigate to the **Employee Pay tab.**
- Select the payroll schedule you wish to remove from the **Create Paychecks table.**
- Choose **Delete Schedule from the Payroll Schedules dropdown menu**. Note: You still have employees on a payroll schedule if you receive a prompt stating that you cannot remove it or make it inactive. Take note of Step 1 and check each employee.

- Click **OK.**

Step 2: Create your paychecks and send your payroll

You must next prepare your paper paychecks or direct deposit forms and sends them to us for processing. You can generate an unscheduled paycheck or a scheduled payroll if you've set up a payroll schedule.

- Scheduled payrolls on a schedule are those you provide to your staff regularly. These payments also include bonuses or other forms of compensation.
- Unscheduled payroll: There may be instances in which you must report fringe benefits, pay commissions, bonuses, and final paychecks to your staff members outside of the regular payroll cycle.

Your payroll agency will determine how to create and process your paychecks. To get started, choose your product below. Uncertain about the payroll service you use? This is how to locate your payroll provider.

- Access your QuickBooks Desktop Company file by logging in as the Payroll Admin or Primary Admin.
- Choose **Employees, followed by the Payroll Center.**
- The payroll service you are utilizing can be found under Subscription Statuses on the Payroll page.

Paying Employees

- Choose **Employees, Pay Employees, and then either Scheduled Payroll, Unscheduled Payroll, or Termination Check as your check types.**
  If you have to run an unscheduled payroll, go to step 3.
- After deciding on the suitable timetable, choose **Start Scheduled Payroll.**
- Check **the dates of the checks, the Pay Period Ends, and the QuickBooks Bank Account.**
- Decide which workers you wish to pay.
- If you are utilizing timesheets, all of their hours for this pay period will already be entered. Alternatively, you can enter hours using the grid. Click on **Open Paycheck Detail** to view each person's salary details.
- To move on to the next employee, pick **Save & Next; alternatively, select Save & Close to return to the Enter Payroll Information box.**
- Click **"Continue."**
- Examine the choices for printing checks and direct deposits.
- After checking each employee's amount, click **Create Paychecks.**
- Print **pay stubs and paychecks** right away, or later if you'd like. Send Intuit your payroll data and direct deposit paychecks if you use QuickBooks Desktop Payroll Assisted or direct deposit payroll.

Editing and Voiding Paychecks

Edit, void, or delete a paycheck, depending on your payroll service and processing time.

Edit a paycheck: This directly updates your pay information for the payroll. If you haven't yet sent us your payroll, you can edit paychecks.

- Navigate to the Banking menu and choose **Use Register.**
- Click **OK** after choosing your bank account.
- Choose the disputed check and open it.
- Click **Paycheck Details**.
- As necessary, update the paycheck.
- Click **OK** when you're ready.
- Choose **Save & Close and then OK.**

Delete a paycheck: The paycheck is deleted from your payroll. If you haven't yet submitted your payroll, you can remove paychecks.

- Navigate to the **Banking menu and choose Use Register.**
- Click **OK after choosing your bank account.**
- Choose the disputed check and open it.
- Select **Delete located at the top of the paycheck.**
- Enter **OK** in the pop-up box.

You can cancel the paycheck if you have already submitted payroll to QuickBooks. The deduction of payroll taxes and direct transfer from your bank account might not be suspended, nevertheless, based on your processing time.

Important: Changes will be necessary if you void a paycheck from a previous quarter or year.

Void a paycheck: Your paycheck will now have zero dollars in it. For your finances to balance, you might need to make some adjustments. This does not reverse the funds and does not halt the processing of a direct deposit. If you have already submitted your payroll, you can cancel checks.

Void direct deposit paychecks

- To edit or void paychecks, pick the **Employees menu and then choose Edit /Void Paychecks.**
- Press the **Tab on your keyboard after changing the Show paychecks through/from dates to the date of the paychecks you need to nullify.**
- After choosing **the check-in question, choose Void.**
- After typing **YES, choose Void.**
- To accept the terms and conditions of nullifying the paycheck, tick the box.
- To include every check that needs to be voided, repeat steps 1 through 5 as needed.

Send the voided paychecks

- To send payroll data, first pick the **Employees menu and then choose Send Payroll Data.**
- Click **Send**. This notifies our system to stop processing paychecks, even though you won't see any direct deposit checks to send.
- After entering your payroll PIN, click **OK.**

Paying Payroll Liabilities

You can write checks and set up scheduled payments in QuickBooks Desktop Payroll to pay benefits and other deductions to your plan administrators, like insurance premiums, garnishments, and 401(k) contributions. This aids in keeping you accountable for your payments and debts.

Set up a pay schedule

- Choose **Payroll Center from the Employees menu.**
- Choose the tab for **Pay Liabilities.**
- Click on **Other Activities and choose Manage or Adjust Payment Methods.**
- Choose **Schedule Payments** after choosing **Benefit & Other Payments.**
- Choose the benefit or liability you wish to create a schedule for under Benefits and Other Payments. Next, choose **Edit.**
- Choose **the Payee (Vendor).**
- Put the Account Number in here. Next, choose the **frequency of payment.**
- To close the window, choose **Finish.**

Add scheduled payments to your calendar

- Select **Pay Liabilities after going to the Payroll Center.**
- Mark the liability payment or payments that require a calendar reminder by placing a checkmark next to them.
- From the dropdown menu, select **Set payment reminder.**
- Choose **"Export Reminder in Calendar File" or "Add Reminder to Calendar."**
    - **Add Reminder to Calendar will launch the default calendar program on the computer of the user.**
    - **Export Reminder in Calendar File will design a calendar reminder file that you can either open on the computer of the user or that you can choose to send to other users so they can add it to their calendar program.**

Note: Payroll tax and other payroll duties, such as garnishments or benefit payments, can be scheduled for reminders by users of Basic and Enhanced Payroll.

Since Intuit currently pays the Federal and State taxes for Assisted Payroll customers, the only option available to them is to create payment reminders for other payroll duties.

Pay your scheduled liabilities

- Select Pay Scheduled Liability after going to Employees and Payroll Taxes & Liabilities.

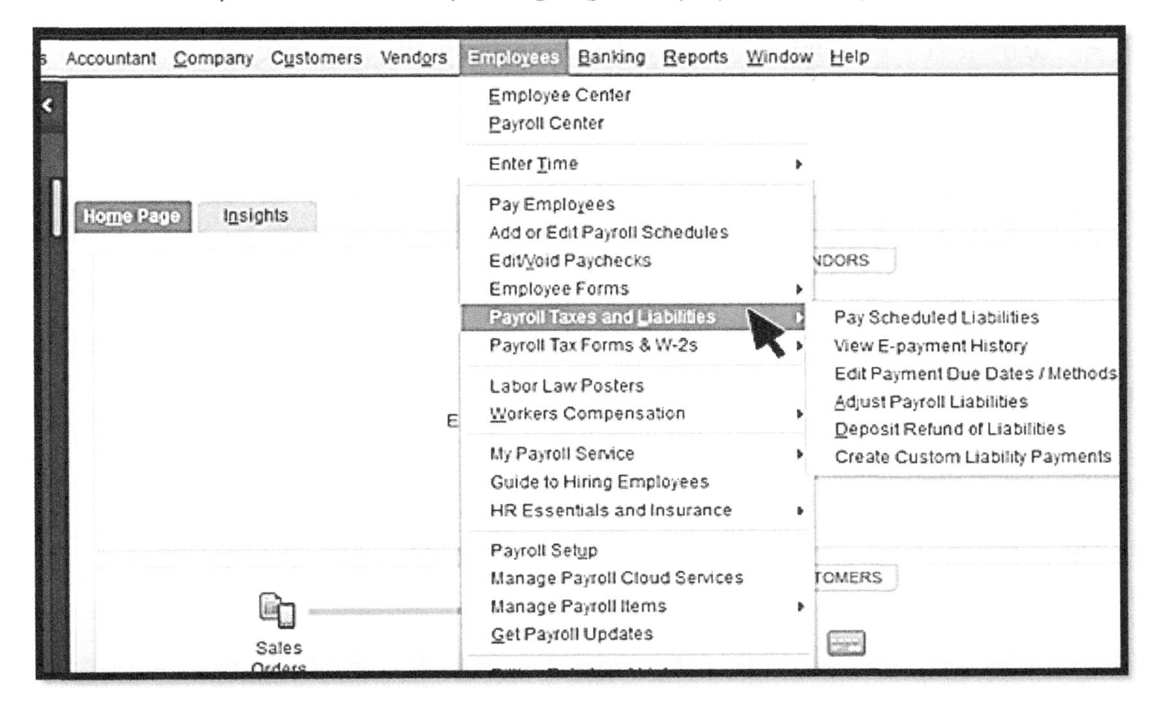

- Choose the tax or other liability you wish to pay from the list in the Pay Taxes & Other Liabilities window. Next, choose View/Pay.
- Examine the due dates and quantities.
- Choose E-pay or Check to continue paying your taxes.

Pay an unscheduled liability or create a custom payment

- Navigate to Employees, then choose Payroll Center > Pay Liabilities.
- Create Custom Payments by selecting it under Other Activities.
- Choose a date range in the Select Date Range for Liabilities window, and then click OK.
- If you would like the liability check to be printed, select To be printed. If you sent a handwritten check, make sure this is evident.
- Choose the date you wish to show on the liability check as well as the bank account.
- You have the option to either create a liability check without examining it or Review your liability check to enter expenses and penalties.
- After choosing the payroll item to be paid, click Create.

Note: When paying into a single agency, several payroll items are consolidated into a single responsibility check. Liability checks will be produced by several agencies. Verify the accuracy of the item list and check the amount under Payroll Liabilities.

- A liability check shows if you choose **Review your liability check** to enter expenses or penalties. You can view the liability check in the check registry if you didn't.
- Verify the quantities and dates are accurate. To print the check, select **Print.**
- To print a check that is handwritten, uncheck the Print Later option. Next, fill in the NO. Field alongside the check number or another reference.
- To indicate obligations settled using Electronic Funds Transfer (EFT), select the **Print Later option and enter EFT in the Liability Check's NO. Field.**
- If you wish to enter costs or penalties on the liability check, select the **Expenses tab.**
- Choose the expenditure account that you use to keep track of payroll costs and penalties from the drop-down menu for the Account field, then type the amount into the Amount column.
- Choose **Recalculate.**

Activity

1. Pay your employee.
2. Edit and void paychecks.
3. Set up and schedule payrolls.

BOOK 4

FINANCIAL CHOREOGRAPHY: STREAMLINING YOUR ACCOUNTING TASKS FOR SUCCESS

CHAPTER 1

FOR ACCOUNTANTS ONLY

You will study the several topics that accountants must or wish to know in this chapter. Unless you have a thorough understanding of your debits and credits, you should avoid doing the activities this chapter discusses. And if you are aware of your debits and credits, this chapter's contents ought to be sufficient for you.

Updating Company Information

Working with Journals

You, as an accountant, may easily record journal entries with QuickBooks. Most journal entries that are automatically entered in the QuickBooks data file are likely familiar to anyone who has worked with QuickBooks for any length of time. For instance, QuickBooks logs the journal entry for a check that is written. Once more, QuickBooks makes a journal entry when someone creates an invoice. However, occasionally a journal entry needs to be made by someone, most often you, to enter a transaction into the QuickBooks data file. Journal entries are used, among other things, to track depreciation, liabilities, and asset disposal.

Follow the steps below to create a QuickBooks Journal entry;

The final option for entering transactions is through journal entries. Use them only if you are familiar with accounting or if you heed your accountant's recommendations. If you require an accountant, you can locate one as well.

- Manually enter credits and debits, same as in conventional accounting systems.
- Money transfers between the accounts for income and expenses
- Move funds to an income or expense account from an asset, liability, or equity account.

Add a journal entry

Here's what to do if you need to write a new diary entry:

- Select the **"Make General Journal Entries"** option from the Company menu.

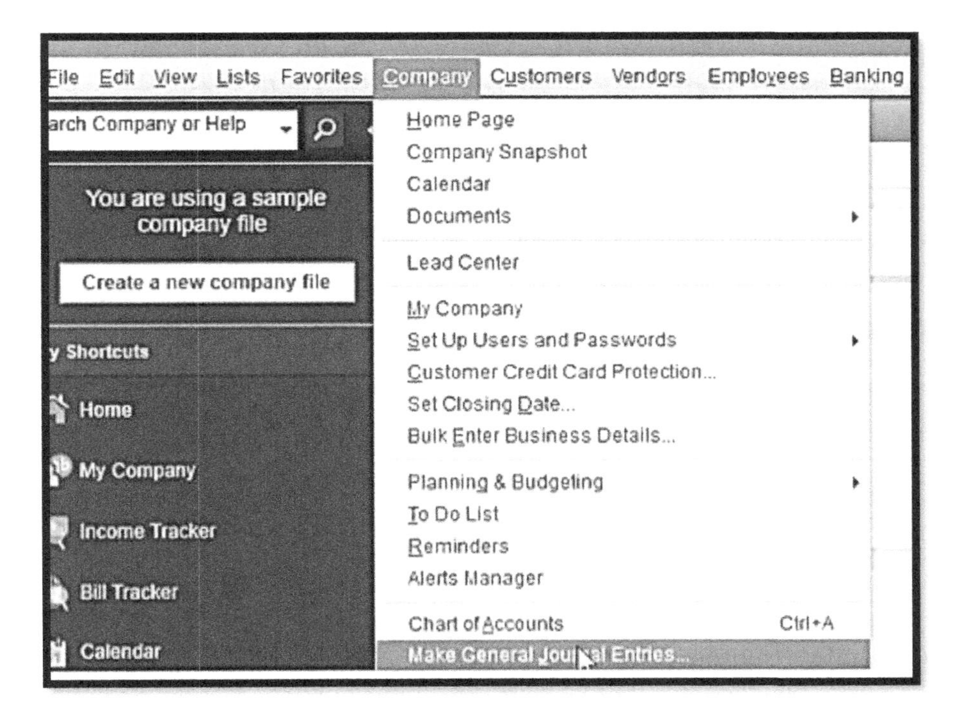

- Complete the areas below to start writing in your journal. When you're done, make sure your debits and credits match.
- Either choose **Save or Save & Close.**

Edit a journal entry

Here's what to do if you need to alter a journal entry:

- Select the "Make General Journal Entries" option from the Company menu.
- **Locate and pick the journal entry that requires editing:**
    - Within Windows QuickBooks: After choosing **Find and inputting the Name, Date, Entry No., or Amount, click Find again.**
    - Locate and pick the journal entry in QuickBooks for Mac from the list on the left side of the **Create General Journal Entries window.**
- After double-clicking the journal entry, **edit it as needed.**
  Choose either **Save or Save & Close** when you're finished.
- Choose **Yes to save the changes.**

Reverse a Journal entry

- Select the **"Make General Journal Entries" option from the Company menu.**
- **Locate and pick the journal entry that has to be reversed:**
    - Within Windows QuickBooks: After choosing Find and inputting the Name, Date, Entry No., or Amount, click Find again.

- In Mac QuickBooks: On the left side of the Create General Journal Entries window, locate and pick the journal entry that you wish to reverse.

- Choose **Reverse.**
- Either choose **Save or Save & Close.**

Any debit and credit amounts have been reversed, and there is an "R" next to the entry number in the reversed journal entry. The date of the new entry is the first of the month that comes after the date of the initial transaction.

Delete a journal entry

Here's how to remove or nullify a journal post if necessary:

- Select the **"Make General Journal Entries" option from the Company menu.**
- **Locate and choose the journal entry that has to be removed:**
  - Within Windows QuickBooks: After choosing Find and inputting the Name, Date, Entry No., or Amount, click Find again.
  - In Mac QuickBooks: From the list on the left side of the Make General Journal Entries window, locate and pick the journal entry that you wish to reverse.
- **To take off the journal entry;**
  - Double-click the journal entry in QuickBooks for Windows; choose **Delete or Void, and then click OK.**
  - In QuickBooks for Mac, choose **Delete General Journal from the Edit menu.**
- Choose **Save & Close.**

Make General Journal Entries is only one of several commands available from the Company menu. For example, accountants may need to run the command Company Information. You can adjust the fiscal and tax year settings, taxpayer identification numbers, the tax form used to declare profits, and the firm name and address using this command.

Working with Memorized Transactions

You can commit many kinds of transactions, including checks, bills, invoices, and sales receipts, to memory in QuickBooks Desktop. You can memorize any transaction that you frequently enter for later usage. Your transactions that you have memorized are always visible. Make sure you pick the Memorized Transaction List from the Lists option.

Creating a memorized transaction

- Every month, enter the transaction the way you want it to appear. Choose not to save. Leave a field empty if the information it contains is subject to change. For instance, on a recurring check, keep the note field empty so you can input a different note as needed.
- Choose **Memorize [Transaction Name] from the Edit menu**. Take Memorize Check, for instance.

- Put a Name Here. Next, decide how you would like QuickBooks to handle that.
    - Add to my Reminders List
    - Your reminders list's Memorized Transactions section will now include the transaction. Please complete the How Often field after selecting this option.
    - Do Not Remind Me
    - The transaction won't be automatically or automatically put on your list of reminders. This can serve as a template for transactions that recur periodically.
    - Automate Transaction Entry
    - When the transaction is due, it will be entered. Don't forget to fill in the Next Date and How Often sections when you select this option.

Note that;

- Make sure your **Next Date** is set to a future day if you have an automatic schedule for a transaction set up.
- Keep in mind that the **Next Date** transaction is included when you put in the Number Remaining.

- Insert any other information as you like, and then choose **OK.**
- Choose **Save & Close or Save & Next.**

Create a memorized transaction group

You can make a transaction group that you can remember if you have transactions with the same due date.

- Choose **Memorized Transaction List from the Lists menu.**

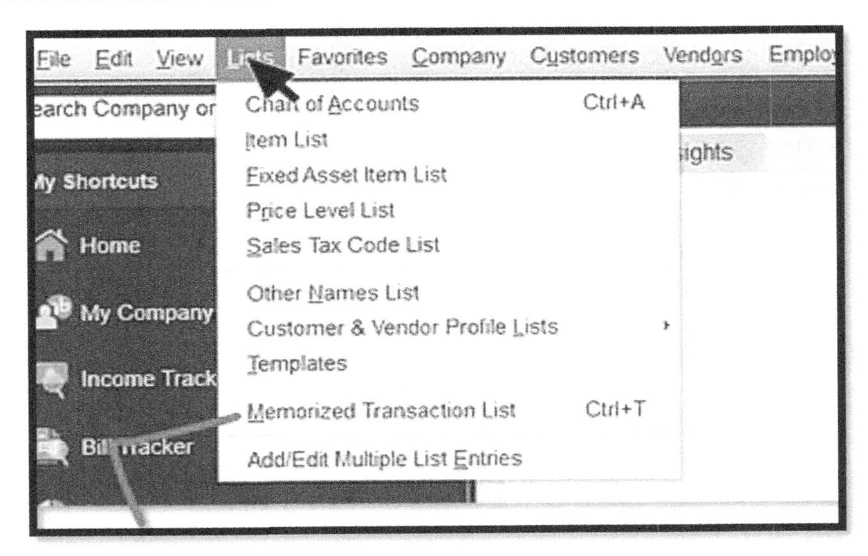

- Choose **New Group** from the Memorized Transaction drop-down menu.
- Add details such as frequency and group name.

- Click **OK.**

Add a transaction to a memorized transaction group

- To memorize a transaction to memory, open it or create one.
- Choose **Memorize.**
- After selecting the **Group Name, click Add to Group.**
- Click **OK.**

Add a transaction you have memorized already

- Choose **Memorized Transaction List from the Lists menu.**
- To edit a memorized transaction, right-click on it and choose **Edit Memorized Transaction.**

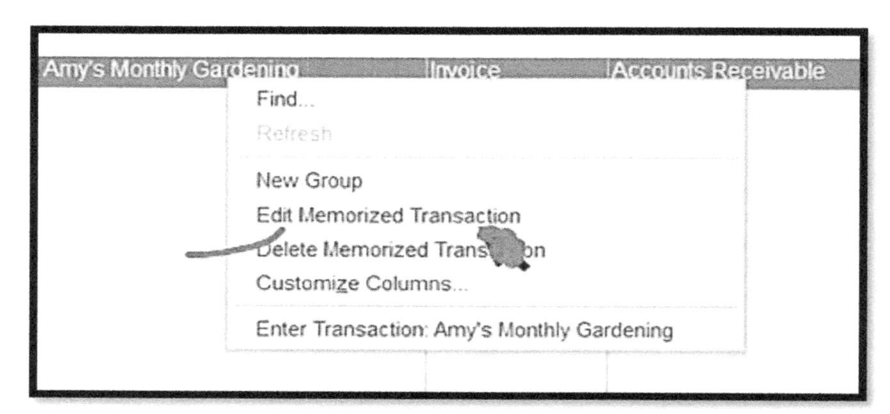

- **After choosing Add to Group, choose the Group Name.**
- Click **OK.**

Edit a memorized transaction

- Choose **Memorized Transaction List from the Lists menu.**
- To edit a remembered transaction, **double-click on it.**
- Make **the desired adjustments.**
- At the top, choose **Memorize.**
- To edit an existing transaction, select **Replace; to create a new one, select Add.**
- Either chooses **Save & Next or Save & Close.**

Delete a memorized transaction

- Choose **Memorized Transaction List from the Lists menu.**
- Choose the transaction that you wish to remove.
- To delete a memorized transaction, first pick the **Memorized Transaction drop-down menu.**

- Click **OK.**

QuickBooks Desktop for Mac

Create a memorized transaction

- Make the transaction you wish to memorize or open it. Fill out the transaction details completely.

Note: Be sure to leave a field blank if it changes for each transaction. For instance, if your monthly utility bill expense varies, you must leave the Amount box empty.

- Select **Memorize from the Edit menu.**
- **Set up the transaction details that you have committed to memory.**
  - **How Often**: this simply is the number of times you would like QuickBooks to remind you about the transaction.
  - **Remind Me**: this helps with the addition of your transaction to your Reminders list.
  - **Automatically Enter:** here QuickBooks will instantly record the transaction when it becomes due.
  - **Next Date**: this is the date the transaction is due next.
  - **Number Remaining**: this is the number of times you would like to record the transaction. For instance; insert the number of payments that are remaining for you if it is a loan transaction.
  - **Days in Advance to Enter:** this is simply the number of days in advance you would like to insert the transaction.
  - **With Transactions in Group and Group Name**: includes the transactions to a memorized transaction group.
  - **Show in Calendar:** here a reminder will be displayed in your Calendar.

To make use of a memorized transaction;

- Select **Memorized Transactions from the Lists menu.**
- Choose the transaction you have committed to memory.
- After choosing Settings, choose **Use.**
- After making the changes, choose **Save.**

Edit or delete a memorized transaction

- Select **Memorized Transactions from the Lists menu.**
- Choose the transaction you have committed to memory.
- Choose **Edit Memorized Transaction from the Edit menu.**
- After making the necessary modifications to the transaction information, choose **Save.**
- Choose **Delete Memorized Transaction** to get rid of the transaction.

Create a memorized transaction group

If the due dates of the memorized transactions coincide, you can group them.

- Select **Memorized Transactions from the Lists menu.**
- Choose **Create +.**
- Put the group name in the Name area. Ensure that the name contains the word "group."
- Enter the information for the transaction group you have committed to memory, and then click **OK.**

Add a transaction to a memorized transaction group

- Select **Memorized Transactions from the Lists menu.**
- Choose the transaction you have committed to memory.
- Choose **Edit Memorized Transaction from the Edit menu.**
- Choose **Using Group Transactions.**
- Choose the group you wish to add from the Group Name drop-down menu.
- Click **OK.**

Reviewing the Accountant and Taxes Reports

Selecting the **Reports > Accountant & Taxes** instruction brings up the Accountant & Taxes menu. You will discover roughly twenty commands and reports in this section that are especially fascinating and practical for accountants.

These reports are listed in the following order:

- **Adjusted Trial Balance**: Naturally, a Trial Balance report as of a specific date is generated by the Adjusted Trial Balance menu command. When compared to the Trial Balance report that follows, this one stands out since the journal entries that need to be adjusted are underlined. (Journal entries that were designated as such need adjustment.) There is an Adjusting Journal Entry check box available in some versions of QuickBooks, including the version you most likely use. To indicate a journal entry adjustment, check that box.
- **Trial balance**: Naturally, a Trial Balance report as of a specific date is generated by the Trial Balance menu command.
- **General Ledger:** A report that only lists the accounts in your Chart of Accounts list and modifies the account for the month, year, or any other accounting period you designate is generated using the General Ledger menu command.
- **Transaction Detail by Account**: The following menu command generates the expected report: a rundown of all the transactions about a specific account.

- **Adjusting Journal Entries**: A list of the journal entries that you or another user designated as modifying journal entries is generated by the modifying Journal Entries command.
- **Journal:** The Journal menu command generates a report that enumerates transactions according to their quantity and type.
- **Audit Trail**: For accountants, especially those who are anxious or afraid that transactions have altered when they shouldn't have, the Audit Trail report is quite crucial. Transactions are listed in the Audit Trail report according to who entered the transactions. The Audit Trail report also indicates who made the adjustments and provides a list of the modifications made to the transactions.
- **Closing Date Exception Report:** The Closing Date Exception Report command finds modifications in closed transactions if you close the books, or conclude the accounting data for the year, which you should do.
- **Customer Credit Card Audit Trail:** For those who have a high volume of credit card transactions that they are unable to understand, a Customer Credit Card Audit Trail report is ideal as it solely includes credit card transactions.
- **Void/ Delete Transaction Detail**: A comprehensive list of all deleted and voided transactions can be obtained by using the Voided/Deleted Transactions Detail command.
- Transa**ction List By Date:** Transactions are listed in the Transaction List by Date report according to the date of entry.
- **Account Listing**: You may see a list of all the accounts in your Chart of Accounts in the Account Listing report. Along with the account amount, the report also shows which line on the tax return the account is reported on.
- **Fixed Asset Listing**: All of the fixed assets in your Fixed Assets list are listed in the Fixed Asset Listing report.
- **Income Tax Summary:** Your income tax preparation data is used by the Income Tax Summary report to indicate which lines of your tax forms should have which amounts on them. QuickBooks examines all of the accounts you use to monitor sales or gross income when you file a Schedule C tax form as a sole proprietor, for instance. The actual value that should be shown on the gross receipts or sales line of your Schedule C tax form is then displayed after adding up the balances in those accounts.
- **Income Tax Detail**: The information provided in the Income Tax Summary report is also included in the Income Tax Detail report; the only difference is that the latter displays the individual accounts that are combined to generate the tax line total.

Creating an Accountant's Copy of the QuickBooks Company File

Find out how to prepare a unique copy of your company file for your accountant to receive.

Note: Only QuickBooks Desktop for Windows is supported by these methods.

Do you want your books reviewed by your accountant? To allow them to make modifications without interfering with your work, you might prepare and email them an Accountant's Copy. You don't have to exchange emails or fret about whose revisions are the most recent when you have an accountant's copy. While your accountant is working on the Accountant's Copy, you can carry on working on your company file. Just import their updates and update your books when they're finished. This is how to make an Accountant's Copy and send it.

Step 1: Set up QuickBooks

Switch off any **Advanced Inventory features** you are currently using before you begin if you use QuickBooks Desktop Enterprise. After sending the Accountant's Copy, you can turn them back on. This step can be skipped if Advanced Inventory is not used, or if you use QuickBooks Desktop Pro or Premier.

Step 2: Create an Accountant's Copy

You have two options for sending an Accountant's Copy to your accountant: either use the Accountant's Copy File Transfer Service to transfer a file over the internet, or create a file to put on a USB or host it online.

Make a file that is USB-compatible

- Hover your cursor over **Send Company File under the File menu.**

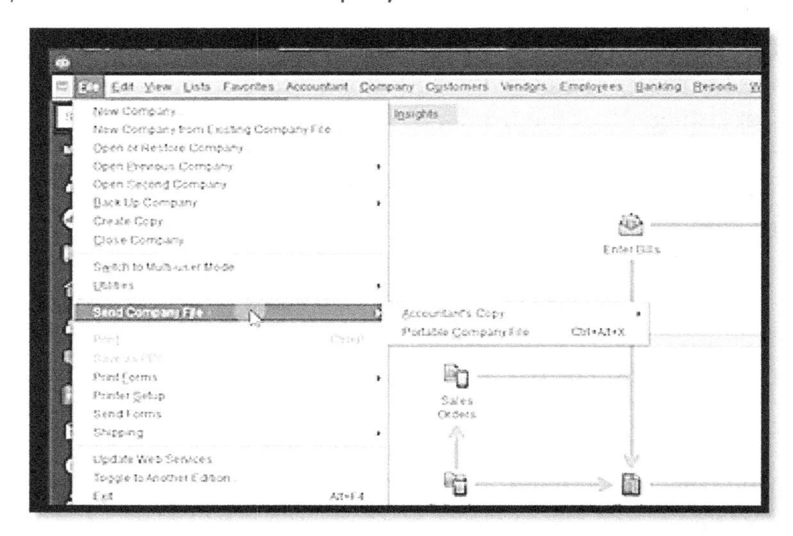

- Hover over **Client Activities after you've hovered over Accountant's Copy.**

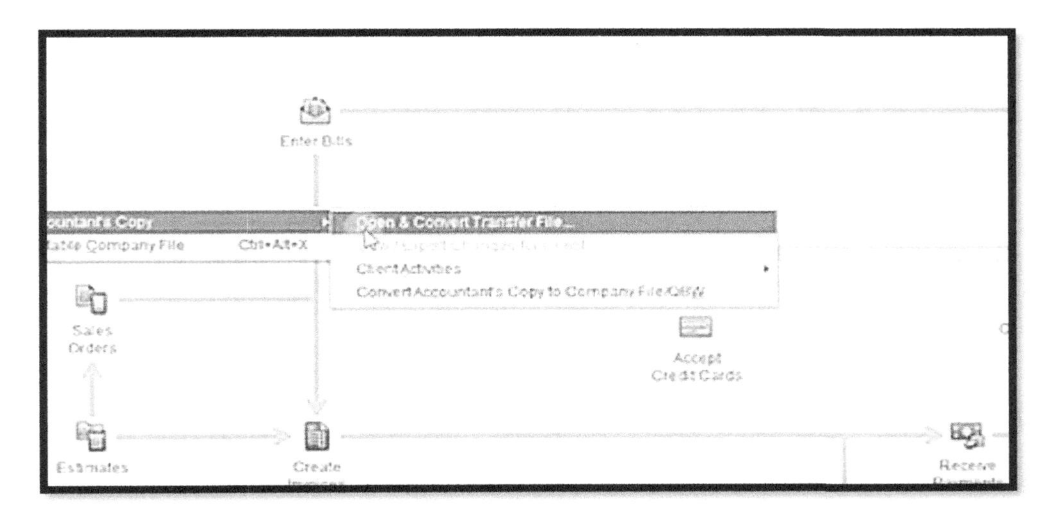

- After choosing Save File, select **Next.**
- After choosing Accountant's Copy, click **Next.**
- Put the dividing date here. Choose **Next.**

Now you have an Accountant's Copy. The filename ends with the extension ".qbx." The file can be shared via a cloud service like Box, attached to an email, or placed on a USB and given to your accountant.

Send a file through the Accountant's Copy File Service

- Hover your cursor over **Send Company File under the File menu.**
- Hover over **Client Activities and Accountant's Copy.**
- After choosing **Send to Accountant, click Next.**

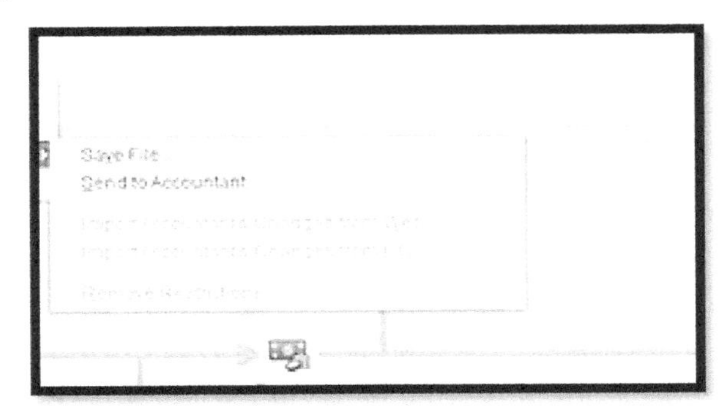

- After choosing **Accountant's Copy, click Next.**
- Put the dividing date and then choose Next.
- Enter the email addresses of both you and your accountant.
- For the file, create a file password. To open it, your accountant requires this.
- Once you're prepared, click **Send.**

QuickBooks sends the file and closes any open windows. The Accountant's Copy you supplied can be downloaded by your accountant throughout the next two weeks.

Regarding accountants: To make modifications, download the Accountant's Copy.

- An email from Intuit with a link to download your client's company file will be sent to you.
- Once you click on the download link, you will get an additional email containing the one-time password that your client supplied when uploading.
- To get the accountant's copy, use this password.
- To make the required adjustments, open the file in QuickBooks.

Switch Advanced Inventory back on

You can omit this step if you don't use Advanced Inventory or if you use QuickBooks Desktop Pro or Premier.

Following file transmission,

Reactivate the Advanced Inventory features. While your accountant is working on their Accountant's copy, you can leave them on. But when you import their adjustments, you'll have to turn them off again for a little while.

Take note:

Your accountant won't have access to your Advanced Inventory details if they add inventory transactions to the Accountant's copy. This comprises lot numbers, inventory locations, and serial numbers, among other things. If necessary, you can manually add this information.

Import your accountant's changes

QuickBooks includes an Accountant's Changes Pending reminder close to your company file name after you transmit the Accountant's Copy. To prevent interference with your accountant's modifications, it also limits specific activities. The notice remains in effect until you either remove the Accountant's Copy limitation or obtain the file back and import your accountant's adjustments.

Use an Accountant's Copy working file in QuickBooks Desktop

To make modifications to your client's books, you must convert the accountant's copy (.QBX) that you receive into an accountant's copy working file (.QBA). Transactions can be readily adjusted and corrected after conversion.

Important: Make sure you use the QuickBooks version (Premier or Enterprise) that your client used to produce the accountant's copy when you accessed it.

Step 1: Ensure that you are using your QuickBooks Accountant Edition

- Choose **Toggle to Another Edition** under the File menu.
- The "Home" option for Premier (or Enterprise Solutions) Accountant Edition ought to be grayed out. If not, press the radio button next to it.
- Click **Next, and then select Toggle**. Rest assured, once you're done, you may go back to your favorite edition.

Step 2: **Convert the accountant's copy to a working file**

- To open and restore the company, choose **Open from the File menu.**
- Click **Next** after selecting **Convert an Accountant's Copy Transfer File.**

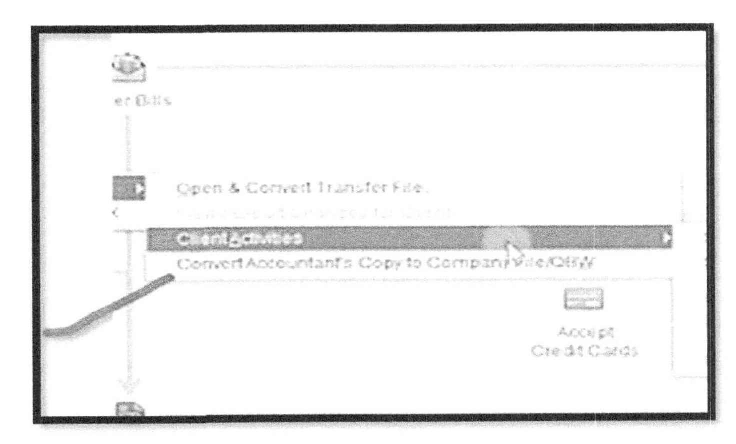

- Go over the Overview and then Next. Proceed similarly with the Can and Can't Dos, and then click **Next.**
- Locate and open the copy of the accountant (.QBX).
- Verify that you truly wish to convert the file.
- Choose **Save** after renaming the file.

Step 3: **Make alterations to the books of your clients.**

Now that you have a working file for an accountant's copy, you can start making the necessary adjustments to your client's books. The following are typical tasks that can be completed with the aid of various accounting tools:

Correct opening balances

The starting balances from the accountant's records for the prior period may not match the balances in a client's books for the review period. This function shows the disparities between the opening balances and recommends changing entries to fix them. There aren't any balances for a previous review period in the accountant's records for the initial review you conducts using this tool. You need to input these balances using the data you obtained from the previous review. When you finish the review after the initial one, the balances are saved. Moving forward from the second review, there won't be any manual balance entry required. The remainder of the procedure is the same after the balances are entered, either manually or automatically.

- **Enter the prior transaction period dates**
  In the fields at the top of the form, provide the from and to dates as well as the rationale for the previous review period. Typically, the current review period begins one day earlier than the previous one. The current period's duration need not match that of the previous review period, but the period's end date must be current.
- **Insert or view balances**
  - The current chart of accounts is used to list the accounts. Enter the amount from the previous review in the relevant column (debit or credit) for each account that has a balance. You have two options when using this tool for the initial review: either manually enter the balances or have it copy every balance from the columns labeled **"Balances from Client's File"** to the columns labeled "Balances in Accountant's Records." When the tool asks if you want to copy the balances, all you have to do is click **Yes.** It is crucial to adjust any previous balances that do not correspond with your records if you allow the tool to duplicate the balances.
  - When you finish reviewing for the previous period using this tool, both sets of balances show up automatically. Until at least one set of previous balances has been manually submitted, the **Last Review Balances** are not automatically displayed.
- **Examine the differences**
  Upon entering both balances, the difference columns are immediately completed.
  - Use the Alt-N shortcut or click the **"Only show accounts with different balances" box at the bottom of the window to view just the accounts with disparities.**
  - For every transaction in the QuickBooks and Difference columns, Quick Zoom is provided. The Transactions by Account report for the chosen account appears when you use Quick Zoom.
  - The Changed Transaction Report is displayed when you click the **View Changed Transactions button.**
  - The CDR Review list changes are seen when you click the **View List Changes button.**

The total of the discrepancies between the balances in the client's file and the accountant's records is displayed by account in the Difference columns of the Troubleshoot Account Balances tool in **Client Data Review.** To view all of the transactions for an account, either Quick Zoom on the entry in the difference column or choose the **View Changed Transactions button.** On occasion, correct items appear as errors in the transaction list of the differences for an account. This typically occurs when entries that ought to have been included in the period are made after the review period. The Transaction Change Report displays all entries made between January 1, 2017, and today, for instance, if the review period was January 1, 2017—

December 31, 2017, and the entry for December 2017 was not finished until January 15, 2018. It can be challenging to distinguish between entries that were made in the first two weeks of January 2018 and those that are part of the balance difference if the list is lengthy. Modify the dates on the Transaction Change Report to today, January 16, 2018, to resolve the issue. The report only includes modifications that occurred after January 15, 2018, even though the evaluation period is still January 1, 2017–December 31, 2017. The list is prepared for review after the period dates have been changed.

- **Request from your client when data entry was completed for the review period**
    - On the Transaction Change Report, use the date one day after that as the start date.
    - Today will always be the expiration date.
- **Correct the balances**

The difference columns will no longer display an account balance if you have made corrections to any underlying transactions and the balances match. You can make an adjustment entry to make up for any balances that are still in the differences columns. To view an adjusting entry with line items for each entry in the differences columns, select the **View Suggested Adjustment button.** All necessary adjustments must be made to the adjusting entry. These include checking that it is balanced, ensuring that any A/R lines have a matching customer, and ensuring that you are not trying to adjust A/R and A/P in the same entry. After making the necessary entry, choose **Save & Close**. If the entry is older than ninety days, you are prompted. You can bring the adjusting entry into the current period by reversing it after saving it. Generally, the entry should be made in reverse. To alter the balances, you can make more than one adjusting entry. The differences columns for the accounts covered by an adjusting entry that modifies some balances are left empty. The remaining accounts can have another adjustment entry made. There needs to be more than one adjustment entry made if the balances of A/R and A/P differ.

- **Checking the balances**

The different columns are updated each time you use this function during a review. There will be zero in the difference column once the balances have been adjusted. It is confirmed that the opening balances for the review period are accurate when there are zero balances in the difference columns.

Write off a group of invoices

To write off several bills, use this program. For every invoice you write off, QuickBooks generates a credit memo. It also appends a memo to the credit memo and the invoice describing the write-off.

- **How to set up write-off item**
    - Select **Add new from the Write off Item drop-down arrow.**

- Keep **Type set to Other Charge in the New Item window.**
- Put a name in the Item Name/Number column, like "write off" or "bad debt."
- Don't change the **Amount or % field from zero.**
- Keep the **Tax Code option selected to Tax.** If the sale was initially nontaxable, don't worry. Taxes are only reversed by QuickBooks on taxable sales.
- Choose the **bad debt expense account by clicking the Account drop-down arrow.**
- Click **OK**.

- Use the Write-Off Invoices tool
    - Select **Accountant > Client Data Review > Client Data Review to open the Write-Off Invoices window from the Client Data Review.**

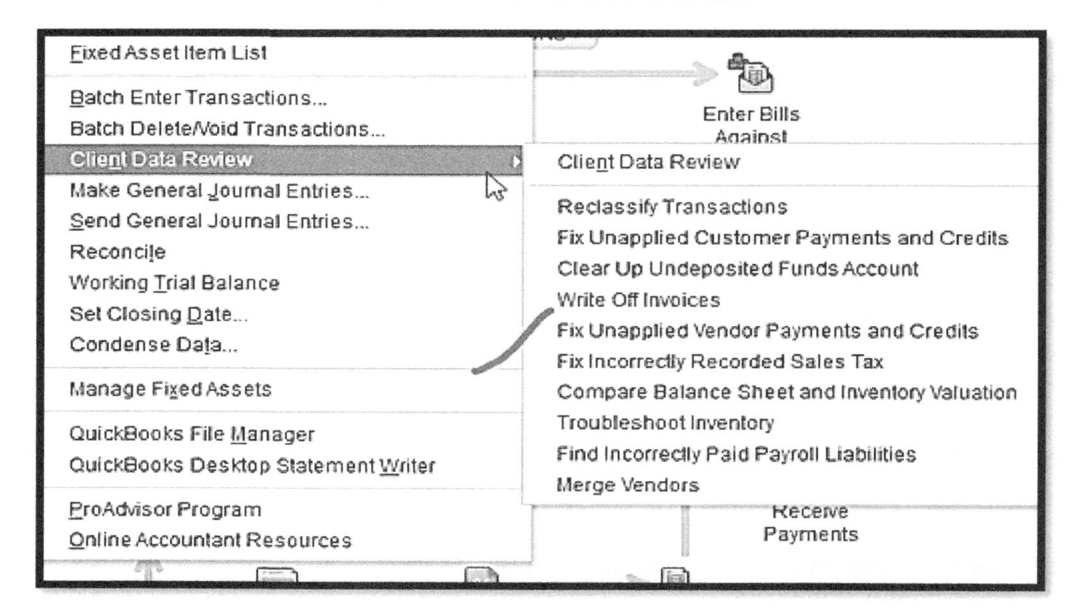

Alternatively, select Accountant > Client Data Review > Write off Invoices to access the window straight away.

- Establish standards for the bills you wish to write off. To narrow down the list of open invoices, use the fields at the top of the window.
- To write off the invoices, choose **the ones in the checkmark column.**
- Choose the write-off item located at the bottom of the window. How is a write-off item set up?
- If needed, adjust the write-off date.
- (Details optional) If you are a class tracker, navigate to the **Class drop-down menu and choose the relevant class.**
- To view the list of bills you are writing off, click **Preview & Write Off. You can still choose to back out.**
- Click **Write Off** when you're prepared to write off the invoices.

- **Enter multiple transactions at once**

Use QuickBooks Desktop's input batch transactions function to copy multiple transactions (checks, deposits, etc.) from one company file to another. You can effectively conserve and manage your time with the aid of this tool. You can use QuickBooks Desktop Enterprise or QuickBooks Desktop Accountant to enter bulk transactions. See Import and Export various lists and transaction kinds for more information about other data types you can import from and export to QuickBooks Desktop. To get this started, follow the set of instructions in the manner in which it has been written;

- **Batch Enter Transactions can be selected from the Accountant menu.**

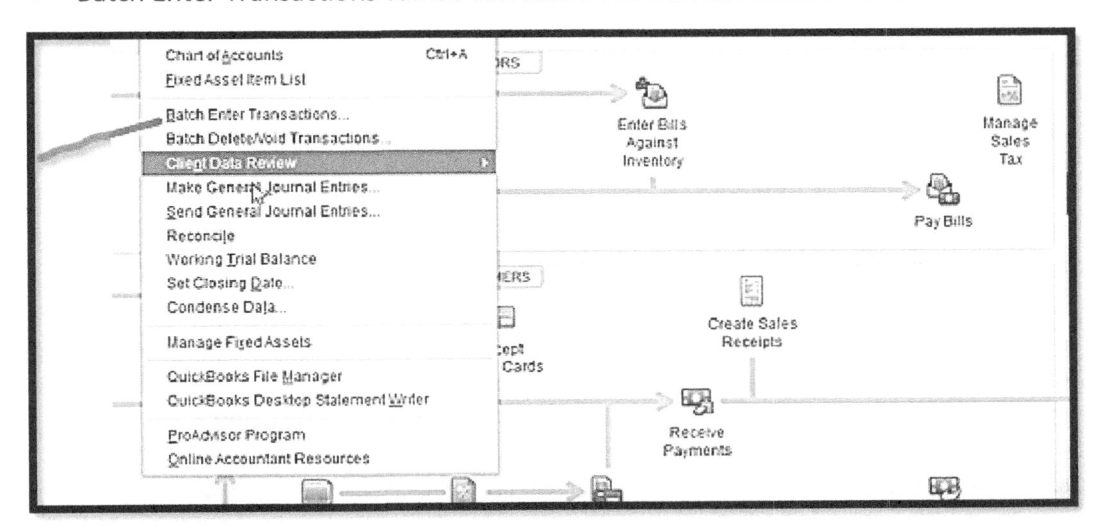

- Select the transaction that has to be entered from the Transaction Type drop-down. You can insert numerous **checks, deposits, credit card charges or credits, invoices, credit memos, bills, and bill credits in any supported version of QuickBooks.**
- Choose the relevant bank, credit card, or AR/AP account using the drop-down menu. To configure the account, you may alternatively select **Add New**.
- To paste the transactions into QuickBooks, open the spreadsheet that contains them.
- Organize your spreadsheet's columns so that they correspond to the QuickBooks Batch Enter Transactions screen's column order.
- Once the transactional data has been highlighted, right-click on it and choose Copy.
- Right-click the first date field in the list in QuickBooks' Batch Enter Transactions screen, then choose Paste.
- The Batch Enter Transactions page shows the data from the spreadsheet.
- Proceed to include every transaction.
- To save, select **Save Transactions and then Yes.**
- The number of transactions saved is shown in a window. Click **OK to complete the import.** While copying multiple transactions from one company file to another in a

manner that can be imported using the enter batch transactions capability, batch transactions cannot be exported.

- **Delete or void transactions by batch**

  To swiftly remove or void several transactions at once, use the Batch Remove/Void Transactions (BDT) program.

  - Batch delete or void transactions
    Important: The transactions below cannot be invalid or batch deleted. They can still be removed one at a time.
    - invoices containing miles, times, costs, or items that were reimbursed
    - Billable time and expense invoices
    - paychecks
    - Checks for Payroll Liability
    - Online Bill Payments with Sales Tax
    - Any deal made within a closed time

Open the transaction, choose Edit, and then delete to remove each one separately.

- Choose **Switch to Single-user mode from the File menu. Avoid selecting Switch to Multi-user mode if it appears.**
- Select the option to **"Batch Delete/Void Transactions" from the Accountant menu.**
- Choose **the transactions from the Available Transactions list that you wish to annul or delete.**
- Choose **Review & Void (or Review & Delete).**
- Choose either **Back Up & Void or Back Up & Delete. You also have the option to choose Void only or Delete only from the dropdowns and forego the backup.**
- Choose Yes to confirm that you would like to delete or void the transactions.

You can print a copy of the deleted or voided transactions by selecting **View Deleted/Voided Transaction Report** after you've deleted or voided the transactions. Certain transaction types are voidable or deletable. Choose a transaction type by selecting the Transaction Type option. These come up on the list for you to nullify or remove. Checks for bill payments, bill credits, bill refunds, refund checks, and finance charges are all included under the bills option. To display transactions related to the specified transaction (such as a paid invoice with an accompanying payment), check the **Show Connected Transactions box**. These can be found in the Linked Trns column of the Available Transactions list. From the Show transactions by menu, choose **Enter date, Last modified date, or Transaction date to filter transactions on the Available Transactions list.**

- **Correct transactions assigned to the wrong accounts or classes**

Facilitate the process of preparing your clients' books for taxation. To locate and fix transactions that have been incorrectly assigned to accounts or classes in your client's books, use the Reclassify Transactions tool. Transactions can be reclassified one at a time or one by one. Here's how it's done.

- Choose the fiscal year you would like to review
  - Select the **Client Data Review option from the Accountant menu.**
  - Choose **Review of Client Data.**
  - After choosing **Modify Review,** click **OK.**

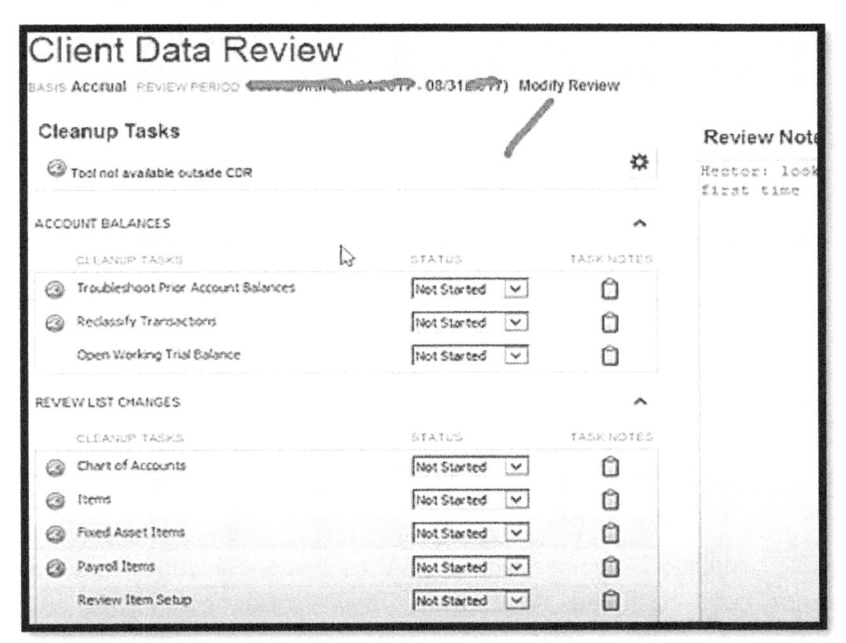

  - Choose the **date range of the transactions you wish to evaluate in the Evaluate Date Range section.**
  - Select either **Cash or Accrual under Review Basis.**
  - Click on **Modify Review.**
  - When you use it for the first time, you'll see Start Review; on subsequent uses, you'll see Modify Review.
  - Locate **Reclassify Transactions under Account Balances**. Choose **"In Progress" from the Status drop-down menu.**
  - Choose **Close.**

- **Review the transactions**
  - Select the **Client Data Review option from the Accountant menu.**
  - Choose **Reclassify Transactions.**

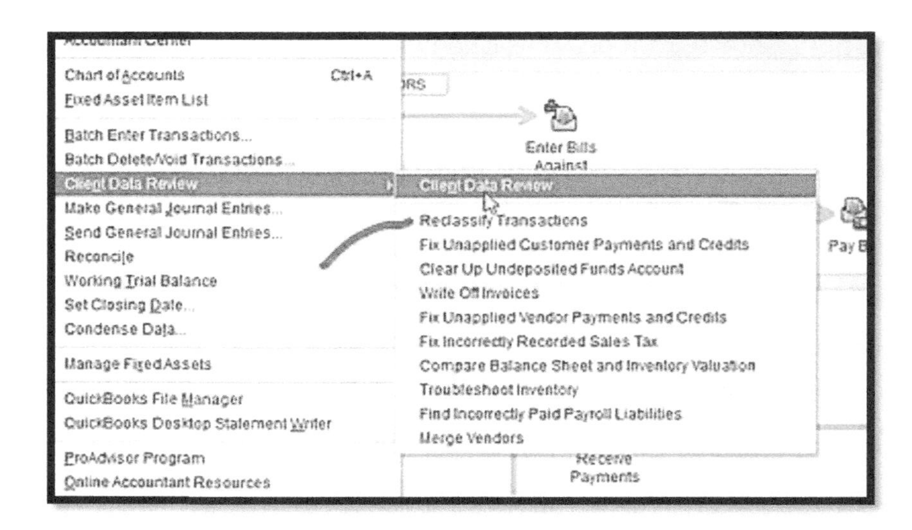

- Choose the **View drop-down menu located in the Accounts section. Choose the account type next.**
- To see the transactions in the right pane, select an account.
- Make your selection from the Name drop-down in the Transactions section.
- Choose the transactions you wish to review from the **Show Transactions drop-down menu.**
- Examine the transaction list.

Note: Transactions such as invoices and bills that involve accounts payable or accounts receivable cannot be reclassified. Additionally, any transaction that is linked to another transaction cannot have its class or account changed.

- **Reclassify transactions**
  You can shift transactions to the appropriate account or class if necessary. Simultaneous reclassification by account and class is also possible.
- Choose **a transaction or Choose All**
- To reclassify by account, check the **corresponding Account to checkbox.**
- For Account to, use the drop-down arrow. Next, identify which account you wish to transfer the transactions to.
- To reclassify by class, select the **Class to checkbox.**
- Next to Class is a drop-down arrow, select it. Next, give the transactions a new class.
- Choose **Reclassify**.
- Visit all list changes

You may view all of the changes made to your lists, including the Payroll Items, Fixed Asset Items, Item List, and Chart of Accounts, by using the Review List Changes tool. You can monitor all of the modifications you've made to your lists in this manner. You will learn how to use it and gain access.

Below is a list of the various things you will be able to review;

Chart of Accounts, Items, Fixed Asset Items, and Payroll Items

You can see and go over the modifications you've made to your things with these listings. You will be able to view the merged, altered, removed, and added objects if you open one of these.

Review Item Setup, Customers, Vendors, and Change Other Name Types

These lists launch the built-in QuickBooks functionality immediately. You can use it to verify the items you have already modified or those you still need to edit.

Gaining access to the tool

- Select the **Client Data Review option from the Accountant menu.**
- Choose **Client Data Review.**
- Choose the list that needs to be reviewed from the **Review List Changes section.**

Note: Every list on your checklist has an editable status.

- Not Started
- In Progress
- Completed
- Not Applicable

* Examine the combined, altered, removed, and added items.
* When you are done going over every item, click **Mark All as Reviewed.**
  It should be noted that once an item is marked as reviewed, it cannot be unreviewed. You can tick the Include Reviewed Items checkbox to view all items.

Changes that are tracked

Chart of Accounts

- Account type, name, and number
- Tax line mapping
- Active or inactive status
- Account or subaccount changes

Items

- Item type
- Cost of goods sold, income, expense, and asset account
- Sales Tax code

- Unit of Measure
- Sales Tax Rate or Agency (for Sales Tax Items only)
- Active or inactive status
- Item or sub-item changes

Fixed Asset Items

- Account type, name, and number
- Tax line mapping
- Purchase date and cost
- Sales date and cost
- Sale expense amount
- Active or inactive status
- Account or sub-account changes

Payroll Items

- Agency
- Accounts assigned to the rate of the item (e.g., Federal unemployment tax rate)
- Limit
- Tax tracking type
- Payment Frequency
- Payroll Schedule
- Status

- **Fix incorrectly recorded sales tax**

Payments that seem to be sales tax payments but weren't recorded using the pay sales tax function are identified using this tool. When a customer pays sales tax with a standard check, this occurs. All or part of the payments can be converted to sales tax checks at once.

Once the list shows up, you can

- To view the check, double-click **on any transaction.**
- To choose a transaction, tick the box next to the transaction line.
- Click th**e "Select All" button to choose every transaction.**
- Click the **Deselect All option** to uncheck every transaction that has been chosen.

Once you've finished choosing transactions, choose **Void & Replace** to make a new sales tax check and void the original one. **On the inside, the following takes place:**

- A sales tax payable check is issued instead of the ordinary check, which is invalidated.
- The amount, date, check number, and reconciliation status of the original check are all retained on the new Sales Tax Payable check.
- Both checks have a memo written in them.

The Sales Tax Adjustment window can be opened immediately by clicking the link Sales Tax Adjustment if you would like to perform a manual adjustment.

- **Correct Inventory errors**

Multiple perspectives on possible inventory issues are included in the Troubleshoot Inventory tool. You can view the things in a way that best fits the client's business by adjusting the inventory criteria and the items that are exhibited. You can quickly Zoom to an inventory item and fix any problems once the inventory list has been displayed. The status column, which sits between the End Qty and Neg Qty? Columns, shows any anomalies in the inventory, like out-of-balance or negative quantity items.

- **Set the display dates**

The review period is the default value for the To and From dates. The dates can be adjusted as needed. Use the tab key or any other click anywhere on the screen to refresh the display after modifying the To date. Only the beginning amount, bought, sold, adjustment, ending quantity, and negative quantity columns are affected by these dates.

Note: CDR automatically sets the earlier date as the From date and the later date as the To date if the entered From date is later than the entered To date.

- **Change the displayed items**

There are multiple inventory views accessible. Select Refresh to see the inventory list with the updated criteria after modifying the view. For readability, the backgrounds of the Type, Cost, Avg Cost, Sales Price, and % Markup columns are all different. There is no particular significance to the background's changing color. There are three choices in the Show Items dropdown box. All shows the whole inventory; All Active shows just the goods that are currently in stock; and Filtered By shows the inventory items that fit the requirements listed below this box. All of the criteria elements are grayed out and unavailable for selection if you select All or All Active. Whether or not the grayed-out items are selected is irrelevant. The Filtered By option is the default. You can use any or all of the criteria to choose which inventory items are shown if the Show Items box is set to Filtered By. The list is filtered by the items you have selected.

The following are the five criteria:

- Quantity Purchased/Build = 0 If there is zero built or purchased quantity, an item is presented.
- Quantity Sold/Used = 0 If there is no quantity utilized or sold, an item is presented.
- **Inverse Quantity:** If the quantity is negative, an item is presented. Under the table, two radio buttons indicate how to represent negative inventory. If you choose the Negative Quantity box and the first button labeled as of "to" date, all items that have a negative quantity at the end of the review period are displayed. Even if an item has a positive amount on the last day of the review period, it will still be displayed if you pick the Negative amount box and click the second button labeled any time in the date range.

- With quantity on hand, inactive If an item has a quantity on hand and is not in use, it is displayed.
- Percentage markup minus...% If the markup is less than the amount entered, an item is displayed. 10% is the default amount. The % Markup box remains visible, but it becomes grayed out if you clear it or select All or All Active under the Show Items option. When it is grayed out, it is retained and not used again, so if you pick the % Markup box or modify the Show Items option, you won't have to enter it again.

- How to fix inventory

Inventory issues can be identified and resolved in the following four ways:

- When the pointer is over the Name, it changes to a Quick Zoom cursor. Double-clicking a **Quick Zoom pointer** will bring up the Edit Item screen where you can make changes. Editing an item will cause the list to refresh.
- Double-clicking the **End Qty or Neg Qty?** The column will display the item's period-specific Inventory Valuation Detail Report.
- By selecting the checkbox next to each inventory item in the first column, you can choose any number of inventory items. Choose **Make Selected Items Inactive** to turn the items you've selected inactive. The entries in the list will become inactive and then automatically refresh. Double-clicking an inactive item will bring up the Edit Item window where you may clear the Item is Inactive box to make it active.
- By selecting Adjust Inventory Quantity/Value on Hand at the bottom of the window, you can change the quantities for every inventory item that is presented. Enter a new amount for any of the products, or the quantity difference, in the new window. One of these items can be entered, and the other will be automatically calculated. At the top of the list, you can add a reference number, job, and class information. You must choose the Adjustment Account. When finished, choose **Save & Close to apply your modifications, or Save & New to apply your modifications while maintaining the window open**. To close the window without making any changes, select **Cancel.** You can get alerts concerning the age of transactions after saving.

Step 4: Send the changes to your client

Export the accountant's copy as the accountant's changes (.QBY) after you've finished editing it. Give your client the file and instructions on how to import the adjustments made by the accountant into their company file.

Export accountant's changes

Once the corrections are recorded, export the Accountant's Changes (.QBY) file. To apply the Accountant's Changes to the company file, the customer must import this file. An Accountant's Changes file can be exported via the Accountant's Copy File Transfer (ACFT) service or by saving it locally. Be aware of this! Accountants and other individuals who manage their clients' financial data export Accountant's Changes (.QBY).

Follow the steps below to have the Accountant's changes (.QBY) exported;

- Click the **Send Company File option from the File menu.**
- To view or export changes for a client, select **Accountant's Copy first and then choose View/Export Changes for Client.**
  Note: Click + to view more details about the adjustments you made.
- (Details optional) To preserve a duplicate of the modifications, choose **Save as PDF or Print.**
- **To save the file locally, follow the steps below;**
  - Click on **Generate Change File.**
  - Select the suitable location for the file's storage and hit the **Save button**. Make sure the file name field is free of asterisks (*).
  - Click **OK.**

If you would like to use Accountant's Copy File Transfer (ACFT) to deliver the file:

- Click **Send Modifications to Client.**
- Put in your name, email address, and the email address of your client.
- If you would want to be notified when the client imports the changes, select **Notify Me.**
- Click **Send.**

Using the Client Data Review Commands

This command is available in QuickBooks Premier and QuickBooks Enterprise Solutions' Accountant Edition versions.

To get the Client Data Review – Start Review dialog box,

- Select **Accountant > Client Data Review > Client Data Review**. This dialog box launches a multi-step process that guides you through cleaning up a client's QuickBooks data file. The utilities in this process include locating and correcting unapplied vendor and customer credits and payments (a common problem for bookkeepers worldwide), reclassifying transactions in bulk (helpful for rectifying bulk errors), clearing out undeposited funds accounts and bad payroll liability account balances (common issues), and writing off uncollectible invoices.

Check out these self-explanatory features if you're using the Accountant Edition of QuickBooks and need some tools to swiftly tidy up some unfortunate client's bookkeeping mess.

Activity

1. What are QuickBooks journal entries?
2. Update the company information.

3. What are memorized transactions and how can they be used?
4. Create an accountant's copy of the QuickBooks data file.

CHAPTER 2

PREPARING FINANCIAL STATEMENTS AND REPORTS

Since there are so many reports in QuickBooks, there aren't detailed descriptions of every report in this chapter. It only includes a few of the tasks that must be completed before financial statements are prepared. Following a review of the fundamentals, you will discover how to create and edit reports as well as some of the helpful tools QuickBooks provides for handling report creation.

Some Wise Words Up Front

It should go without saying, but keep in mind that the quality of the reports you generate in QuickBooks depends entirely on the data file. Your reports should be rather decent if your QuickBooks data file has rich, high-quality information, is error-free, and has all of the transactions entered. This seemingly insignificant discovery has a significant consequence: gathering all the information is frequently the first step in creating accurate financial statements and insightful reports. Stated differently, you should confirm that all of the checks, purchase orders, invoices, and other paperwork have been entered. Additionally, you should confirm that any unique accounting transactions—like those related to accruals, asset sales, or depreciation—have been recorded.

Producing a Report

Several reports are available in QuickBooks Desktop to meet your business requirements. A Report set is a set of instructions that determines how reports are shown in QuickBooks Desktop. This instruction set is used to extract data from the data file and display it as a series of transaction lines. The report set defines which transactions' lines are included in the report and whether Source, Targets, or both are included.

The report set comprises:

- The structure of the report is hardcoded into QuickBooks Desktop.
- The embedded filters are part of this structure.
- Default filters.
- Settings on the Display and Filter tabs.

QuickBooks examines individual transaction lines when creating reports. A line is added to the report if it matches the report set. It should be noted that different reports interpret transactions differently, thus even while two reports seem to indicate the same amount, they can reflect different amounts. To apply accounting principles and procedures, such as documenting transactions and presenting reports, QuickBooks Desktop additionally makes use of a notion known as Source and Targets. Gaining an understanding of Sources and Targets enables you to make the most of Report Filters, leading to faster, more sophisticated discoveries and more successful reports.

- **Source**: here is a transaction summary of information. It includes all of the source data, including the source amount, source memo, source name, and source account.
- **Targets**: Provide all target data, such as target accounts, target names, target memoranda, target amounts, etc., along with the transaction's specific details.
- Pressing **Ctrl+Y** on your keyboard opens the transaction journal report for any saved transaction in QuickBooks, such as an invoice or a check. The report's source data is displayed in the first line, and the target data is shown in the subsequent lines.
- Except for general journal entries, where a line can be inserted before the first line, all transactions have a fixed source of data. By doing this, QuickBooks will recognize every line on the general journal entry as target data.

Working with the Report Window

Ten options are usually available in the Report window: Comment on Report, Print, Email, Excel, Hide Header, Collapse, Refresh, Print, Memorize, and Share Template. You can experiment to see what these command buttons accomplish.

Working with Report window buttons

Customize Report

This button shows the Modify Report dialog box. So much won't be explained in this section as there is a later aspect that talks more about this.

Comment on Report

The Comment on Report window appears after clicking the **Comment on Report button**. You click the report value you like to annotate with a comment to activate the Comment on Report dialog box. A comment box appears at the bottom of the window when QuickBooks launches. After typing your comment, click **the "Save" button.** You must save the annotated report after you have finished your comments. To accomplish this, select the Save button located in the top-left corner of the screen. You are prompted by QuickBooks to save the report with a distinct report name. You can add your comments after you print the report. (Accountants and bookkeepers who wish to interpret numbers for other financial statement readers may find this tool very helpful.) Selecting the report from the **Reports > Commented Reports submenu** allows you to print a saved commented report.

Share Template

Once you've made any modifications to a report, QuickBooks will enable the Share Template button. From there, you may share your modified report settings—not the data—with other QuickBooks users. QuickBooks shows the Share Template dialog box (not visible) when you press this button. Give your report template a name, use the provided option buttons to indicate whether you want to stay anonymous, give your customized report a brief description, enter your name and email address, and save the dialog box. QuickBooks publishes your report template to an Intuit website so that others can download and utilize it when you click the **Share button.**

Memorize

The Memorize Report dialog box appears when you click the **Memorize button**. You can store, or commit to memory, a specific set of report-generating preferences using this dialog box. Once you commit these configurations to memory, you may generate the same report by selecting the stored report from the **Reports > Memorized Reports submenu.**

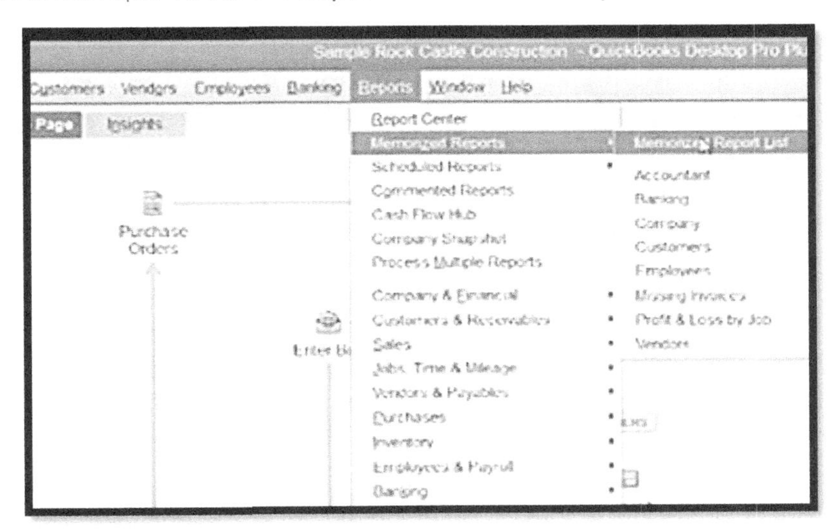

Memorized reports can be saved in the Memorized Report Group. Checking the **Save in Memorized Report Group box will accomplish this**. Then choose the report group that the memorized report should be saved in using the **Save in Memorized Report Group drop-down box.**

Print

Report and Save As PDF are the two choices in the drop-down list that appear when you click the **Print command button** on the top menu bar.

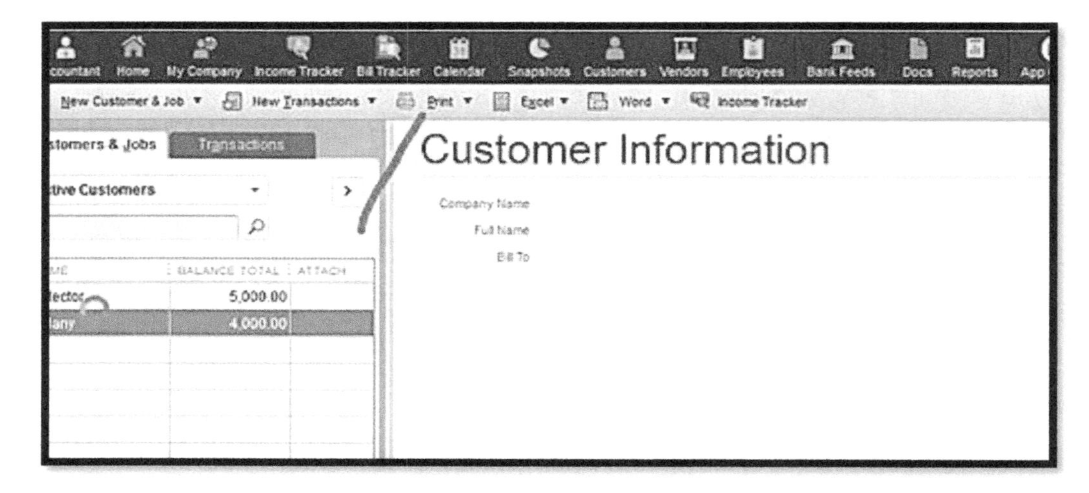

When you select Report, QuickBooks (often to your disgust) opens the Print Reports dialog box where you can select where and how you want the report to print. For example, the Settings tab allows you to select the printer, choose between portrait and landscape page orientation, indicate if you want to print a certain range of pages from the report, manage page breaking, and change the report's width and height. QuickBooks presents the **Save Document as PDF dialog box**, which allows you to produce a PDF of the report document when you select **Save as PDF** by selecting the drop-down arrow to the right of the Print button. You can set the margins that QuickBooks ought to utilize on the printed report pages in the Print Reports dialog box by selecting the Margins tab. The top, right, bottom, and left margins are all given in inches. To view the Preview window, which displays the appearance of your printed report pages, click the Preview button. The window also has buttons that allow you to print the report, zoom in and out of it, and page to the previous and next pages. Click **Print** after determining how QuickBooks should print a report using the **Settings and Margins tabs**. Your printer receives the report from QuickBooks.

Email

You can email a PDF or Microsoft Excel workbook version of a report to another person as an attachment by using the Email command button.

Excel

QuickBooks presents a submenu when you click the **Excel button**, where you may select **Create New Worksheet or Update Existing Worksheet**.

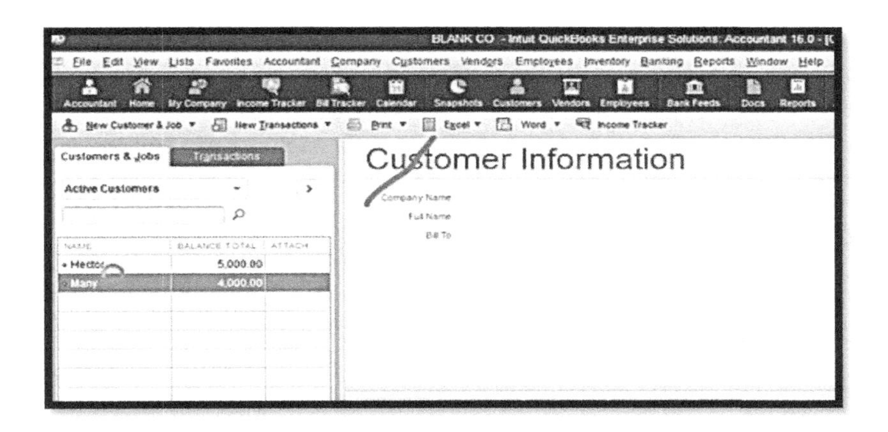

To open the Send Report to Excel dialog box, select **Create New Worksheet**. With the help of this dialog box, you can copy data from a report to a file that can be opened with ease by a spreadsheet application like Excel. The copy can be sent to an Excel spreadsheet that's already open, a new Excel spreadsheet, or a.csv (comma-separated values) file that can be opened by almost any database or spreadsheet application. Click the **Create New Worksheet radio button** to copy the report to a new workbook. From there, you can either create a new sheet in an existing file by selecting the In Existing Workbook radio button, or you can create a new Excel spreadsheet by clicking the **In New Workbook option**. After selecting the radio button, QuickBooks will open a text box where you can enter the path and name of the workbook. (Alternatively, you can utilize QuickBooks's built-in dialog box to find the workbook file if you don't know the path or name of the workbook.)

To copy the report to an already-existing Excel spreadsheet, choose the option button labeled "Update an Existing Worksheet." Excel updates the previously exported worksheet when QuickBooks runs. Choose the **Replace an Existing Worksheet radio button** if you want to replace a current Excel spreadsheet with the new report you're sending to Excel. Next, when QuickBooks opens a text box with the Browse button added, you may type the workbook's name and path in the text box or choose the Browse button, find the workbook, and choose it. Lastly, click the **Create a Comma Separated Values (.csv) File radio button** if you want to copy the report data to a.csv file (a file type that can be viewed by any spreadsheet or database tool). QuickBooks shows the **Advanced Excel Options dialog box** when you choose the Advanced command button on the **Send Report to Excel dialog box**. This dialog box gives you the ability to set up some basic workbook printing information in Excel (using the Printing Options radio buttons), manage what formatting QuickBooks copies to Excel (using the QuickBooks Options checkboxes), and turn certain Excel formatting features on or off. Everything here has to do with how Excel functions. Make the modifications you desire if working with Excel is comfortable for you. If you don't feel comfortable using Excel, follow QuickBooks's default recommendations. All of this is readily and laterally editable in Excel. If you work with QuickBooks, you should be aware that Excel is an excellent tool for further exploring your data.

To be more precise, I presume that you will be transferring data between QuickBooks and Excel in a few chapters of this book. Consider purchasing Excel and investing the time to become familiar with that potent spreadsheet program if you haven't already done so or if you haven't read those chapters. Remember that you might be able to purchase Microsoft Office together with your PC the next time you buy one. Excel comes with Office.

Hide Header

The report's appearance in the Report window and, if printed, on the page can be altered using the **Hide Header and Collapse buttons.** To get rid of header details like the firm name, click the Hide Header option. You can change the header by clicking the **Hide Header button** once again after hiding it.

Collapse

Report details can be collapsed by using the Collapse button. In a collapsed report in QuickBooks, just accounts are displayed, not subaccounts. Click the **Expand button** to uncollapse a report that you have already collapsed. When the Report window displays a collapsed report, QuickBooks substitutes the **Expand button for the Collapse button.** Don't waste time attempting to understand the functions of the Collapse/Expand and Hide Header buttons. To ask a question, simply select the command button next to the report that you would like more information on. You can see what the command button performs by looking at the changes in the Report window.

Refresh

When changes occur in the QuickBooks data file, the Refresh button instructs QuickBooks to update the report's data accordingly. Although it may seem absurd at first, report windows can be left open. Let's say a profit and loss statement from a week ago appears in a report window. The report's data might not be accurate if you've entered many transactions in the previous week. QuickBooks is aware that it should refresh the report with the most recent modifications when you click the **Refresh button.**

Using the Report window controls

Five controls are available in the Report window: Dates, From, To, Columns, and Sort By. You may also modify the information displayed in the Report window as well as how it looks by checking these boxes. You can choose to display the report on an accrual or cash basis by selecting the Report Basis radio button. To view the data that the report is filtering, click the blue-text; **Show Filters link that appears next to the Report Basis radio button.**

Dates, From, and To

You can instruct QuickBooks as to the reporting interval you would like the report to display using the Dates, from, and To settings. Stated otherwise, you input the month, quarter, year, or any other period for which you wish to generate a report into QuickBooks using these boxes.

Show Columns

A selection of column options is shown via the Show Columns drop-down list. QuickBooks, depending on the period you choose, shows a report with a single total column by default. For example, you can tell QuickBooks that you want to view monthly columns by using the Columns drop-down option when creating a report that summarizes annual income and cost data. In this case, QuickBooks displays an annual income statement along with columns for January, February, March, and so on, giving more information about a certain period, customer, or vendor. The first quarter's profit and loss statement, which includes the months of January, February, and March, is displayed in the window.

Sort By

In a report, you may select the information's order using the Sort By drop-down box. The Sort By drop-down list offers no useful alternatives for many types of reports. However, the Sort By drop-down list offers useful options to arrange report data for different kinds of reports.

Report Basis

This addition lets you quickly switch the report's accrual basis and cash basis. You can tell QuickBooks to create a report on an accrual basis or a cash basis by using the Report Basis option buttons, Accrual and Cash. To be honest, clicking these buttons won't automatically switch between accrual-basis accounting and cash-basis accounting. QuickBooks cannot fully understand accrual-basis accounting or cash-basis accounting on its own. For example, you have to use QuickBooks' Accounts Payable tool and record revenue and expense transactions as soon as you incur expenses and earn money if you employ accrual-basis accounting. However, it's quite useful to be able to easily switch between profit statements that focus on cash and financial statements that resemble accruals thanks to the Report Basis buttons.

Modifying a Report

Any report you create with QuickBooks Desktop can be tailored to your preferences. The data can be altered, columns can be added or removed, information can be changed for the header and footer, and the report's font and style may all be customized. Since each report/group of reports pulls data differently from the company file, available columns and filters vary as well. When screening reports, it's very crucial to understand the source and objectives.

Follow the steps below to customize reports;

- Run a report.
- Choose Custom Report on the report window.

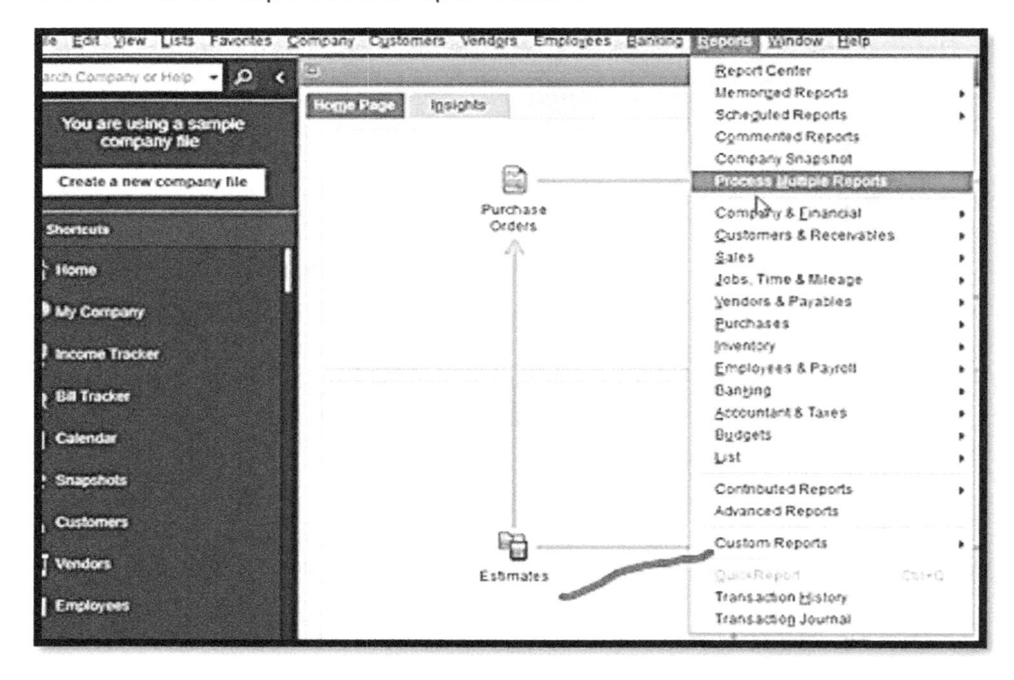

- Locate the **Modify Report window,** navigate to the tab/s you would like to update, and then choose OK when you are through.

Display tab

The information shown in the report is chosen by the Display tab. Depending on the report you run, there are a few elements that you can modify.

Report date range: The dates that the report covers are selectable. You can manually select the date by clicking on the calendar icon in the From and To fields, or you can use the Dates drop-down menu to select from the available date range. You receive data as of the To date if you enter a To date but leave the From date blank.

Report basis: choose either Accrual or Cash to choose the report basis.

Columns: based on the report that is being executed, you will have any of the following choices in this section;

- Display columns by Only the Display columns by drop-down menu, where you may choose how you want the columns to show across the top (by total, by day, by item type, etc.), is available for reports like Profit and Loss and Balance Sheet. On the other hand, the Unpaid Bills Detail Report and the Open Invoices Report include a list that can be used for columns. Custom fields that you have set up and added to your form templates with data will also show up in the column list. Select the data to pick (or remove) a column. You've selected the ones with a checkmark.

- **Sort by**: You can select the sorting method (Default, Total, etc.) for the data display using a sort-by drop-down menu. It establishes the report's subtotal sorting order. Both ascending and descending order sorting are also available.
- **Add subcolumns**: some reports also offer the option to include subcolumns.
- **Advanced**: Depending on the report, different options are available when you pick the Advanced button. The following options are available for reports such as General Ledger, Custom Summary, Custom Transaction Detail, Sales by Customer, Sales by Item, Sales by Rep Detail, Customer Balance Detail, Supplier Balance Detail, and so on:
    - **Include:** this choice informs QuickBooks of the very accounts, items, names, etc. that should be added to the report.
    - **All:** this choice makes a list of all list and account elements.
    - **In Use:** in this choice, just the elements and accounts that have activity in the period chosen are selected.
- **Open Balance/Ageing:** inform QuickBooks of how the effective date of the report shows a transaction's open balance of the effective date.
    - **Current**: displays open balance as of Today, irrespective of the date range of the report.
    - **Report Date**: displays open balances based on the date range that has been chosen for the report.

You can specify which rows and columns to include in the QuickBooks reports for Profit and Loss, Balance Sheet Standard, Statement of Cash Flows, and Customer and Supplier Balance Summary by using the Display Rows and Display Columns feature.

- **Display rows/ Display columns**
    - **Active**: Regardless of balance, include all rows or columns with activity within the chosen date frame.
    - **All:** this contains all the available rows and columns. When this option is chosen it will override the filters.
    - **Non-Zero:** this includes just the rows and columns that have a non-zero balance.
- **Reporting calendar:** By selecting Calendar Year, the balance is shown from January through December. The information you enter in your company's information determines the Fiscal or Income Tax Year.

Filters tab

You can use filters to restrict report data to particular criteria. This is especially crucial if you want to tailor the report to your requirements or identify the root cause of a problem while troubleshooting.

To get a report filtered;

- Choose **the desired filter from the Filter list.**
- Select or provide any additional data that QuickBooks need for the filter to function properly on the Filter Detail Information screen.
- (Details optional) Select **the filter** you wish to remove by highlighting it in the current filter choices column, then click **Remove Selected Filter.**
- Click **OK.**

Note

- QuickBooks provides a synopsis of a chosen filter. Click **Tell Me More...** to get more information about the filter.
- When customizing a report, choose the class that is linked to all classes if you see two classes on the filters.

Header/Footer tab

You can change the data that is displayed at the top and bottom of the report using this tab. The text that appears above the report data is known as the header information. The text that shows up beneath the report data is called the footer. Only a print preview or a printed copy of the report contains footer content. If you would want to add or remove information, check or uncheck the corresponding item. To update the data, use the field that is supplied. Use the Alignment drop-down menu to adjust the alignment.

Font & Numbers tab

You can alter a report's appearance and style on this tab. The typeface, font size, and font style can all be changed for specific sections of the report.

To change the font:

- Choose the desired region to modify from the Change Font For column.
- Choose **Change Font**
- Modify the font's Font, Font Style, Size, Effect, and Color in the Column Labels window.
- Click **OK**.
- When asked to apply the modifications you made to every label, click **Yes**.

Titles must not exceed 57 characters. The date range is no longer visible, but you can still add characters to the subtitle. To view details about the base report that was used to create a customized report, navigate to the Help menu and choose QuickBooks Desktop Help.

Collapse Columns

You can collapse report columns about jobs or classes in QuickBooks Desktop. This eliminates the need for you to export your report to Excel or browse through a lot of text to view totals per task or class.

- Click **the** - to the left of the columns you wish to collapse to collapse just one job or class.
- Select **Collapse Columns** from the report menu bar to collapse all jobs or courses.
- Click **the plus symbol (+) or Expand Columns** to view every information once again.

Note: Only when sub-jobs or sub-classes are in use is this feature usable.

Processing Multiple Reports

The Process Multiple Reports dialog box appears in QuickBooks when you select the **Reports > Process Multiple Reports option.**

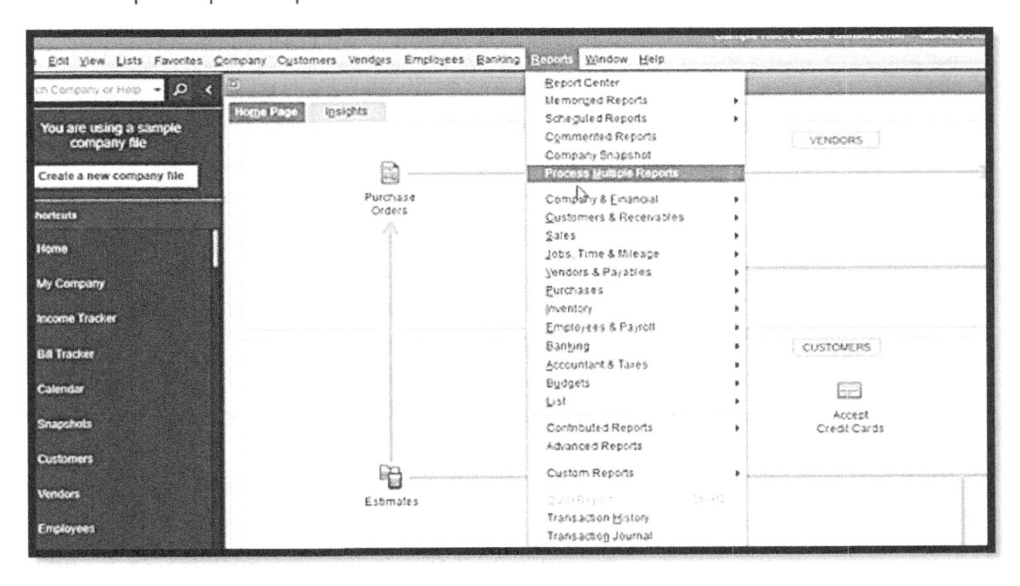

You can request many reports that you have previously commented on or memorized at once using this dialog box. Select a report group from the drop-down list at the top of the dialog box before using it. Next, pick the reports you want from the report group and mark them as completed on the list. If a report that QuickBooks displays as selected (shown by a check mark) and you would like it removed, click the check mark. Next, confirm that the From and To boxes for the reports you have chosen accurately display the report interval. You can choose the Display button to have QuickBooks show the report windows for each of the reports you've chosen once you've chosen the reports and entered the report interval dates. As an alternative, you can click the **Print option** to request that QuickBooks print copies of each of the reports you've chosen on paper.

A Few Words about Document Retention

Below are a few things you can think about when it has to do with keeping documents as an accountant;

- Consider whether the other party to a transaction is ever going to want the information. It makes sense to hold onto vendor bills and any documentation of your payment for as long as the dispute may persist, for example, if you and the vendor are having frequent arguments over whether or not you have paid a bill. This implies that, if there is no issue, you are not required to keep any records of vendor invoices and payments.
- Consider tax accounting requirements. Many people are unaware that businesses must keep accounting records to report their income, deductions, profits, and losses to the Internal Revenue Service. Therefore, you should keep all documentation necessary to compute your profits or support certain aspects of your calculations. However, there is a statute of limitations that usually lasts for three years from the date you last filed the return. This implies that, for the most part, documents related to returns that are more than three years old don't need to be kept on file. Putting this another way, if your 2019 tax return was submitted on March 15, 2020, and you have data from that year, you shouldn't (generally) need to retain all of that old documentation by March 16, 2023. It should be possible for you to get rid of the older material because of the statute of limitations. **However, there are a few exceptions to this three-year statute of limitations, so proceed with caution:**
    - Six years is the statute of limitations if you were extremely careless and, as a result, omitted gross income exceeding twenty-five percent of what your return indicates.
    - There is no statute of limitations if a fraudulent return is filed or if no return is filed at all.
    - States without income taxes—like the state of Washington, where a lot of people work and live—have distinct laws and may have lengthier statutes of limitations. For instance, Washington state states that the statute of limitations is four years rather than three.
- Think about the old documents you could use later on to figure out a tax return item. It is necessary to keep these records. For instance, if you purchased a factory thirty years ago, hold onto your purchase documentation for three or six years following the factory's sale.
- Remember that there may be additional document-retention laws or restrictions in place in particular businesses. Physicians are required to retain their previous patient records, which may contain patient accounting data, for some time greater than three

years. The remaining document-retention guidelines differ by industry. Find out the regulations that apply to your sector.

- Think about the dangers of keeping private information around for too long. Lastly, keep in mind that there are hazards associated with this strategy even if you consider all the previously mentioned factors and decide that you should save your financial data forever. In certain situations, it may be easier for financial documents to be misplaced or stolen the more you archive. For example, you wouldn't want to retain so much data over several years that you have to hire a warehouse in a seedy area of town merely to store it.

Activity

1. Produce and modify a report.
2. Process multiple reports.
3. What is document retention?

CHAPTER 3
PREPARING A BUDGET

Budgets give managers and business owner's effective tools for running their companies. The owner or manager of the company can more easily and quantitatively manage the employees with the use of a budget. Often, a budget can see issues or possibilities early on. Ultimately, a budget provides the management or owner with a means to plan the year's operations, prioritize tasks, and put a number on what the company should accomplish.

Reviewing Common Budget Tactics

It's ideal to understand how to quickly identify and explain three extremely helpful and popular budgeting strategies: top-line budgeting, zero-based budgeting, and benchmarking, before diving into a full discussion of how to establish a budget and use that budget within QuickBooks. These three strategies are not difficult at all. At least two of these you most likely already know about and comprehend. All these strategies, though, must be taken into account when creating official or informal business budgets.

Top-line budgeting

The most basic budgeting method, known as a top-line budget, uses the figures from the previous year or month to create the budget for the current year. Naturally, a top-line budget may use an inflation factor to inflate the numbers from the previous year or month if inflation has happened. On the other hand, if the company has had a slowdown or bad circumstances, the figures from the prior year or month may have dropped somewhat.

Top-line budgeting provides at least a few benefits, despite the negative reputation it frequently gets from those who dislike the way it maintains the status quo:

- **Top-line budgeting is easy**. One of its main advantages is that it is simple. Some budgeting strategies may require a lot more effort.
- **Top-line budgeting is based on reality.** The figures from the previous month or year are accurate. This is a special advantage of top-line budgeting that is not provided by other budgeting strategies (which will be discussed in the paragraphs that follow). Thinking about what you'll spend this month can be greatly aided by knowing the reality of the true, actual amount you spent, say, $2,000 on rent last month.

However, top-line budgeting has a well-known flaw in that it frequently reinforces prior poor budgetary choices. For example, even though it no longer makes sense (or never made sense), top-line budgeting may continue to budget the $10,000 yearly expense for an advertisement in a special industry journal if someone determined long ago to spend that amount.

Zero-based budgeting

The reverse of top-line budgeting, known as zero-based budgeting, operates from the bottom up. Individual income, spending, asset, liability, and owner's equity accounts are the first to be included in a zero-based budget. It looks at a certain account, like postage expense, and then tries to use logic and common sense to determine a reasonable budget amount for mail expense. For instance, the budgetary estimate might predict that the company will mail 1,000 letters a year, with an average postal cost of 50 cents per letter. In this instance, the zero-based budgeting technique estimates the estimated $500 postage expense for the upcoming year. This sum is determined by multiplying 1,000 letters by the postage cost of 50 cents for each letter, as determined by the zero-based budget. Zero-based budgeting has the advantage of tending to correct previously planned sums that were not accurately calculated; it does not just repeat prior budgetary errors. New budgeted amounts are determined by applying basic mathematics and common sense, which frequently yields very accurate results. That is just amazing.

Making those who utilize or benefit from a budgeted amount accountable for it is another clever component of zero-based budgeting. According to top-line budgeting, a manager who incurred $50,000 in travel expenses the previous year is eligible to spend $50,000 this year. In contrast, zero-line budgeting requires the manager to demonstrate that $50,000 in travel expenses is appropriate for this year by using basic math and common sense. Though it has a drawback, zero-based budgeting isn't flawless; budgeters often forget numbers or perform calculations incorrectly. In the example of a budgeter who estimates that $500 will be spent on postage in the upcoming year., this estimate is based on an approximation of the annual letter-sending volume (1,000) and the typical letter postage cost (50 cents). The postage-expense budget figure is off if one of those figures is off, or if—heaven forbid—the budgeter multiplies one figure by the other improperly. The budgeter will surely make a few mistakes if they are budgeting hundreds or even thousands of budgeted amounts.

Benchmarking

Benchmarking is a very effective, but sadly rarely applied, strategy that involves comparing your actual or preliminary budgeted data with those of companies in your industry that are of a comparable size. For example, CPA firms invest money in a tax library. A tax library's annual fees might range from as little as $100 or $200 to as much as $10,000. (Note that these sums represent fees for a lone entrepreneur.) How do you determine the right amount to budget for? You can probably budget what you should or can spend on a tax library if you know what other CPA firms or sole proprietor CPAs are spending on it. Of course, obtaining that comparative data is the difficult part. Fortunately, more people understand how simple it is to obtain this information.

Two sources are available to you for information regarding comparable firms' financial statistics:

- **Your local library**: Generally speaking, there are several reliable sources available that provide general financial statistics regarding companies in different industries and sizes. Annual summaries of financial information and ratios are published by Dun & Bradstreet, the Risk Management Association, Robert Morris & Associates, and a fellow by the name of Leo Troy. These summaries are based on multiple sources. You can ask the librarian for assistance in finding one or more of these reference sources if you head over to the library and stop by the reference desk. All of a sudden, you have access to a multitude of knowledge. For example, you can see how much the typical bar spends on peanuts and beer. The amount that the typical restaurant spends on advertising is shown. Stated differently, you have access to comprehensive financial data about a company that is identical to yours.
- **Industry associations:** Numerous professional associations and industry associations gather and disseminate industry-specific financial data in addition to the broad information found in reference materials frequently kept on hand at your local library.

Taking a Practical Approach to Budgeting

Regretfully, business budgeting entails more than just putting projected income and expenses on paper. Usually, a balance sheet is also made. Budgeting with a balance sheet is too complex to be completed on the back of a cocktail napkin or in the early hours before the kids get up. You can budget in a really basic and unrefined way if all you want to do is track revenue and cost figures. For example, you could write the predicted income figures for each account on the back of a cocktail napkin.

Using the Set up Budgets Window

You can plan and make informed company decisions with the aid of forecasting and budgeting features found in QuickBooks Desktop.

Review last year's data

Ensure that your fiscal year has been selected correctly before creating a budget or projection.

- Select **My Company from the Company menu.**
- After choosing the pencil icon, click **Report Information.**
- Verify that the first month of your accounting year is the right one.

Next, go over the financial reports from the previous fiscal year.

- Hover your mouse over **Company & Financial and go to the Reports menu.**
- Based on what you want to budget or forecast, **choose either Profit & Loss Detail or Balance Sheet Detail.**
- Click on the **Dates option and choose Last Fiscal Year.**

- Click on **Refresh.**
- (Preferable) You can save this report so you can memorize it for later use.

Set up a budget or forecast

You now own reports that you can utilize to create a prediction or a budget. Alternatively, you can start a budget for the following year using the Profit and Loss information from the previous year.

- Hover your cursor over **Planning & Budgeting on the Company menu. Choose Set Up Budgets after that.**

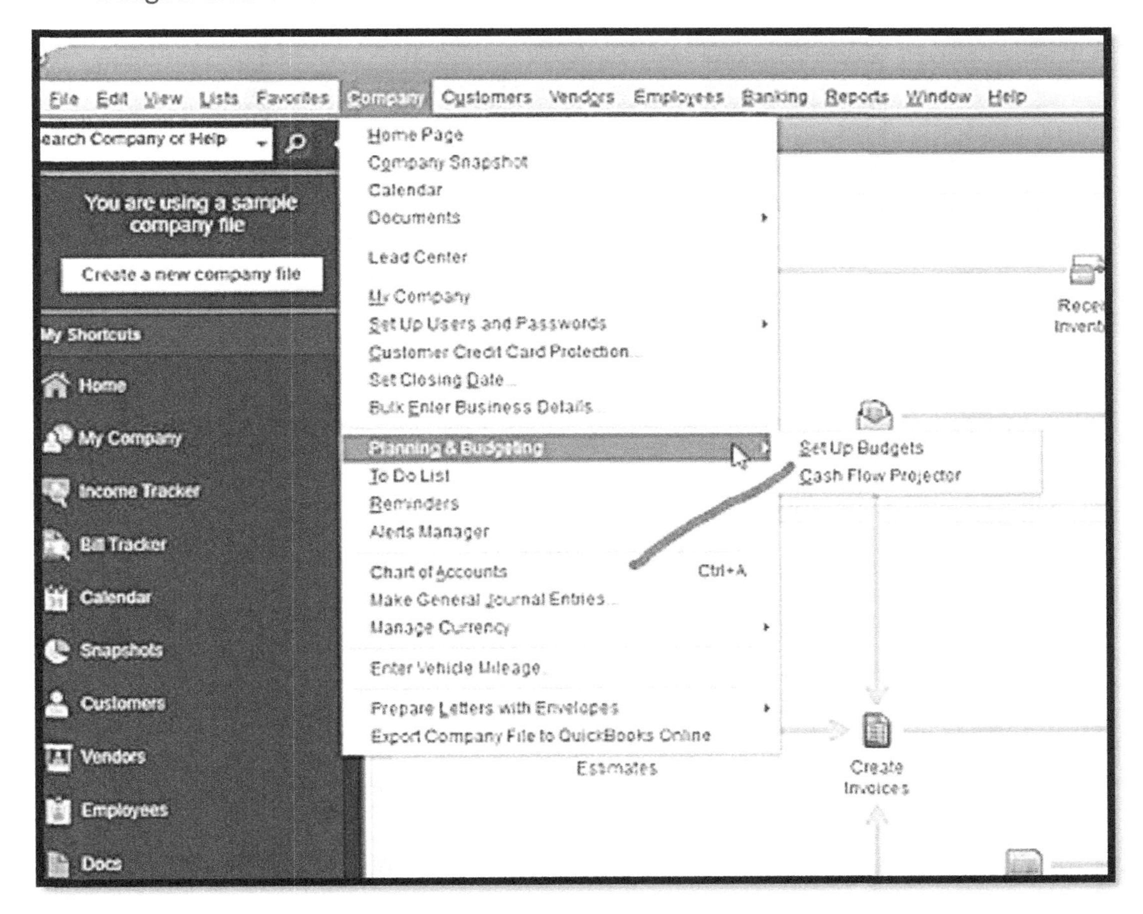

- Choose to **Create a New Budget.**

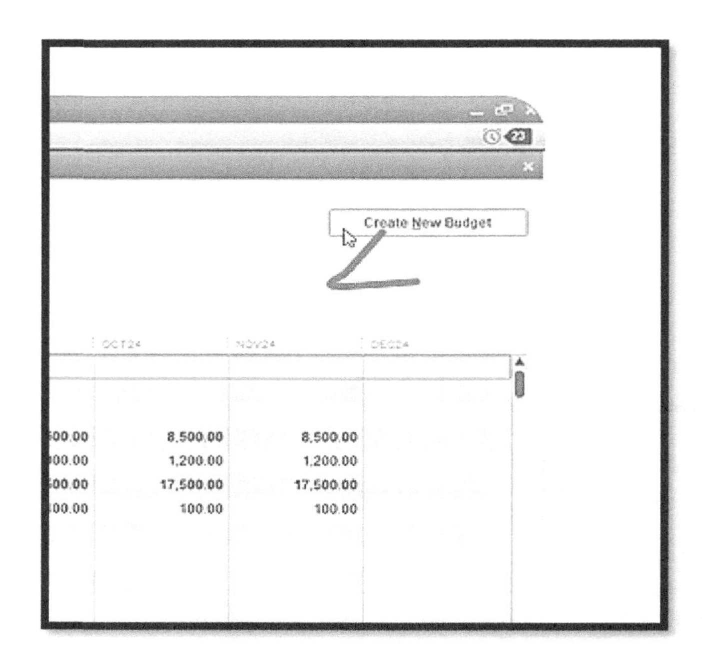

- Select the **Balance Sheet or Profit and Loss** after setting the budget's fiscal year. You have the option to add more criteria, such as Jobs or Class monitoring if you choose **Profit and Loss.**

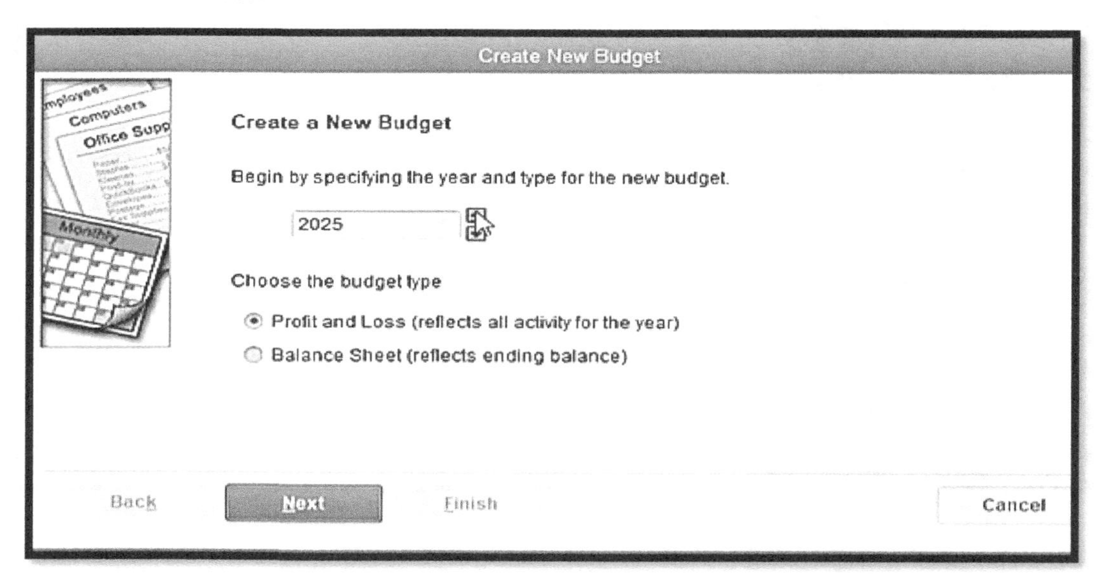

- Choose between creating a budget from scratch or using the existing data from the previous year if you choose Profit and Loss.
- Choose **"Finish."**

Create a forecast

You can also make projections to project future income and cash flow if you use QuickBooks Desktop Premier, Accountant, or Enterprise. A financial projection can be made from scratch or using information from the previous year.

- Hover your cursor over **Planning & Budgeting on the Company menu. Choose Set Up Forecast after that.**
- Click on **Create New Forecast.**
- For the forecast, select the fiscal year. It is optional for you to provide other criteria, such as Jobs or Class monitoring.
- Either creating a forecast from scratch or creating a forecast using actual data from the previous year should be selected.
- Choose **"Finish."**

Edit an existing budget

Follow the steps below to have an existing budget modified;

- Click on **Company > Planning & Budgeting > Set Up Budgets**. This opens the Set Up Budgets window in QuickBooks. During the year you are budgeting for, you utilize this window to enter the amount you anticipate for each month's revenue and expenses.
- Choose a **budget or create a new one**. Select the desired budget from the Budget drop-down menu located at the window's top. Choose the **Create New Budget button** to begin creating a new budget (you are allowed to have as many as you like).
- (Optional) Select a customer. Usually, you allocate money to accounts. You can utilize the Current Customer: Job drop-down list to identify individual customers from whom you expect revenue or for whom you incur costs if you wish to budget more precisely by including predicting amounts for jobs, classes, or customers.
- Make a record of the budgeted amounts for each month of the fiscal year. In the corresponding month columns, enter the budgeted amounts for each account. Remind yourself that the monthly expected amount is budgeted for the revenue and expense accounts. The quantity of assets, liabilities, and owner's equity is budgeted as the anticipated month-end account balance.
- Click the **Copy across button** to transfer the monthly budget into the text boxes for the following months.
- (Optional) Adjust row amounts. If the annual sum for an account turns out to be less than your expectations, you have two options: either use the Adjust Row Amounts button or go back and adjust each month's amounts to get the total up to your desired amount. The dialog box labeled Adjust Row Amounts appears when you click this button. Select the month you wish to begin with (either the first month or the month that is currently selected) using the **Start At** drop-down list. Next, enter a dollar number

or a percentage to indicate how much you wish to increase or decrease the amounts budgeted. When you're done, click **OK** to have QuickBooks exit the dialog box.

Managing with a Budget

Once your budget has been entered into QuickBooks, you can use the Budgets & Forecasts section to compare your actual and budgeted numbers by selecting commands. QuickBooks offers several budgeting reports that are detailed in the list below when you select the **Reports > Budgets & Forecasts command**

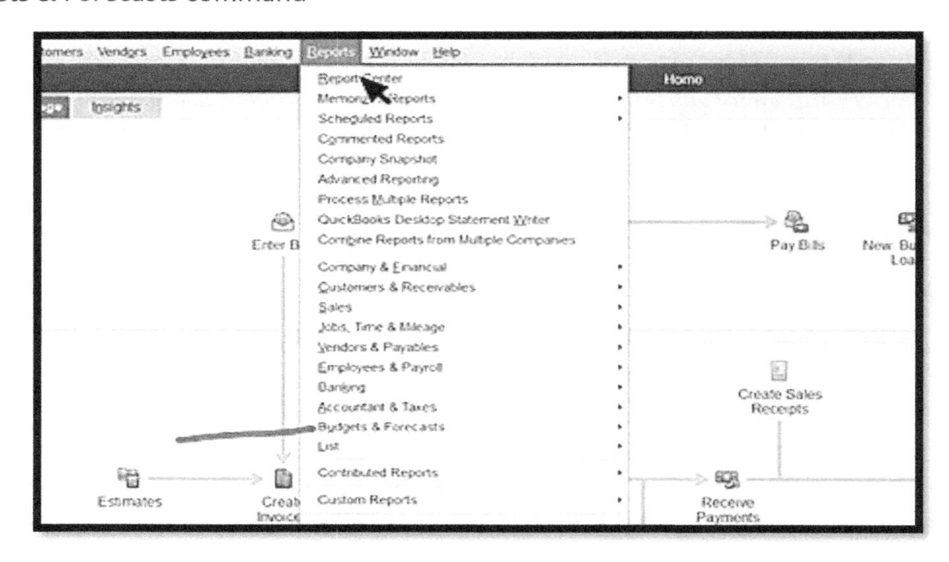

- **Budget Overview**: The sums you budgeted are compiled in this report. It can be used to review and double-check your budget.
- **Budget vs. Actual:** You can compare the information on the budgeted and actual income statements with this report. You may thus compare your anticipated and actual revenue and expenses using the report.
- **Profit & Loss Budget Performance**: You can compare your actual revenue, costs, and profits to your planned revenue, costs, and profits with this report.
- **Budget vs. Actual Graph**: This graph is a chart that displays actual and budgeted data; it is not a report.
- **Forecast Overview**: A QuickBooks projection is summarized in this report. In essence, a forecast is an estimate of your expected future cash flow and revenue. Forecasts are used in "what if" scenarios.
- **Forecast vs. Actual**: In this report, actual events are compared with a forecast.

Getting the most out of your budgeting efforts depends on how you use the information in budgeting reports. You can search for differences between your budget and your actual financial outcomes if you have a well-crafted, sensible budget. Utilizing your budget will help you identify instances when, for instance, an asset item is too high, an expense item is too low, or a revenue figure is falling short of your projections. Unexpected findings are shown by differences between expected and actual results. Unexpected outcomes frequently point to issues or opportunities. **Consider the variances in the following cases and any conclusions that can be drawn from them:**

- **Monthly revenue is $40,000 instead of & $50,000**: Twenty percent less monthly revenue than anticipated could be a sign of issues with your product, your sales team, or your customers. Either way, you should probably take quick corrective action if sales are under 80% of your expectations.
- **Inventory balances are averaging $50,000 at month's end rather than $100,000 at month's end**: A lower-than-expected inventory balance might be advantageous or disadvantageous. If your closing inventory balance is less than half of what you anticipated, it could mean that you're selling things considerably faster than you anticipated. In this case, you should buy more inventories and boost your inventory investment. However, a low inventory investment could also indicate that you're just not receiving supplies from your suppliers quickly enough, which puts you at serious risk of losing sales due to insufficient stock levels.
- **Research and development expenses equal $50,000 a year instead of $25,000 a year:** Double your expected costs for research and development seems like a bad idea. Spending twice as much as you anticipate on an expense can't be good, right? However, it can be a good idea to double your research and development spending if you find yourself investing in some unexpectedly intriguing new idea, technology, or product.
- **Sales to a particular class of customer are 50 percent higher**: Let's say you tracked sales to clients both domestically and internationally using classes. Sales to clients outside the nation may represent a chance to expand internationally if you discover, perhaps surprisingly, that they are 50% higher than anticipated. Perhaps if you put in more time and effort, clients from outside the nation could contribute even more to your company. Variances might occasionally point out chances that you might otherwise overlook.

Some Wrap-Up Comments on Budgeting

Below are very simple take-home tips about the subject of budgeting;

- One use of the proverb "Plan your work and then work your plan" is what budgeting is all about. Money limits aren't shackles. Budgets are not a prison. Simply said, budgets are planning instruments that help you decide wisely about the financial matters of your company for the upcoming year.
- You shouldn't engage in budgeting if it isn't beneficial to you. Alternatively, you ought to modify your current approach. I won't dispute that budgeting is a good idea if it

doesn't yield any benefits. Nonetheless, I believe that most organizations do receive value. I don't think you should budget if you can run your company without one - I provide a tip after the chapter that works well for this. When managing your business, you make use of the tools that offer the most value to you. That's what budgeting does for a lot of folks. Don't do the work if it doesn't work for you.

- When it comes to overseeing individuals who have measurable financial obligations, budgets can be quite useful. Alright, I realize that budgets aren't flawless and that they receive a terrible rap, but guess what? You can use a budget to manage employees who have financial obligations that you can measure for yourself. Let's say you have salesmen who are expected to bring in $25,000 in sales each month. You can use a budget to compare actual sales generated by each individual with the planned sales expected for them, provided that you budget per salesperson (you will likely need to set up a class or revenue account for each salesperson).
- I've found that people who enjoy budgeting usually concentrate on negative deviations. I bring up this example because, while unfavorable variations frequently point out issues that require correction, good deviations are occasionally more fascinating and insightful to examine. Let's say you own a business and you want your salespeople to bring in $25,000 a month. Ade's sales figures of $75,000 each month are quite intriguing. Monique most likely possesses knowledge, abilities, or a method that the other salespeople lack. If you're lucky, you might be able to determine why Ade performs so effectively. You could then utilize this newfound understanding to motivate your other salesmen to close more deals each month.
- Usually, there is a modest collection of important budgeting metrics to keep an eye on. You could be able to operate your business just fine by looking at only a few figures, even if a budget according to QuickBooks may include hundreds of numbers. Perhaps in your company, sales are the most important thing. You might not have much incentive to monitor how much you pay for your phone bill or postage each month if sales drive all other factors in your business, including expenses and earnings. Your budgeting and financial analysis will be a lot easier if you can reduce your financial plan to a few numbers that you need to keep an eye on.

Activity

1. Briefly highlight common budgeting tactics.
2. Set up budgets using the budgets window.
3. How can you manage with a budget?

CHAPTER 4
USING ACTIVITY-BASED COSTING

It can be said that the greatest innovation in accounting during the last thirty years is activity-based costing. This is crucial because, contrary to popular belief, ABC provides businesses with an improved method of estimating the earnings of goods and services. Many firms struggle with the issue of running or overhead costs that aren't directly related to their goods or services. Businesses are unable to decide which goods are profitable and which are not without a proper distribution of overhead and operational expenses. ABC uses the capabilities of the computer (QuickBooks, in this case) to directly link overhead expenses to goods and services to solve this issue. Interestingly, ABC completes this duty in a quite direct and uncomplicated manner.

Reviewing Traditional Overhead Allocation

Prices for products must be set by businesses so that they may turn a profit and pay for all direct and indirect costs. Either activity-based costing or traditional costing is the two costing systems that might influence pricing decisions, which are based on a variety of factors. Finding the right costing system for your business or client will be made easier if you can pinpoint your unique requirements and limits. Allocating overhead (or indirect) production costs is the foundation of the traditional costing system, an accounting technique used to calculate the cost of producing goods to turn a profit. This method works by applying predefined overhead rates to a given measure after they have been calculated. Estimated overhead rates are used in traditional costing techniques for a given cost driver. **A cost-generating component of the manufacturing process is something like this:**

- Managerial expenses
- Packaging
- Machine hours
- Machine setups
- Quantity of materials required
- Cleaning and maintenance

How to make use of the traditional costing method with a worked example

Follow the steps below to calculate costs with the use of the traditional costing method;

- **Identify overhead costs:** Production expenses known as overhead are those that do not directly affect the final product. Both manufacturing and non-manufacturing costs may be included. Let's take fresh for Fido, a tiny business that offers organic dog food, as an example. The business occupies a small factory. The company's overhead expenses comprise the salaries of maintenance personnel, cleaning supplies, and factory utilities.

- **Estimate the overhead costs for a specific period:** These expenses can be projected for a month, a quarter, or a year. In the same case, the proprietors of Fresh for Fido project that their annual overhead costs will be $30,000.
- **Choose a cost driver to use in your calculations:** When it comes to highly automated production, the cost driver should be closely related to machine hours.
  Fresh for Fido chooses labor hours as its cost driver since the company mixes and prepares its dog food by hand.
- **Estimate the figure for the cost driver:** The time frame you select for the calculation of overhead expenses and the expected term for the cost driver should coincide.
  Let's go back to the example: Eight workers at Fresh for Fido put in 40 hours a week for 40 weeks a year. This comes to 12,800 work hours annually.
- **Calculate the predetermined overhead rate**: Your estimates form the basis of the predefined overhead rate. Divide the projected overhead costs by the estimated amount or quantity of the cost driver to find the rate.
  The following computation is used by Fresh for Fido in our case to compute the predetermined overhead rate:
  Predetermined overhead rate = estimated overhead cost/cost driver amount
  Predetermined overhead rate = $30,000 / 12,800 labor hours = 2.34
- To calculate the projected overhead costs for the product, multiply the selected measure by the fixed overhead rate. The projected overhead costs for Fresh for Fido can be computed using the specified overhead rate of 2.34. For example, we may calculate the total overhead expenses for each pound of dog food if the work required is two hours per pound. Overhead costs per pound of dog food = 2 hours of labor per pound of dog food x $2.34 per hour = $4.68. For the specified period, this amount represents an estimated $4.68 in overhead costs per pound of dog food. Assume for the moment that the direct costs for a pound of dog food are $0.80. You can add $0.80 to $4.68 to get $5.48, which is the estimated total cost to create one pound of dog food. The entire cost, if Fresh for Fido is charging $10 for a bag of dog food, is $54.80. Fresh for Fido makes an estimated profit of $5.20 for each bag when selling its 10-pound bag for $60. The company will turn a profit of $26,000 if it sells 5,000 bags of dog food annually.

Differences between traditional costing and activity-based costing?

Both activity-based costing (ABC) and traditional costing identify how much overhead should go toward a particular product. Every approach, though, has unique benefits and drawbacks.

The following are the ways that ABC and conventional costing are different:

Calculations

The primary distinction between traditional costing and activity-based costing is the considerations you make when assigning costs to products. In traditional costing, the predicted overhead costs are computed using a single cost driver and the predetermined overhead rate. All overhead expenses are combined into a single, approximate cost that is applied uniformly to every product. All cost drivers involved in producing a product or goods are taken into account by activity-based costing. Included in this are non-manufacturing expenses like facility upkeep. Additionally, activity-based costing more accurately divides overhead expenses among goods. It makes a distinction, for instance, between goods that take three machine hours to produce and goods that take just one machine hour. In this manner, the expenses can be divided into suitable amounts for every product. The labor hours are the sole cost driver required by the typical costing method in the Fresh for Fido example. The business will make use of each of the determined cost drivers if it decides to employ activity-based costing instead.

Time

Since it involves fewer variables than activity-based costing, traditional costing allows for faster cost estimation. To get the required estimations, ABC is frequently complicated and time-consuming, needing participation from multiple departments.

Accuracy

Traditional costing is less accurate than activity-based costing because it requires less specific information. When it comes to costing, ABC is more comprehensive and can offer more insight into business expenses like facility costs, which can assist managers in finding areas where costs can be cut.

Expense

Certain activity-based costing computations could get so complicated that you have to utilize pricey specialized software to complete them. Managers and accountants must also put in a lot of work to accomplish ABC. Traditional costing is less complicated and so involves less labor and input, which lowers its cost.

Understanding How ABC Works

An accounting method called activity-based costing (ABC) seeks to make clear precisely where and how a business generates profit. ABC allocates expenses to every resource required to complete a certain business task. Indirect ("soft") operating costs are also taken into consideration. As a result, a more complete financial picture is obtained than is typically the case with conventional accounting techniques (like standard costing), and a helpful differentiation between value-adding and non-value-adding operations is made. ABC proponents utilize it to guide strategy for a wide range of topics, including capital investment, price, product mix, organizational change, and product mix. They also utilize it to assist in identifying and managing expenses, boost productivity, and boost earnings. Activity-based management, or ABM, is another name for ABC, which is becoming increasingly popular as a useful tool for evaluating an organization's overall performance and guiding its long-term strategy when implemented properly. In the 1980s, ABC gained notoriety as businesses attempted to reduce expenses while simultaneously enhancing their offerings. Their outstanding outcomes have led to ABC's rising popularity, especially in the manufacturing industries.

What is involved with ABC?

An ABC costing involves the following five fundamental steps:

- Identify the product or service
- Identify every resource and process needed to make the product or service, and work out the cost of each
- Remember to include "cost drivers" for each resource and process
- Gather information such as the time taken up by each process or resource, as well as cost data
- Use all the information and data to work out the total cost of products and services.

ABC is incredibly adaptable. The majority of activities, including company operations, service delivery, and industrial processes, can be accessed with it. It also produces a more comprehensive picture since it considers a far larger variety of parameters than other costing approaches. ABC can take a long time because it requires gathering a lot of data. Additionally, there's a chance that managers will become so engrossed in monitoring expenses that they lose focus on the task at hand. Businesses have successfully employed ABC to calculate the relative expenses of electronic vs. more conventional means of managing transactions to demonstrate the financial benefits of e-commerce. Banks, for instance, utilized it to verify that ATMs save money and offer consumers a service they desire. Another illustration would be publishers weighing the advantages and disadvantages of publications published online versus on paper. Companies that provide advisory or legal services can use ABC to verify their charge-out expenses, which helps them determine their actual profit margin more precisely. For example, healthcare providers have utilized ABC very successfully to assess profits, justify expenses, and prepare for change. A medical practice will find it much easier to determine how much to charge for services if it is aware of the true cost of each component. In this instance, specific doctors could be considered cost centers. If expenses can be linked to a particular service, they are assigned to the doctor who makes money or spends money on that service. It is possible to distribute fixed overheads and indirect costs proportionately or evenly among cost centers.

Identifying under- or over-staffed operations within an organization is one of ABC's special benefits. Such analysis is especially helpful to knowledge-based enterprises, whose human expenditures are always their highest; the more efficiently a staff member is deployed, the more likely the business is to make a profit. Lastly, ABC analysis can help establish important performance benchmarks for an organization or even help a business assess how much its internal processes and procedures cost in comparison to industry averages.

Implementing a Simple ABC System

ABC can be intricately designed. Moreover, you can wind up with something quite powerful and extremely complex if you go out and hire an outside consultant — someone who wants to charge you thousands or even tens of thousands of dollars to set up one of these systems. Nevertheless, ABC systems don't have to be that difficult, especially if all you want is improved overhead cost allocation rather than a system that looks at the activities or cost drivers that go into your overhead expenses. ABC is usually rather simple, particularly in a small or medium-sized business.

Overhead costs

Make sure you have sufficient overhead to be concerned about. ABC could not make sense for you if your company has extremely minimal overhead and large profit margins. Rather than being the result of sound accounting, the incremental value you obtains by more accurately allocating overhead can just be the result of an OCD.

Identify the big overhead cost

If you choose to use an ABC strategy to allocate some or all of your overhead, you must take this action. If the penny-ante amounts are easy to assign and can be completed concurrently with the larger project, don't waste time attempting to assign them precisely. Seek out the greatest value for your money. Make an ABC system that distributes a significant portion of your overhead with little work on your part. Don't become overly formal.

Note the principal activities that use up the overhead costs

You only have one task to complete in the straightforward example of the made-up hot-dog stand: serving customers. There will undoubtedly be more activities for you than that. However, it's not necessary to compile a list of 80 tasks. Determine the major tasks that allow you to distribute your overhead. Your accounting will be easier the fewer activities you need to do this. Identify a small number of tasks that enable you to precisely and fairly assign overhead to product lines. It is the whole picture.

Track the activities of products with the use of the appropriate measures

Make sure to utilize the appropriate measure, sometimes referred to as a cost driver, to tie the overhead expenses to the product lines or service lines after you've identified the few activities that allow you to link them to items. You can use an ABC system as a tool to control the profitability of your sold goods and services as well as your overhead expenses. Ultimately, what you need is an ABC system that generates meaningful data, which will enable you to think more creatively and practically about your organization. From a practical standpoint, you should concentrate on the large overhead expenses.

Seeing How QuickBooks Supports ABC

This is all you have to do to set up a basic ABC system in QuickBooks at this moment. Put another way; simply continue to use a strong, respectable chart of accounts to track your running expenses. That makes up 90% of all you need to do.

There will also be a need for you to take care of one or two minor additional items;

- Turn on the QuickBooks Class Tracking feature. You can group revenue and expense transactions into specific classes in addition to income and expense accounts by using class tracking.
- When you record an expense, note the class into which the expense falls.

Turning on Class Tracking

The word "class tracking" may be unfamiliar to many QuickBooks users. So, before diving right into the setup procedure, it is best to give you a quick overview of this word. Essentially, class tracking enables you to monitor account balances by department, business office or location, distinct properties, or any other significant business segment. Additionally, it enables you to monitor specific portions that you wish to pay particular attention to. You may quickly establish classes in QuickBooks that are linked to the transactions. This enables you to monitor the account balance by department, company office or location, individual user properties, etc.

Businesses with several departments can benefit greatly from this functionality, which makes it easier for them to use classes to report account balances for each department. Although class tracking may initially seem like a laborious task, it ultimately pays dividends. Users can see how their money is being spent and receive an incredible overview of the company's spending, which finally makes budget management simple. Now that you are familiar with class tracking and its extensive array of advantages, you can get started on setting it up on QuickBooks desktop. Make sure you pay close attention to the instructions and carry them out carefully.

Before looking at the individual stages for enabling class tracking, there are a few things to keep in mind:

- The withholding tax account and item only need to be set up once. Using the current withholding tax item would suffice the next time you want to charge off withholding tax.
- Create classes according to the kind of reporting you want to do and take into account how you want to view the business segments on reports.
- Finally, create a class called "other" to categorize transactions that fall outside of any certain category.

Follow the steps below to switch on class tracking;

- Opening the company file should be done first.
- Next, select the preferences option from the edit menu.
- Selecting accounting is the next step, after which you go to the page for company options.
- After completing that, make sure to check the box for using class tracking for transactions.
- Additionally, selecting the prompt to assign classes checkbox is advised if you need a reminder at the moment if you forgot to assign a class.
- To finish, select the **OK tab.**

Using Classes for ABC

Using classes is simple once class tracking is enabled. For the product or service lines that you wish to track profitability for, you create classes. If you can, you categorize transactions as belonging to a specific class at the time they occur, or later on if you need to adjust the activity and cost driver calculations.

Setting up your classes

For every good or service you wish to track profitability for, you create a class. Simply type the name of the class into the box that displays in the window where you record invoices, create checks, and enter journal entries to set up a class.

- You may also select **Lists > Class List as an alternative**. Click the **Class button** at the bottom of the window when QuickBooks opens the Class List window, then select New from the menu that appears. To describe the new class, use the **New Class dialog box that displays.**

Classifying revenue amounts

Use the Class box that shows up in the Create Invoices and Enter Sales Receipt windows to categorize revenue as falling into a specific class. (You enter sales information in these two windows.)

Classifying expense amounts

In addition, you can utilize the Class column to determine which product line or service the expense falls under to write a check that covers an expense that is related to a specific activity.

Activity

1. How does ABC work?
2. Implement a simple ABC system
3. Use classes for ABC

CHAPTER 5
SETTING UP PROJECT AND JOB COSTING SYSTEMS

Numerous companies work on tasks or projects. For example, one approach to conceptualizing a home builder's company is a sequence of construction projects. Books, brochures, and posters can be printed for clients by a manufacturer, like a commercial printer. Every single one of those things stands for tasks completed for particular clients. Accounting procedures may operate somewhat differently when a company divides its workload into jobs or projects. A company may occasionally need to manage income and expenses by jobs or projects in addition to using a normal chart of accounts. Thankfully, job costing, also known as project costing, is simple with QuickBooks.

Setting Up a QuickBooks Job

Choose the **Customers >Customer Center command** to configure a QuickBooks job. The window for the Customer Center appears in QuickBooks. Right-click on the consumer and select the Add work menu command from the shortcut menu to set up a work for that specific customer. QuickBooks opens the New Job window when you do this. Give the work or project a name using the work Name box before setting it up for a customer. For instance, a home builder can use the house's address as the job. (Maybe the street address will do.) You may determine the job status and type using the drop-down lists on the Job Info tab of the New Job. You can also input the job start date, estimated end date, and actual end date using the text boxes on this tab. You can also tick the Job Is Inactive checkbox if a job is no longer active and you would like it to no longer show up in the list in the Customer Center window.

Tracking Job or Project Costs

Tracking costs associated with a job and contrasting them with income is known as job costing. The job costing tools in QuickBooks Desktop allow you to see the costs and revenues associated with each job. The methods listed below will help you ensure that your job costs are accurately documented.

Set up a Customer: Job for each of your jobs

Establish a separate job specifically for each customer, even if you only have one for them. This makes it possible for you to monitor your earnings and outlays for each project separately and can make bookkeeping easier if you take on additional work for that client down the road.

Get all of your expenses assigned to jobs

Assigning all of your costs to jobs will allow you to see the whole cost picture of the job. Every time you enter an invoice, check, or timesheet, make sure the right job is selected in the Customer: Job field.

- **For billable time**: Either uses a single activity entry or a weekly timesheet to track the hours worked. Assign the hours to the work or the client. Every entry in the form's Billable column is immediately verified. It should be noted that timesheets are not posted. For time to be included in the Job Profitability or Company Financial Reports, it must be imported into a bill or invoice.
- **For job-related purchases:** (Products acquired for a project, outsourced services) To document the purchase, use a bill, cheque, or credit card charge. Enter each item or service you have purchased on the Items tab. Make sure to assign each item or service to the appropriate customer or task in the Customer: job column.
- **For overhead expenses:** Here's how to compute and manage overhead fees if you decide to assign them to particular jobs. Before making any modifications to your company file, please consult your accountant.

Tracking overhead

If you have the right accounting software, keeping track of everything should be rather simple. However, the precise classification of overhead expenses varies depending on the type of firm. Shipping and office supplies are two examples of variable overhead that your company may have even if the majority of overhead expenditures are set. These expenses vary from month to month and occasionally may even be $0. Additionally, you can have semi-variable expenses like seasonal variations in your power bills, commission-based sales wages, and overtime. Some businesses believe that dividing overhead expenses into the manufacturing and administrative subcategories is beneficial, and occasionally even required. Maintaining their separation gives the company the ability to charge manufacturing expenses according to completed goods or ongoing projects.

The company can perform a more complete analysis of its profitability by isolating manufacturing overhead from other categories of overhead expenditures. You now have more knobs and levers to adjust with. For instance, it is difficult to modify administrative expenses without making major adjustments to the company's infrastructure, such as cutting staff. On the other hand, proactive maintenance could reduce manufacturing overhead and save repair costs. Alternatively, you could figure out how to accomplish things more quickly so that machines run on less energy. You may calculate the overhead rate of your company as a percentage of revenue once all costs have been correctly categorized. To calculate this, total overhead expenditures are added up, broken down by month, and then the monthly sales ratio is divided by the total.

The following is the formula:

(Overhead ÷ monthly sales) x 100 = overhead percentage

Example:

- Company A, a consulting company calculates they have $120,000 in monthly overhead costs.
- They make $800,000 in monthly sales.
- Company A's overhead percentage would be $120,000 divided by $800,000, which gives you 0.15.
- Multiply that by 100 and your overhead percentage is 15% of your sales.

This indicates that for Company A, overhead costs account for fifteen cents of every dollar the business makes. Given that most businesses have an average profit margin of 10%, 15% is a noteworthy percentage. This is the reason controlling your overhead expenses is crucial. Finding the overhead % in connection to labor costs is also helpful. The overhead allocation rate is the term for this. The monthly labor costs are then divided by the monthly overhead costs, and the result is multiplied by 100.

The following is the formula:

Total overhead ÷ total labor hours = overhead allocation rate

If Company A employed 700 people a month, that is how that would look:

$120,000/700 = $171.42

Based on this, Company A needs to set aside $171.42 for overhead for each hour of consultation. The more efficiently a company uses its resources, the lower the percentage in both of these scenarios. Even if overhead expenses are just a component of "the cost of doing business," no company can afford to overlook them. Gaining control over your overhead costs allows you to see your whole financial situation and your needs for cash flow. It assists you in determining the best prices to charge, identifying potential cost-cutting opportunities, and making more informed business decisions in general.

- **For mileage:** In the Enter Vehicle Mileage window, note the mileage. You can adjust the amount on the invoice if you would like to charge the customer more than the normal rate for this expense.
- **For other expenses:** (Postage, freight costs, etc.) To document the costs, use a bill, cheque, or credit card charge. Enter every expense under the Expenses tab. Make careful you allocate each expense to the appropriate customer or job in the Customer: Job column.

Enter your estimates in QuickBooks Desktop

- Your estimates can be made either inside or outside of QuickBooks. You can just enter summary estimates into QuickBooks if you would rather generate estimates manually or using a spreadsheet rather than the application.
- You may easily convert estimates into invoices by entering your invoice details in the make estimates window if you make estimates outside of QuickBooks but invoices inside of the program.
- Certain job costing reports don't require estimates to be entered into QuickBooks Desktop. To ensure that your project budget is on track, you can access the whole suite of Job Cost reports by entering estimates into QuickBooks. You can assess the estimates' accuracy and make the necessary adjustments for upcoming projects.

It should be noted that you must select one timesheet or bill to transfer to an invoice if you enter time and expenses on estimates as well as timesheets or bills. For instance, in adding time from an estimate to an invoice, QuickBooks Desktop will not immediately correlate the two times. This needs to be done manually.

Create appropriate invoices

- When creating invoices, be sure to select the appropriate Customer: Job.
- If you would rather not use QuickBooks Desktop to create invoices, make sure that each invoice is at least partially entered into the application so that the revenue is included in the Job Profitability reports.

Run job costing reports to have a view of how your business is doing on a job-by-job basis

Job Reports can be used to determine which jobs are profitable and which are not. It assists you in improving estimates, evaluating the financial status of each task, and identifying problematic jobs before it's too late to save them.

To view different work reports:

- Select the **Reports option.**
- Choose **Jobs, Duration, and Mileage.**

A greater selection of task costing reports is available in QuickBooks Premier Contractor Edition and Accountant Edition; they can be found here:

- Select the **Reports option.**
- After choosing **Industry Specific, choose Contractor Reports again.**

Job Cost Reporting

If you want to see payroll wages, taxes, deductions, and contributions broken down by job, run Job Reports. The same report can also be used to determine which jobs are profitable and which are not.

- Navigate to **Reports, Jobs, and Time & Mileage.**

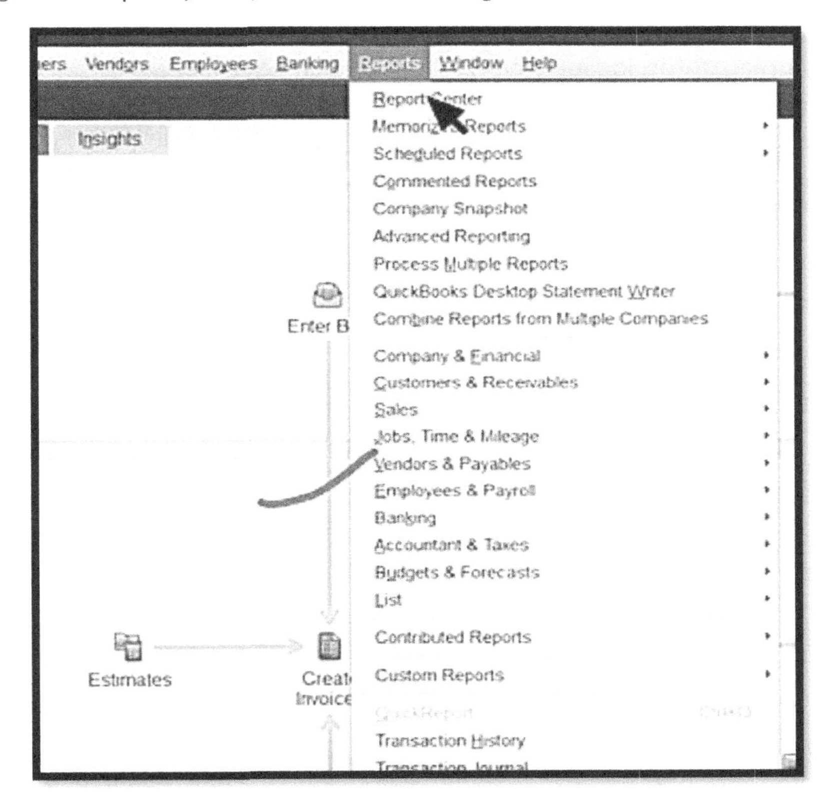

- Choose the **Job Profitability Summary option.**
- To view the earnings, taxes, deductions, and contributions for each job, double-click the job amount.

A submenu of over two dozen reports that provide task costing data is displayed by QuickBooks. Certain reports list the profitability of a job, while other reports include the estimations related to a certain job. In other reports, the expenses of the jobs are compared with the estimates. Naturally, if you are going to start using job costing, you should play around with these reports. You can use these reports to manipulate your job accounting data in a variety of ways. These reports should provide you with most of the information you need to manage job expenses and make informed decisions about job pricing, even with some adjustments.

Using Job Estimates

A bid, proposal, or quote is made using an estimate. Afterward, the estimate may be converted into an invoice or a sales order. These are the procedures for making an estimate.

Turn on estimates

You must ensure that the Estimates feature is enabled before creating an estimate.

- As an administrator, log into the QuickBooks company file.
- Pick Preferences from the QuickBooks Edit menu.
- Select Jobs Estimates from the left pane, then select the Company Preferences tab.

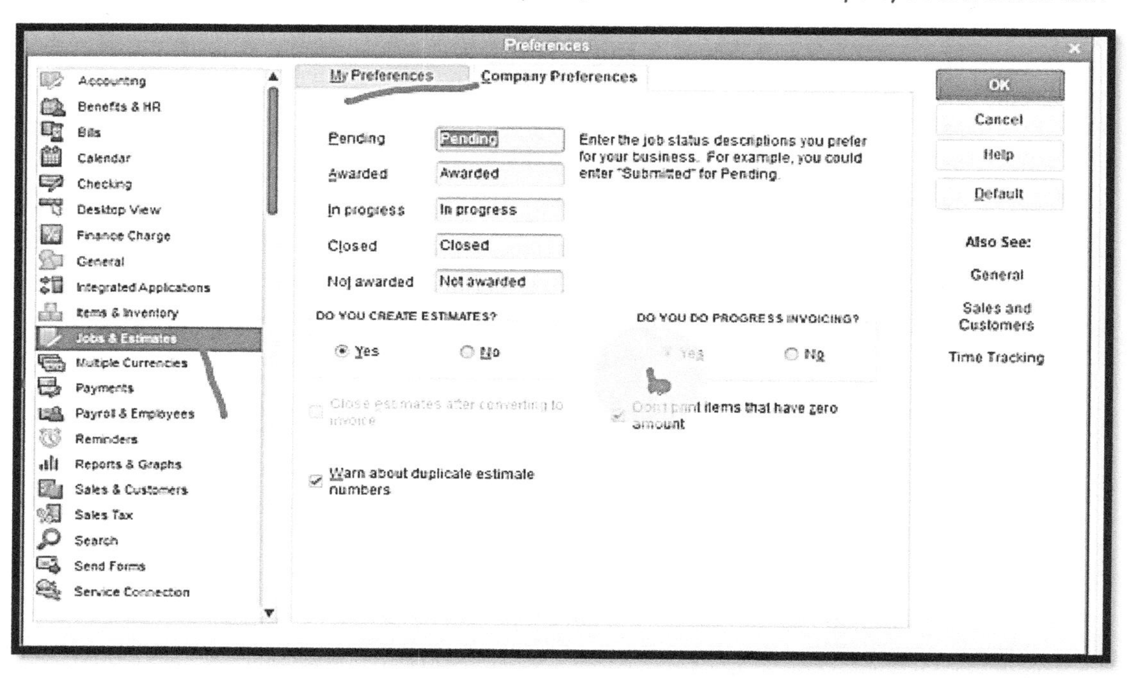

- To answer the question, "Do you create estimates?" choose Yes.
- Click OK.

Create an estimate

- Choose Estimates / Create Estimates from the Customers menu or the QuickBooks Home page.
- Choose a customer or customer job from the Customer: Job drop-down menu. You can choose Add New if the client or task is not yet on the list.

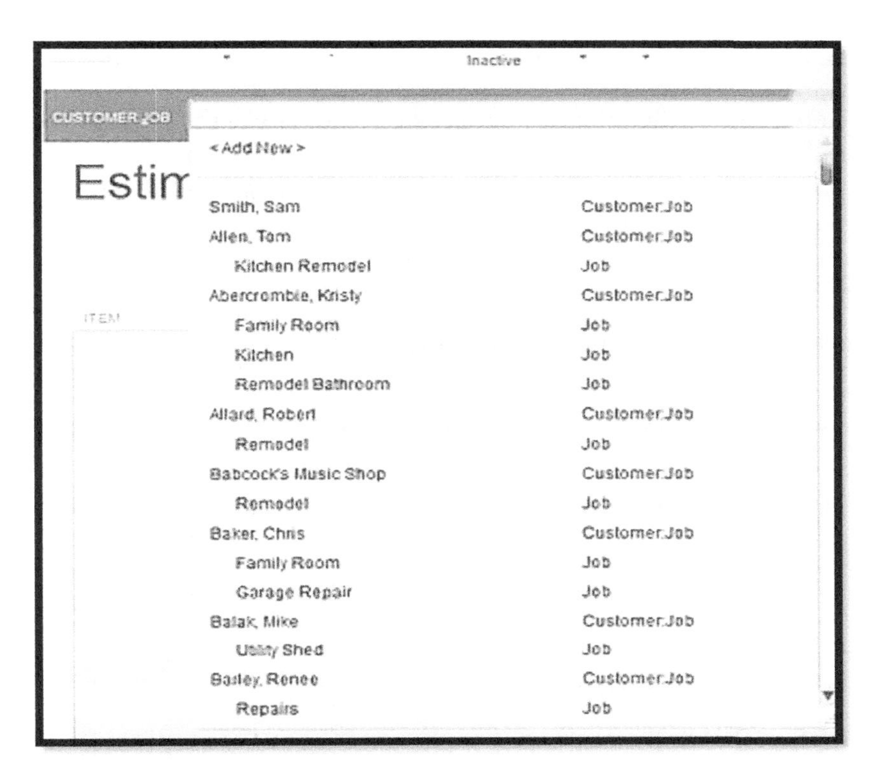

- Enter the pertinent data, such as the date and estimate number, at the top of the form.
- Choose the item or items you plan to sell in the detail section.

Note: Depending on the details and unit cost supplied when the item was set up, the quantity and description immediately appear when you pick or add an item. This is something you can change or remove when making Estimates.

- (Optional) You must create a discount item to apply for a discount.
  - Select **Item List from the QuickBooks Lists menu.**
  - Anywhere you right-click, choose **New.**
  - Choose **Discount from the Type drop-down menu in the New Item box**.
  - Add **the item's name or number and a succinct description.**
  - Enter the amount or percentage of the discount in the Amount or % area. You might choose to enter the discount amount directly on your sales forms and leave the Amount or % column empty if your discount amounts vary.
  - Select the income account you wish to use to track the discounts you offer to clients using the Account drop-down menu.
  - After choosing the proper tax code for the item, click **OK.**
- Choose **Save & Close**

Progress Billing

You can divide an estimate into as many invoices as necessary with progress invoicing. You can invoice customers for partial payments rather than expecting complete payment at the start of a job. Add things from the initial estimate to progress invoices as you finish the work. This maintains project payments linked and arranged from the beginning to the end.

Turn on progress invoicing

In case you haven't done so yet, activate progress invoicing.

- Log in as an administrator to QuickBooks Desktop.
- Select **Switch to Single-user mode from the File menu.**
- Navigate to the **Preferences menu by selecting Edit.**
- From the list of menu options, choose **Jobs & Estimates**.
- Click the **tab for Company Preferences**.
- In the "DO YOU CREATE ESTIMATES"? Box, click Yes. Next, in the DO YOU DO PROGRESS INVOICING? Area, choose **Yes.**
- To close and save your preferences, click **OK.**
- Return to the File menu and choose Switch to Multi-user mode if necessary.

Create an estimate

- Click on **Customers and choose Create Estimates.**
- Select **a customer**.
- Complete **the remainder of the estimate**.
- Choose either **Save & Close or Save & New**.

Before you begin making progress invoices, add the estimate to the work using the jobs tool.

Create progress invoices from the estimate

Instead of following the standard invoice method, you work from your estimate for progress invoicing.

- Choose the **Customer Center from the Customers menu.**
- Locate and pick your customer from the roster.
- On the customer's page, locate and open the estimate.
- On the toolbar, choose **Create Invoice.**

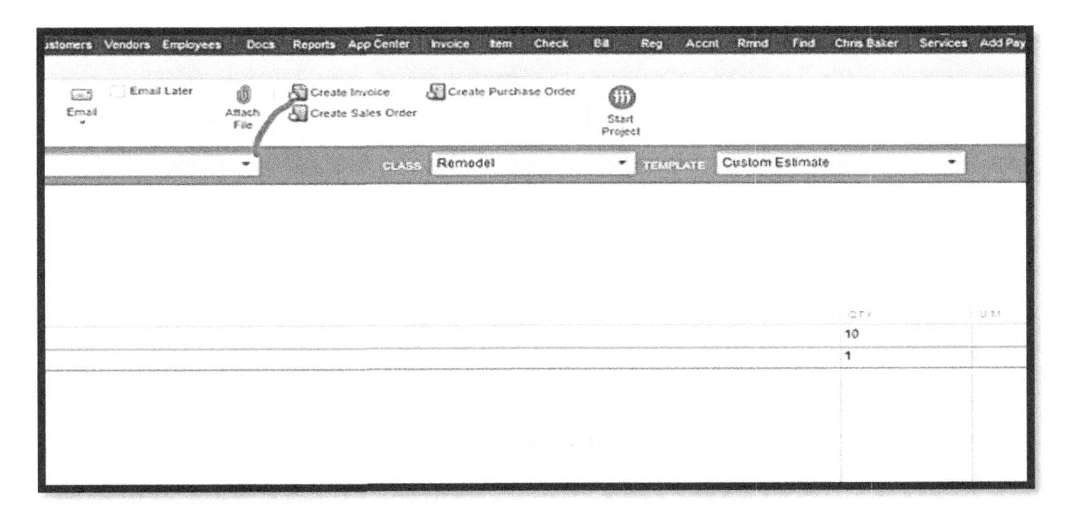

- Choose the amount that you wish to charge for the invoice. For some things, you can charge a set sum or a percentage. Next, choose **OK.**
- Complete the other part of the invoice and forward it to your customer.

Progress invoices for a job on Mac

- Click **Open Estimate**, choose **Customers, and then click Create Invoice.**
- Choose the information that should be on the invoice. Choose OK after that.
  - Sums still outstanding on the estimate.
  - The estimate as a percentage.
  - Only certain things or each item's proportion.
- Once you have identified the data required for the estimate, click **OK.**
- After you've confirmed the quantities you wish to see on the invoice, click **Save.**

Proceed to Step 1 to prepare the next progress invoice for this task. After that, the remaining sum on the estimate is added to the subsequent invoice, continuing where you left off. Useful information is provided by the estimate panel, such as the total number of open estimates for a client. Choose the **Transactions tab** and navigate to the **Related Transactions** section to view every progress invoice you generated from an estimate.

Activity

1. Set up a quick book job.
2. Track job or project costs.
3. What does progress billing mean?

BOOK 5

FINANCIAL SYMPHONY: ARTFULLY MASTERING THE ELEGANCE OF WEALTH MANAGEMENT

CHAPTER 1
RATIO ANALYSIS

When you can compare figures from your financial accounts with other figures and external benchmarks, the statistics make greater sense. You will discover how to conduct this type of analysis, known as ratio analysis, in this chapter. Despite your lack of mathematical skills, ratio analysis can be useful to you. Even those who are not quantitative can benefit from ratio analysis's ease of use and ability to help them comprehend the data in financial statements. Here's a little demonstration of ratio analysis. The gross margin %, which is calculated by dividing your gross margin by your total sales, is one especially helpful ratio. This ratio can be quite helpful, even though it might not seem like it at first. You'll know this isn't good if, for example, you look at your gross margin percentage and notice a reduction from the previous year. Reduced gross margin translates into lower operating, interest, and profit margins. However, you know it's a good thing if you compare your dropping gross margin % to that of your competitors and find that theirs is declining even faster than yours. This contrast suggests that you might not be in such bad shape after all. Unlike your rival, at least you are not in pain. This is the kind of information that ratio analysis may offer. They allow you to contextualize figures from your balance sheet and income statement.

Uncovering Some Caveats about Ratio Analysis

There are two major things worth considering before you happen to dive into the world of ratio analysis;

- **Ratios become relevant through comparison**. You should have realized earlier that your financial ratios become most significant when they are compared to your competitors' numbers, your numbers from a year ago, and the numbers that a bank loan agreement specifies you must maintain to maintain good standing with the bank. Because your figures are frequently just numbers if they cannot be compared with outside standards, you must compare them with other ratios.
- **The ratios are just as good as your inputs**. Naturally, any ratios you compute using the data from your QuickBooks financial statements will be more accurate the more accurate your accounting records in QuickBooks are. Is this not what makes sense? Trash in, trash out. Your financial ratios aren't as good as they may be even if your financial records are spotless and contain anything slightly odd, like an exceptionally large transaction that skews all the data.

Some industries commonly make reports that help to summarize financial ratio information for other firms that are also in the industry. The industry in which you work likely has a professional association. Be alert to the likelihood that this organization or group generates and disseminates reports that contain financial ratios. These reports might be helpful resources for you as a business manager.

Note: When you use financial ratios to compare your company with other companies, you are comparing it to companies that are similar in size. Comparing, say, a million-dollar company with a billion-dollar one is usually illogical.

Simple financial ratios are automatically provided by certain QuickBooks financial statements. For example, the regular income statement and balance sheet can have the gross margin % (as well as other percentage measurements) added to it.

Looking at Liquidity Ratios

The ease and comfort with which a company can meet its short-term financial obligations and take advantage of emerging possibilities is gauged by liquidity ratios. If all else is equal, the company with the bigger cash reserve will be better able to pay its bills and seize any fantastic opportunities that present themselves. (A very liquid corporation with large amounts of cash can more easily take advantage of such an opportunity, for example, if a competitor slips into problems and wants to sell important assets at fire-sale rates.)

Current ratio

A comparison of a company's current assets and current liabilities is made using the current ratio liquidity measure. Cash, inventory, accounts receivable, and any other assets that can be swiftly converted into cash are examples of a company's current assets. While they might have some, like short-term investments, most small firms don't have many other current assets. Payables that need to be paid in the upcoming year include accounts payable, salaries payable, taxes payable, and if you're taking out a long-term loan, like a bank loan, the principal amount due in the upcoming year. These are examples of current obligations.

The precise formula used to determine the current ratio is as follows:

- current assets/current liabilities

Regarding current ratios, the following general guidelines apply: A company's current ratio ought to be at least 2. Stated otherwise, the present assets of the company need to equal or exceed the current liabilities of the company.

Acid-test ratio

The quick ratio also referred to as the acid-test ratio, determines if a company has the resources to pay its short-term obligations by analyzing information from its balance sheet. A corporation can typically fulfill its short-term obligations if its ratio is 1.0 or higher; if it is less than 1.0, it may find it difficult to do so. The acid-test ratio is sometimes preferred by analysts over the current ratio, sometimes referred to as the working capital ratio, because it takes into account assets like inventory that could be challenging to swiftly liquidate. Thus, a more cautious metric is the acid-test ratio. Businesses that have an acid-test ratio below 1.0 should be handled carefully because they do not have enough liquid assets to cover their current liabilities. The current assets of a corporation are heavily reliant on inventories if the acid-test ratio is significantly lower than the current ratio. This isn't always a negative thing, though, as certain business strategies are built around inventory. For example, retail establishments may have extremely low acid-test ratios without necessarily being dangerous. Various businesses will have various acceptable ranges for acid-test ratios, and you'll find that peer companies in the same industry make the most meaningful comparisons. In most cases, the acid-test ratio ought to be higher than 1.0. Conversely, a high ratio isn't always advantageous. It can mean that instead of being reinvested, distributed to shareholders, or used for other beneficial purposes, cash has accumulated and is now sitting idle.

Calculating the Acid-Test Ratio

There are other methods to define the numerator of the acid-test ratio, but understanding the company's liquid assets realistically should be the main focus. Included should be short-term assets like marketable securities as well as cash and cash equivalents. While accounts receivable are typically included, not all industries should use this. For instance, accounts receivable in the construction sector may require a longer period to recover than in other sectors, thus mentioning it could give the impression that a company's financial situation is more stable than it is.

The formula is:

Acid Test = Cash + Marketable Securities + A/R

Current Liabilities

Where: A/R = Accounts receivable

An alternative method of computing the numerator involves deducting illiquid assets from all current assets. The most crucial thing to remember is that inventory needs to be deducted; yet, because retail enterprises hold so many inventories, this will negatively distort the picture. If some items, such as advances to suppliers, prepayments, and deferred tax assets, cannot be utilized to fulfill liabilities shortly, they should be deducted from the balance sheet. All current debts, obligations that are due within a year and liabilities should be included in the denominator of the ratio. It is significant to remember that the acid-test ratio does not take time into account. A corporation may be in considerably worse shape than its ratio would suggest if its accounts payable are almost due but its receivables are taking months to arrive. Contrarily, things can also be true.

Difference between current and acid-test ratios

A company's short-term ability to earn enough cash to pay off all of its debts should they come due all at once is measured by both the acid-test ratio and the current ratio, also referred to as the working capital ratio. However, because it does not account for goods like inventories, which could be challenging to swiftly liquidate, the acid-test ratio is regarded as being more conservative than the current ratio. Another significant distinction is that assets that can be turned into cash in less than 90 days are excluded from the acid-test ratio, whereas assets that can be turned into cash in a year are included in the current ratio. In essence, the quick ratio, also known as the acid test, determines whether a business can generate enough cash to cover its short-term debt and other immediate liabilities. In most cases, the acid-test ratio ought to be higher than 1.0. Companies should be handled carefully if their ratio is less than 1.0 since it indicates that they do not have enough liquid assets to cover their present liabilities. An indication that a company's current assets are heavily reliant on inventories is an acid-test ratio that is significantly lower than the current ratio. Conversely, an excessively high ratio can mean that money has accumulated and isn't being reinvested, distributed to shareholders, or used productively.

Divide a company's current cash, marketable securities, and total accounts receivable by its current liabilities to find its acid-test ratio. The balance sheet of the business contains this data. The fast ratio, often known as the acid-test ratio, is a ratio used to determine whether a business can sell assets for cash within ninety days of incurring costs. Analysts often feel that a company can cover its short-term costs if the ratio is greater than 1.0. It cannot if it is less than 1.0. Like many other financial statistics, this one's reliability is dependent on the industry the company you're examining works in, thus it's ideal to use it when comparing similar businesses.

Looking at Leverage Ratios

A leverage ratio is any of several financial metrics that examine the amount of capital that is in the form of debt (loans) or evaluate a company's capacity to pay its debts. Because businesses rely on a combination of debt and equity to fund their operations, the leverage ratio category is crucial because it helps determine a company's ability to repay debt as it becomes due. Leverage ratios are typically used to evaluate a company's ability to pay its debts. An organization and its investors may be at risk if they have too much debt. On the other hand, debt might support expansion if a business's operations can yield a higher rate of return than the interest paid on its loans. Credit downgrades or even worse outcomes may result from unmanaged debt levels. However, having too few debts might also cause problems. Operating margin constraints may be indicated by a reluctance or incapacity to borrow. To determine how changes in output may impact operating profits, a company's mix of operating expenses can also be measured using a leverage ratio. The consumer leverage ratio is an additional ratio of leverage. This ratio, which examines consumer debt to disposable income, is utilized by policymakers and economists alike.

The secret to grasping leverage is realizing how debt magnifies returns. Having debt is not always a terrible thing, especially if it is used to finance investments that will yield profits. Thus, leverage can increase returns, but if returns are negative, it can also increase losses.

Banks and Leverage Ratios

In the US, banks are some of the most leveraged institutions. A banking environment with minimal lending risks has been created by the combination of Federal Deposit Insurance Corporation (FDIC) protection and fractional-reserve banking. The Federal Reserve, the Comptroller of the Currency, and the FDIC, three independent regulatory agencies, evaluate and limit the leverage ratios for US banks to make up for this. These organizations impose limits on the amount of money banks can lend to the capital they invest in their assets. Because banks can "write down" the capital component of their assets if total asset values decline, capital levels are crucial. Debt-financed assets cannot be written down because the money is owed to the bank's depositors and bondholders. Leverage ratio laws in banking are intricate. Bank holding companies are subject to criteria established by the Federal Reserve, which differ based on the bank's rating. Generally speaking, banks that grow quickly or run into operational or financial issues must keep their leverage levels higher.

There are quite several leverage ratios. Below are some of the common ones;

The Debt-to-Equity (D/E) Ratio

The debt-to-equity ratio is arguably the most well-known financial leverage measure. This can be stated as:

$$\text{Debt-to-Equity Ratio} = \frac{\text{Total Liabilities}}{\text{Total Shareholders' Equity}}$$

For instance, United Parcel Service had $20.0 billion in total shareholder equity and $19.35 billion in long-term debt as of the quarter that ended on June 30, 2023. For the quarter, the company's D/E was 0.97. A high debt-to-equity ratio typically denotes an active use of debt to finance a company's expansion. Because of the added interest expense, earnings may become variable as a result of this.

The likelihood of a default or bankruptcy may rise if the company's interest expense increases excessively. A D/E ratio larger than 2.0 generally denotes a risky situation for investors, though industry-specific standards may differ. Large capital expenditure (CapEx) businesses, such as manufacturing and utility corporations, would need to obtain more loans than other types of businesses. To better comprehend the statistics, it's a good idea to compare a firm's leverage ratios with companies in the same industry and with prior performance.

Debt-to-capitalization Ratio

The amount of debt in a company's capital structure is measured by the debt-to-capitalization ratio. It is computed as follows:

$$\text{Total debt to capitalization} = \frac{(SD + LD)}{(SD + LD + SE)}$$

Where;

- SD = short-term debt
- LD = long-term debt
- SE = shareholders' equity

Operating leases are capitalized in this ratio, and equity consists of both common and preferred shares. An analyst evaluating a firm's capital structure may choose to use total debt as a substitute for long-term debt. Minority interest and preferred shares would be included in the denominator of the formula in this scenario.

The Consumer Leverage Ratio

The ratio of the average American consumer's debt to disposable income is measured by the consumer leverage ratio. According to some economists, one reason why corporate revenues have grown over the past few decades is the sharp rise in consumer debt levels. Some attributed the Great Recession to the high amount of consumer debt.

$$\text{Consumer leverage ratio} = \frac{\text{Total household debt}}{\text{Disposable personal income}}$$

The Debt-To-Capital Ratio

One of the more significant debt ratios is the debt-to-capital ratio, which emphasizes the relationship between debt liabilities and a company's entire capital base. It is computed by taking the entire debt plus the total shareholders' equity of a corporation and dividing it by the total capital. All obligations, both short- and long-term, are considered debt. This ratio is used to assess the funding methods and financial structure of a company. Generally speaking, the risk of default increases with the debt-to-capital ratio. The cost of debts and liabilities may exceed earnings if the ratio is extremely high. Once more, the industry determines what a reasonable debt-to-capital ratio is because different industries use different amounts of leverage.

The Debt-To-EBITDA Leverage Ratio

The ratio of debt-to-EBITDA leverage gauges the amount of revenue earned and available for debt repayment before a company's depreciation, amortization, interest, and tax charges. This ratio, which is often utilized by credit agencies, measures the likelihood of defaulting on issued debt and is computed by dividing short- and long-term debt by EBITDA. The number of years of EBITDA needed to pay off the entire debt can be found using this ratio. In general, if the ratio is greater than 3, it may be concerning; however, and this can differ based on the sector.

The Debt-To-EBITDAX Ratio

The debt-to-EBITDA ratio and the debt-to-EBITDAX ratio are comparable. Instead of using EBITDA, it only compares debt to EBITDAX. Earnings before interest, taxes, amortization, depreciation (or depletion), and exploration expense are referred to as EBITDAX. By taking out exploration costs—a regular expense for oil and gas companies—it increases EBITDA. The full cost method vs. the successful efforts method are two distinct accounting methods for exploration expenses that are often normalized in the US using this ratio. Financial statements often list exploration, abandonment, and dry-hole costs in addition to other costs. Impairments, deferred taxes, and the accretion of asset retirement liabilities are additional noncash expenses that need to be added back in.

The Interest Coverage Ratio

The interest coverage ratio is another leverage ratio that deals with interest payments. Examining a company's overall debt obligations alone has the drawback of providing no information regarding the company's capacity to repay its debt. The interest coverage ratio is specifically designed to address this. The ability of the business to pay interest is demonstrated by this ratio, which is calculated by dividing operational income by interest expenses. While this varies by industry, a ratio of 3.0 or greater is often preferred.

The Fixed-Charge Coverage Ratio

An alternative to the interest coverage ratio is times interest earned (TIE), sometimes referred to as a fixed-charge coverage ratio. The purpose of this leverage ratio is to show how cash flow compares to interest paid on long-term liabilities. Finding the company's profits before interest and taxes (EBIT) and dividing it by the interest expenditure of long-term obligations will yield this ratio. Since interest is tax deductible, use pre-tax profits; you can use all of your earnings to pay interest at a later date. Once more, higher figures are preferable. Different methods are used to calculate the different types of leverage ratios. It frequently entails dividing a company's debt by another variable, like total capital, shareholders' equity, or EBITDA. Tools like leverage ratios are helpful. They offer a straightforward method of determining how much a business depends on debt to finance its operations and growth. Debt is a significant issue. It can produce a better rate of return than its costs when applied properly. However, having too much might be risky and result in default and financial disaster.

Industry-specific leverage varies. More corporations than others rely on debt, and banks are even restricted in the amount of leverage they can keep. The optimum use case for leverage ratios is historical comparison.

Looking at Activity Ratios

One kind of financial indicator called an activity ratio shows how well a business is using the assets on its balance sheet to create cash and revenue. Activity ratios, also known as efficiency ratios, are frequently used by analysts to assess a company's inventory management practices, which are crucial to the smooth running and overall financial health of the business.

- Any financial indicator that aids investors and research analysts in determining how effectively a business uses its assets to create revenue and cash is referred to as an activity ratio.
- Activity ratios can be used to compare two distinct companies operating in the same industry or to track the financial health of a single company over time.
- Activity ratios are further classified as return on equity measurements, merchandise inventory turnover ratios, total assets turnover ratios, and a variety of other indicators.

Activity ratios are particularly helpful when used to compare two rival companies in the same industry to see how a specific company stands out from its competitors. However, activity ratios can also be used to monitor changes over time by tracking a company's financial development over several recording periods. These figures can be plotted to give an outlook for the future performance of an organization.

Activity ratios are subdivided into the subsequent categories:

Accounts Receivable Turnover Ratio

The ability of an organization to collect money from its clients is measured by the accounts receivable turnover ratio. The average accounts receivable balance during a certain period is divided by the total credit sales. A low ratio points to a potential problem with the collection procedure.

Merchandise Inventory Turnover Ratio

The frequency with which the inventory balance is sold throughout an accounting period is gauged by the merchandise inventory turnover ratio. The average inventory for a certain period is divided by the cost of items sold. Higher computations imply that a business can move its goods more easily.

Total Assets Turnover Ratio

The effectiveness with which a company uses its assets to tender a sale is gauged by the total assets turnover ratio. To calculate how well a company uses its assets, total sales are divided by total assets. Lower ratios could mean that a business is having trouble selling its goods. It is not possible to compare the total assets turnover ratio you determine for your company to any external benchmark or set of accepted guidelines. You contrast your ratio with that of comparable-sized companies in your sector. The most important thing to think about is how well you're leveraging your resources to generate sales in comparison to your rivals. Your company will do better if it can generate more sales with a certain amount of assets.

Inventory Turnover Ratio

The number of times the inventory balance sells out within an accounting period is measured by the inventory turnover ratio.

The following is the formula:

$$\frac{\text{Cost of goods sold}}{\text{Average inventory}}$$

It is not appropriate, strictly speaking, to utilize the ending inventory balance. An average inventory balance is what you ought to use. An average inventory balance can be determined in all the standard, practical ways. For example, you can take the inventory balance from the balance sheets for this year and the prior year, and then take the average of them. As you may have seen, the revenue statement's measurement period determines the inventory turnover period. By definition, an inventory turnover ratio of 1.2 indicates that a company sells 120 percent of its balance of inventory in a given year, assuming the income statement is an annual statement and the cost of goods sold (COGS) amount is an annual COGS amount. The inventory turnover period is one month if the COGS amount from a monthly revenue statement is used by the inventory turnover ratio. A company with a 1.2 inventory ratio sells 120 percent of its goods in a month with a monthly COGS amount. There are no standards for inventory turnover ratios. An optimal inventory turnover ratio is contingent upon the actions of your industry's competitors. You need an inventory turnover ratio that is at least somewhat comparable to your rivals' ratios if you wish to remain competitive.

Average Collection Period Ratio

The length of time it takes a business to collect its receivables is shown by the average collection period ratio. This ratio might be seen as an indicator of the caliber of a company's credit and collection practices. To put it another way, this ratio demonstrates how astute a company is in selecting whom to give credit to. This ratio also demonstrates how well a business collects from clients.

This is how the average collection period ratio formula looks:

$$\frac{\text{Average accounts receivable}}{\text{Average credit sales per day}}$$

The general rule regarding the typical collecting period is that it ought to correspond with your terms of payment. Your terms of payment should be something like net 60 days if, for example, your average number of days of credit sales in accounts receivable equals 60 (i.e., consumers are required to pay you in 60 days or fewer). Stated differently, the majority of your clients should be paying on time based on your usual collection period. It's important to keep in mind that while some of your clients will pay on time, others will undoubtedly pay a little later. Ideally, clients will pay on schedule most of the time.

Asset Turnover Ratio

The asset turnover ratio is a statistic that shows how much money a business makes for every dollar it has in assets. This number, which can be easily computed by dividing sales by total assets, shows how well a business uses its assets to produce revenue.

Activity Ratios vs. Profitability Ratios

Both activity ratios and profitability ratios are essential analytical instruments that assist investors in assessing various aspects of a company's financial health. Profitability ratios show how much money a company makes, whereas efficiency ratios assess how well it uses its resources to get those profits. By analyzing a company's success across multiple reporting periods, profitability ratios can assist analysts in comparing its profits to those of its industry competitors.

Looking at Profitability Ratios

Using information at a single point in time, profitability ratios are a class of financial measurements that are used to evaluate a company's capacity to generate profits over time about its revenue, operating costs, balance sheet assets, or shareholders' equity. These are some of the most often-used metrics in the field of financial analysis. Ratios of profitability can provide insight into the health and financial performance of an organization. Ratios are not useful as measures on their own; instead, they work best as comparison tools. Efficiency ratios, which evaluate how successfully a business uses its internal resources to generate income (as opposed to after-cost profits), can be used in conjunction with profitability measures. The efficiency with which a company's management runs its operations can be inferred from profitability ratios. They can be used by investors in conjunction with additional research to assess a company's potential suitability as an investment.

Higher profitability ratios, in general, might indicate a company's advantages and strengths, such as its capacity to keep lower expenses and charge more (or less) for items. The most insightful comparisons for a company's profitability ratios are those with comparable companies, the company's past performance, or typical ratios within the industry. A greater number in comparison to the prior value typically denotes a successful business.

Types of Profitability Ratios

Profitability ratios fall into two distinct categories; margin ratios and return ratios. Margin ratios provide information about a company's capacity to convert sales into profit from several distinct perspectives. Return ratios provide some methods for assessing how successfully a business uses the capital that its shareholders have contributed to produce a return for them.

Some common examples of the two types of profitability ratios include;

- Gross margin
- Operating margin
- Pretax margin
- Net profit margin
- Cash flow margin
- Return on assets (ROA)
- Return on equity (ROE)
- Return on invested capital (ROIC)
- Price to sales (P/S) ratio

Margin Ratios

A company's profitability is measured at different cost levels of inquiry using different profit margins. The gross margin, operating margin, pretax margin, and net profit margin are some examples of these profit margins. As costs are low, the margin between profit and costs increases; as layers of extra costs (such as taxes, operational expenditures, and cost of goods sold, or COGS) are added, the margins contract.

Gross Margin

One of the most popular profitability measures is gross margin, sometimes referred to as gross profit margin. The difference between sales revenue and the previously indicated cost of goods sold is known as gross profit. Gross profit and revenue are compared using the gross margin. A business that has a higher gross margin than its competitors is probably able to charge more for its goods. It can suggest that the business has a significant competitive edge. Conversely, a trend of diminishing gross margins could indicate heightened competition. Seasonality is a reality for several sectors. For example, during the year-end holiday season, shops usually see a big increase in sales and profits. Comparing a retailer's fourth-quarter profit margin to that of its competitors or its own from the prior year would therefore be the most instructive and helpful.

Operating Margin

The percentage of sales that remain after deducting COGS and typical operational costs (such as marketing, general, and administrative costs) is known as the operating margin. It contrasts revenue with operating profit. An organization's operating margin can provide insight into how well it runs its business. That can reveal information about how effectively management controls expenses and maximizes profits. One could argue that a business is better able to manage its fixed costs and interest on liabilities if it has a bigger operating margin than its competitors. It can probably charge less than its rivals. Furthermore, it is better equipped to withstand the consequences of a faltering economy.

Pretax Margin

The pretax margin indicates the profitability of a business after all costs, including non-operating costs like loan payments and inventory write-offs, have been deducted, except taxes. Pretax margin is a ratio that evaluates the difference between revenue and expenses. It can demonstrate management's capacity to operate a company profitably by increasing sales while cutting expenses. A corporation might be deemed financially sound and capable of setting its prices for goods and/or services appropriately if it has a higher pretax profit margin than its competitors.

Net Profit Margin

After all costs and taxes are deducted, a company's capacity to turn a profit is shown by its net profit margin, also known as its net margin. By dividing net income by total revenue, it may be calculated. One indicator of a company's overall financial health is its net profit margin. It can show whether the management of the business is controlling all expenditures and making a sufficient profit from sales. One of its limitations as a tool for peer comparison is that, due to its comprehensive accounting of spending, it can include one-time costs or the sale of assets that would boost earnings temporarily. The one-off transactions won't happen to other businesses. For this reason, in addition to net profit margin, it's a good idea to look at additional ratios like gross margin and operating margin.

Cash Flow Margin

The ability of a business to convert sales revenue into cash is gauged by its cash flow margin. It illustrates how operations, cash flows, and sales are related to one another. Since cash is needed to pay for expenses and purchase assets, cash flow margin is an important ratio for businesses. Because of this, managing cash flow is crucial. A higher cash flow margin means that there is more money available to pay vendors, debt repayments, shareholder dividends, and capital asset purchases, among other things. Even if it is making money from sales, a company with negative cash flow is losing money. This may imply that it will require borrowing money to continue running. A brief period of negative cash flow may arise from using funds to finance, say, a significant investment that will aid in the company's expansion. Over time, cash flow and cash flow margin should benefit from that, as one might anticipate.

Return Ratios

Return ratios offer data that may be utilized to assess how successfully a business makes money for its investors and produces returns. These profitability measures contrast net income with equity or asset investments. These metrics may show how well a business can handle these investments.

Return on Assets (ROA)

Profitability is evaluated by expenditures and costs. It is compared to assets to determine how well a business uses assets to produce revenue and profits. The ROA measure's use of the phrase "return" typically refers to net profit or net income, which is the amount of earnings from sales after all, costs, expenses, and taxes have been deducted. Divide net income by total assets to get ROA. A company's potential for profit and sales increases with the number of assets it has amassed. Returns may increase faster than asset growth as economies of scale help reduce costs and boost margins, eventually raising ROA.

Return on Equity (ROE)

Since it gauges a company's capacity to generate a return on its equity investments, return on equity (ROE) is a crucial number for investors. Net income divided by shareholders' equity, or ROE can rise in the absence of new equity investments. Higher net income from a larger asset base financed by debt may cause the ratio to increase. A corporation with a high return on equity (ROE) may be viewed favorably by investors. It may suggest that a business can make money on its own and is not dependent on debt.

Return on Invested Capital (ROIC)

This return ratio shows how successfully a business uses the capital it has access to from all sources—including shareholders and bondholders—to produce a profit for those investors. Because it takes into account factors other than shareholder equity, it is seen as a more sophisticated indicator than ROE. ROIC measures the difference between total invested capital (loan and equity again) and after-tax operating profit. It is employed internally to evaluate the proper use of capital. Investors utilize ROIC for value as well. A corporation that may trade at a premium and create value is indicated by a return on invested capital (ROIC) that is greater than its weighted average cost of capital (WACC). The significance of profitability ratios lies in their capacity to reveal a company's ability to generate consistent profits (after deducting expenses) and its proficiency in managing investments to yield returns for its investors. They may serve as an indicator of the company's overall financial health as well as the management's capacity to meet these two objectives. The gross margin, operating margin, and net profit margin are the profitability ratios that are frequently seen as being the most significant for a company.

Activity

Define the following;

- Ratio analysis
- Liquidity ratios
- Leverage ratios
- Activity ratios

- Profitability ratios

CHAPTER 2
ECONOMIC VALUE-ADDED ANALYSIS

You might not be making any money, even though your QuickBooks profit and loss statement indicates a profit. Economic Value Added Analysis (EVA) is a tool that you must use. This chapter explains the purpose of EVA and shows you how to run an EVA analysis using the data you create in QuickBooks. Interesting stuff, although a little theoretical. Fortunately, EVA is really useful when you reduce it to its most basic form.

Introducing the Logic of EVA

EVA analysis puts what you intuitively know into a formula. You're not doing yourself or your family any financial favors by owning your own business if you can make more money by selling it, reinvesting the money, and finding another job somewhere. EVA is a metric used to quantify an organization's economic profit after deducting operating profit and capital costs. To put it simply, it's a method of figuring out the actual economic value that a business generates for its owners.

It accounts for the cost of the capital employed to create that profit, making it a more accurate indicator of a company's performance than conventional financial metrics like net income or return on equity. Let's take an example where Company A generates $1 million in net profits with $5 million in capital. According to conventional financial measures, the company's return on equity is 20%. But if Company A's cost of capital is 10%, then its actual economic profit—or EVA—is just $500,000. This means that, after deducting the cost of the capital employed to produce that profit, the corporation is only producing value for its owners of $500,000. Conversely, suppose that firm B requires $3 million in capital and generates a $1 million net income.

By applying conventional financial measurements, the company's return on equity would be 33.33%. However, if business B has an 8% cost of capital, and then its actual economic profit—or EVA—is $200,000. This means that after deducting the cost of the capital utilized to produce that profit, firm B is generating $200,000 in value for its shareholders. This example demonstrates how EVA can be used to determine a company's actual economic profit as well as the value it is generating for its owners. When evaluating the performance of several businesses and formulating strategic plans, this can be quite helpful. In summary, EVA is a financial performance statistic that accounts for both operating profit and the cost of capital to determine a company's actual economic profit. It can help compare the success of various businesses and make strategic decisions because it provides a more accurate assessment of a company's performance than traditional financial indicators.

How EVA is calculated

The computation of EVA involves deducting the cost of capital from the operational profit of the business. The operating profit of the business is its net income before interest and taxes (NOPAT), whereas the cost of capital consists of the cost of debt and equity. **The EVA formula is as follows:**

- EVA = NOPAT – (Cost of Capital x Capital Employed)
- To understand how this formula works, let's take a look at an example.
- Assume that Company X has a NOPAT of $1,000,000 and has $5,000,000 in capital employed (a combination of debt and equity). The cost of capital for the company is 10%.
- The cost of capital for the company can be calculated using the following formula:
- Cost of Capital = (Cost of Debt x (Debt/Total Capital)) + (Cost of Equity x (Equity/Total Capital))
- Assume for this example that the corporation has $2,500,000 in equity and $2,500,000 in debt. 15% is the cost of equity and 5% is the cost of debt.

Now, calculate the cost of capital for Company X:

- Cost of Capital = (5% x (2,500,000/5,000,000)) + (15% x (2,500,000/5,000,000)) = 10%
- Next, use this information to calculate EVA for Company X:
- EVA = 1,000,000 – (5,000,000 x 10%) = $50,000

This indicates that after accounting for the cost of the capital utilized to produce that profit, Company X is adding $50,000 in value for its owners. Remember that EVA is a relative indicator of a company's performance and those changes in the cost of capital and interest rates can have an impact on it. Furthermore, there are other techniques for computing the cost of capital, such as the Weighted Average Cost of Capital (WACC) and the Capital Asset Pricing Model (CAPM).

In summary, the computation of EVA involves deducting the cost of capital from the net present value of the enterprise. There are various methods available for calculating the cost of capital, which encompasses the cost of debt and equity. It is a means of calculating a business's actual economic profit and the value it is generating for its owners.

Seeing EVA in Action

Given that it considers both the cost of capital and operational profit, EVA is a valuable tool for assessing a company's financial performance. Additionally, it can be used to evaluate how well other businesses are performing. EVA's ability to assist in identifying businesses that are adding value for their shareholders is one of its primary advantages. A business that has a positive equity value (EVA) is adding value for its owners by producing a return that exceeds its cost of capital. Conversely, a negative EVA indicates that a business is not producing enough value for its shareholders because it is not making enough money to pay for its capital costs.

Using Company A as an example, let's say that its EVA is $50,000 and that of Company B is $30,000. This suggests that compared to Company B, Company A is producing greater value for its owners. Managers and investors may find this information helpful in formulating their strategic plans. EVA also aids in bringing management and shareholder interests into alignment, which is another advantage. Financial measures like net income or return on equity are commonly used to assess and pay managers. These measures, however, can result in decisions that are not optimal for shareholders because they fail to account for the cost of capital. Managers are encouraged to make choices that will increase value for shareholders by using EVA as a performance metric. EVA has additional applications in forecasting, budgeting, and performance assessment. A business might utilize EVA as a performance metric to budget and set goals for upcoming periods. EVA can also be used by the business to assess how well certain initiatives or divisions are performing. Many firms, both large and small, use EVA to assess their financial performance and formulate strategic plans. It is also used by analysts and investors to evaluate the performance of various businesses and make investment choices.

Among the most well-known businesses using EVA is the multinational American corporation General Electric (GE). Since the 1990s, GE has used EVA as a performance indicator. By utilizing EVA as a crucial tool for assessing its business divisions and formulating strategic plans, GE has been able to dramatically increase its performance. Pfizer, a pharmaceutical corporation, is another example. Pfizer makes strategic decisions and assesses the performance of its various business units using EVA. Pfizer can determine which business units is adding value for shareholders and which ones aren't using EVA, and can then adjust its strategy accordingly. It is also used by analysts and investors to compare the performance of various businesses. Investors and analysts can determine which companies are generating value for shareholders and which ones are not by comparing the EVA of several companies within the same industry. Investment decisions can be made using this information. To sum up, businesses frequently utilize EVA to assess their financial performance and inform strategic choices.

Reviewing Some Important Points about EVA

The straightforward goal of an EVA analysis is to determine whether running your own company is profitable for you.

To ensure that your investigation is progressing as planned, you need usually take into account the following factors:

- How good are the numbers? This is a crucial factor to remember. Do the figures on your income statement and balance sheet accurately reflect the profit you made (one of the numbers in your calculation) and the potential sale price and subsequent reinvestment value (another significant figure in your calculation)? There will always be some degree of imprecision in your numbers. That is a reality. However, a great deal of uncertainty in those two figures taints the outcomes. The worth of your owner's equity should be compared to what you would likely receive from a sale of your company. You should generally utilize the cash-out value in your EVA analysis rather than the owner's equity value if the amount on your balance sheet differs significantly from the owner's equity value.

- How good is the cost of capital percentage? The cost of capital value is a major factor in the computation of capital charges. To be honest, it's difficult to come up with this figure. A staff of PhDs would most likely be required to calculate a number for a billion-dollar company, which is not possible for a small one. As a result, using a range of values is advised. A common belief is that a small firm, defined as any company with revenues under, say, $50 million, ought to generate returns of 20 to 25 percent annually. That range of data appears to be appropriate for use in EVA analysis. It could also be of interest to you to know that the cost of capital rates for a large corporation often ranges from 10 to 12 percent. You don't want to be so miserable. Lastly, keep in mind that venture capital returns, or the returns produced by the most prosperous and quickly expanding small companies, often range from 35 to 45 percent per year. Therefore, it would seem that your EVA analysis's cost of capital rates should be significantly lower than this. The cost of capital rates should be significantly lower than 35 to 45 percent, at least for the majority of firms.
- What about psychological income? When analyzing an owner-managed company, it is acceptable to take psychological income into account. Economics cannot be disregarded. A sound firm should eventually turn a profit and cover its capital expenditures, particularly if it is your own.
- Have fluctuations occurred? The fact that in many small firms is another crucial point. Therefore, you cannot decide to move on from a single, possibly extremely difficult year. In a similar vein, you shouldn't base your decision to purchase the French villa in the south of France on a single stellar year. When the inputs accurately represent the overall state of the company—that is, the overall level of profits, the overall amount that can be cashed out, the overall cost of capital estimate, and so forth—EVA analysis is effective.
- Is your business in a special situation? Everyone acknowledges that EVA analysis is extremely difficult and in certain cases may not be achievable. Even EVA analysis enthusiasts would quickly acknowledge that, for example, it is not very useful in the context of a fledgling company. The majority of these individuals also acknowledge that the rapid growth of a company might cause problems for EVA analysis. The issue in each of these situations is that the income statement simply cannot provide a reliable indicator of the value the business is creating. It is therefore impossible to ascertain the precise type of economic profit the company has generated. Once more, this ought to make natural sense. It's reasonable to assume that the company will either turn a loss or generate very little revenue in the first year or two.

Using EVA When Your Business Has Debt

The computational load of EVA analysis increases in very large businesses. While I don't go into great length about potential issues in this chapter, one prevalent issue that comes up frequently is debt. This is the situation. Borrowing can be utilized to increase EVA if a company can restructure its bank loans, credit lines, mortgages, and other debt. As a result, and very helpful, you can identify this additional wrinkle using a little more complex EVA model.

Should your company be able to freely reorganize its debts, you might choose to modify the EVA study in two ways:

- It can be necessary to employ a comprehensive cost of capital. Both the cost of equity and any debt are taken into account in a comprehensive cost of capital analysis.
- You utilize an adjusted net income figure that accounts for both the amounts paid to lenders and the amounts paid to shareholders.

Presenting Two Final Pointers

Below are two closing pointers specifically for business owners who would like to make use of EVA analysis to brood over the economics of their businesses.

- As a thinking tool, EVA analysis is most helpful to business owners and managers, or at least to those of small and medium-sized companies. To put it another way, EVA makes sense as a method to consider how you should operate your company and whether making adjustments makes sense, even if you don't scratch down the numbers on the back of an envelope. It's a good idea to compare your company's net income to what you could make by selling the capital and reinvesting the proceeds somewhere else.
- EVA analysis isn't just for commercial evaluations; it can also be used to assess a company holistically. With a little bit of tweaking, EVA analysis may be used to assess a company unit, a certain product line, your management, and other entities.

When you think about it, this is quite neat. EVA analysis can be used to divide your company's revenue-generating operations. You can probably identify which activities should be prioritized because they generate an economic profit and which should be discontinued (possibly) because they don't by using EVA analysis to examine the economic profit of these various profit activities. Managers and customers can be assessed in the same manner. Working with a chart of accounts that enables more in-depth income statements and balance sheets will help you undertake this more thorough EVA analysis. Stated differently, if you intend to divide your company into two business units, make use of a chart of accounts that facilitates the easy viewing of the income statement for each unit. Similarly, for your balance sheet, utilize a chart of accounts that displays the capital investment for each of the two business units. Keep in mind that each line item in the chart of accounts must have its account for it to show on an income statement or balance sheet.

Activity

1. Explain what economic value-added analysis is all about.
2. How can you make use of EVA when your business is in debt?

CHAPTER 3
CAPITAL BUDGETING IN A NUTSHELL

Allocating capital, or money, is an issue for every business. Though your financial resources are restricted, your thoughts and prospects are frequently boundless. To put it briefly, capital budgeting aids in sorting through all of these concepts and chances. With capital budgeting, you can respond to inquiries such as these: Should I buy a new delivery vehicle or replace that important piece of equipment that the factory uses? Should we purchase the structure that houses our offices? Or should we buy that rival business because it's for sale?

Introducing the Theory of Capital Budgeting

In capital budgeting, initiatives that improve a company's worth are selected. Almost anything can be included in the capital budgeting process, such as buying property or fixed assets like a new truck or piece of equipment. Businesses monitor a prospective project's performance using multiple measures, and capital budgeting can be done in several ways.

- Investors assess a proposed investment projects worth through a method called capital budgeting.
- Net present value (NPV), internal rate of return (IRR), and payback period (PB) are the three methods of project selection that are most frequently used.
- The payback period establishes the amount of time that a business would need to see sufficient cash flows to cover the initial expenditure.
- The projected return on a project is known as the internal rate of return; if it exceeds the cost of capital, the project is worthwhile.
- The most efficient of the three approaches is probably the net present value, which compares a project's profitability to alternatives.

Every year, businesses depend on finance leadership to assist in the preparation of annual or long-term budgets and frequently interact across departments. These budgets, which usually describe how the company's revenue and expenses will be distributed over the next 12 months, are operational. But capital budgeting is another facet of this financial strategy. The long-term financial strategy for higher outlays is known as capital budgeting. Like other budgeting methods, capital budgeting is predicated on a number of the same core techniques. Nevertheless, capital budgeting faces several particular difficulties. First off, capital budgets are frequently only cost centers; they need outside funding, such as money from another department, and do not generate income while the project is underway. Second, there are greater risks, uncertainties, and potential problems because capital budgets are long-term in nature. For long-term projects, capital budgets are frequently created and then revised as the project or endeavor progresses. As a project progresses, businesses frequently update their capital budget projections. A capital budget should proactively plan for big cash inflows that, once initiated, shouldn't be stopped unless the business is prepared to incur significant expenses or losses in the event of a project delay.

Why do businesses need capital budgeting?

Since it establishes measurability and accountability, capital budgeting is crucial. Owners or shareholders would view as reckless any company that attempts to commit its resources to a project without fully appreciating the risks and rewards involved. Moreover, a company would likely have little chance of surviving in the cutthroat industry if it had no means of gauging the success of its investment choices. Businesses are frequently faced with situations when resources are scarce and choices must be made in concert. Typically, management has to decide how to divide up labor hours, capital, and resources. In this process, capital budgeting is crucial since it sets project expectations. To determine which project or projects are most suited, these expectations can be compared to those of other projects. Apart from nonprofit organizations, businesses exist to make money. Businesses may quantify the long-term financial and economic profitability of any investment project by using the capital budgeting method. While projecting sales for the following year may be easy for a business, estimating the outcome of a $1 billion, five-year industrial head office redevelopment may be more challenging. As a result, capital budgeting is essential for organizations to evaluate risks, make plans, and anticipate difficulties before they arise.

Method used in Capital Budgeting

There isn't just one way to do capital budgeting; in fact, businesses can find it useful to combine a number of the approaches covered below to create a single capital budget. In this manner, the business can spot holes in a single analysis or analyze the effects of other approaches that it might not have otherwise considered.

- **Discounted cash flow analysis**: Given that a capital budget frequently covers several months or even years, businesses frequently employ discounted cash flow methodologies to evaluate the dollar's effects in addition to the timing of cash flows. Currency values frequently decline over time. The idea that a dollar now is worth more than a dollar tomorrow because a dollar today can be utilized to create revenue or income tomorrow is a fundamental idea in economics that faces inflation. The project's inflows and outflows are included in discounted cash flow as well. Most of the time, businesses may have to pay a one-time, upfront cash investment for a project. In other cases, there can be a string of withdrawals signifying recurring project payments. Either way, businesses can try to work out a target net cash flow amount or a goal discount rate at the end of a project.
- **Payback analysis**: Payback techniques of capital budgeting plan around the timing of when specific benchmarks are attained, as opposed to just assessing money and returns. Certain companies wish to monitor when their business breaks even, or when it has paid for itself. Others are more concerned with the exact moment at which a

capital project turns a profit. Capital budgeting requires extra caution when projecting cash flows for repayment strategies. This approach necessitates greater attention to timing because any variation in an estimate from one year to the next may significantly affect when a business reaches a payback metric. If a business wants to combine capital budget approaches, it can also combine the payback method and discounted cash flow analysis method.

- **Throughput analysis**: Throughput analysis-based capital budgeting techniques offer a radically different approach. Throughput methods are frequently used to analyze revenue and expenses not only for individual projects but also for the entire corporation. Operational or non-capital budgeting can also make use of throughput analysis via cost accounting. Throughput methods involve deducting variable costs from a company's revenue. Using this method, the amount of profit that can be attributed to fixed costs is calculated for each sale. Any throughput that remains after a business has paid all of its fixed costs is retained as equity. Businesses could aim to have a target amount of capital available after variable costs in addition to making a specific amount of profit. These monies can be used to pay for operating costs, and management may set a goal for the amount that capital budget initiatives must return to the operations.

Metrics Used in Capital Budgeting

One of the first things a company does when faced with a capital budgeting choice is assess the project's potential profitability. The most popular strategies for choosing projects are payback period (PB), internal rate of return (IRR), and net present value (NPV). While it is ideal for all three criteria to point to the same capital budgeting strategy, these methods frequently yield inconsistent outcomes. There will be a preference for one strategy over another based on selection criteria and management preferences. However, these popular approaches to valuation come with a shared set of benefits and drawbacks.

Payback Period

The time needed to recover the initial investment is determined by the payback period. For instance, the PB indicates the number of years needed for the cash inflows to equal the $1 million outflow if a capital budgeting project necessitates an initial cash outlay of that amount. A quick payback period (PB period) is ideal since it suggests that the project would "pay for itself" in a shorter amount of time. Payback periods are usually applied when there is a significant issue with liquidity. A corporation may only be able to work on one large project at a time if its funding is restricted. As a result, management's first goal will be to recoup their original investment before moving on with new initiatives. The fact that the PB is simple to compute after the cash flow estimates are created is another significant benefit of employing it. The PB measure has limitations when it comes to capital budgeting considerations. First off, the temporal value of money (TVM) is not taken into consideration by the payback period.

Merely computing the PB yields a statistic that equally prioritizes payments obtained during the first and second years.

One of the cornerstones of finance is broken by this kind of mistake. Fortunately, there is a simple solution to this issue: using a discounted payback time model. In essence, the discounted PB period takes TVM into account and gives one a discounted cash flow basis for estimating the time it will take to repay the investment. The fact that cash flows that happen at the end of a project's life, such as the salvage value, are ignored by both payback periods and discounted payback periods is another disadvantage. As a result, the PB does not directly represent profitability.

Calculating the Rate of Return on Capital

The return on invested capital (ROIC) measures how well a business allocates its money to lucrative ventures. Net operating profit after tax (NOPAT) is divided by invested capital to determine it. ROIC indicates how effectively a business is turning a profit on its capital. If a company's weighted average cost of capital (WACC) is compared to its ROIC, it can be determined if invested capital is being used efficiently.

Quick tips!

- A measure called returns on invested capital (ROIC) is used to assess how well a business deploys its resources to successful ventures or investments.
- In other words, return on invested capital (ROIC) is the amount of money a business makes over the average cost of its debt and equity capital.
- Net operating profit after tax (NOPAT) is divided by invested capital to get ROIC.
- ROIC is a useful metric for estimating the worth of other businesses.
- If a business's ROIC is higher than its weighted average cost of capital (WACC), it is deemed to be creating value.

There are multiple methods for figuring out this number. One way to calculate total assets is to deduct cash and non-interest-bearing current liabilities (NIBCL) from total assets. This includes tax liabilities and accounts payable, provided they are not subject to interest or fees. An alternative approach to determining invested capital is to deduct non-operating assets such as cash and cash equivalents, marketable securities, and assets of discontinued operations from the book value of a company's debt and then add the book value of its equity to that amount. To compute invested capital, one last method is to take the working capital and deduct current liabilities from current assets. Subtracting cash from the working capital figure you just computed yields non-cash working capital. Eventually, a company's fixed assets are increased by non-cash working capital.

There are other methods for calculating the value in the numerator as well. Dividends can be subtracted from a company's net income in the simplest method. However, it is frequently preferable to look at net operating profit after taxes (NOPAT) because a company may have profited from a one-time source of income unrelated to its main business—a windfall from swings in foreign exchange rates, for example. To compute NOPAT, one must first adjust the operating profit for taxes.

NOPAT = (operating profit) x (1 – effective tax rate)

ROIC is typically expressed as an annualized or trailing 12-month value and is always computed as a percentage. To assess if a business is producing value, it ought to be contrasted with its cost of capital. A corporation is creating value and will trade at a premium if its return on invested capital (ROIC) exceeds its weighted average cost of capital (WACC), which is the most widely used cost of capital indicator. A return that is two percentage points higher than the firm's cost of capital is a standard benchmark for demonstrating the generation of value. While they might not be destroying value, some businesses operate at a zero-return level, meaning they have no extra cash to invest in expansion in the future. You can compare businesses that are in the same industry to have a better understanding of what constitutes a respectable or acceptable ROIC. A corporation is usually better managed and more successful if it consistently produces a higher return on invested capital (ROIC) than its peer group. Comparing the ROIC of an established, mature company to its historical ROIC can also is helpful. Finally, ROIC is a well-liked financial indicator. It provides information on a company's capital allocation and whether or not it is generating value from its investments. A company's return on invested capital (ROIC) needs to exceed its cost of capital, minimum. The business model is unsustainable if it isn't consistently the case.

When analyzing businesses that make significant capital investments, ROIC is especially helpful. In addition, similar to many measures, it provides more insight when compared to other organizations in the same industry. Businesses having the highest ROICs in a given sector will frequently trade at a premium.

Calculating the rate of return with Excel

In Microsoft Excel, simply input the cash flows generated by the investment to get the rate of return. You can create this worksheet even if you've never used Excel before; all you need to do is launch Excel (just like you would launch any other Windows application). The investment's cash flows are then entered. To input one of these values, in case you're unfamiliar with Excel, simply click the box, which is formally referred to as a cell, and type the value. You click the cell and write -65000 to enter the $65,000 down payment needed to purchase the building. Press Enter once you've typed this number. To calculate the rate of return, you enter the other net cash-flow variables in the same way.

Measuring Liquidity

The efficiency or convenience with which a security or asset can be turned into quick cash without negatively impacting its market price is referred to as liquidity. Cash alone is the most liquid asset. As a result, the primary factor determining how well a market functions is the availability of funds for these conversions.

- An asset may be converted back into cash more quickly and easily the more liquid it is. More time and money may be spent on less liquid assets.
- The ease with which a security, or asset, can be changed into quick cash without depressing its market value, is known as liquidity.
  Of all the assets, cash is the most liquid, whereas tangible goods are less liquid.
- Market liquidity and accounting liquidity are the two primary categories of liquidity.
- When assessing liquidity, current, quick, and cash ratios are most frequently employed.

Put differently, liquidity is the extent to which an item may be readily purchased or sold on the market at a price that accurately reflects its inherent value. Because it can be changed into other assets the quickest and easiest, cash is usually regarded as the most liquid asset. Real estate, fine art, and collectibles are examples of tangible goods that are not very liquid. Other financial assets lie at different points on the liquidity continuum, from partnership units to stocks. Cash, for instance, is the asset that can be utilized to buy a $1,000 refrigerator the most readily. A person is unlikely to locate someone ready to sell the refrigerator for their $1,000 rare book collection if they have no cash but the collection is valuable. Rather, they will have to sell the collection and pay for the refrigerator with the proceeds. That might not be an issue if the buyer has just days to make the purchase, but it might be if they can wait months or years. Rather than waiting for a customer who is prepared to pay the full amount, they could have to sell the books at a discount. An example of an illiquid asset is rare books.

Market Liquidity

The degree to which assets can be purchased and sold at steady, transparent prices on a market—like the stock market of a nation or the real estate market of a city—is referred to as market liquidity. In the aforementioned scenario, there is no market for refrigerators in return for rare books since it is so illiquid. Higher market liquidity, however, is what distinguishes the stock market. The price that a buyer offers per share (the bid price) and the price that a seller is ready to take (the asking price) will be very close to each other if an exchange has a significant volume of activity that is not dominated by selling. Consequently, investors won't have to forfeit unrealized gains in exchange for a speedy sale. The market is more liquid when the difference between the ask and bid prices narrows; when it widens, the market becomes more illiquid. Compared to stock markets, real estate markets are typically significantly less liquid. The size and number of open exchanges on which other assets can be traded determine the liquidity of those markets. Examples of these assets include derivatives, contracts, currencies, and commodities.

Accounting Liquidity

Accounting liquidity quantifies how easily a person or business may pay off debts when they become due by using their liquid assets to meet their financial commitments. The rare book collector in the aforementioned example has somewhat illiquid assets, thus in an emergency, they probably wouldn't be worth their entire $1,000 value. Matching liquid assets to current liabilities, or debts that are due within a year, is the process of evaluating accounting liquidity in the context of investments. Accounting liquidity is measured by several ratios, each of which has a different definition of what constitutes liquid assets. These are used by investors and analysts to find companies with high liquidity. It is regarded as a depth measure as well.

Measuring Liquidity

Financial analysts consider a company's capacity to pay short-term obligations with liquid assets. In general, a ratio larger than one is preferred when utilizing these calculations.

Current Ratio

The easiest and least restrictive ratio is the current ratio. It compares current obligations to current assets or those that might be profitably turned into cash in a year.

Its equation would be as follows:

Current Ratio = Current Assets ÷ Current Liabilities

Quick Ratio (Acid-Test Ratio)

A little stricter is the quick ratio, often known as the acid-test ratio. It does not include current assets like inventory, which are less liquid than cash and cash equivalents, short-term investments, and accounts receivable.

The equation is:

Quick Ratio = (Cash and Cash Equivalents + Short-Term Investments + Accounts Receivable) ÷ Current Liabilities

Acid-Test Ratio (Variation)

A slightly more generous version of the quick/acid-test ratio is obtained by simply deducting inventory from current assets:

Acid-Test Ratio (Variation) = (Current Assets - Inventories - Prepaid Costs) ÷ Current Liabilities

Cash Ratio

Of all the liquidity ratios, the cash ratio is the strictest. It defines liquid assets strictly as cash or cash equivalents, excluding accounts receivable, inventory, and other current assets. The cash ratio evaluates an entity's ability to remain solvent in the worst-case scenario—an emergency—more so than the current ratio or acid-test ratio because even extremely lucrative businesses might face difficulties if they lack the liquidity to respond to unanticipated circumstances. Its equation is;

Cash Ratio = Cash and Cash Equivalents ÷ Current Liabilities

Liquidity Example

Equities are one of the most liquid asset classes when it comes to investments. However, when it comes to liquidity, not all stocks are made equal. On stock exchanges, some shares trade more frequently than others, indicating a larger market for those shares. Put another way, traders and investors are more consistently drawn to them. The daily volume of these liquid equities, which can number in the millions or even hundreds of millions of shares, typically identifies them. A high volume indicator for a stock indicates that there are a lot of buyers and sellers in the market, which facilitates the buying or selling of the stock by investors without having a big impact on its price. Conversely, low-volume equities could be more difficult to purchase or sell since there might be fewer market players and, thus, less liquidity. For instance, 69.6 million shares of Amazon.com Inc. (AMZN) were exchanged on exchanges on March 13, 2023. In contrast, the volume of merely 48.1 million shares for Intel Corp. (INTC) suggests that it was a little less liquid. Among these three equities, Ford Motor Co. (F) was the most active and likely the most liquid with a volume of 118.5 million shares that day.

Why is Liquidity Important?

It is more difficult to sell or convert securities or other assets into cash when markets are not liquid. For example, you could possess a highly precious and uncommon family treasure valued at $150,000. It is meaningless, though, if there is no market for your item—that is, no one will purchase it for anything approaching its estimated value—because it is extremely illiquid. It might even be necessary to pay an auction house to locate possible buyers and serve as a broker, which will be expensive and take time. On the other hand, liquid assets can be sold cheaply and rapidly for their full worth. Additionally, businesses need to maintain a sufficient level of liquid assets to meet their immediate liabilities, such as payroll or bills; failing to do so put them at risk of a liquidity crisis and insolvency. The most liquid asset is cash, followed by cash equivalents such as time deposits, money market accounts, and certificates of deposit (CDs). Marketable securities can be sold quickly through a broker and are frequently very liquid, such as stocks and bonds listed on exchanges. You may easily sell gold coins and some valuables for cash. Over-the-counter (OTC) securities, including some sophisticated derivatives, are frequently highly illiquid. A house, a timeshare, or a car are all somewhat illiquid assets for individuals since it might take weeks or months to locate a buyer and then additional weeks to complete the deal and get paid. Furthermore, broker fees are typically high (a real estate agent typically pays between 5% and 7%).

Thinking about Risk

Knowing about risk is very important. Even with low-risk assets like bank CDs, there is a risk involved. However, when it comes to capital investments, no government organization is watching out for your best interests or cleaning up the mess if something goes south.

So take a moment to consider risk assessment and management as they relate to capital expenditures. The following three points are crucial to take into account:

- Consider every option carefully and thoroughly when creating cash flows. The more thoughtful and accurate your estimation of the cash flows from a capital expenditure, the more accurate and valuable the results will be. Accurate cash-flow projections lead to accurate rate-of-return calculations.
- Try something out. You must test your presumptions. Make adjustments and see the impact on the rate of return and cash flow metrics.

For instance, if the amount sold for a profit in a given year represents the building investment's single largest cash flow. It would be fascinating to observe the impact of a reduced rate of inflation or appreciation on the final rate of return. An inflation rate of two percent would have a significant impact on this investment's cash flows and rate of return calculation. In the same way, a 5 or 6 percent inflation rate during those 20 years would completely alter the situation.

- Consider the discount rate you choose to apply. Although the discount rate isn't normally discussed in great detail, you should infer the risk that you are taking when investing. "Your discount rate should equal the rate of return that similarly risky investments produce," goes the statement. This straightforward advice contains a wealth of knowledge. You would never choose an investment that yields a lower rate of return than its degree of risk. In addition, you ought to employ a smaller discount rate when examining investments with lower levels of risk. It is not reasonable to use a discount rate that would be suitable for a very dangerous investment in brand-new, cutting-edge technology when evaluating a comparatively low-risk investment, such as an office building.

You should experiment with various discount rates. You can test how different discount rates affect an investment's quality (and implicitly alter your assumptions about the investment's risk) by playing not just with your cash-flow figures but also with your discount rates.

What Does All This Have to Do with QuickBooks?

Utilizing QuickBooks isn't directly related to capital budgeting. In certain respects, capital budgeting is similar to a crucial financial management activity that you must consider. However, QuickBooks doesn't offer direct support for this task. Having said that, keep in mind that a lot of the information you've gathered using QuickBooks is frequently quite helpful for obtaining accurate estimations of the costs and savings related to certain capital expenditures. When investing in an office building, for instance, you need to know how much you've been paying in rent and how much you might be able to save by purchasing your building. QuickBooks' extensive financial database provides just the kind of information you need. Your cash flow estimates are usually far more detailed. If you are thinking about investing in a building, you should account for a variety of costs associated with upkeep and repairs. If you have been renting space in someone else's building, you have to take into account a variety of costs related to that, such as additional insurance that the landlord requires you to purchase, the additional money that you must spend since the space doesn't quite match your needs, and so forth. QuickBooks provides you with this kind of data.

Activity

1. What does capital budgeting mean?
2. How can the rate of return on capital be calculated?
3. How can risk be mitigated?

BOOK 6

STRATEGIC CANVAS: CRAFTING THE BLUEPRINT FOR BUSINESS BRILLIANCE

CHAPTER 1
COST-VOLUME-PROFIT (CVP)

Profit-volume-cost analysis is an effective technique for estimating break-even points and how a company's profits fluctuate in response to changes in sales volumes. (The sales revenue level at which there is no profits is known as the break-even point.) Analysis of profit, volume, and cost frequently yields unexpected findings. The analysis typically demonstrates that minor adjustments to a company's sales volume result in significant adjustments to its earnings. Profit-volume-cost analysis is an effective technique for estimating break-even points and how a company's profits fluctuate in response to changes in sales volumes. (The sales revenue level at which there is no profits is known as the break-even point.) Analysis of profit, volume, and cost frequently yields unexpected findings. The analysis typically demonstrates that minor adjustments to a company's sales volume result in significant adjustments to its earnings. Businesses like hotels and airlines frequently experience unexpected swings in their profits based on comparatively little changes in their sales income. Now that you know this, you'll undoubtedly note that investment analysts frequently utilize slight variations in hotel occupancy and airline load factors—the proportion of occupied seats on an aircraft—to explain large variations in profits.

Seeing How Cost-Volume-Profit (CVP) Works

A cost accounting technique called cost-volume-profit (CVP) analysis examines how different cost and volume levels affect operational profit.

- A method for determining how changes in variable and fixed costs impact a company's profit is through cost-volume-profit (CVP) analysis.
- Businesses can utilize CVP to determine the minimal profit margin they must meet or the number of units they must sell to break even (pay all expenditures).
- The sales price, fixed costs, and variable costs per unit are all taken for granted in CVP analysis.

The formula for calculating this is; profits = **(sales x gross margin percentage) - fixed cost**

The breakeven point for various sales volumes and cost structures is found using the cost-volume-profit analysis, usually referred to as the breakeven analysis. This information can be helpful for managers making immediate business choices. Several presumptions are made in CVP analysis, such as the constant sales price and fixed and variable costs per unit. Several equations for cost, pricing, and other variables are used when doing a CVP analysis, and the results are plotted on an economic graph. The breakeven point can also be determined using the CVP formula. The quantity of units sold or the amount of sales income needed to cover the costs of manufacturing the product is known as the breakeven point. The margin of product contribution is also managed by CVP analysis. The entire revenue minus the total variable costs is the contribution margin. The contribution margin must be greater than the total fixed costs for a business to be profitable. One option is to compute the contribution margin on a per-unit basis. Simply said, the unit contribution margin is the amount left over after deducting the unit variable cost from the unit sales price. The calculation of the contribution margin ratio involves dividing the total sales by the contribution margin.

The breakeven point of sales is ascertained using the contribution margin. It is possible to determine the breakeven threshold of sales in terms of total dollars by dividing the total fixed costs by the contribution margin ratio. For instance, to break even, a business with $100,000 in fixed expenditures and a 40% contribution margin needs to bring in $250,000 in sales. To do a CVP analysis on the intended result, profit may be added to the fixed expenses. For instance, if the prior business wanted to make $50,000 in profit, the required total sales revenue can be calculated by dividing $150,000—the total of the fixed costs and the intended profit—by the 40% contribution margin. Based on this example, $375,000 in sales revenue is needed. The application of cost-volume-profit analysis helps to ascertain whether a product's manufacturing is economically justified. The breakeven sales volume is the number of units that must be sold to pay the costs of manufacturing the product and reach the goal sales volume required to provide the intended profit. To this amount is added a target profit margin. Next, to choose whether to manufacture the product or not, the decision maker could compare the product's sales estimates to the goal sales volume.

The assumptions used by CVP, such as the constant sales price and stable and variable cost per unit, are what give it its dependability. Costs are set within a predetermined production threshold. Since it is anticipated that every unit produced will be sold, every fixed cost needs to be constant. Another supposition is that variations in activity level cause all variations in expenses. It is necessary to divide semi-variable expenses between expense categories using statistical regression, scatter plotting, or the high-low approach.

Contribution Margin

It is possible to express the contribution margin as a gross or per-unit amount. It shows the additional revenue made for each product or unit sold following the deduction of the variable costs incurred by the business. In essence, it displays the percentage of sales that goes toward paying the fixed expenses of the business. Profit is defined as any amount of revenue left over after fixed costs are paid. Therefore, the contribution margin must be greater than the total fixed costs for a business to be profitable.

Calculating Break-Even Points

Break-even analysis is the process of evaluating sales revenue to fixed operating expenses. The goal of the study is to determine the amount of revenue that will be needed to pay for all fixed expenses for the company to turn a profit. As a result of this activity, an entity's margin of safety based on collected revenues and related expenses is also calculated and examined. A

seller would gain a great deal of understanding about their selling capabilities via a demand-side analysis.

- The number of units of a product that must be sold to pay the fixed and variable costs of manufacturing is determined by break-even analysis.
- The margin of safety is thought to be gauged by the break-even point.
- Break-even analysis is widely utilized in many areas, including corporate planning for a range of initiatives and stock and options trading.

Determining the production level or a targeted ideal sales mix can be accomplished by computing the break-even analysis. Since the metric and computations are not utilized by outside parties like investors, regulators, or financial institutions, the study is intended solely for use by a company's management. The break-even point (BEP) is calculated in this kind of analysis. The price per unit less the variable costs of manufacturing is divided by the total fixed costs of production to determine the break-even point. Expenses known as fixed expenses don't change based on how many units are sold. In a break-even analysis, the amount of fixed costs is compared to the profit generated by producing and selling each extra unit.

A corporation with lower fixed costs will typically have a lower point of sale at which it breaks even. When the first product is sold, for instance, a business with $0 in fixed costs will instantly have broken even, provided that variable costs do not exceed sales income. Two equations may be used in the break-even analysis computation. Divide the total fixed expenses by the unit contribution margin in the first computation. Assume for this example that all of the fixed costs total $20,000. The break-even point is 500 units ($20,000 divided by $40) with a contribution margin of $40. After 500 units are sold, all fixed costs will have been paid, and the business will record a net profit or loss of $0. Alternatively, the total fixed expenses are divided by the contribution margin ratio to determine the break-even point in sales dollars. The division of the contribution margin per unit by the sale price yields the contribution margin ratio.

Numerous organizations, including financial analysts, companies, government agencies, and entrepreneurs, use break-even analysis.

- **Entrepreneurs:** For founders and entrepreneurs, break-even analysis helps figure out the lowest revenues required to cover expenses. For a business in its early stages, this is crucial.
- **Financial Analysts**: Break-even analysis is a profitability and risk assessment used by these experts. Break-even analysis is used by financial analysts in their business valuations and recommendations.
- **Investors**: Investors use break-even analysis to assess a company's financial health. They choose their assets with greater knowledge after reading this material.
- **Stock and Option Traders**: For stock and option traders, knowing how much money is required to cover their costs on each transaction is essential, which is why break-even

analysis is so important. They were able to ascertain which assets would yield the highest earnings for them and how much money to allocate to a deal thanks to this analysis.

- **Business**: Break-even analysis is a tool that many different types of businesses utilize to have a better understanding of their pricing, cost structure, and operational efficiency.
- **Government Agencies**: Break-even analysis is a tool used by government organizations to assess the financial viability of projects and programs. It provides a solution to the following query: What is the minimal volume of sales or income necessary to pay expenses?

Businesses use the break-even point component of break-even analysis in a variety of ways. Businesses can use the break-even threshold to help with cost management, growth strategies, sales forecasts, and price decisions. Businesses can determine the lowest price they must charge to pay their costs by using the break-even point. Businesses can enhance their pricing strategy by comparing this point to the market price. A common financial tool used by both stock and option traders and corporations is break-even analysis. Break-even analysis is crucial for organizations to identify the minimal sales volume needed to break even and cover all costs.

It supports companies in making defensible choices about operations, cost control, and pricing policies. Break-even analysis is also a crucial tool in stock and options trading because it helps identify the minimal price movements needed to pay trading expenses and turn a profit. Break-even analysis is a useful tool for traders to control risk, set reasonable profit targets, and make wise trading decisions. It is a crucial instrument for financial analysts and investors to assess a company's financial health and make well-informed investment decisions. Investors can successfully control risks and make lucrative investment decisions by being aware of the break-even point. All things considered, break-even analysis is a vital instrument in the financial industry for companies, investors, traders of stocks and options, financial analysts, and even government organizations.

Using Real QuickBooks Data for Cost-Volume-Profit (CVP) Analysis

To run a profit-volume-cost analysis, you need three types of data: sales revenue, gross margin percentage, and fixed cost. Finding these kinds of data is usually not too tough if you have experience with QuickBooks. However, there are several inconsistencies between this data and the line items found in a QuickBooks income statement.

Sales revenue

You want to experiment with different sales revenue levels; therefore they are the ones you use in the calculation. They most likely indicate potential sales income levels for your company, if not likely ones. Thus, QuickBooks is not where the sales revenue amounts originate from. If you want to know what sales revenue levels are fair or likely, you could wish to review previous income statements. However, the calculation inputs are not derived from a QuickBooks income statement; they are most likely approximations.

Gross margin percentage

As previously shown, you may find the gross margin % by deducting your variable costs from your sales revenue and then dividing the remaining amount (the gross margin) by the sales revenue. The costs of the goods you sell, such as inventory, commissions, shipping, and other related expenses, are included in the variable costs.

Here are a few examples to go over because figuring out the gross margin percentage might be a little tricky the first few times:

- **Boat building**: If you sell $100,000 boats and your material, labor, and commission costs come to $40,000 per boat, you can use this method to find the gross margin percentage: $ ($100,000 - $40,000) ÷ ($100,000). The result of the computation is 0.6, or 60%, which represents the boat-building industry's gross margin percentage.
- **Tax return service**: Assume, for another example, that you are a proprietor of a personal services company and that your primary source of income is tax return preparation. Assume further that the small-business tax return you prepare costs $200, and the only variable expense is the $40 fee you must pay the tax software provider. In this instance, the formula is used to determine the gross margin percentage.
  ($200 - $40) ÷ $200
  The result of this formula is 0.8, or 80 percent. In this instance, your tax return preparation business's gross profit percentage is eighty percent. The crucial idea is that variable expenses change in response to sales income. If a sale happens, variable costs result. There are no variable costs if there is no sale.

What does all of this mean, then? Well, the cost of goods sold (COGS) figure that appears on your QuickBooks revenue statement is usually equal to the variable costs. If your company resells inventory, this COGS figure most likely include the inventory products you sell in addition to other costs like freight and sales fees. As a result, the QuickBooks income statement contains most, if not all, of the variable cost information. It could be necessary for you to adjust the COGS figure that appears on the income statement in QuickBooks. Some of the costs you've listed in the COGS area of your income statement might not be variable since, as you may recall, variable costs are those that change based on sales. Some of the expenses shown in your income statement's regular operating expenses section are changeable. As a result, you might wish to consider the expenses listed in your income statement's COGS and operational expenses sections. Make some changes if you find that the COGS value isn't a reliable indicator of variable costs. Naturally, a fixed cost that is part of the COGS figure needs to be deducted. Additionally, the COGS figure could need to be increased by a variable cost that is included in the other operating expenses.

Fixed costs

All other non-variable costs are included in your fixed costs. In short, because they remain constant regardless of sales volume, fixed costs are just that—fixed. Rent for an office or factory, wages for permanent staff, insurance overhead and other expenses are examples of fixed expenditures.

Recognizing the Downside of the Cost-Volume-Profit (CVP) Model

Cost-volume-profit (CVP) analysis is a valuable tool, but before using it exclusively for strategic decision-making, organizations should be aware of its limits.

Firstly, CVP analysis assumes that all costs incurred by a business are either fixed or variable.

In actuality, some costs—like advertising—can fluctuate in response to variations in volume even when they are not directly correlated with sales. Certain expenses, like mixed costs that have fixed and variable components, are neither fixed nor variable. If these expenses are not properly taken into account, this restriction may lead to calculations that are not accurate.

Another limitation of CVP analysis is that it assumes that the sales mix ratio remains constant

It indicates that a company's share of sales from each good or service it provides remains constant. But this is frequently unachievable, especially for businesses that offer a broad range of goods and services. The break-even threshold will fluctuate in tandem with changes in the sales mix ratio, which could result in erroneous inferences.

Moreover, CVP analysis assumes no changes in market conditions

This covers client preferences and competition. Given that these modifications may have an impact on price, cost structure, and sales volume, this restriction may have a major effect on the analysis's accuracy.

CVP analysis is based on the assumption of perfect costs and revenue behaviors

In actuality, several things influence revenues and costs. This involves, among other things, differences in client demand, technological advancements, and economies of scale. When this assumption is broken, the analysis's conclusions may diverge significantly from real-world situations.

Others include;

- Several presumptions, including constant sales prices, variable costs, and fixed expenses, are crucial to CVP analysis. The analysis may become less accurate and trustworthy if these presumptions turn out to be false.
- The greatest candidates for CVP research are companies with straightforward cost structures. It does not take into consideration companies that produce many items and have complex products with varying costs. It is assumed in the analysis that the cost structure of each product is the same.
- The main purpose of CVP analysis is to assist in making immediate decisions. It ignores long-term trends that could have a big influence on a company's financial performance, like inflation and technology advancements.
- Financial information, including expenses and revenues, is the main emphasis of CVP analysis but it disregards non-financial aspects that can affect corporate decisions, like staff morale, customer happiness, and environmental effects.
- All costs, revenues, and profits are assumed to be linearly proportional in CVP analysis. This presumption ignores elements like economies of scale or diseconomies of scale, which cause the unit cost to change depending on the volume of production.
- In a world where relationships play a major role in corporate success, CVP analysis might not take network effects or partnerships into consideration. It falls short of giving a full picture of the possibilities and activities of a corporation.

Using the Profit-Volume-Cost Analysis Workbook

You may estimate break-even points, chart break-even, and profit-volume-cost data, and estimate profits for a range of sales revenue volumes using the Profit-Volume-Cost Analysis workbook. The remaining pages of this chapter will teach you how to utilize the Profit-Volume-Cost Analysis workbook as well as how to comprehend and evaluate the workbook's results, which include a break-even analysis and a profit-volume-cost analysis. A brief overview of the charts that visually represent the outcomes of the profit-volume-cost analysis will also be covered.

Collecting your inputs

More data points are gathered by the worksheet than you might anticipate. The majority of this data, however, is only a somewhat more detailed method of gathering the three fundamental inputs—estimates of sales revenue, the percentage of gross margin, and fixed costs—that are necessary for any profit-volume-cost analysis. The Profit-Volume-Cost Analysis workbook covered in this chapter doesn't require you to be an Excel whiz, but you will need to know how to open and close the program and insert values into worksheet cells.

Follow the steps below to make use of the Profit-Volume-Cost Analysis workbook;

- Check for the Profit-Volume-Cost Analysis workbook online and download it. Once downloaded, open it.
- Make a description of the sales revenue you would like to test.
  Three pieces of information are required to accomplish this: the unit sales price, the low unit sales volume, and the high unit sales volume. In cell E5, type the unit sales price. For example, if you sell something for $1,500, you enter $1,500 into cell E5. To determine the range of sales quantities that you wish to test, use the low unit volume tested and high unit volume tested inputs displayed in cells E6 and E7, respectively. The worksheet determines the lowest revenue volume by multiplying the low unit volume tested value by the unit sales price. The greatest sales revenue volume tested is equal to the high unit volume tested times the unit sales price amount. Which sales revenue volumes you wish to study is indicated in the workbook by the three revenue inputs that you gather and enter into cells E5, E6, and E7.
- Describe the variable costs.
  Real-world profit-volume-cost analyses reveal that your variable costs may be classified into two groups: those that are stated as a percentage of the sales price and those that are indicated as an amount per unit. The data required to characterize these kinds of variable costs is gathered in the worksheet range E10:E18.
  Enter the first set of variable costs into cells E11, E12, E13, and E14. It is referred to as vary-with-unit costs. Cell E11 should contain any direct labor expenses related to the product you are selling. E12 includes direct material expenses. Cell E13 is used for variable factory overhead expenditures, which are determined by units sold. You put the amount per unit for any additional vary-with-unit charges you may have in cell E14. Businesses frequently incur variable expenses, which are best described as a proportion of revenue, in addition to vary-with-unit costs.
  These variable expenses, which are referred to as vary-with-revenue costs, are provided with space to be described and recorded in the Profit-Volume-Cost Analysis workbook in worksheet range E16:E18. For instance, the spreadsheet may display in cell E16 a 5% sales commission. Cell E17 in the spreadsheet displays a sales tax of 8%. Additionally, the workbook contains other vary-with-revenue-costs values in cell E18 as a catch-all category for other vary-with-revenue costs.

- Record your fixed costs.
- Estimate any variable costs that may vary with profits.

Activity

1. What is profit volume cost analysis all about?
2. What are break-even points and how can they be calculated?
3. Employ the use of the profit volume cost analysis workbook.

CHAPTER 2

CREATING A BUSINESS PLAN FORECAST

Pro forma financial statements, which include cash-flow statements, balance sheets, and income statements, are essential to budgeting and corporate planning. You will therefore learn a little bit about how to make these pro forma (or as if) statements. But right away, you should be aware that in addition to QuickBooks, you also need another program to generate these kinds of statements. In particular, you'll need a spreadsheet application, such as Microsoft Excel. Google Sheets and Excel for the Web offer a free online version of Microsoft Excel if you don't have a license for the program.

Reviewing Financial Statements and Ratios

Before you get started fully, here is a refresher on some very important things you need to take note of. One of the various schedules and summaries of economic data might be referred to as a financial statement. However, the phrase usually refers to a group of documents that comprise a cash-flow statement, a balance sheet (also known as a statement of financial condition), and an income statement (also known as a statement of operations). An income statement lists a company's gains and losses for a given time frame. Let's say you would like to know how much money your company made or lost last month. You create an income statement that details your monthly earnings and losses as well as your income and expenses.

Now onto the ratios!

Relationships between the amounts shown in the financial statements are expressed by financial ratios. The ratios can provide information about a company's financial health. The reasonableness of a forecast's implicit assumptions can also be determined by the ratios. You can compare the financial features of your company with those of other companies by comparing its ratios with those of similar companies. You can also verify the plausibility of your modeling assumptions by contrasting the ratios in your pro forma model with industry norms and averages. Financial ratios can be broadly classified into two categories: intra-statement or inter-statement ratios and common-size ratios. Common size ratios change the unit of measurement from dollars to percentages in a financial statement, typically an income statement or balance sheet. The assets, liabilities, revenue, owner equity, and expenses of companies of different sizes can all be compared according to common size ratios. The comparison might be made as a trend throughout time or at a specific moment in time. Relationships between quantities from several financial statements or various sections of the same financial statement are measured by intra-statement or inter-statement ratios, respectively. Ratios, both intra-statement, and inter-statement, are attempts to take into consideration the fact that numbers are typically not interpretable in isolation but rather need to be considered about other significant financial events and circumstances. Generally speaking, comparisons with industry norms and trends yield the greatest value for both types of ratios.

Using the Business Plan Workbook

To use the workbook, there is a need for you to develop and insert information about the following;

- Assets
- The creditor and owner's equities at the start of the forecasting horizon
- Expected changes in the assets and equities over the forecasting horizon
- Revenue and expenses for each period on the forecasting horizon

Although the workbook has a lot of functions, its operation is rather simple. The worksheet creates a balance sheet based on the information you enter about your initial assets, liabilities, owner's equity balances, and anticipated changes in these amounts throughout the forecasting horizon. When you enter data about sales and costs of sales, operating expenses, interest income, and expenses, and marginal income tax rates, the workbook creates an income statement. The workbook then creates a cash-flow statement based on the balance sheet and income statement. The following procedures will allow you to enter your data into the business planning beginning worksheet.

Enter positive balances or rises as positive amounts and negative balances or reductions as negative amounts:

- **Open the business plan workbook in Excel.** The default inputs are originally present in the beginning workbook.
- **Insert the cash as well as the equivalent balance for the start of the forecasting horizon**. The total amount of cash held at the start of the forecasting period is the value you provide for Cash and equivalents. If you're projecting future values based on present circumstances, you can obtain the Cash & Equivalents figure from QuickBooks. Of course, the money you start with is the same money you have in your possession right now.
- **Make an input of the forecasted period yield that you expect the cash and equivalents to get delivered.** The cash and equivalents balance is multiplied by the cash and equivalents yield in the model to predict the period interest income.
- **Insert the accounts receivable balance for the commencement of the forecasting horizon**. The starting accounts receivable balance, or balance at the start of the forecasting horizon, minus any allowance for uncollectible amounts, is the value that you record for accounts receivable (A/R).
- **Insert the number of periods of sales in accounts receivable**. The number of periods, or fraction of a period, for which sales are held in accounts receivable is the value that you give for # Periods of Sales in A/R, or number of periods of sales in accounts

receivable. If your forecasting periods are months and accounts receivable normally equals thirty days of sales, then you have one period (one month) of sales in accounts receivable. Alternatively, you hold one-twelfth of a period of sales in accounts receivable if, for example, you use years as your forecasting periods and accounts receivable normally equal around thirty days of sales.

- **Insert the dollar amount of the inventory held at the beginning of the forecasting horizon**. The total monetary amount of goods manufactured or bought for resale and retained at the start of the forecasting horizon is known as the starting inventory balance or inventory value.
- **Insert the forecasted dollar amount of inventory bought or produced for each period of the forecasting horizon**. The total monetary amount of goods bought or produced over the period is the inventory purchased/produced value.
- **Insert the amount of the current assets held at the commencement of the forecasting horizon**. The Additional Current Assets The entire dollar amount of any additional current assets with which you start the forecasting horizon is known as the beginning balance. These additional current assets could be vendor deposits, short-term investments, and prepayments for expenses.
- **Insert the amount of the change in the other current assets for each period in the forecasting horizon**. The total dollar amount of increases or reductions in the accounts included in the initial Other Current Assets balance represents the value for Chgs in Other Current Assets or changes in other current assets during the period.
- **Insert the amount of the plant, property, and equipment at the commencement of the forecasting horizon**. The initial balance for Plant, Property, and Equipment is the total amount of money allocated to fixed assets. This sum covers things like real estate, furniture, Learjet, and manufacturing equipment.
- **Insert the amount of the change in plant, property, and equipment (P, P, & E) for each period of the forecasting horizon**. The entire dollar amount of losses or rises in the plant, property, and equipment accounts during the period is known as the Chgs in P, P, & E value. Increases in these accounts are most likely the result of buying more fixed assets. These accounts' decreases are most likely the result of asset sales.
- **Insert the amount of the accumulated depreciation on plant, property, and equipment at the commencement of the forecasting horizon**. The depreciation charges charged to date on the assets listed in the starting P, P, and E balance are represented by the starting Accumulated Depreciation balance.
- **Insert the amount of the change in the accumulated depreciation for each period of the forecasting horizon**. The Changes in Total. The total cash amount of all of the period's increases and declines in the accumulated depreciation account is the depreciation value. The current-period depreciation expense is most often the cause of increases in the accumulated depreciation balance. Removing the accumulated depreciation associated with a fixed asset that you sold off is most likely the cause of decreases in the accumulated depreciation balance.

- **Insert the amount of the other noncurrent assets at the commencement of the period.** The total amount of money held at the beginning of the forecasting period in other noncurrent assets is known as the starting Other Noncurrent Assets balance. A few more noncurrent assets may be goodwill, patents, and copyrights.
- **Insert the amount of the change in the other noncurrent assets for each period of the forecasting horizon.** The total dollar rise or decrease for the period in the accounts included in the initial Other Noncurrent Assets balance is the Chgs in Other Noncurrent Assets value.
- **Insert the amount of the accounts payable balance at the commencement of the forecasting horizon**. The total amount of money owed to vendors for inventory at the beginning of the forecasting period is known as the starting accounts payable (A/P) balance. Using the cost of sales volumes as a basis, this beginning workbook computes future accounts payable balances. The model assumes that accounts payable represent debt incurred for the cost of sales to increase prediction accuracy.
- Insert the number of periods of the cost of sales in accounts payable. The number of periods, or fraction of a period, for which the cost of sales is retained in accounts payable is indicated by the #Periods Cost of Sales in A/P entry. If your forecasting periods are months and accounts payable usually equals thirty days of cost of sales, then you have one period, or one month, of cost of sales in accounts payable. Alternatively, you store one-twelfth of a period of cost of sales in accounts payable if, for example, accounts payable normally amounts to roughly thirty days of cost of sales and you use years as your forecasting periods.
- At the beginning of the forecasting horizon, enter the balance of accumulated expenses. The total amount of money owed to vendors for operational expenses at the beginning of the forecast period is known as the starting Accrued Expenses (A/E) balance. Based on the amounts of operational expenses, this beginning workbook computes future Accrued Expenses balances. The model assumes that accumulated expenses are debt incurred for operating expenses to increase prediction accuracy.
- In accumulated expenses, enter the number of operational expenditure periods. The number of periods, or portion of a period, for which operating expenses are retained in accumulated expenses is indicated by the # Periods Operating Expenses in A/E value. You maintain one period of operating expenses in accumulated expenses if, on average, accrued expenses equal thirty days of operating expenses and you utilize months for your forecasting periods. Alternatively, you store one-twelfth of a period of operating expenses in accumulated expenses if accrued expenses normally equal roughly thirty days of operating expenses and you use years as your forecasting periods.
- At the beginning of the forecasting period, enter the total amount of the other current liabilities. The entire amount of all other current liabilities held at the beginning of the forecasting period is known as the Other Current Liabilities starting balance. Income

tax payable, product warranty responsibility, and the current element of a long-term liability are examples of additional current liabilities.

- For every forecasting horizon period, enter the change in the other current liabilities' amount. The total dollar amount of increases or decreases for the period in the accounts included in the initial Other Current Liabilities balance is the Chgs in Other Current Liabilities value.
- At the beginning of the forecasting horizon, enter the balance of long-term obligations. The total amount of debt that will be repaid in cash at some point after the next year is the initial Long-Term Liabilities balance.
- For each forecasting horizon period, enter the amount of the long-term liability change. The change in the amount of outstanding long-term debt over a certain period is represented by the value of Changes in Long-Term Liabilities. These adjustments could include reductions brought about by principal amortization through debt service payments and additions brought about by extra money supplied by creditors. Since the principal component of debt service payments reduces the amount of long-term liability, you must report them as negative values.
- At the beginning of the forecasting horizon, enter the total amount of the other noncurrent obligations. The entire amount of all other noncurrent liabilities held at the beginning of the forecasting period is known as the Other Noncurrent Liabilities starting balance. These could include capitalized leasing commitments, deferred income tax, and employee pension plan liabilities.
- For each forecasting horizon period, enter the change in the other noncurrent liabilities' amount. The total dollar amount of increases or decreases for the period in the accounts included in the initial Other Noncurrent Liabilities balance is the Chgs in Other Noncurrent Liabilities value. These adjustments could include reductions brought about by principal amortization through debt service payments and additions brought about by extra money supplied by creditors.
- For each forecasting horizon period, enter the amount of the change in the owner's equity balance due to increased capital contributions, dividends, and other exceptional distributions to owners. The value of the changes in owner equity is the total dollar amount of all owner equity declines and rises over the period, except those resulting from corporate earnings. Additional issues of common or preferred stock as well as transactions involving U.S. Treasury stock may result in increases in the Owner Equity balance; dividends and other distributions to stockholders may result in declines in the Owner Equity balance.
- For each predicted period of the forecasting horizon, enter the expected sales revenue. The sales revenue figures show how much money the company expects to make from sales throughout each forecasting horizon period.
- For each forecasting horizon period, enter the estimated cost of sales. The estimated costs of the inventory sold during the forecasting horizon are represented by the Cost of Sales numbers.

- For every period of the forecasting horizon, enter the costs that fit into the first, second, and third operating expenditure classifications or categories. The operational expenses for the forecasting horizon are represented by the operating expenses for Cost Centers 1, 2, and 3. These numbers could represent three different business operational expense categories or the sum of the three groups' expenses.
- Add the interest cost of any debt that was taken on to finance activities or the acquisition of assets. The interest costs incurred throughout carrying any business-related loan are represented by the Interest Expense values.
- Enter the income tax rate that determines the income tax expense (or savings) when multiplied by the period's profit or loss. The proportion that determines the income tax expense is known as the Income Tax Rate value, and it is multiplied by the operational profit (or loss). The fact that corporate income taxes are progressive makes this computation a little more difficult. The tax rates applicable to an individual entrepreneur vary based on their income level, ranging from 0% to around 35 percent. The income tax rates for a typical corporation range from 15 to 34 percent.

Understanding the Workbook Calculation

The inputs forecast, Balance Sheet, Common Size Balance Sheet, Income Statement, Common Size Income Statement, Cash Flow Statement, and Financial Ratios Table are the seven sections that make up the business plan workbook. A brief explanation of the Excel calculations that take place in each of these sections is provided below so that, should you have any queries or wish to make any changes, you can tailor the starter workbook to work better for your particular scenario. Do not worry if you are not familiar with Excel and do not wish to learn it; you may bypass this talk. This is primarily for readers who wish to know how the workbook functions internally and who might need or wish to alter the calculations in the workbook.

Forecasting inputs

One set of formulas can be found in the inputs section of the beginning workbook for business planning. The time for which the results are derived is indicated in the second row. The periods for which values are input are numbered by the period identifier. Cell D3 stores the integer 0 at the beginning of the first period. Subsequent periods are stored as the preceding period + 1. Similar algorithms are used for the period IDs in the schedules for the cash flow statement, income statement, common size income statement, balance sheet, and financial ratios table. The word "Period" appears before each period in the cells containing the period identifiers, which are formatted using a unique number system. Use a different number format to reformat the cells to get rid of it. The simplest way to accomplish this is to first select a cell, and then you can click a formatting button (such as the Currency or Percent Style buttons) in the Excel toolbar.

Balance Sheet

There are 19 rows of computed data in the Balance Sheet schedule; the first row only has text labels that correspond to the period numbers. The period identifier in the business planning beginning workbook numbers the intervals, for which values are predicted, much like in the inputs section. The next paragraphs provide descriptions of the remaining values on the Balance Sheet.

Cash & Equivalent

The estimated cash on hand after each forecasting period is displayed in the Cash & Equivalents data. The amount you enter in the business planning starter workbook's inputs section is the starting balance. The balance is computed and taken from the Cash Flow Statement schedule for the first and subsequent periods.

Accounts Receivable

The net receivables held after each forecasting period are displayed in the Accounts Receivable (A/R) data. The amount you enter in the business startup worksheet's inputs planning section is the starting balance. The Sales Revenue and the #Periods of Sales in A/R numbers that you enter in the inputs section of the Business Planning Starter Workbook determine the balance for the first and subsequent periods.

For the first period, the formula is;

- E8*E32
- The formula for the second period is
- =F8*F32, and so on.

Inventory

The monetary amount of the inventory maintained after each forecasting period is displayed in the inventory values. The amount you enter in the business planning starter workbook's inputs section is the starting balance. The balance from the previous period plus any inventory purchases or production costs less any cost of sales is the balance for the first and future periods.

For the first period, the formula is;

=D46+E10 – E33

The formula for the second period is

=E46+F10 – F33; and so on.

Other Current Assets

The monetary amount of the other current assets held after each forecasting period is displayed in the Other Current Assets data. The amount you enter in the inputs section of the business planning beginning workbook represents the starting balance for Other Current Assets. The prior balance plus the balance change represents the balance for the first and subsequent periods.

For the first period, the formula is;

=D47+E12

The formula for the second period is

=E47+F12

And so on.

Total Current Assets

The dollar amount of current assets after each forecasting horizon is displayed in the Total Current Assets data. The total of cash and equivalents, accounts receivable, inventory, and other current assets is the balance at any one time.

The beginning Total Current Assets balance is calculated using the formula;

=SUM (D44:D47)

The formula for the first period is

=SUM (E44:E47)

And so on.

Plant, Property, & Equipment

After each forecasting horizon, the Plant, Property, and Equipment figures display the original dollar cost of the plant, property, and equipment. You enter the initial Plant, Property, and Equipment balance in the business planning starter workbook's inputs section. The prior balance plus any additions to the accounts for plant, property, and equipment make up the balance for the first and subsequent periods.

For the first period, the formula is;

=D49+E14

The formula for the second period is

=E49+F14

And so on.

Less: Accumulated Depreciation

The plant, property, and equipment's cumulative depreciation costs levied during the current period are displayed in the Accumulated Depreciation numbers. The amount you enter in the business planning starter workbook's inputs section is the starting balance. The prior balance less the adjustments in accumulated depreciation for the current period is the balance for the first and future periods.

For the first period, the formula is;

=D50 – E16

The formula for the second period is

=E50 – F16

And so on. The positive figure extracted from the forecasted inputs is subtracted since the cumulative depreciation is displayed as a negative amount.

Net Plant, Property. & Equipment

After each forecasting horizon, the Net Plant, Property, and Equipment numbers display the difference between Plant, Property, and Equipment and Accumulated Depreciation.

The beginning balance formula is;

=D49+D50

The formula for the first period is

=E49+E50

And so on. You only add these two figures to the formula for the Net Plant, Property, and Equipment amount because the Accumulated Depreciation balance is displayed as a negative amount.

Other Noncurrent Assets

The monetary amount of any additional noncurrent assets held after each forecasting period is displayed in the Other Noncurrent Assets data. The amount you enter in the business planning starter workbook's inputs section is the starting balance. The balance from the prior period plus the account's change in the current period constitutes the balance for the first and future periods.

For the first period, the formula is;

=D52+E18

The formula for the second period is

=E52+F18

And so on.

Total Assets

The dollar amount of all the assets held after the forecasted periods is displayed in the Total Assets numbers. Any given time's balance is the total of the following: Net Plant, Property & Equipment; Other Noncurrent Assets; and Current Assets.

The beginning balance formula is;

=D48+D51+D52

The formula for the first period is

=E48+E51+E52

And so on.

Accounts Payable

The debt associated with the cost of sales that remains unpaid after each forecasting period is displayed in the Accounts Payable data. The amount you enter in the business planning starter workbook's inputs section is the starting balance. For the first and later periods, the equilibrium is Sales Cost for the specified period's #Time Frames Sales Cost in A/P.

For the first period, the formula is;

=E20*E33

The formula for the second period is

=F20*F33

And so on.

Accrued Expenses

The debt associated with the operating expenses that remain unpaid after each forecasting period is displayed in the Accrued Expenses numbers. The amount you enter in the business planning starter workbook's inputs section is the starting balance. Operating expenses times one is the amount for the first and subsequent periods. #Operating Expense Periods in A/E.

For the first period, the formula is;

=E22*SUM (E34:E36)

The formula for the second period is

=F22*SUM (F34:F36)

And so on.

Other Current Liabilities

The dollar amount of other outstanding debts after the forecasted periods that will be settled during the current year or business cycle is displayed in the Other Current Liabilities data. The amount you enter in the business planning starter workbook's inputs section is the starting balance. The prior balance plus the change from the current period is the balance for the first and following periods.

For the first period, the formula is;

=D59+E24

The formula for the second period is

=E59+F24

And so on.

Total Current Liabilities

After each forecasting period, the Total Current obligations statistics display the total amount of all current obligations in dollars. Accounts Payable, Accrued Expenses, and Other Current Liabilities add up to the balance at any given time. The beginning balance formula is;

=SUM (D57:D59)

The formula for the first period is

=SUM (E57:E59)

And so on.

Long-Term Liabilities

After each forecasting period, the Long-Term Liabilities statistics display the total dollar amount of outstanding long-term debt. The amount you enter in the business planning starter workbook's inputs section is the starting balance. Any changes in the Long-Term Liabilities balance in the current period are added to the previous balance for the first and subsequent periods.

For the first period, the formula is;

=D62+E26

The formula for the second period is

=E62+F26

And so on.

Other Noncurrent Liabilities

The dollar amount of any additional noncurrent outstanding debt after each forecasting period is displayed in the Other Noncurrent Liabilities statistics. The amount you enter in the business planning starter workbook's inputs section is the starting balance. The balance from the previous period plus the change from the current period equals the balance for the first and following periods.

For the first period, the formula is;

=D63+E28

The formula for the second period is

=E63+F28

And so on.

Total Noncurrent Liabilities

After each forecasting period, the dollar amounts of long-term debt and other outstanding noncurrent debt are displayed in the Total Noncurrent Liabilities numbers. The total of Long-Term Liabilities and Other Noncurrent Liabilities is the balance at any given time.

The beginning balance formula is;

=D62+D63

The formula for the first period is

=E62+E63

And so on.

Owner Equity

After each forecasting period, the owner equity figures display the dollar totals of the owner equity accounts. The amount you enter in the business planning starter workbook's inputs section is the starting balance. The balance for the first and subsequent periods is equal to the balance from the previous period plus the period's net income after taxes plus any extra adjustments, like dividends and additional capital contributions.

For the first period, the formula is;

=D65+E30+E113

The formula for the second period is

=E65+F30+F113

And so on.

Total Liabilities and Owner's Equity

After each forecasting period, the dollar totals of Current Liabilities, Noncurrent Liabilities, and Owner Equity are displayed in the Total Liabilities and Owner's Equity figures.

The beginning balance formula is;

=D60+D64+D65

The formula for the first period is

=E60+E64+E65

And so on.

Common Size Balance Sheet

The Common Size Balance Sheet schedule shows the percentages that each asset represents the total assets, each liability represents the total liabilities, and each owner's equity represents the total equity in balance sheet format. You can determine the relative strength or weakness of your company's finances by comparing these percentages with those of your industry counterparts. The overall financial health of your company may be improving or declining based on trends in the percentages over time. Nineteen rows of calculated data, representing line-item amounts as percentages of the total, make up the Common Size Balance Sheet schedule. Assets are shown as a proportion of total assets on the asset side of the balance sheet. Equities are stated as a percentage of total liabilities and owner's equity on the creditor and owner equity side of the balance sheet. The Balance Sheet values are simply converted to percentages by the algorithms for all rows, except for Total Assets, Total Liabilities, and Owner Equity.

The initial period's Cash & Equivalents formula is;

=D44/D$53

The formula for the first period is

=E44/E$53

And so on.

The sum of the percentages for Current Assets, Net Plant, Property and equipment, and Other Noncurrent Assets determines the Total Assets % at any given period. The outcome is always 100 percent. Similar to this, the sum of the current, noncurrent, and owner equity percentages determines the total liabilities and owner's equity proportion at any one time. There is always a 100% outcome.

Income Statement

There are thirteen rows of computed data in the Income Statement schedule. The period identifier in this schedule is just a numerical representation of the periods used to calculate values. Cell E96 stores the first period as an integer of 1, and subsequent periods are kept as the preceding period plus 1. The following paragraphs describe how the other values in the Income Statement are calculated.

Sales Revenue

The estimations that you submit in the business planning beginning workbook's inputs section are the Sales Revenue statistics. The value you enter in the inputs section of the business planning starting worksheet is the amount for the period.

Less: Cost of Sales

The cost of sales estimations that you submit in the business planning starter workbook's inputs section is the cost of sales statistics.

Gross Margin

The amounts remaining from sales proceeds after deducting the cost of sales are displayed in the gross margin data. Your profit figure is obtained by deducting your other expenses from the gross margin amount. Sales Revenue for the period less Cost of Sales is the formula for calculating gross margin.

For the first period, the formula is;

=E97+E98

The formula for the second period is

=F97+F98

And so on.

You'll see that the Gross Margin formula just adds the Sales Revenue figure to the negative Cost of Sales figure since the Cost of Sales figures are pulled into the Income Statement schedule as negative quantities.

Operating Expenses: Cost Centers 1, 2, and 3

The amounts for each operating expenditure classification or category that you enter in the inputs section of the business planning beginning workbook are displayed in the Operating Expenses figures for Cost Centers 1, 2, and 3.

Total Operating Expenses

The Total Operating Expenses numbers display the totals of the operating expenses for each of these three operating-expense groups or classifications that you provide in the business planning beginning workbook's inputs section. The aggregate of the operational costs for Cost Centers 1, 2, and 3 determines the total for each period.

For the first period, the formula is;

=SUM (E102:E104)

The formula for the second period is

=SUM (F102:F104)

And so on.

Operating Income

The dollar amounts of sales that remain after covering operating expenses and cost of sales are displayed in the operating income data. The amounts shown in the Operating Income numbers are what you keep after deducting your income tax and financing charges from your total earnings. The Gross Margin for the period less the Total Operating Expenses number equals the amount for each period.

For the first period, the formula is;

=E99 – E105

The formula for the second period is

=F99 – F105

And so on.

Interest Income

The interest income data reflects the profits from using the company's capital for investments. The starting Cash and equivalents balance from the inputs section of the business planning starter workbook is multiplied by the period yield on Cash and equivalents to get the amount for each period.

For the first period, the formula is;

=D44*E6

The formula for the second period is

=E44*F6

And so on.

Interest Expense

The costs of using borrowed money for operations and asset purchases are displayed in the Interest Expense statistics. The figure you enter in the inputs section of the business planning starter worksheet is the amount for each period.

Net Income (Loss) Before Taxes

The operating income that remains after paying interest expenses and collecting any interest income is displayed in the Net Income (Loss) Before Taxes numbers. Each period's total is equal to the sum of the operating income, interest income, and interest expense for the respective periods.

For the first period, the formula is;

=E106+E108 – E109

The formula for the second period is

=F106+F108 – F109

And so on.

Income Tax Expenses (Savings)

Using the estimated Net Income (Loss) Before Taxes and Marginal Income Tax Rate numbers that you predicted in the inputs section of the business planning beginning workbook, the income tax expenses (or savings) are displayed. Observe that when there is a net loss before taxes, the model computes savings in income taxes for the present period. This could occur if a loss from the current period is carried over to a prior period or if it is combined with the income from connected firms for the current period. Because you can deduct a loss in one business from the earnings of another, the model essentially implies that a net loss before income taxes results in a current-period tax refund or overall tax savings. However, you adjust the calculation if a current-period loss does not result in a current-period income tax savings. The amount for every period is calculated by multiplying the marginal income tax rate by the net income (loss) before taxes.

The initial period's formula is;

=E38*E110

The formula for the second period is

=F38*F110

And so on.

Net Income (Loss) After Taxes

The numbers for Net Income (Loss) After Taxes determine the earnings a business makes after deducting taxes. Net Income (Loss) Before Taxes less Income Tax Expenses (Savings) equals the amount for each period.

For the first period, the formula is;

=E110 – E112

The formula for the second period is

=F110 – F112

And so on.

Common Size Income Statement

Each income statement line item's percentage of total sales revenue is listed in income statement format on the Common Size Income Statement schedule. By contrasting these percentages with those of your industry counterparts, you may determine how well your company is doing financially in comparison. Trends in the percentages throughout the forecasting horizon can reveal if your company's financial performance is improving or declining. Thirteen rows of calculated data, representing the component line-item value for each period as a percentage of the sales revenue number for that period, make up the Common Size Income Statement schedule. The Income Statement data are simply converted to percentages by the algorithms for all rows, except Sales Revenue. The Sales Revenue numbers include the percentages of Net Income (Loss) After Taxes, Interest Income, Interest Expense, Cost of Sales, and Total Operating Expenses. Every time, the outcomes are 100%. Keep in mind the percentages for expenses and profits are added to the sales revenue computations. Expenses that are displayed as negative amounts are deducted.

Cash Flow Statement

There are sixteen rows of computed data in the Cash Flow Statement schedule. The periods for which values are calculated are numbered by a period identifier, much like in other schedules. Cell E136 stores the first period as an integer 1. Subsequent periods are stored as the preceding period + 1.

Beginning Cash Balance

The anticipated cash and equivalents balance at the beginning of each forecasting period is displayed in the Beginning Cash Balance data. The amount you enter in the business planning starter workbook's inputs section is the starting balance. The ending cash balance of the preceding period becomes the beginning cash balance for the following periods.

Net Income after Taxes

The sums determined as the firm profits for each forecasting period in the Income Statement schedule are displayed in the Net Income after Taxes statistics.

Addback of Depreciation

The change in the total depreciation balance for each forecasting period is displayed in the Addback of Depreciation statistics. This adjustment is typically related to the period depreciation expense; as the depreciation expense is cashless, it needs to be included back into the Net Income after Taxes calculation. The amount you enter as the change in accumulated depreciation in the inputs section of the business planning beginning workbook represents the depreciation added back for each period.

Accounts Payable Financing

The data for Accounts Payable Financing indicate the variation in the Accounts Payable balance throughout the given period. When sales expense is paid throughout the period at a lesser cost than what was incurred, this balance increases. If the amount paid for sales expenses exceeds the amount incurred, this balance will decrease. The model accounts for variations between the actual cash disbursements for the cost of sales expenses and the accrual-based accounting of those charges in the Income Statement by recognizing the changes in this account balance. The balance of accounts payable after each period, as opposed to the balance at the end of the preceding one, is the accounts payable financing figure.

The first formula is =E57 – D57

The formula for the second period is

=F57 – E57

And so on.

Accrued Expenses Financing

The accumulated Expenses Financing data indicate how the accumulated expenses balance has changed throughout the period. When the amount paid for operational expenses during the period is less than the amount incurred, this balance increases. When operating expenses are paid during the period and exceed incurred expenses, this balance decreases. The model accounts for discrepancies between accrual-based accounting expenses on the Income Statement and real cash disbursements for operating expenses by recognizing changes in this account balance. The difference between the amount at the end of the current period and the Accrued Expenses balance at the end of the previous period is the Accrued Expenses Financing figure for each period.

The initial period's formula is;

=E58 – D58

The formula for the second period is

=F58 – E58

And so on.

Other Current Liabilities Financing

The balance change for the period is displayed in the Other Current Liabilities Financing data. When cash is earned through borrowing, either directly or indirectly, this quantity rises. When cash is utilized, either directly or indirectly, to settle short-term debt, this quantity goes down. Every period's Other Current Liabilities Financing number is calculated by subtracting the Other Current Liabilities balance after the prior period from the amount at the end of the current one.

The initial period's formula is;

=E59 – D59

The formula for the second period is

=F59 – E59

And so on.

Long-Term Liabilities Financing

The quantity of long-term obligations during the period is shown as changes in the Long-Term obligations financing data. This amount rises whenever long-term borrowing generates cash, either directly or indirectly. When cash is utilized, either directly or indirectly, to settle long-term debt, this quantity goes down. Each period's Long-Term Liabilities Financing number is calculated as the difference between the balance at the end of the previous period and the current period's balance for Long-Term Liabilities.

The initial period's formula is;

=E62 – D62

The formula for the second period is

=F62 – E62

And so on.

Other Noncurrent Liabilities Financing

The balance of Other Noncurrent Liabilities over the period is shown as changes in the Other Noncurrent Liabilities Financing data. When more long-term borrowing generates cash, either directly or indirectly, this amount rises. When cash is utilized to settle other long-term debt, either directly or indirectly, this amount is reduced. Every period's Other Noncurrent Liabilities Financing number is calculated by subtracting the Other Noncurrent Liabilities balance after the prior period from the balance at the end of the current one.

The initial period's formula is;

=E63 – D63

The formula for the second period is

=F63 – E63

And so on.

Accounts Receivable Investments

For every forecasting period, the change in the accounts receivable balance is displayed in the Accounts Receivable Investments data. When the sales revenue realized during the period is less than the revenue reported, this amount rises. When the sales revenue received during the time exceeds what was recorded, this amount drops. The approach accounts for discrepancies between real cash receipts for sales and the accrual-based accounting of sales revenue on the income statement by identifying changes in the account balance. The amount of the Accounts Receivable Investments for every period is the difference between the balance at the end of the current period and the balance at the end of the previous one.

The initial period's formula is;

=E45 – D45

The formula for the second period is

=F45 – E45

And so on.

Inventory Investments

Each forecasting period's change in the inventory balance is displayed in the Inventory Investments numbers. When inventory is sold for less than it was purchased, this sum rises. When inventory is acquired less than it is sold, this amount falls. The model detects changes in inventory balances and the resulting cash consequences by identifying changes in this account balance. The difference between the inventory balances after the previous and current periods is the inventory investments figure for each period.

The initial period's formula is;

=E46 – D46

The formula for the second period is

=F46 – E46

And so on.

Other Current Assets Investments

The numbers for other current assets investments illustrate how the balance of other current assets changed throughout the period. When cash is used to purchase current assets, either directly or indirectly, this quantity rises. This sum falls as current assets are converted to cash, either directly or indirectly. The balance of Other Current Assets after each period, as opposed to the balance at the end of the preceding one, is the Other Current Assets Investments figure for each period.

The initial period's formula is;

=E47 - D47

The formula for the second period is

=F47 – E47

And so on.

Plant, Property, & Equipment Investments

The numbers for Plant, Property, and Equipment Investments illustrate how the Plant, Property, and Equipment balance has changed throughout the period. When money is spent on purchasing plants, real estate, and equipment, either directly or indirectly, this sum rises. When plants, property, and equipment are converted into cash, either directly or indirectly, this sum is reduced. Each period's Plant, Property, and Equipment Investments figure is calculated as the difference between the balance at the end of the previous period and the current period's end.

The initial period's formula is;

=E49 – D49

The formula for the second period is

=F49 – E49

And so on.

Other Noncurrent Assets Investments

The figures for other noncurrent assets illustrate how the balance of other noncurrent assets changed throughout the period. When cash is used—directly or indirectly—to purchase additional noncurrent assets, this quantity rises. When cash is made by turning other noncurrent assets into cash, either directly or indirectly, this quantity decreases. The balance of Other Noncurrent Assets after each period, as opposed to the balance at the beginning of the next, is the Other Noncurrent Assets Investments number for each period.

The initial period's formula is;

=E52 – D52

The formula for the second period is

=F52 – E52

And so on.

Other Owner Equity Changes

The cash flows from any further capital contributions made by the owners to the company, as well as from dividends and other distributions made by the company to the owners, are displayed in the Other Owner Equity Changes statistics. The value you provide in the inputs section of the business planning beginning workbook is the Other Owner Equity Changes figure for each period. In the Uses of Cash section, the Other Owner Equity Changes data are presented as negative values. This is because a positive change in owner equity, such as an additional capital contribution from a stock offering, for instance, doesn't require cash; rather, it provides cash.

Net Cash Generated (Used)

Based on the specified cash sources and uses, the Net Cash Generated (Used) numbers display the entire cash flow for each forecasting horizon period. Each period's total is equal to the cash sources minus the cash spent during that time.

For the first period, the formula is;

=SUM (E140:E146) – SUM (E149:E154)

The formula for the second period is

=SUM (F140:F146) – SUM (F149:F154)

And so on.

Ending Cash Balance

The anticipated cash and equivalents balance after each period is displayed in the Ending Cash Balance numbers. The sum of the period's Net Cash Generated (Used) and Beginning Cash Balance figures is the balance.

For the first period, the formula is;

=E137+E155

The formula for the second period is

=F137+F155

And so on.

Financial Ratios Table

There are eleven rows of calculated data in the Financial Ratios Table. The periods for which values are calculated are numbered by the period identifier, just like in other schedules. Cell E159 stores the first period as an integer of 1, and subsequent periods are kept as the preceding period plus 1. The methods outlined in the ensuing paragraphs are used to calculate the other values in the Financial Ratios Table.

Current Ratio

This current ratio displays the current ratio of liabilities to assets. One way to assess a company's ability to pay its short-term debts is through the current ratio. The balance of current assets from the balance sheet schedule divided by the total amount of current liabilities yields the current ratio for each period.

The first-period formula is;

=E48/E60

The formula for the second period is

=F48/F60

And so on.

Quick Ratio

The Quick Ratio numbers display the ratio of current liabilities to the total of cash and equivalents plus accounts receivable. Compared to other ratios, the fast ratio offers a stricter assessment of a company's capacity to satisfy its immediate financial obligations. Each period's Quick Ratio is calculated by dividing the total current liabilities by the sum of the accounts receivable and cash and equivalents figures.

For the first period, the formula is

= (E44+E45)/E60

The formula for the second period is

= (F44+F45)/F60

And so on.

Working Capital to Total Assets

The ratio of working capital, or current assets less current liabilities, to total assets, is displayed in the Working Capital to Total Assets numbers. The Working Capital to Total Assets ratio provides insight into how a company's assets are allocated between liquid and non-liquid resources and is another indicator of a company's capacity to pay its debts. For every period, the ratio of Working Capital to Total Assets is determined by dividing the difference between Current Assets and Current Liabilities by Total Assets.

The initial period's formula is;

= (E48 – E60)/E53

The formula for the second period is

= (F48 – F60)/F53

And so on.

Receivables Turnover

The ratio of sales to the balance of accounts receivable is displayed in the Receivables Turnover numbers. The effectiveness of sales collections is shown by the Receivables Turnover Ratio. The fact that the ratio denominator may contain both credit and cash sales presents an issue with the metric as it is typically used.

There are two possible issues with this strategy:

- The cash sales may give the impression those receivables collections are occurring more quickly than they are.
- Even when the effectiveness of the receivables collection procedure hasn't changed, the ratio may still be impacted by simple adjustments in the proportion of credit and cash sales.

Each period's Receivables Turnover figure is computed by dividing the Sales Revenue figure by the balance of accounts receivable that is still outstanding after the period.

For the first period, the formula is;

=E97/E45

The formula for the second period is

=F97/F45

And so on.

Times Interest Earned

The ratio of the total net income after taxes + interest income to interest expense is displayed in the Times Interest Earned row. The ratio shows how easily the company can cover its financing expenses in comparison. By dividing the total of the Operating Income and Interest Income numbers from the Income Statement schedule by the Interest Expense figure, the Times Interest Earned ratio for each period is determined.

For the first period, the formula is;

= (E106+E108)/E109

The formula for the second period is

= (F106+F108)/F109

And so on.

Sales to Operational Assets

The ratio of sales revenue to net plant, property, and equipment is displayed in the Sales to Operational Assets row. The ratio shows how well a company generates sales revenue from its operational assets. The Sales to Operational Assets ratio for each period is calculated by dividing the Net Plant, Property, and equipment value from the Balance Sheet schedule by the Sales Revenue amount entered in the inputs section of the business planning beginning workbook.

For the first period, the formula is;

=E97/E51

The formula for the second period is

=F97/F51

And so on.

Return on Total Assets

The ratio of the total assets to the sum of the interest expenditure and net revenue after taxes for each period is displayed in the Return on Total Assets row. As a rate of return on the company's assets, the ratio shows the total operating profitability of the enterprise.

For the first period, the formula is;

= (E113+E109)/E53

The formula for the second period is

= (F113+F109)/F53

And so on.

Return on Equity

The net income after taxes divided by the owner's equity for each period is displayed in the Return on Equity row. The ratio shows how profitable the company is as an investment for the owners. Each period's Return on Equity ratio is calculated by dividing the Owner Equity value from the Balance Sheet schedule by the Net Income (Loss) After Taxes figure from the Income Statement schedule.

The initial period's formula is;

=E113/E65

The formula for the second period is

=F113/F65

And so on.

Investment Turnover

The ratio of sales revenue to total assets is displayed in the Investment Turnover row. A ratio, like the Sales to Operational Assets ratio, shows how well a company uses its resources—in this case, its total assets—to produce revenue. The Sales Revenue number you submit in the business planning beginning workbook's inputs field is divided by the Total Assets value from the Balance Sheet schedule to determine the Investment Turnover ratio for each period.

For the first period, the formula is;

=E97/E53

The formula for the second period is

=F97/F53

And so on.

Financial Leverage

The difference between the return on owner's equity and the return on total assets is displayed in the Financial Leverage row. The ratio shows how borrowing affects an equity return, either more or less. By utilizing financial leverage, the return on the owner's equity can be improved; a negative value denotes a decline in the return on the owner's equity. The Return on Total Assets less the Return on Equity equals the Financial Leverage for each quarter.

For the first period, the formula is;

=E170 – E169

The formula for the second period is

=F170 – F169

And so on.

Customizing the Starter Workbook

The business plan workbook can be used for a variety of business projections; however, you might wish to modify the initial workbook to better fit your needs. For example, you can include text that explains your company and the forecasted horizon. Additionally, you have the option to change the number of periods. For example, if your periods are months and you want to anticipate a full year, you may change the number of periods to 12. Unprotect the document before making any changes to the beginning workbook aside from the forecasting inputs. Select the Review tab and press the Unprotect Sheet button to accomplish this.

Change the number of periods

Changing the number of forecasting periods is a simple process. The last column's borders can be removed to increase the number of periods. Next, copy the existing last column to the right as needed. To reduce the amount of periods, just remove any columns from the schedule that aren't needed from the right side.

- To remove a column, click at the top of the column to highlight the entire column. Next, select Delete from Excel's shortcut menu by using the right-click menu. Once these are done, you can add new borders to the right and reactivate cell protection if necessary.

Performing ratio analysis on existing financial statements

To do a financial ratio analysis on a group of current financial statements, copy the contents of column E from the business plan workbook's inputs area (row 32) including the sales revenue projection through the final row of the ratios table and paste it into column D. The columns for periods 1 through 10 (columns E through N) should then be removed. You have the option to remove the Cash Flow Statement and add the necessary column titles later on.

Use the amended beginning workbook by filling in each of the unshaded cells in column D's inputs area of the business planning starter workbook with the appropriate Balance Sheet and Income Statement data.

Calculating taxes for a current net loss before taxes

When you have a current period net loss before income taxes, you can use the MAX function to change the formula in cell E112, which calculates the income tax expense (or savings) for the first period, so that it takes the maximum of the calculated expense amount, or zero using the MAX function;

=MAX (E38*E110, 0)

Once this is completed, you can duplicate the formula into the remaining forecasting horizon cells that determine the income tax savings (or expense).

- Click the **Home button, select the cell containing the formula you wish to copy, and then click the Copy button. After that, click the Paste button after selecting the range of cells into which you wish to copy the formula.**

Combining this workbook with other workbooks

Just a brief, and somewhat apparent, note: You might want to create other workbooks to provide figures for the business plan workbook covered in this chapter. To reflect your complete investment in plant, property, and equipment, you can create an asset depreciation schedule using the straight-line depreciation standard for a $25,000 asset. You can then utilize this data in the business plan workbook. Workbooks should be combined into a single workbook if you wish to use them together in this way. Copying a worksheet from one workbook to a blank worksheet in the other workbook is the simplest method of copying one workbook to another. (This approach is made simple and achievable by using only one worksheet in each of the starter workbooks.)

Activity

1. Take a review of financial statements and ratios.
2. Customize your starter workbook.
3. Employ the use of the business plan workbook in guiding your business plan creation.

CHAPTER 3
WRITING A BUSINESS PLAN

If you do projects, you should know how to create a complementary business plan. Here are some helpful tidbits regarding company plans as well as advice on crafting a strong business plan.

Defining What the Term Business Plan Means

A business plan is a written document that outlines the objectives of an organization and its approach to achieving them. Established businesses as well as startups might benefit from business strategies. A business strategy can be crucial for businesses to attract potential investors and lenders.

One can help established businesses stay focused and avoid losing sight of their objectives.

- A business plan is a written document that outlines the operations of a firm and its aims and strategies.
- Business plans are used by startups to get off the ground and draw in outside investors.
- A business plan can assist established organizations in maintaining executive team focus and progress toward both short- and long-term goals.
- While there isn't a set framework for a business plan, most organizations will wish to include a few essential components.

A business plan ought to be in place before any new venture starts. Before they consider lending money or providing capital to start-up companies, banks, and venture capital organizations frequently request to see a business plan. A business plan can assist an organization in staying focused on its objectives even if it isn't trying to acquire more capital. "Entrepreneurs who write formal plans are 16% more likely to achieve viability than the otherwise identical non-planning entrepreneurs," according to a 2017 Harvard Business Review article. A business plan should ideally be reviewed and modified regularly to take into account any changes or accomplishments of goals. An established company that wishes to take a different course for itself may draft a whole new business plan. The act of drafting and adhering to a carefully considered business strategy has many advantages. These include the capacity to consider concepts thoroughly before making large financial commitments to them and to identify any potential roadblocks to achievement. A business may also provide its business strategy to dependable third parties to obtain their unbiased opinion. A business plan can also assist in ensuring that the executive team of a company is in agreement over strategic action items and priorities.

Common Elements of a Business Plan

A business plan's length might differ significantly depending on the type of firm. In any case, it's preferable to condense the essential details into a 15–25 page document. Patent applications and other important documents that require a lot of space can be included as appendices and linked inside the main text.

Below are some of the most common elements in most business plans;

- **Executive summary**: This section provides an overview of the business, including its mission statement and pertinent details about its locations, leadership, staff, and operations.
- **Product and services**: The business should include the goods and services it now provides or intends to launch here. Information about cost, product life, and special advantages for the customer may be included. This part may also take into account the company's intellectual technology, any applicable patents it may hold, and its production and manufacturing procedures. Research and development (R&D)-related information may also be placed here.
- **Market analysis**: A business must be well aware of the competitive landscape and the state of its industry at the moment. This part must elucidate the company's positioning, the kinds of clients it intends to court, and the likelihood or difficulty of unseating competitors for market share.
- **Marketing strategy**: This part can include any projected marketing and advertising initiatives, as well as the company's plans for bringing in and retaining customers. It should also outline the route or channels of distribution it plans to employ to offer its goods and services to customers.
- **Financial plans and projections**: Balance sheets, financial statements, and other pertinent financial data are examples of established enterprises. For the first several years, financial targets and estimations might be provided by new enterprises. You may have included any financing requests in your strategy as well.

In addition, a business plan refers to three separate things;

- **A strategic plan:** a discussion or description of the overall strategy of a firm.
- **A new venture plan:** the fundraising document that entrepreneurs employ in the promotion of a new venture to investors.
- **A white paper plan:** An entrepreneur will utilize a 50-page (or even 100-page) document to thoroughly outline a new business possibility, including all pertinent risks and prospects.

Types of Business Plans

Despite their diversity, business plans can be broadly classified into two types: traditional and lean startup. The conventional business plan is the more prevalent of the two, as reported by the U.S. Small Business Administration (SBA).

- **Traditional business plans**: Compared to lean startup plans, these plans are typically much lengthier and contain a lot more detail. Because of this, they demand more work from the company, but they may also persuade and reassure potential investors more.
- **Lean startup business plans**: These make use of a condensed format that emphasizes important details. These one-page business plans are brief and only include the most

essential information. If a business chooses to employ this type of plan, it should be ready to offer more information upon request from a lender or investor.

Why Business Plans Fail

A business plan does not guarantee success. It's possible that the plan's initial assumptions and estimates were implausible. Unexpected changes may occur in the markets and the economy as a whole. A rival may launch a ground-breaking new product or service. Because of this, your plan needs to be somewhat flexible so that you can change direction when necessary. The nature of the business will determine how often a business plan needs to be updated. An established company may wish to examine its plan once a year and adjust it as needed. In a highly competitive market, a startup or rapidly expanding company may wish to change it more frequently, perhaps quarterly. If a business would rather provide a brief overview of its operations, it can choose the lean startup business plan. For instance, a recently established business could believe it doesn't have much information to offer just yet. A value proposition, the company's main operations and benefits, personnel, capital, and intellectual property, a list of partnerships, client categories, and income streams are a few examples of sections.

Explaining Briefly about Strategic Plans

In this section, you will learn about various strategies used by different firms all over the world;

Cost strategies

A cost plan or strategy is essential for merchants to succeed. Businesses like Costco and Amazon are great at offering their customers things at reasonable prices. They pass on a large portion of the economic gains to their clients in the form of reduced costs. However, not all of the cost savings are transferred to the customers. Thanks to extraordinarily effective operations, a considerable amount of the cost savings is kept by the company and turn into profits. One of the three fundamental methods is low-cost operation or such cost leadership. Any business can use this method, but those who have attained economies of scale can benefit most from it. A low-cost strategy's main drawback is that to outperform its rivals in terms of profit, the company must keep some of the cost reductions. Therefore, it is insufficient to be a low-cost producer. A company must be able to manufacture goods and services at a low cost while maintaining the ability to charge enough for them so that a portion of the cost savings is kept in the form of profits.

Differentiated products or service strategies

Differentiating your products is the second fundamental tactic. Product differentiators are frequently used to market highly unique goods or services. A notable example is the department store chain Nordstrom, which provides exceptional service and, more often than not, a superb and high-quality range of merchandise. Although Nordstrom products are more expensive, customers are willing to pay the difference. Why? Because they receive a lot more value for their money. A business that uses difference as a strategy competes by showcasing the unique qualities of its goods and services. Being able to charge your consumers more for those unique features than the special features cost you is essential to making this plan work. For differentiation to be effective, revenue growth must outpace expense growth.

Focus Strategies

In actuality, the focus strategy is a cross between the differentiation and cost strategies. This tactic claims that a company excels at both cost management and product or service differentiation in certain aspects. A company may decide to employ this hybrid strategy if it has experience with a certain market, client niche, or product category. Put another way, the company can outperform all competitors in a specific market by using this targeted approach. This company will excel in filling a certain niche. As with other strategies, the focus strategy must, once more, result in higher revenue than the strategy's increased cost or bigger cost savings (for the company) than lower costs passed on to customers. What exactly is a retailer's focus strategy? In my opinion, Target is. In my view, Target caters to middle-class suburbanites by providing them with nearly the ideal blend of unique products and cost savings.

Look Ma: No Strategy

If you have not been exposed to so much strategic thinking before, you will feel all of this doesn't make sense. But when you contrast companies with these strategies—cost leaders like Amazon and Costco, differentiation leaders like Nordstrom, and focus leaders like Target—with companies without a distinct strategic emphasis, the strategies and their advantages become abundantly evident. In business, strategy refers to a method (usually one of the three general methods) to outperform your competitors: cost, differentiation (often through superior product quality), and focus. It does not relate to a concept you may have. You succeed if you can carry out a plan more skillfully than everyone else. Businesses who have chosen a strategy will consistently outperform you if you try to do a little bit of this or a little bit of that, or if you neglect or can't bring yourself to choose a certain plan. The cost leaders win the cost game against you. The differentiators win the differentiation game against you. Additionally, you fall short when competing against businesses that specialize in certain niches.

About Tactics

When you hear individuals discussing strategy, they usually mean tactics rather than strategy in the first place. The decisions that businesses make to successfully implement strategy are referred to as tactics. Ironically, those who misapply the term "strategic"—referring to actions as strategies—frequently lack a strategy themselves. As is to be expected, tactics are ineffective and only make sense in support of a specific strategy. For instance, if you want to follow a cost leadership plan, you need to make sure that all of your techniques align with that approach. If some of your techniques support a differentiation strategy some support a cost strategy, and some support a focus strategy, you jeopardize your chances of successfully implementing that approach. You end up being a master of none and a jack of all trades in this scenario.

Below are certain key points worth considering;

- **Know the three strategies**. A firm can execute just one of three business strategies;
    - Cost-based strategy
    - Differentiation-based strategy
    - Focus-based strategy
- **Pick a strategy.** Choosing a strategy is the initial stage, the action you conduct before deciding on suitable methods. All other tactical decisions flow from the strategic decision.
- **Support the strategy with appropriate tactics**. Of course, any strategic plan needs to have a well-defined strategy. Next, it has to include all of the techniques that the strategy is supported by. That's truly all there is to it. Also take note of this crucial point: only techniques that complement one of these tactics are appropriate.
- **Stick to your strategy**. Disciplining oneself (or the company) to choose a strategy and follow through on it is the difficult part of creating a strategic plan. Few businesses desire the discipline required to adhere to a strict plan of concentration, differentiation in the product, or cost. You might easily find yourself in a situation where you're attempting to be a little bit of this or a little bit of that. Choosing a specific approach implies that you will have to turn down some opportunities, refuse some clients, and refuse some items.
- **Read about competitive strategy**
- **Take a look at every Evergreen Small Business blog.**

Looking at a White-Paper Business Plan

When someone knows they need a strategic plan but is unwilling to make the difficult decisions required to create one, they frequently create a white-paper company plan. To cover up the lack of a strategic plan, the person in this dilemma drafts a lengthy white-paper company plan. I suppose it should go without saying, but before writing a white-paper business plan, you should draft a strategic strategy. By the way, a strategic plan just needs to be one or two pages long. The difficult aspect of creating a strategic plan is making the sacrifice of giving up comfortable or familiar tactical tactics, markets, and opportunity areas. When writing a white-paper business plan, maybe the most crucial thing to keep in mind is this: Numerous additional locations have thorough documentation of this procedure. You can initiate a wizard that guides you through the process of creating a white-paper business plan by selecting

- **Company > Planning & Budgeting > Use Business Plan Tool** if you have QuickBooks Premier or QuickBooks Enterprise Solutions.

Additionally, the U.S. Small Business Administration (SBA) website, www.sba.gov/business-guide/plan-your-company/write-your-business-plan, has comprehensive advice on developing a business plan in the majority of languages. There's a page on drafting a business plan that you may view on the SBA website. It offers connections to other pages with in-depth details about the steps involved in creating a business plan, like one that offers guidance on strategic planning and another that offers step-by-step directions for actually developing your plan. Moreover, a comprehensive framework for crafting a white-paper business plan may be found in Microsoft Word and PowerPoint, which are widely owned by computer users due to their inclusion in nearly all versions of Microsoft Office. (You can explore the template libraries by selecting **File > New** to access these business-plan outlines.) These templates offer excellent beginning outlines, so don't let anyone fool you into believing that something Microsoft offers Word and PowerPoint users for free is somehow less effective than what actual organizations utilize. Microsoft has done a great job of illustrating what details are appropriate for a business plan included in a white paper.

Google Slides is a free tool for creating slideshows if you don't have a licensed copy of Microsoft Word or Microsoft PowerPoint. A pro forma financial forecast is typically required for new venture and white-paper company strategies. You might also wish to draft a fresh venture plan once you have a strong, well-thought-out strategy and a rudimentary white-paper business plan. How to do this is covered in the next section.

Creating a New Venture Plan

Writing a white-paper plan requires a different methodology than writing a new venture plan. To give potential investors the information they need to decide whether to look into your venture further as a potential investment, new venture plans address five fundamental questions. These five questions are explained in depth in the following sections.

Is the new venture's product or service feasible?

While it may not always be necessary to ask, the response is crucial to take into account if a company is considering investing in a novel or untested idea. The scenario that best exemplifies this is when a company intends to develop and then commercialize some novel technology. Is it possible to develop a better mousetrap? is a crucial question to ask if you're considering launching a business to make one. Practically speaking, there are two ways that you can respond to this question. Of course, building a better mousetrap first is the best way to address the feasibility challenge. You'll find it simple to convince potential investors that the product is viable once you've constructed the superior mousetrap. You can place your mousetrap on the desk and walk through its operation. If a product or service has not yet been developed or proven to be deliverable, assembling a team of individuals with prior experience building similar goods is the next best thing to do. This strategy is frequently employed by technology companies. The reasoning behind this strategy is that investors may typically be certain of a team's performance history if they have experience developing comparable technology.

Investors can reasonably assume that a group of skilled engineers who have created new and enhanced mouse traps will eventually be able to create an even better one. The technology is understood by the engineers. They are aware of the issue. They have expertise in coming up with fresh approaches to problems. You can see how accepting of the possibility it is.

Is the product something the market wants?

If your company does have a workable, viable product or service, you must address another important issue up front: Do customers desire the service or product? That is, is there a need for the company's offering among the general public? Demand seems to be one of those things that is difficult to quantify. A new business should ideally demonstrate the existence of demand by having existing consumers purchase the product. Such concrete evidence of demand is hard to get by if a new business hasn't completed the product or service. Here's what you can do instead: Doing independent market research studies will allow you to state, "Yes, we've held multiple focus groups, and participants say they'll purchase a better mousetrap," as evidence of the market's desire. In certain cases, demonstrating that customers or businesses presently buy a comparable good or service and would reasonably buy a noticeably better version of the good or service is another way to demonstrate market demand. People are already purchasing a large number of superior mousetraps. Therefore, by showcasing the superiority of the new product, you could essentially demonstrate market demand if you did manufacture better mousetraps.

Can the product or service be profitably sold?

The first two inquiries concern whether a good or service is marketable and whether consumers would be interested in it. Does that suffice? It's not at all. The third and most crucial issue is: Is it possible to sell the goods you're offering profitably? To demonstrate that the revenue from products or services less the cost of items sold generates a gross margin sufficient to cover the company's operational costs as well as leave room for profit, you must run some approximate calculations. This demonstration of the company's ability to sell its goods or services successfully is accomplished by the business pro forma financial outlook. If you oversee the new company, factor in reasonable compensation for your work while calculating profitability. Until your company can pay you (as well as other team members) a reasonable compensation and the kind of fringe benefits that are realistically expected, it isn't profitable. You need to know enough accounting to create a set of forward-looking financial statements that make a strong case for a profitable enterprise to write a good new venture plan.

Is the return on the venture enough for the prospective investors?

Oddly, it's not always sufficient to merely demonstrate that a company's effort will be lucrative. Additionally, a company must produce earnings that meet or exceed the investors' desired return on investment. Investors have very specific expectations about what a risky investment should yield in the event of a new business. Angel investors typically want yearly rates of return in the range of 20 to 25 percent. Owners of small businesses and entrepreneurs frequently have comparable expectations for rates of return. Professional and institutional venture capital investors, such as those you read about in Inc. magazine and The Wall Street Journal, frequently demand yearly rates of return of 45 to 55 percent, sometimes even 65 percent. When you consider what all of this entails, you'll quickly realize that some investors won't be satisfied with even a pretty darn fantastic business that generates an annual rate of return of 30 to 35 percent, which is fairly good when you think about it. Anything that yields a measly 30 percent annual return won't pique the interest of an institutional venture capital investor, who, for example, wants a 50 percent annual return on their investment.

You give the prospective investor information on a new business plan that allows them to calculate the rate of return. The potential investor might then assess how well this return meets their needs. Examining the returns that your new venture plan is subtly recommending is not a terrible idea. Verify that you aren't attempting to convince investors who demand a 50% yearly return on an investment with a 25% annual return. In the same way, you might not have to present a proposal paying a fifty percent yearly return to investors' content with a twenty-five percent return.

Can existing management run the business?

It doesn't matter how good your business idea is, how many customers are giddy with anticipation over your product, how much money your venture will make, how much potential there is for profit, how wonderful the return on investment is for your investors, or how many customers you have before you run out of steam. There is one more important question that a new venture plan needs to pose and address. Any new venture plan must persuade potential investors that the current management group, which consists of the president or founder and their vice presidents or lieutenants, can successfully run the company. Put another way, even a fantastic business opportunity needs a capable management team that is prepared to carry out the strategy.

Here are two methods to demonstrate that the management group won't cause you any trouble:

- Assemble a management team that has experience running a business that is comparable to the new endeavor. It will be considerably easier for you to persuade potential investors that the management team is capable of building a $25 million company that sells better mousetraps if they have previously built a $25 million company that did just that.
- Demonstrate that the majority of the management team members are successful individuals. A management team with a track record of major accomplishments gives investors' confidence that they are a winning team. This has less to do with being an Eagle Scout and more to do with having an MBA from Stanford or several years of

managerial experience in a large, well-regarded organization. In summary, if some teams members have demonstrated their business acumen and cognitive abilities, or, better still, have effectively led a significant division in another company, you're effectively telling potential investors, "Hey, this management team will bring home a win for us."

Activity

1. What does a business plan mean?
2. Create a new venture plan.

BOOK 7

DATA PROTECTION & TROUBLESHOOTING SKILLS ON QUICKBOOKS

CHAPTER 1
ADMINISTERING QUICKBOOKS

QuickBooks gathers and provides financial data, which is a crucial function for the profitability of your company. Because of this, you should be well-versed in safeguarding both the assets that QuickBooks tracks and the data that it gathers and retains. All of this is explained in this chapter.

Keeping Your Data Confidential

A lot of the time, accounting data is private information. Your QuickBooks data displays your bank account balance, your debt to creditors, and the amount of profit—or lack thereof—that your business makes. Maintaining the privacy of your data is your top priority while managing a QuickBooks accounting system because this information is private. You have two complementary ways to protect the privacy of your QuickBooks data. The first strategy for confidentiality protection makes use of Microsoft Windows' built-in security measures. The alternative approach makes use of QuickBooks's security features.

Windows Security

Windows' security features allow you to limit a program's or data file's accessibility to particular users. This implies that you can control who has access to the QuickBooks data file and who cannot by using Windows-level security. If Windows-level security is already in place, you (or someone in your company) are aware of how to use it to stop illegal users from accessing or using programs and data files. You can use your current general knowledge of the QuickBooks program file or the QuickBooks data file to enable Windows-level security for QuickBooks. You don't have to take the time to master Windows' intricate security architecture if you already use Windows-level protection. You can use QuickBooks which is more basic security.

QuickBooks Security

Password security

QuickBooks Desktop needs passwords for data files to meet specific complexity standards to protect your important data.

The following are the bare minimums for complicated passwords:

- At least 7 characters (letters, numbers, or special characters).
- At least 1 number.
- At least 1 upper case letter.

Every ninety days, complex passwords need to be reset. Both on the day of expiration and close to the end of the 90 days, QuickBooks encourages you to update your password.

Password protection

When users sign in to their files following the update, they will be prompted to create a complicated password if their files contain sensitive information such as credit card numbers, Social Insurance numbers, employer identification numbers, or information if Credit Card Protection is enabled. It should be noted that every 90 days, only administrators will need to reset their password.

The QuickBooks Desktop password requirements are listed below. Passwords are case-sensitive, so take note.

- Between 8-16 characters in length
- At least 1 uppercase character (A-Z, plus all uppercase characters in the Latin-1 Supplement set)
- At least 1 lowercase character (a-z, plus all lowercase characters in the Latin-1 Supplement set)
- At least 1 special character (! " # $ % & ' ( ) * + , - . / : ; < = > ? @ [\ ] ^ { | }~)
- At least 1 number (0-9)
- Password cannot contain the username (case sensitive)
- The username cannot contain the password (case sensitive)
- No spaces

It is required to set a password for people who have credit card protection or sensitive information. It guarantees that your data is only accessible to authorized people. You can use QuickBooks File Manager to manage your passwords for every file if you use QuickBooks Desktop Accountant or Enterprise Accountant.

- If any user has not created a password, the Administrator will be informed. By asking for or providing other users with a password, this will assist the Administrator in keeping the file secure.
- The Automated Password Reset Tool can be used by users who have forgotten their password, including the Admin password and its related password reset hint.
- Make sure that everyone using QuickBooks Desktop in multi-user mode has updated the security update and is running a supported version of the program.

By giving a QuickBooks corporate data file a password, you can safeguard the privacy of your data. This can be done while setting up QuickBooks.

- By selecting the **Company > Change Your Password instruction, you may also establish a password. The command to change your password in QuickBooks non-enterprise** versions is **Company > Set up Users & Passwords > Change Your Password**. The Change Your Password dialog box appears in QuickBooks when you select this command.

The process of creating a password involves inputting the same password into the New Password and Confirm New Password text boxes. Keep in mind that the login "Admin" is linked to your password (which stands for administrator). A Current Password text box won't appear if you haven't set up a password and don't have an old password. You also need to submit a challenge question and response if you're using an Administrator password.

Reset user password

- Launch **QuickBooks.**
- As the admin user, log in.
- Choose **Users** then **Set Up Users and Passwords under Company**.
- Click on **Set up Users. Next, type the admin password once more.**
- Choose the user who needs to update their password from the User List. Next, choose **Edit User.**
- Make a fresh password entry.
- After selecting next twice, choose **Finish.**

QuickBooks won't open the company data file until it has received a username and password. For instance, if you set a password for your company data file, QuickBooks will prompt you to enter your username and password before clicking **OK** each time it launches. The data file is opened in QuickBooks. QuickBooks won't open the data file if you can't provide the password.

Using QuickBooks in a Multiuser Environment

You don't need to use a single password to restrict access to your QuickBooks data file. Multiple passwords can be configured for the QuickBooks data file. This approach is pretty cool since it lets you set QuickBooks to only allow specific users and passwords to accomplish specific tasks. Although it seems difficult, this is not at all. For instance, the owner of the company might have a password that gives them complete control. However, a fresh accounting clerk can own a password that restricts their ability to enter bills into the system.

Create and manage users and roles in QuickBooks Desktop Enterprise

You can add a user with a specified role to manage your books in QuickBooks Desktop Enterprise. A user with particular access and roles can be created. This is how a user is created and assigned a role. It should be noted that only administrators can add and modify users. Make sure you log in to the company file as the admin user.

Follow the steps below to add a QuickBooks user, and then assign a role to it;

- Navigate to the **Company menu and choose Users.**
- Click on **Set up Users and Roles.**

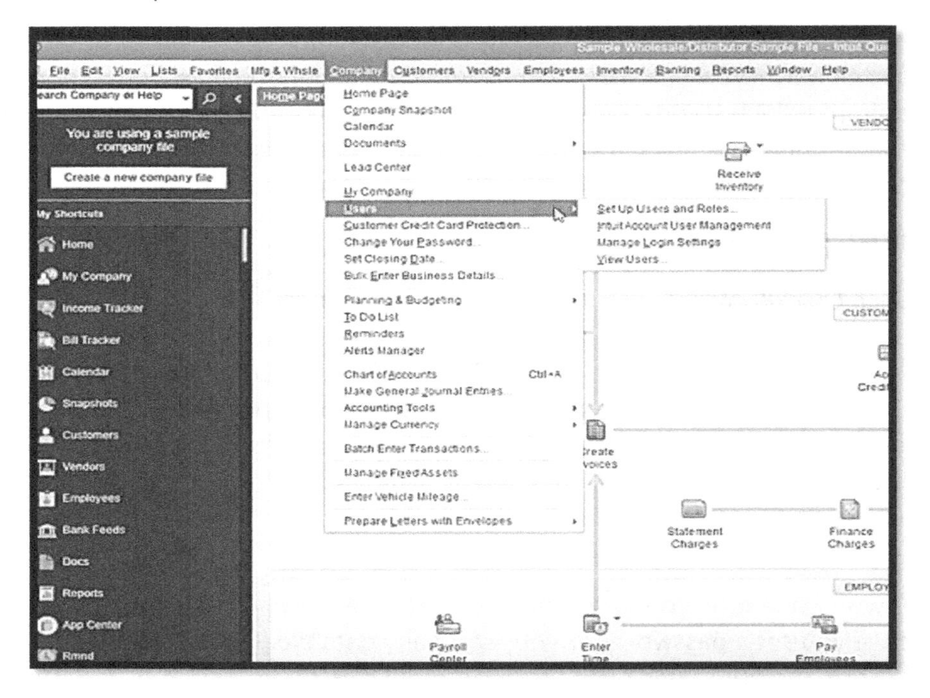

- After entering the admin password, click **OK.**
- Click the **User List tab and choose New.**
- Put in your username and, if desired, a password.
- Choose the roles that belong to the user in the Available Roles section, then click **Add.**
- Click **OK.**

Invite Intuit account users

You can ask users who don't use QuickBooks frequently to create an Intuit account if they just require access to linked services like Capital, Workforce, Payroll, and QuickBooks Time.

This is the method.

- Navigate to the **Company menu and choose Users.**
- Click on **User Management for Intuit Accounts.**
- Choose **Add User from the Users tab.**
- Choose a role from the list of available roles, enter the user's email address, and click **Add.**
- Click **Add User.**
- Click **OK.**

Ask them to check their inbox, click Accept Invite, and then enter their user ID or email to log in.

Use predefined roles

There are 14 predefined roles to choose from. These include typical roles that most businesses have. Asterisk (*)-designated roles can view any transaction in your account without any limitations. Additionally, established roles can be customized to provide you access to some pre-existing permissions. Remember that the changes you make will affect every user who possesses that role.

- Navigate to the **Company menu and choose Users.**
- Click on Set Up **Users and Roles.**
- After entering the admin password, click **OK.**
- Pick the tab for the role list.
- To check a user's permissions, select it and then click **Edit.**
- Choose an account area from the **Area and Activities section**. To adjust the access level, choose **Partial, Full, or None.**
- To save after adjusting the permissions, choose **OK.**

Create a new custom role

You can start from scratch when creating new jobs. This enables you to control which certain sections of your accounts are accessible.

- Navigate to the **Company menu and choose Users.**
- Click on **Set up Users and Roles**.
- After entering the admin password, click **OK.**
- Click the **Role List tab and choose New.**
- Give the position a title and an explanation.

Note: Give it a name that conveys the degree of permission it has.

- Choose an account area from the **Area and Activities section**. After going over each section, choose **None, Full, or Partial** to establish the role's rights.
- Choose **OK** to save after granting rights for each section.

Review roles and permissions

Do a Permission Access by Roles report if you need to see every role and its permissions. This is how to go about it;

- Navigate to the **Company menu and choose Users.**
- Click on **Set up Users and Roles.**
- After entering the admin password, click **OK.**
- Choose **View Permissions a**fter selecting the **Role List tab.**

- After choosing the roles you wish to review, click **Display.**

A permissions audit may be necessary every few months or years, depending on your bookkeeping procedures and employee turnover. Former workers or bookkeepers shouldn't have any positions that allow them to alter data in your file. It's probably best if they had no duties at all! The View Permissions window in QuickBooks provides a convenient method to view this data online. To print a copy of the permissions data, simply **click the Print button in the window.**

Adding users in QuickBooks Pro and Premier

In QuickBooks Pro and QuickBooks Premier, take the following actions to add more users:

- Select **Company >Set Up Passwords and Users > Set Up Users**. The Users and Roles List dialog box appears in QuickBooks and lists all of the users who are presently logged in and for whose QuickBooks access has been configured.
- By clicking the **Add User option**, you can inform QuickBooks that you wish to add a user. The first Set up User Password and Access dialog box appear in QuickBooks (not shown).
- Provide **the password and the user's identity.** Enter a brief name, such as the user's first name, in the User Name box to assign a username to each user for whom you are creating a password. Once the person has been identified, you input their **password in the Password and Confirm Password text boxes.**
- Next, select if you wish to restrict the new user's access by clicking **Next.** Select whether you wish to restrict the user's access and rights when QuickBooks shows the second Set up User Password and Access dialog box (not shown). Choose the Selected Areas of QuickBooks radio button if you wish to restrict access and permissions (which are essentially the things that a user is allowed to accomplish). The All Areas of QuickBooks radio button should be selected if you want the user to have complete control. You can skip the next steps and finish configuring the user password if you specify that the new user should have access to every part of QuickBooks.
- Choose **Next** to proceed and then make a description of access to sales and accounts receivable information and tasks. The third Set up User Password and Access dialog box (not shown) appears in QuickBooks. This is the first in a series of dialog boxes that guide you through an interview by posing specific questions about the level of access that each user should have to different areas. For instance, QuickBooks inquires about access to transactions (such as invoices, credit notes, and accounts receivable information) to sales activity. You can check the No Access radio button to let the user know that they shouldn't have access. To indicate that the user should have full access, check the box next to Full Access.
- Choose **Next** and then make a description of the purchases and accounts payable rights.

- Choose Next and then make a description of the user rights and access that is left. QuickBooks shows multiple versions of the Set Up User Password and Access dialog box that it uses to ask you questions about user privileges and access when you click the Next button at the bottom of each version. QuickBooks inquires about the checking and credit card areas when you specify the rights that are appropriate for the user, for example, in the purchases and accounts payable section. It then queries the inventory area. Payroll is the next topic it inquires about, then general, delicate accounting operations. Lastly, QuickBooks queries access to the tools for financial reporting. Just as you do with sales and accounts receivable, purchases and accounts payable, you restrict privileges in each of these other areas as well. I won't go into detail on how to repeatedly choose the **No Access option button,** the Full Access option button, or the Selective Access button. Just keep the user's rights in mind as you navigate through the screens. While you don't want to grant users more privileges than they require, you do want to grant them the rights they require to carry out their duties.
- Indicate if the user can alter or remove transactions. QuickBooks shows the Changing or Deleting Transactions page of the Set Up User Password and Access dialog box (not pictured) after you've navigated through about six different iterations of the dialog boxes that inquire about various aspects of accounting. You can specify whether a user can alter transactions that were recorded before the closure date on the Changing or Deleting Transactions page. Limiting a user's access to alter or remove transactions is often a good idea.
- Choose **Next and then make a review of your rights decisions.**
- Choose **Finish** when you are done with the review of user rights and access.

Using Audit Trails

You'll value the QuickBooks Audit Trail function, which maintains track of who makes modifications to the QuickBooks data file if you choose to grant several users access to the file. You can use this feature, which is always on, to find out if any information in the file has changed and, if so, who made the changes. Please take note that archiving and condensing data is the only way to remove transactions from the Audit Trail list or history.

- Select **Reports > Accountant and Taxes >Audit Trail** to generate an Audit Trail report.

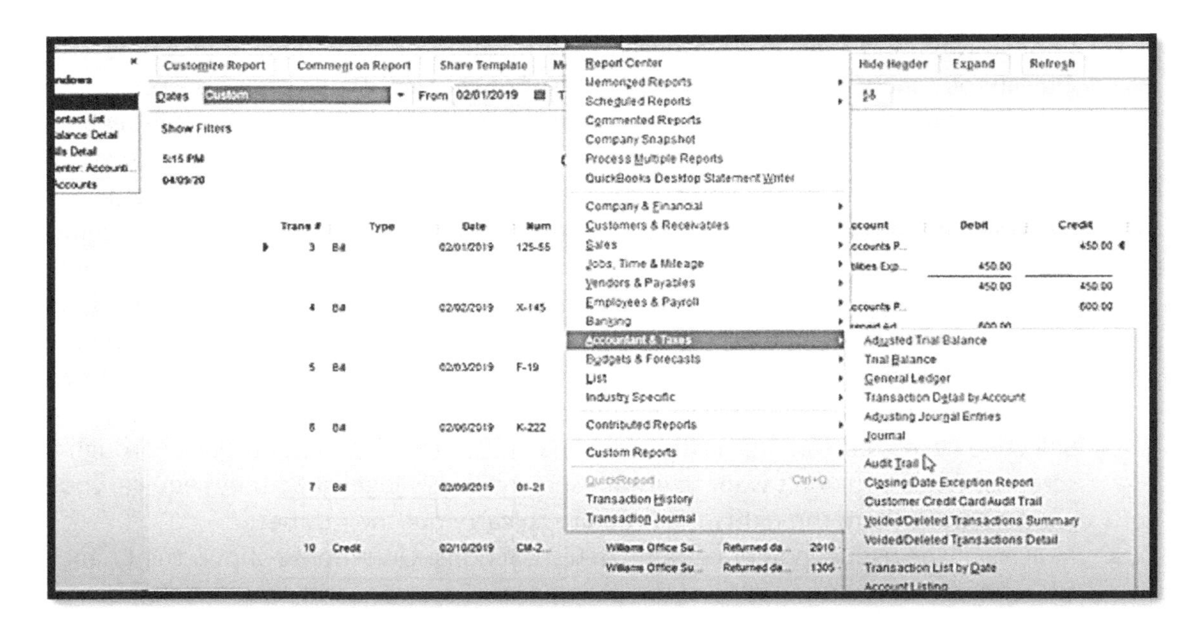

Viewing transaction changes in Audit history

The adjustments made to a particular transaction are all documented in the audit history.

The following data is available in the audit history:

- Who altered?
- When the modifications were implemented.
- What has changed?

It is worth noting that only users who have complete access rights will be able to see the Audit history.

- Launch the transaction that should be investigated.
- Choose More.
- Get the Audit trail opened by choosing Audit History.
- Choose Show All for a much expanded view and choose Compare for a side-by-side comparison.

Enabling Simultaneous Multi-User Access

Sometimes, even when multiple employees use QuickBooks, all you need is one computer and one copy of the software. For example, one copy of QuickBooks operating on a single personal computer can be sufficient if all that's needed for a small firm is access to a QuickBooks data file by the proprietor and an administrative assistant. Nonetheless, QuickBooks does support many users using the QuickBooks data file at once. It should come as no surprise that you must first set up many users, as this chapter has already covered.

Once multiple users have been configured, you can install the QuickBooks program on additional computers. If these computers are connected to a Windows network, you can then use the additional copies of QuickBooks to access the QuickBooks data file that is stored on the primary computer. You must also instruct QuickBooks to accept simultaneous use if you want to utilize it in a setting where numerous users are using it at the same time.

- Select the **File > Switch to Multi-User Mode command to accomplish this. (Select File > Switch to Single User Mode once more if you wish to disable Multi-User Mode later.)**

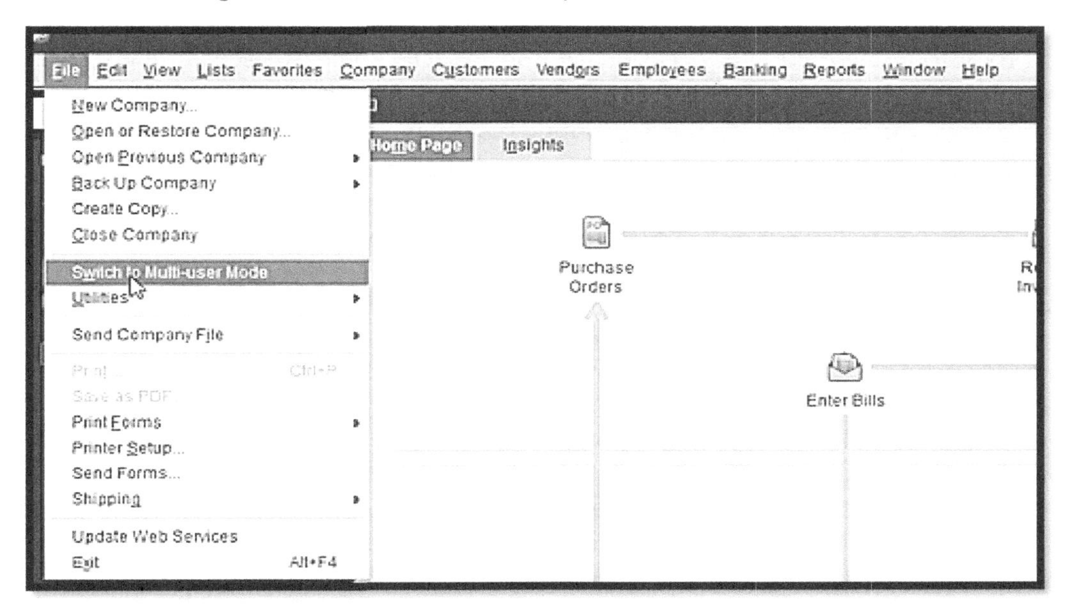

Thanks to a feature called record locking, which locks just the records you're working with and not the QuickBooks data file as a whole, QuickBooks allows several people to utilize it simultaneously. It's acceptable if you wish to collaborate with Company A and another user prefers to work with Company B. QuickBooks permits it. However, working on the same firm (A or B) simultaneously is not something you and the other user can accomplish. This would imply that the client record you are working with is the same.

Note

It is illegal to have a QuickBooks system with numerous users if the same copy of QuickBooks is installed on several computers. For any computer that has QuickBooks installed, a copy must be bought. It should be noted, though, that Intuit does provide various QuickBooks editions for numerous users, wherein you must purchase five licenses for a single QuickBooks package. (The other versions of QuickBooks offer multiple-user networks with a maximum of 5 simultaneous users; the Enterprise version supports up to 40 simultaneous users.) If sales reps in your company produce bids for clients or bills, you might want to have multiple QuickBooks users. You might wish to create QuickBooks accounts for each salesperson in this situation. But keep in mind that these salespeople should only be able to make invoices or maybe invoice estimates that they can create and print. Giving inexperienced accounting users complete access to the accounting system should be done with extreme caution, for reasons that are covered in more detail in the next section of this chapter.

Maintaining Good Accounting Controls

In the chapter's earlier paragraphs, you must have learned how QuickBooks supports multiple users. Once they reach a certain size, many firms must accommodate several users who want access to accounting data and, occasionally, the capacity to create accounting transactions. Regrettably, the business owner faces risk when there are several users of the accounting system. Users who get access to the accounting system may, regrettably, purposefully mislead a company or unintentionally introduce faults into the system. For these reasons, there is a need for you to learn a few QuickBooks control strategies that an owner or management of a company can employ to reduce inadvertent mistakes and theft opportunities.

Regularly compare physical inventory counts with the use of inventory accounting records

Unfortunately, inventory decreases. Inventory theft is a common occurrence among individuals, including shoplifters and occasionally employees. Thus, you should routinely verify physical inventory counts with what your accounting records indicate to reduce inventory losses and preserve correct accounting records. For example, a small convenience shop could want to compare the inventory of cigarettes every day, wine and beer every week, and all other grocery products every month or every year.

By regularly tallying the most valuable and readily pilfered goods, this method achieves two goals:

- Shrinkage in inventory is promptly detected.
- By determining the kind of goods that are most frequently taken or even the times when it is most frequently stolen, the business owner can reduce inventory shrinkage.

Reconcile bank accounts

One thing that owners of businesses should do is reconcile their bank accounts. Accounting staff members frequently commit employee theft when they learn how to write checks on the business bank account without the owner's knowledge. A reliable method to identify a fake or fraudulent transaction is to have the owner balance the bank account. The owner can compare the bank's accounting for the account with the business's QuickBooks accounting records if they reconcile the bank statement. Since any glaring differences may be resolved, the QuickBooks accounting records are more accurate. Additionally, when the business owner attentively examines checks, any shady or questionable activities usually come to light.

Segregate accounting from physical custody where this can be done

It might be challenging to keep the accounting for some activities distinct from the physical possession or accountability for those activities in a small business. It's challenging to keep inventory accounting separate from actual possession or access to the inventory. For instance, a cashier at a business would have little trouble stealing cigarettes and manipulating inventory records by using cash register sales. However, built-in error checking happens everywhere physical possession and accounting may be separated. The accounting clerk indirectly verifies that the asset is being properly cared for by the physical custodian. The accountant can discover, for instance, that the physical custodian is pilfering cigarette cartons when they cross-reference the accounting records with the physical inventory accounts. Similar to this, even if someone has full access to cash accounting records, they cannot simply take cash if they do not have access to cash or a bank account. To assist you in separating the accounting and bookkeeping responsibilities from the physical custody of assets, consult your CPA. You absolutely ought to take this action. Sadly, employee theft occurs frequently.

Train employees on how to use QuickBooks

If you own a business of any size, you should teach staff members how to use QuickBooks for two main reasons:

- The likelihood of unintentional mistakes is lower for someone proficient with QuickBooks. Although QuickBooks is not hard to use, you cannot just pick it up on your own without any assistance. Certain transactions can be quite complex, especially for specific types of firms. Therefore, it makes sense to offer employee assistance, training, or both, if at all possible. These tools make it easier and more accurate for users to utilize QuickBooks' features to create financial data that improves business management.
- A disorganized accounting system might mask employee theft. One common observation following employee theft is severely damaged accounting records. That's why you can end up with an accounting system that is disorganized and encourages employee theft due to under-trained staff. Thus, receiving training increases the accuracy of your accounting records and decreases the likelihood of having an atmosphere that encourages theft or embezzlement.

Set a closing date

If you enroll in a Principles of Accounting course, you will learn that closing refers to a series of bookkeeping operations that are carried out to balance the revenue and expenditure accounts to make it easier to compute revenue and expenses going forward. In QuickBooks, the term "closing" has a distinct meaning. Nevertheless, to protect the integrity of your data, you should still close the QuickBooks file.

Here's how to do it:

- Select the Accounting option in the Preferences dialog box, choose the **Company Preferences tab, and click the Closing Date Set Date/Password button after selecting the Edit > Preferences command**. When QuickBooks asks, enter your password and closing date. QuickBooks forbids or restricts users from editing or adding transactions dated before the closure date once you supply this information.

Manage your QuickBooks accounting system

The accounting system is seen by many business owners as nothing more than a means of generating payroll, invoices, and the data needed for the yearly tax return. Regretfully, company owners frequently don't feel the need to actively supervise what happens with the accounting system because of their remote relationship with it. You should utilize an accounting system as a tool to help you operate your company more effectively. And that is a possibility. But, you must manage the system if you want it to be a tool for improving business management. Put another way; assume accountability for making sure staff members are taught how to protect your accounting system (e.g., backing up the data file).

Activity

1. Get your data confidential.
2. Make use of audit trails.
3. Keep good accounting controls.

CHAPTER 2
PROTECTING YOUR DATA

You will discover how to safeguard your QuickBooks data in this chapter. Essentially, backing up your data is necessary for data protection. By backing up your data, you ensure that you always have a backup in case something happens to or corrupts the original data file. You will also learn about archiving in this chapter because data file compression and archiving are important to backing up and restoring QuickBooks data files. A permanent record of the data files is created when you archive QuickBooks data files. Condensing the active working data file is another option available to you.

Backing up the QuickBooks Data File

Creating a backup of the QuickBooks data file is a crucial operation that you or a colleague must accomplish. I humbly propose that not many things on the hard drive of your computer are as important as the QuickBooks data file. The QuickBooks data file is a literal description of the financial matters of your company. You mustn't misplace the data file. If the data file is lost, you may find yourself without any idea of how much money you have, whether you are making money or not, and unable to easily and accurately prepare your yearly tax returns.

Follow the steps below to backup the QuickBooks data file;

Store firm files in a backup. Right now, save everything to your corporate file. Your accounting information, templates, letters, logos, pictures, and associated files (Loan Manager, Cash Flow Projector, Business Planner, and QuickBooks Statement Writer) are all included in this. It does not, however, support your payroll forms. There are two methods for data backup. You have the option of backing up your data automatically or manually.

Schedule automatic backups

Allow QuickBooks to automatically back up your company file rather than doing it by hand.

- Go to the **File menu** in QuickBooks and choose **Switch to Single-user Mode.**
- Navigate back to the **File menu and select Backup Company**.

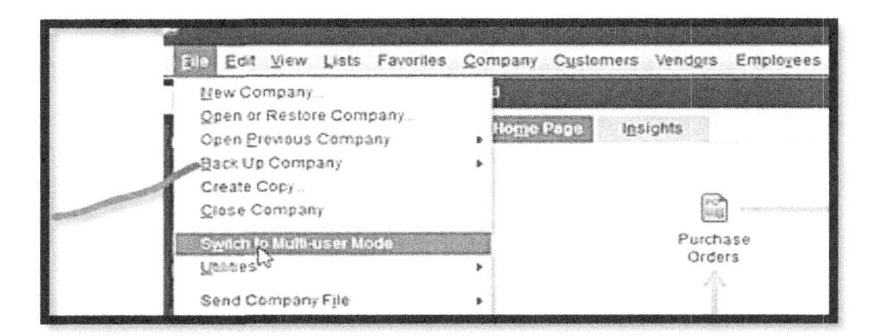

- Next, choose to **Create a Local Backup.**
- Choose **Local Backup** from the window, then click **Next.**

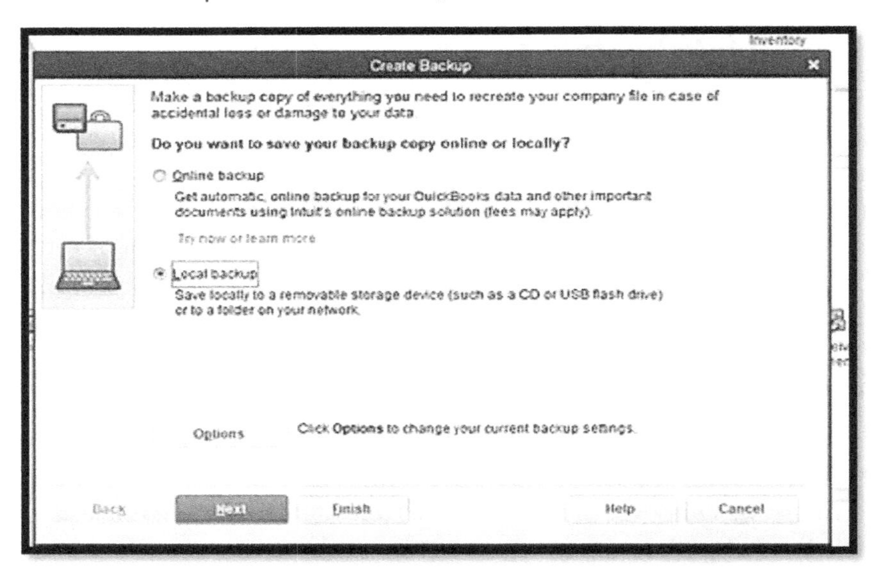

- Choose **Browse in the Local Backup Only option**, and then choose the location to save your backup company file.
- Decide how many backups you wish to retain. You can choose not to do this. You don't have to mark it down in your calendar. To create backup reminders, utilize the settings found in the Online and Local Backup sections.
- Choose **Complete Verification** under the Online and Local Backup section. Before you save, this test to make sure your backup file is intact.

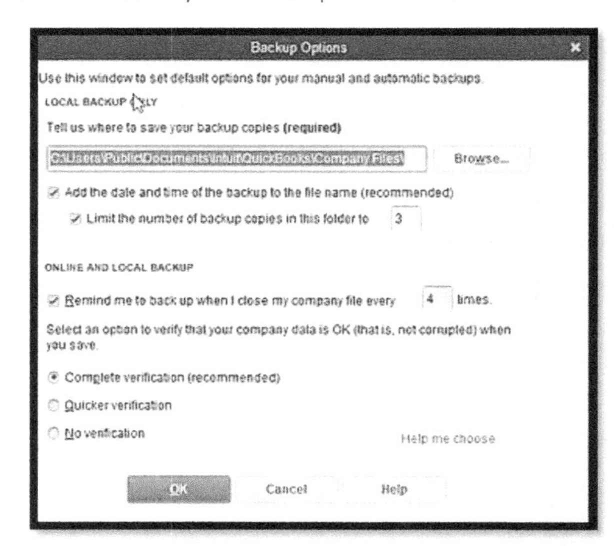

- Click **OK** when you're ready.
- Choose **Next**, then **Save it now and schedule backups for later**. Or choose only to schedule future backups if you would rather not save a backup right now.
- Click the button labeled **"Save backup copy automatically when I close my company file."** Next, decide how long it will be between backups.
- Click **New** to start creating a schedule. Complete the fields with data to generate a backup schedule. A particular hour or day of the week can be specified.
- Click **OK** once your schedule has been created. You are prompted by QuickBooks to enter your Windows sign-in password. This permits QuickBooks to perform the planned backup.
- Click **Finish** when you're ready to start creating your backup.

QuickBooks schedules your future backups and makes a backup at the same time. You receive a confirmation message after it's finished.

Backup your company file manually

You have the option to periodically backup your company files on your own.

- Go to the **File menu** in QuickBooks and choose **Switch to Single-user Mode.**
- Navigate back to the **File menu and select Backup Company**. Next, choose to **Make a Local Backup.**
- Choos**e Local Backup** from the window, and then click **Next.**
- Choose **Browse** in the **Local Backup Only option,** and then choose the location to save your backup company file.
- Decide how many backups you wish to retain. This is a choice. You don't have to mark it down in your calendar. To create backup reminders, utilize the settings found in the Online and Local Backup sections.
- Before saving, this performs a test to ensure that your backup file is intact.
- Choose **OK** once you're prepared.
- Click on **Save Now and Proceed.**

Adjust your backup settings

Curious about the last time you backed up your company file? Hover your cursor over Back up Company in the File menu. The date and time are displayed at the top of the menu.

To modify your preferences for backups:

- Hover over the **Backup Company after selecting the File**. Next, choose to make a **Local Backup**.
- Choose **your options.**
- **Implement your alterations and choose OK.**

Restoring a QuickBooks Data File

Find out how to use your QuickBooks Desktop backup company file (.qbb) to restore your company file. You can recover your accounting data using a backup company file if your computer crashes or if you need to reverse recent modifications. If an issue arises, this allows you to return to one of your safe places. QuickBooks creates a new company file (.qbw) during the restoration process using the backup company file (.qbb).

Important: You must first transfer your backup company file to your local hard drive if it is currently stored on an external device, such as a USB, or a hosting service, such as Box. then carry out the instructions.

Follow the steps below to move your company file to another computer;

- Make certain that you install QuickBooks Desktop on the new computer before you begin.
- On your original computer, follow the instructions to generate a backup company file.
- Give the backup file a distinctive name when you store it to make it easy to find. Additionally, this stop unintentional overwrites.
- Store the backup file on your Windows desktop or wherever else you can find it quickly.
- Transfer the company file backup to your new PC. The backup can be stored on an external device or a flash drive. If your new computer is connected to the same network, you can also share it.
- On your new computer, follow the instructions to restore the backup. Recall that the file name ought to be distinct.
- After moving your file, get the most recent tax table if you utilize payroll.

To move your company files to a different location on the same computer;

- To build a backup company file, follow these instructions.
- Give the backup a distinctive name when you save it to make it easy to find. Additionally, this stop unintentional overwrites.
- Store the backup file on your Windows desktop or another immediately accessible location. Keep in mind that you should store the backup on your home hard disk if your company file is located on a network. Save it off of your network.
- To restore the backup to the new folder or location, follow the instructions. Recall that it needs to have a distinct filename.

Use the backup as your new primary company file after you've restored it. We advise you to rename your initial company file as well. To let you know that it should be retired, append the word "old" to the filename.

The last alternative is for you to move your whole QuickBooks data folder;

Alternatively, you can just relocate your complete QuickBooks folder if you don't want to make a backup of your company file.

- Launch QuickBooks and the desired company file to transfer.
- The Product Info window can be opened by pressing **F2 (or Ctrl+1).**
- Examine the File Information area. This indicates the location on your hard drive where your corporate file is kept.
- Launch **File Explorer** after selecting it from the Windows Start menu.
- Locate the folder containing the company file.
- Choose **Copy** by right-clicking **on the folder.**
- Open the new location on your hard drive or the external device you plan to use to transfer the files. Next, choose **Paste.**

Your complete folder has now been copied to you. It can be moved to a different location on your hard drive or transferred to a new computer. Next, choose "Open or Restore an Existing Company" when you launch QuickBooks. Locate the folder you just copied on your computer, and then open the company file that was copied.

After have done any of the above to keep the company file, you can then make use of the instructions below to restore a backup company file;

- Go to the **File menu** in QuickBooks and choose **Open or Restore Company.**
- Next, choose to **restore a backup copy.**
- After selecting **Local Backup, press Next.**
- Look for your company file backup on your computer. It needs to be like this: [Name of your firm].qbb.
- To determine where to save your repaired company file, choose a folder. Choose **Open** after that.

You run the risk of overwriting your data if you open the backup in the same folder as your current company file. You can give the backup file or your current company files a distinctive name to prevent overwriting anything. Alternatively, you might save the backup in an entirely different folder.

- Once you're prepared, choose **Save**. Choose the one that best suits your needs if you receive any warnings about potentially overwriting your data. Unless you are certain that you want to, don't overwrite anything.

Online Backup

There are probably two reasons why I would recommend an online backup choice;

Stress-free

As long as you have a dependable Internet connection, online backup can make the process of backing up easier and more frequent. It's not necessary to keep track of backing up and then remember to bring the backup disc home.

Reasonable cost

The cost of online backup is very affordable (it may even be free if you have QuickBooks Desktop Pro Plus, Premier Plus, or Enterprise). The price varies depending on the amount of time you want to back up (monthly subscriptions are more expensive than annual ones) and whether you want to back up all of your PC's files or just QuickBooks. Using an annual subscription to back up all files appears to be the best deal. Backup files can be kept in a folder that synchronizes with a cloud-based backup service like Dropbox, Google Drive, or OneDrive from Microsoft. If you utilize any of these services for free storage spaces, you can get a free set-and-forget cloud backup. Users with limited resources or on a tight budget should consider this kind of service.

Styles to coping with backups

Most of the time, backing up is just basic sense. Having stated that, allow me to provide you with some suggestions for how, when, and possibly why you ought to back up:

Make it easy

Making backups simple is the most crucial thing you can do with QuickBooks data file backups. This likely implies looking into the online option, but if you decide to go local, you should have a removable, high-density storage device that you can utilize in conjunction with the computer that QuickBooks is installed on. I make use of a tiny USB flash disk. Select the device that best suits your needs, but you should have a storage device that is as simple to use. In this instance, ease of use indicates a higher likelihood of backing up.

Backup regularly

Every time you enter a transaction in the QuickBooks data file, it is advised that you make a backup. You won't want to back up, of course, if it takes a lot of work. However, you can and should regularly perform backups if you have an easy way to do so and a handy storage device to store your backups. Not too frequently is daily.

Store a backup copy of the QuickBooks data file offsite

One other crucial issue that is worth mentioning is that many of the things that can damage or destroy your data file are specific to your computer, such as a virus, a hard disk failure, a user error, and so on. However, some occurrences are location-specific and could corrupt or destroy your QuickBooks data file. You can lose both the QuickBooks data file and its backup due to fire, flood, or theft. You should keep a duplicate of the backup offshore because of this. For example, you might wish to take the flash drive home at the end of the week and put it in your purse or shirt pocket. Make sure the backup QuickBooks data file is not destroyed if something corrupts or destroys the original QuickBooks data file. This is even more justification for online storage of your backups.

Condensing the QuickBooks Company Files

The procedure of QuickBooks file condenses accomplishes two goals:

- A permanent copy of the QuickBooks data file is produced by the QuickBooks Condense command. (This version of the file is referred to as an archive copy.) A snapshot of the firm file at a specific moment in time is what an archival copy of the file is. When a federal or state auditor, your accountant, or another third party has a query later on, you can use the archival copy of the data file to demonstrate what the company file looked like at a specific moment in time.
- By condensing numerous closed, detailed transactions that require monster journal entries, the file condensing procedure reduces the size of the data file.

Let me briefly outline the steps involved in condensing the QuickBooks Company file because this process of archiving and condensing can be a little unclear.

During the procedure, QuickBooks usually performs the following tasks:

- Retains a copy of your company's files in the archive: An archival copy of the QuickBooks company file is saved by QuickBooks when it is condensed.
- Eliminates completed transactions: You have the option to delete outdated, closed transactions from the current, operational version of your QuickBooks company file as part of the condensation process. Keep in mind that the QuickBooks company file is created as an archive copy when archiving. However, the current, operational version of the QuickBooks company file remains and it is this version that is cleaned up, or reduced in size, by eliminating outdated, closed transactions.
- Condensing usually generates summary monthly journal entries for the old, closed transactions and inserts these summary transactions in the current, operational version of the QuickBooks data file. This is done because the old, closed transactions are eliminated from the QuickBooks data file. You can keep creating monthly financial statements with these summary journal entries. By archiving, you can still generate financial statements for January 2021 in 2024, even though it eliminates all of the

previous, completed transactions from, say, January 2021. The summary monthly journal entries are used by QuickBooks to generate the monthly financial statements for January 2021.

- Removes the audit trail; QuickBooks keeps a record of who inputs what information. The audit trail is one practically unnoticed consequence of the QuickBooks data file cleansing. Before the date of "removed closed transactions on or before," QuickBooks removes the audit trail from a company file that has been cleaned up and indicated to be condensed. Put another way, when QuickBooks deletes old, closed transactions, it also deletes the audit trail for that period.

Your company's data file can be made more efficient and perform better using the Condense Data application. Learn more about the process of condensing.

Condense data while keeping all transactions

- Choose **File, followed by Utilities.**
- Click on **Condense Data.**

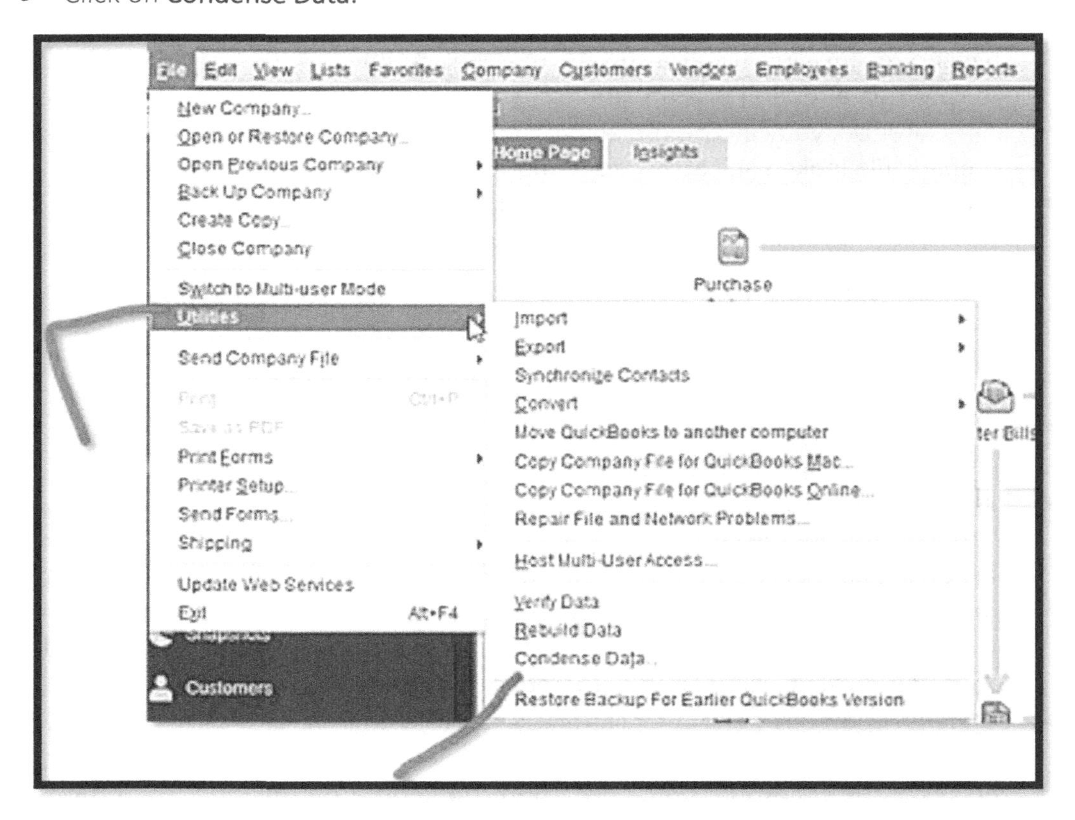

- Choose **Keep all transactions**, but delete the most recent audit trail data.

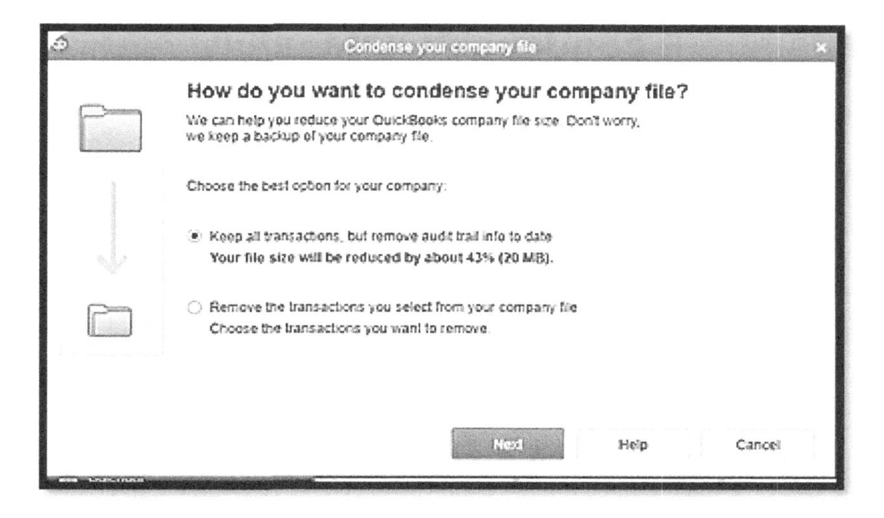

- Click on **Next.**
- Allow the procedure to finish. Choose **Close**.

Condense data by taking off selected transactions

- Choose **File, followed by Utilities.**
- Click on **Condense Data.**
- Click on **Remove the selected transactions from your company file**. Click on **Next.**
- After choosing the transactions you want to delete, click **Next.**
- After choosing the summary option for transactions, click **Next.**
- After choosing the inventory reduction method, click **Next.**
- After choosing the recommended transactions you want to delete, click **Next.**
- After choosing the List of entries you want to eliminate, click **Next.**
- After choosing **Begin Condense**, watch for the procedure to finish. Choose **Close.**

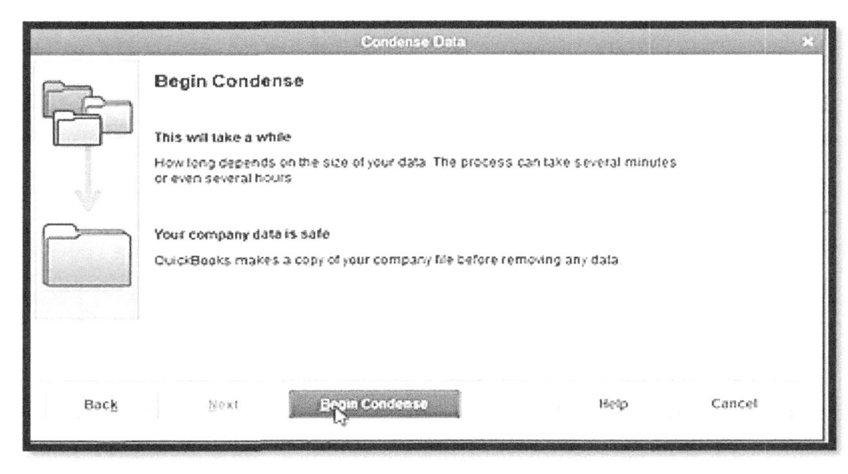

Basic facts about condensed data utility

It is not reversible

Your company file cannot be undone once it has been condensed. Consider alternative options before implementing the final one. Here are a few good explanations for doing so:

- Your data file is quite big.
- Your list is almost at its max.
- Your hardware has been updated.
- After talking over various choices, your accountant and technical support have decided to move forward with condensing.

It may or may not affect the size of your company file

- Due to the removal of list entries and transaction details, the size will be smaller.
- Neither the file size nor the number of open transactions will be impacted.
- If the file size doesn't significantly change, Condense won't be available.

It doesn't affect various reports

Activity

1. Back up your QuickBooks data file.
2. Restore a QuickBooks data file.
3. Condense the QuickBooks company files.

CHAPTER 3

TROUBLESHOOTING

Using the QuickBooks Help File and This Book

You might run into problems at any point and you can count on the QuickBooks Help file or you can also count on this book for that solution. The best course of action in this kind of situation is to learn more about QuickBooks and give it another go. For instance, learning more about printing and reports may help you resolve issues if you're having trouble printing a report. Most of the time, the table of contents and index will allow you to locate the material in this book. Additionally, the QuickBooks Help file normally contains the information (although in a less user-friendly manner). Select **Help > QuickBooks Desktop Help/Contact Us** to bring up the QuickBooks Help window and access information.

Click the **button** that resembles a magnifying glass after entering the word or phrase you wish to look up in the search box at the top of the window. QuickBooks provides you with a list of clickable links to aid you with any issue you may be experiencing.

Browsing the Intuit Product-Support Website

The QuickBooks product help website from Intuit is yet another excellent source for troubleshooting. This website is a vast resource of troubleshooting knowledge that you can access by either using the Help > Ask Intuit command within QuickBooks or by typing https://quickbooks.intuit.com/learn-support in your web browser. Select any other topic you require assistance with, or choose Account Management from the drop-down box, for assistance with downloads, billing updates, and password resets. Depending on the version you are using, you can select QuickBooks Desktop or Online by scrolling down. Use the search box at the top of the page if you are unable to find the solution in the list of topics. Input your query or search terms into the search field and hit Enter or Return. A collection of troubleshooting articles that might assist in resolving your issue is displayed on the product-support website.

Checking Another Vendor's Product-Support Website

Remember that your issue might not even be with QuickBooks itself, but rather with the hardware or Windows on your computer. The incredibly informative Microsoft product-support website can be found at https://support.microsoft.com. A great place to start is by totally shutting down your computer, waiting a full minute, and then turning it back on—especially if you suspect that something other than QuickBooks is the source of your problem. You might be able to make sense of things with this easy method. You can find troubleshooting instructions on the hardware or software manufacturer's product-support website if your issue is hardware or operating system-related. Generally, a decent Internet search engine will make it easy for you to locate the hardware manufacturer's product support page. For instance, use a search engine like https://google.com to find the Dell Computer product support page by typing in something like Dell Computer product support. The vendor's product-support web page's URL (address) is nearly always returned when a search engine looks for that keyword. The Microsoft product support website has troubleshooting advice for Intuit products. If the remedies provided by the website are not particularly comforting, you can at least ascertain whether other users have encountered the same issue. Microsoft might only advise getting in touch with the supplier (Intuit in this example) or updating to a more recent version of the QuickBooks program. Frequently, though, it's helpful to know that the issue you're having is one that Microsoft has acknowledged, documented in its product-support Knowledge Base, and provided a technical description for.

Tapping into the Intuit Online and Expert Communities

You have at least two additional options for getting direct product help in addition to visiting the Intuit product-support website:

Online Community

To get in touch with a sizable community of generally cordial QuickBooks users, go to https://quickbooks.intuit.com/learn-support and choose an option from the Community menu. In addition to viewing other people's questions and answers, you can post your questions on the website by logging in using your Intuit sign-on credentials, which you also use to register. (After using QuickBooks for a while, you might even be able to assist other users with their questions!)

Professional adviser

Through the QuickBooks website, you can get in touch with a professional counsel for QuickBooks. In summary, QuickBooks professional advisers are individuals (often, consultants and accountants) who became Intuit partners to receive discounted copies of the QuickBooks software, a listing on the QuickBooks product-support website, and access to exclusive training. (A few of these individuals additionally clear a certification exam to get the title of QuickBooks Pro Advisors.) You pay these experts their regular consulting costs, however, let me say that this assistance option can be quite helpful if your issue is more with how to utilize QuickBooks to fix an accounting issue than it is with a technical issue with the program.

Activity

Highlight various ways you can find help when making use of QuickBooks.

CHAPTER 4

EXCEL WORKFLOWS

If you've worked with Excel extensively, even for a short while, you most likely have all of these abilities. However, please spend some time reading this appendix if you're even the slightest bit unsure about your ability level. You can use Google Sheets or Excel for the Web if you don't have a licensed copy of Microsoft Excel. All of the programs offer the same basic functionality as Microsoft Excel, with a few small variations. They can be downloaded for free by registering on the Google or Microsoft websites.

Starting Excel

There are two methods to begin using Excel, and neither is particularly tough. You have two options: open an Excel worksheet or select the Start button, followed by the Excel tile that shows up in the list of apps on the Start menu. To utilize the Excel tile, just locate it (you might have to browse the list of tiles on the Start menu) and click on it. Excel can be launched by selecting an **Excel workbook** from a menu or a folder window. Excel workbooks and other documents are frequently displayed on Windows and program menus. Double-clicking the workbook will open it if Windows shows the list of documents in a folder window. Windows launches Excel and instructs it to open the worksheet when you open an Excel workbook.

Stopping Excel

Click the **Close box in the Excel window** to end the program. Excel closes any active workbooks before shutting down.

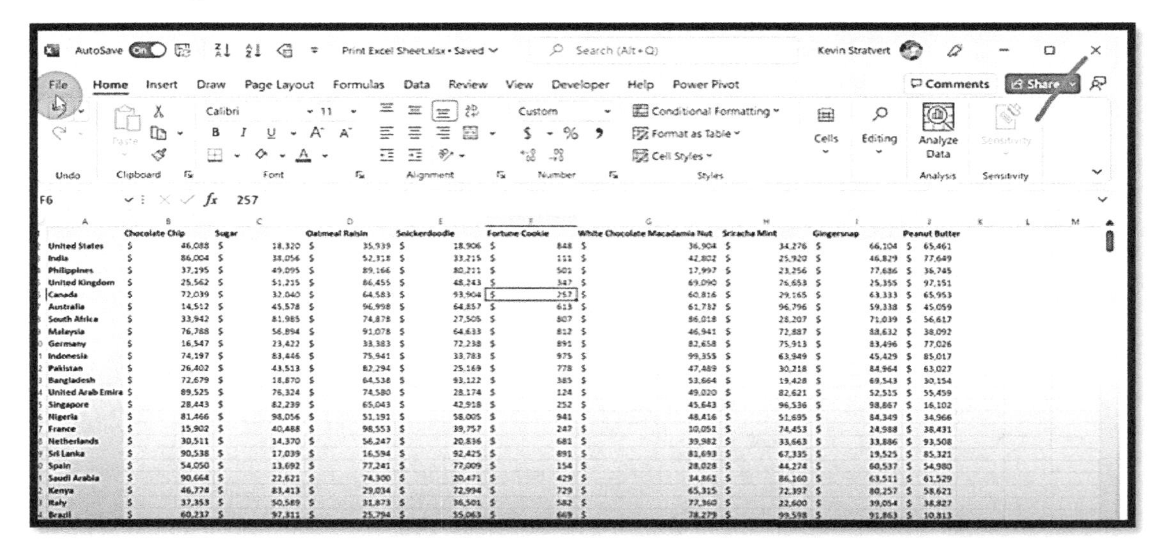

The button with an X in the upper-right corner of the Excel window is the Close box.

Explaining Excel Workbooks

Excel opens in a blank workbook with a single worksheet in the document window. A spreadsheet is a workbook in Excel. Lettered columns and numbered rows make up a spreadsheet. The spreadsheet's left edge displays the row numbers, while the top edge displays the lettered columns. Numbers go from 1 for the first row to 2 for the second, and so forth. The letter A is used to identify the first column, the letter B to identify the second, and so on. Cells are formed by the intersections of rows and columns. To describe a cell location, use the row number and column letter. For instance, the workbook's top-left cell, designated A1, is labeled.

Putting Text, Numbers, and Formulas in Cells

By inserting text labels, numbers, and formulas in the cells that make up a workbook, you can create a spreadsheet, also known as a workbook.

These things are listed in the following order:

- **Text labels**: this includes any characters and digits you wish to avoid using in computations. Text labels include things like your name, a phone number, and a description of the budget and expenses. These data points are not utilized in any computations.
- **Numbers**: Numbers or values are bits of information that you might need to employ in a calculation at a later time. For example, the actual amount you allocated for a certain expense will always be expressed as a number or value.
- **Formulas**: Additionally, they are input into worksheet cells. Excel computes the formula result and shows it in place of displaying the formula when you input =2+2 into a cell. Although the formula result is presented, the formula itself is saved in the cell.

Excel's core function is this stuff about formulas entering workbook cells. Excel workbooks are incredibly useful tools, even if they were used for nothing else. Spreadsheet programs were limited to computing cell formulas when they first came out. It only takes a mouse click to input a text label, value, or formula into a cell; after that, you simply type the text label, value, or formula into the cell. Excel enters your formula, value, or label into the cell when you **click or hit Enter**. It only needs that.

Writing Formulas

You must have studied formulae in the previous part, which also included an example of a simple formula. However, to apply formulas practically, you also need to know a few other things.

In particular, there are a few factors you should keep in mind while typing formulas into workbook cells:

- **Formulas should start with the equal sign (=)**: Excel is informed that the formula that follows should be calculated using the equal sign.
- **You can make use of any of the standard arithmetic operators in your formulas**: The addition sign (+) is used to add numbers. The subtraction operator (–) is used to subtract numbers. The multiplication operator (*) can be used to multiply numbers. The division operator (/) is used to divide numbers. The exponential operator (^) can be utilized to do exponential computations as well.
- **You are in no way limited to making use of values in your formulas**: Cell addresses are another option. When a formula contains a cell address, Excel utilizes that cell's value or formula to result in the computation. When two values are stored in cells A1 and B1, respectively, the formula =A1+B1 yields the value 4. Put differently, the formula equals =2+2.
- **Remember standard rules of operator precedence when you build complicated formulas**: You might recall from junior high math that exponential operations are carried out initially. Operations involving division and multiplication are carried out second. The third set of operations is addition and subtraction. Put the actions you wish carried out first inside parentheses to override these normal operator precedence rules.

Scrolling through Big Workbooks

Only a small percentage of the Excel workbook is represented by the cells that you view inside the Excel program window. In actuality, an Excel worksheet offers more: 16,384 columns and 1,048,576 rows. As there are only 26 letters in the alphabet, a new naming scheme is required, which begins in column 27. Excel uses two letters to mark columns 27 and upwards. The labels for the 27th, 28th, and 29th columns are AA, AB, and AC, respectively. This pattern continues into the 702nd column, denoted as ZZ. Excel goes one step further and uses three letters to identify the 703rd and following columns. The labels for the following columns are as follows: 703 is labeled AAA, 704 is labeled AAB, 705 is labeled AAC, and so on. An Excel workbook's last column, or rightmost column, is designated XFD.

There are multiple ways to scroll the visible area of the Excel worksheet:

- Use the horizontal and vertical scroll bars that show along the bottom edge and at the right edge of the worksheet window: The scroll bar has three buttons: click, drag the scroll marker, and hit the scroll-bar arrow icons that are located at either end. Spend some time experimenting with scroll bars if you're not familiar with how they operate.
- Scroll the viewable portion of the Excel worksheet by dragging the cell selector: Excel employs a dark rectangular border called the cell selector to indicate which cell is active. The cell that appears when you type something is the active cell. Excel allows

you to move the cell selector by using the arrow keys. The cell selector travels in the direction indicated by the arrow. Press the arrow keys repeatedly to find out what the cell selector is if you're not sure.
- Move the viewable portion of the worksheet up and down by tapping the Page Up and Page Down keys

Copying and Cutting Cell Contents

It's simple to copy and paste the contents of worksheet cells, and you should do both because using these abilities makes creating worksheets much simpler.

Follow the steps below to copy cell contents;

- **Choose the cells you would like to copy**. Click the cell you want to pick. Click the cell in the top-left corner of the range and drag the mouse to the cell in the bottom-right corner to choose a range of cells—a range is a collection of adjacent cells.
- **Get the selection copied by choosing the Copy icon**. To see the Home icons, first, if needed, click the Ribbon's Home tab. (You might need to do this since the Home tab is where the Copy icon, which you use for copying, displays.) Excel saves a copy of the selection's contents to the Office Clipboard, a temporary storage location.
- **Choose the location where you would like to position the data you have copied.** Click the cell in the upper-left corner of the range that you want to transfer the data into an Excel to specify where you want the selection to go.
- **Paste the copied range selection by choosing the paste icon**: The range selection that you previously copied from the Office Clipboard is copied by Excel to the workbook location that you specified in Step 3.

You may notice that the Paste icon resembles a clipboard with a piece of paper stuck to it.

There are options for you to move, or cut the contents of cells and ranges when you follow the steps below;

- Choose the cells that you would like to move.
- Select the cut command. When you select the Cut command, Excel moves the contents of the selection to the Office Clipboard. To ensure that you can see the Cut icon, click the Home tab on the Ribbon. Otherwise, click the Cut icon that appears on the Ribbon to instruct Excel to cut your selection.
- Choose the specific location where you would like to position the data you are moving.
- Paste the data by selecting the Paste command. Another option is to use the Paste toolbar button. Excel then copies the range selection that was previously transferred from the Office Clipboard to the workbook location that you specified in Step 3.

Formatting Cell Contents

You may format the data in the cells of a spreadsheet in Excel. For a workbook or range, you can select the font, the point size, and any additional effects that you want, such as boldfacing, underlining, or italicizing. You can also add conventional punctuation to values and formula results, such as dollar signs, percentage symbols, decimal points, and commas to separate thousands. To format a cell or range, you can either pick the range or use the formatting boxes and buttons on the Home tab, or you can launch the Format Cells dialog box by hitting Ctrl+1. For example, you may choose the font for the selected range using the Font box on the Ribbon's Home tab. To define the point size of text and numerals within the chosen range, the Home tab additionally offers a Font Size box. For formatting the contents of cells, the Format Cells dialog box offers tabs containing boxes and buttons. To modify the typeface employed in a range selection, select the Format Cells: Font icon and utilize the boxes and buttons on the Font tab to make the necessary adjustments. The small arrow in the lower-right corner of the Font section on the Ribbon's Home tab is the Format Cells: Font icon.

Recognizing That Functions Are Simply Formulas

Basic measurements can be easily calculated with Excel's readymade formulas, known as functions, even though you may create more complex formulas using the common arithmetic operators. One of Excel's functions makes it simple to determine an arithmetic mean, or average, for instance. It also offers a feature for figuring out auto loan payments. A function can be used to do specific calculations. The SUM function is used to add a set of values. Next, you provide the individual values, individual cell addresses, or range selections as function arguments or function inputs. There are instances when functions are so basic that you won't want assistance to recall the arguments the function requires or how they should appear. For example, spreadsheet users create the SUM function so often that, after only a few applications, they usually memorize its syntax. However, some functions—like those that determine a loan payment—require many arguments in a specific order. The Insert Function command is usually the best choice for more complex functions. Click the Formulas tab, and then select the Insert Function icon to utilize the Insert Function command.

If you're not sure what function you need, you can search for a function by typing a brief description of what you want to compute in the text box that appears at the top of the dialog box, and then clicking Go. As an alternative, you can select a function category from the Or Select a Category drop-down menu. Numerous function categories are available in this list, including text, mathematical and trigonometric, date and time, financial, and statistics. Excel provides you with a list of potential functions at the bottom of the Insert Function dialog box, based on what you input in the first text box or select from the drop-down list. You look through this list to find the desired function. Excel provides a brief function description and the arguments required for the function to compute when you select a function from the list.

Saving and Opening Workbooks

If you've used other Microsoft Office programs, like Word, you probably know that Excel saves and opens workbook documents consistently.

Follow the steps below to save a workbook;

A workbook can be saved by selecting **File >Save**. When saving a workbook for the first time, you have the option to select **File > Save or File > Save As**. Either way, Excel asks you where you want to store your workbook and lets you choose the storage location when it shows the store As dialog box (not shown). Excel displays the conventional Save As dialog box when you click Browse. Utilizing the File Name box, you give the workbook a name. Usually, all you need to do is click the Save button on the Save As dialog box, without worrying about any of the other buttons or boxes. Excel uses the supplied name and saves your workbook in the designated place. You can choose **File > Save** again to save a workbook after you've saved it the first time. Excel saves the workbook using the same name and location when you do this.

Select File >Save As if you wish to save a copy of the workbook with a different name or location. If you notice a folder you wish to save it in, click on it. Excel shows you some recent directories you might have used. If the folder is not visible, click Browse to open the standard Save As dialog box and choose a different location. You select a file location in the Save As text box and give the workbook a name in the File Name text box, just like you would the first time you save a workbook.

Opening a workbook

You can either open Excel or select **File > Open** to open an existing workbook or you can show the contents of the folder containing the spreadsheet.

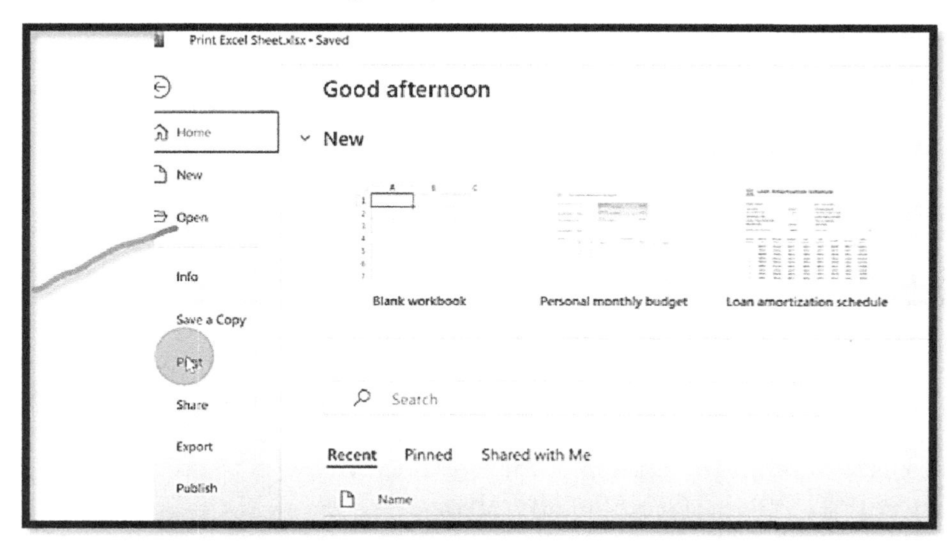

Open the folder's window first if you wish to open Excel workbook documents directly from Windows. Double-click the Excel workbook when Windows displays it in a folder window. This will launch the workbook. Excel is launched by Windows and instructed to open the workbook. Workbook documents can also be opened by selecting **File > Open**. This will display the Open screen, where you can click on the location to locate the workbook's storage place (such as your computer). Excel shows the Open dialog box when you choose the storage location. Click Open after selecting the desired workbook from the list Excel presents.

Printing Excel Workbooks

Workbooks in Excel can be printed similarly to other documents. To begin with, launch Excel and select the document you wish to print, which is a workbook in Excel's case. Excel will open the workbook; select **File > Print** after that.

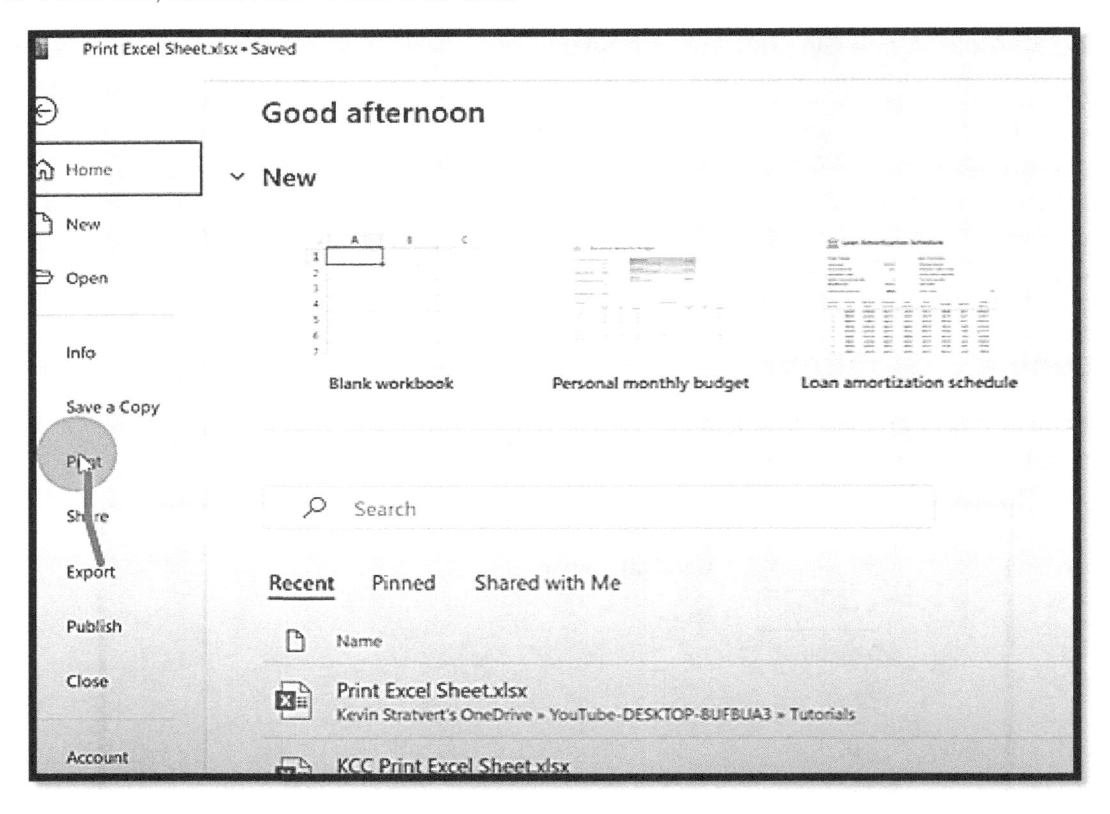

Excel presents the Print page, which includes boxes and buttons to control printing and depicts how the workbook will appear when printed. To indicate how many copies of the workbook you wish to print, use the Copies combo box. From the Printer drop-down list, select the printer you wish to use. To select the portion of the workbook you wish to print, use the drop-down menus and Settings buttons. Click **Print** after that.

Click the **question mark (?)** button in the upper-right corner of the page if you have any questions about any of the buttons or boxes on the Print page. Then, click the **button or box** that you're not sure about. Help tailored to the circumstances is displayed as a text box. Frequently, workbooks that appear flawless on screen may not fit on a single piece of paper because they are a little too wide. When this occurs, Excel prints twice as many pages as you believe you are printing, forcing you to either reprint or stap all of those sheets into an impromptu banner. You might avoid all this trouble (as well as time, ink, and paper) with a quick preview.

Activity

1. Start and stop an Excel application.
2. Insert text, numbers, and formulas in cells.
3. Format cell contents.
4. Save and open a workbook

Conclusion

In the current market of businesses, there are diverse accounting management software that provides various efficient features and functions. QuickBooks 2024 is a superb accounting management software that provides very effective features and functions that can be used in solving real-time accounting issues. QuickBooks 2024 is compatible with every kind of business irrespective of the number of users; some plans suit your needs. With QuickBooks 2024, you have better security, efficient growth, and visible productivity. QuickBooks 2024 aids you in enabling financial records, ensures that your daily tasks are automated, and also helps you to make efficient decisions that help to promote the growth of your business. Get the QuickBooks 2024 today and become more efficient at what you do!

INDEX

B

C

D

E

F

G

H

I

J

N

O

P

Q

R

S

T

U

V

W

Y

Z

Made in the USA
Las Vegas, NV
09 July 2024